Sex and Sexuality in
Early America

Sex and Sexuality in Early America

EDITED BY

Merril D. Smith

New York University Press

NEW YORK AND LONDON

NEW YORK UNIVERSITY PRESS
New York and London

© 1998 by New York University
All rights reserved

Library of Congress Cataloging-in-Publication Data
Sex and sexuality in early America / edited by Merril D. Smith.
p.   cm.
Includes bibliographical references and index.
ISBN 0-8147-8067-9 (cloth : acid-free paper)
ISBN 0-8147-8068-7 (pbk. : acid-free paper)
1. Sex customs—America—History. 2. America—History—To 1810.
I. Smith, Merril D., 1956–
HQ18.A37 S48 1998
306.7'0973—ddc21   98-19767
                                       CIP

New York University Press books are printed on acid-free paper,
and their binding materials are chosen for strength and durability.

Manufactured in the United States of America
10 9 8 7 6 5 4 3 2 1

For my mother, Sylvia L. Schreiber
and in memory of my father, Lee L. Schreiber

Contents

Acknowledgments   *ix*

Introduction: Perceptions and Realities   1

PART I: European/Native American Contact,
         1492–1710   7

1 Sexual Violation in the Conquest of the Americas   9
   Stephanie Wood

2 Native American Sexuality in the Eyes of the
   Beholders 1535–1710   35
   Gordon Sayre

3 Her Master's Voice: Gender, Speech, and Gendered
   Speech in the Narrative of the Captivity of
   Mary White Rowlandson   55
   Steven Neuwirth

PART II: Regulating Sex and Sexuality in Colonial
         New England   87

4 The Regulation of Sex in Seventeenth-Century
   Massachusetts: The Quarterly Court of
   Essex County vs. Priscilla Willson and
   Mr. Samuel Appleton   89
   Else L. Hambleton

5 Sarah Prentice and the Immortalists: Sexuality,
   Piety, and the Body in Eighteenth-Century
   New England   116
   Erik R. Seeman

PART III: Race, Sex, and Social Control in the
Chesapeake and Caribbean in the
Eighteenth Century   133

  6 William Byrd's "Flourish": The Sexual Cosmos of a
     Southern Planter
     Richard Godbeer   135

  7 The Sexual Life of an Eighteenth-Century Jamaican
     Slave Overseer
     Trevor Burnard   163

  8 Sex, Sexuality, and Social Control in the Eighteenth-
     Century Leeward Islands
     Natalie A. Zacek   190

PART IV: Images of Masculinity, Femininity, and
Sexuality in the Eighteenth Century   215

  9 Soldiers in Love: Patrolling the Gendered Frontiers
     of the Early Republic
     Wayne Bodle   217

 10 "Imperfect Disclosures": Cross-Dressing and
     Containment in Charles Brockden
     Brown's *Ormond*
     Heather Smyth   240

 11 "Insidious Murderers of Female Innocence":
     Representations of Masculinity in the Seduction
     Tales of the Late Eighteenth Century
     Rodney Hessinger   262

 12 "The Fruit of Unlawful Embraces": Sexual
     Transgression and Madness in Early American
     Sentimental Fiction
     Karen A. Weyler   283

     Selected Bibliography   315
     Contributors   333
     Index   337

Acknowledgments

Editing a collection of essays sounds much easier than it is. Despite the times I couldn't stand to look at these pages any longer, I'd still like to thank Larry Eldridge, who originally came up with the topic for this book. I also want to thank Jennifer Hammer, my editor at New York University Press, for seeing me through the editing process. Despina Papazoglou Gimbel, managing editor, and her assistant, Andrew Katz, showed great patience while waiting for my revised manuscript. In addition, I offer grateful thanks to the authors who contributed to this volume. Not only have they written great essays, but they returned revisions on time and without arguments.

My husband, Doug, read drafts of the manuscripts and helped with computer problems. My daughters, Megan and Sheryl, let me work without too many distractions as my deadline neared, at least most of the time. The love of the three of them keeps me going.

Deborah Mosley-Duffy provided much-needed encouragement and support when needed.

Thanks to all of you.

Introduction
Perceptions and Realities

In 1683, Priscilla Willson, a sixteen-year-old orphan from Hammersmith, Massachusetts, was convicted of fornication. Samuel Appleton, the presumed father of her child, was not. Several witnesses suggested he had forced himself on Willson, whom neighbors testified had "behaved herselfe soe modestly and Civilly all her time before this transgression." The notion that pregnancy could result only from consensual sex was so pervasive, however, that despite evidence to the contrary, no one in the village actually accused Appleton of rape. The people of this Puritan community assumed that Priscilla Willson had misbehaved, even if she had been led astray by Appleton. The reality of the situation, that Appleton most probably seduced or raped the much younger Willson, was lost to a canon that condemned premarital sex, but permitted class and gender double standards. Although Appleton did have to pay half the court costs, as well as expenses incurred with the birth, his status as a gentleman and his connections to the judges enabled him to maintain his honor.[1]

Similarly, Virginia planter William Byrd's standing as a gentleman affected both his public and private personas. Although he was concerned with how those in the larger world perceived him, he conducted his intimate relationships, too, with an awareness of his social status. Indeed, as Richard Godbeer points out, Byrd considered his sexual performance a significant aspect of his self-image as a "gracious yet masterful gentleman." This elite position gave him additional advantages in sexual encounters. Within the transatlantic world of an early eighteenth-century Virginia planter, Byrd had access to the bodies of servants and slaves who worked for him—and like Appleton had the power, if not the inclination, to coerce sex with them.[2]

1

Power and status also played a part in the conquest of the Americas, where the rape and domination of native women by European men aided in the implementation of new structures of authority. The intersection of and boundaries between class, race, and gender form one theme of the essays in this book. But the *perception* of these categories forms another. Thus, as Stephanie Wood notes, European men who committed acts of sexual violation and degradation against indigenous women may have felt it was permissible precisely because they were native women—some kind of "other." In contrast, New England Puritans knew that the northeastern woodland Indians did not rape their white captives. Still, Mary Rowlandson regarded the fact that she had not been sexually abused during her captivity as a miracle.

Thus, images and impressions about sex and sexuality link the essays in this volume. As Gordon Sayre comments in the case of Native American sexuality, "the eyes of the beholder" could reveal opposing views. For instance, French missionaries to the New World tended to emphasize the chastity of their new converts, while explorers and colonial promoters stressed the promiscuity of native women—often to titillate their readers with visions of naked and submissive virgins.[3]

But "the eyes of the beholder" have perceived differing images of sexuality in many places and times. The prying eyes of Puritan Massachusetts, seeing the pregnant Willson, recognized her as a wrongdoer, while ignoring the misdeeds of the predatory Appleton. Those ogling the naked black "Bum-boat women" of Antigua were understood to be observing a local attraction; however, when their lascivious stares turned to a neighbor's wife, it meant disruption of the Leeward Islands' moral code, and possible prosecutions.[4]

Some of the essays in this volume focus on the perception of the body itself. In addition to the above examples of how Europeans viewed the female bodies of indigenous and slave women, two chapters in particular connect images of and beliefs about the body to politics and theology in New England. In the case of Mary Rowlandson's narrative, the body, particularly the female body, is portrayed as sinful and easily corrupted. Mary admits to indulging her body's need for food, but not its sexual desires. Sarah Prentice and the Immortalists, however, attempt "to make the body holy and incorruptible" through their celibacy.

Despite the objectification and subjugation of women evidenced in many of these essays, strong and independent women do appear. And female sexuality is expressed in many guises. Through Steven Neuwirth's exploration of gendered speech, for example, we hear Mary Rowlandson's "female voice," as she speaks out against her male oppressors. Erik Seeman's essay on Sarah Prentice presents readers with a woman who left her husband and church to embrace celibacy and a hope for immortality. The fictional Constantia Dudley, studied by Heather Smyth, is a well-educated and independent woman in late eighteenth-century Philadelphia. Wayne Bodle's examination of post-Revolutionary gender roles depicts women who ably master life in western Pennsylvania, much to the bemusement of their male counterparts, as the quick-witted Bella Barclay demonstrates. In other cases, women, such as Thomas Thistlewood's slave mistress, used their sexuality to make the best of a bad situation.

In addition to illuminating women's roles, several essays study how societal beliefs both shaped literary genres and influenced common gender practices. For instance, Karen A. Weyler observes that in this period of changing values, where the line between public and private was being recast, both medical theory and the novels that drew upon these theories consigned women who committed sexual transgressions to certain madness. Heather Smyth discusses shifting tensions in the late eighteenth century in her study of cross-dressing in the novel *Ormond*, and at the same time explores the construction of gender in early America. Further examining eighteenth-century novels and stories, Rodney Hessinger notes that by the late eighteenth century, mass fears of unattached and mobile young men helped spur a common motif of seduction literature: the immorality of men, as compared with the natural virtue of women.

Yet in reality, as Wayne Bodle recognizes, not all young men were seducers. At least one of these unattached and mobile young men, Erkuries Beatty, in his confusing quest to find his place in the new republic, seems totally befuddled by women and not very successful in his few attempts at seduction. Although more successful in his quest for sexual conquest, the sex-obsessed William Byrd, at times seems just as confused by women as Beatty does. Nevertheless, while his own sexual appetites and sometimes obsessive interests dominate his thoughts, they also lead to introspective meditations, as Richard Godbeer shows in his perceptive interpretation. Examining the lives of Jamaican slaveholders and slaves, Trevor Burnard draws a vivid portrait of Thomas Thistlewood, a man just as obsessed with sex as William Byrd. Like Byrd, Thistlewood noted every conquest; however, he did so with a singular lack of emotion and insight.

This examination of masculinity in various times and places in early America is one of the strengths of this volume. Byrd's, Thistlewood's, and Beatty's thoughts are interpreted through their own words in diaries and letters. Natalie A. Zacek provides additional insights into the codes of conduct for white men and women in the Leeward Islands by analyzing records of the courts and colonial office and contemporary accounts of island life. But literature also interprets the sexuality of its characters within a particular time and place. Thus, the fictional characters in Rodney Hessinger's and Karen Weyler's essays, as well as the cross-dressing Ormond, discussed by Heather Smyth, serve as commentators on eighteenth-century society and values. Such interpretations give us a much broader view of both male and female sexuality in the early national period.

These examples indicate the wide range of subjects and issues in this book. I have chosen to interpret sex and sexuality broadly to include a variety of sexual activities and what they meant to a particular culture. How was coerced sex interpreted? Seduction? Transvestism? What was involved in the choosing of mates? What did it mean to be a man or a woman in this society, and how did that affect the sexuality of men and women? And conversely, how did the choices they made about their sex lives affect their communities or cultures? For example, when Sarah Prentice embraced celibacy, it meant that she was consciously rejecting further procreation, thereby upsetting Puritan ideals of women's role and creating additional fissures in an area already shaken by the Great Awakening. She distanced herself even more from traditional standards by traveling and preaching throughout the country.

The history of sex and sexuality is still a fairly new area of research. Even less has been studied about sexuality in early America. This volume's central purpose is to advance that knowledge. Through the essays printed here, we come to know much more about the sex lives, practices, and attitudes of the men and women living in North America and the Caribbean between 1492 and 1800. In some cases, what the authors have found confirms knowledge gathered by other scholars, but sometimes previous notions are challenged. For example, Stephanie Wood entreats historians to consider rape as a weapon of war and a tool of conquest. Else L. Hambleton asks was illicit sexuality and premarital sex really as common in colonial New England as others have suggested? Natalie A. Zacek disputes the belief that society in the Leeward Islands was one in which "anything goes."

Some of the subjects in these essays overlap, and some of the essays cover many topics. I have chosen to group the chapters roughly by time period, geographical area, and subject. In this book, "early America" means the period of time from approximately 1492 to 1800. Thus, the book opens with Stephanie Wood's essay on the conquest of the Americas and ends with an examination of gender roles in the eighteenth century. Sexuality in New England is explored in one set of essays, while that of the Chesapeake and the Caribbean are examined in another. The authors of these essays come from diverse backgrounds in history, literature, and cultural studies. They have used sources ranging from diaries and letters to court papers, promotional tracts on the New World, religious works, eighteenth-century literature, and paintings and drawings. Quotations have not been modernized except where an author has used a published edition of a work already modified. Further questions about dates, spelling, or sources used are discussed by individual authors in their notes.

NOTES

1. M. G. Thresher, ed., *Records and Files of the Quarterly Court of Essex County, Massachusetts*, 9:64, cited in Else L. Hambleton's essay in this volume.

2. See the essay by Richard Godbeer in this volume.

3. For more on the conquest of the Americas, Mary Rowlandson, and Native American sexuality, see the essays by Stephanie Woods, Stephen Neuwirth, and Gordon Sayre in the first part of this volume. The reference to the "eyes of the beholder" comes from Gordon Sayre's essay in this volume.

4. The reference to the "Bum-boat women" comes from the essay by Natalie A. Zacek in this volume.

European/Native American Contact, 1492–1710

When Europeans crossed the Atlantic and encountered "the New World," they attempted to master the land and its peoples. Conquest meant bringing men, animals, and goods from Europe and Africa; imposing European systems of government and religion; and interbreeding, often forcibly, with the native women. Unfortunately, few documents record the feelings and reactions of the native Americans to their conquest by these early European explorers, soldiers, and priests. Lost entirely to the modern world is how they viewed various sexual activities and concepts, such as virginity, transvestism, homosexuality, and rape.

Stephanie Wood discusses these problems in her study of conquest and sexual coercion, noting, too, that most often sexual assaults were committed secretly or in private. Moreover, even the definition of what constitutes a sexual violation may differ between two cultures, as it may differ between men and women. Wood, therefore, has for the most part had to deduce the reactions of the indigenous population by interpreting European narratives. She determines that although rape may not have been a consciously promoted tool of conquest, it did become part of the apparatus of conquest. Political and military leaders did not announce rape as an aspect of their policies, but common soldiers considered the indigenous women part of their "spoils" of war. Those in authority did little to curb sexual abuses and in fact may have even tacitly encouraged sexual coercion as a means to impose power over the people they were trying to conquer.

Gordon Sayre's essay concerns the representation of Native Americans by European explorers and missionaries. He observes that characterizations of the Americas and Americans are filled with erotic overtones. Moreover, the accounts of these early eye-witnesses were highly influenced by their preconceptions, as well as by their own behavior. Like

Wood, Sayre finds that historians of today must rely upon the biased sources of the conquerors. Sayre further notes that these sources are colored by the particular observer's prejudices, fears, and desires. Thus, accounts of Native American sexuality written by missionaries differ from those of explorers and promoters. Using the example of the *berdache*, the Indian men who dressed as women and took on the role of females, Sayre shows how Native American sexuality is still being disputed and debated by present-day scholars.

Stephen Neuwirth presents a different aspect of Native American and European encounters in his analysis of Mary Rowlandson's captivity narrative. By revealing Rowlandson's "female voice," Neuwirth determines that here was a woman who spoke out, albeit subtly, against both the Native American and the European men who controlled her life. At the same time, Rowlandson redeems herself as a proper Puritan matron. By invoking stereotypical images of the Indians as drunken, lusty savages pursuing her, Rowlandson presents it as a miracle that she, a weak woman susceptible to the devil, remained chaste. Thus, Neuwirth's essay gives us additional insights into gender roles, the body, and religion in colonial New England, topics that will be explored further in part 2.

Chapter 1

Sexual Violation in the Conquest
of the Americas

Stephanie Wood

Underlining the essential link between sexuality and conquest, historian R. C. Padden writes: "Biologically speaking, it was neither microbe nor sword nor mailed fist that conquered Mexico. It was the *membrus febrilis.*" He credits the "love-making" between the "donjuanistas," who were "in their masculine prime," and indigenous women with transforming Mexico into a European colony. He suspects that the "Spaniards commonly left more pregnancies in their camps than they did casualties on the field of battle."[1] Indeed, one conqueror recalled a compatriot who had sired thirty children by indigenous women in only three years.[2]

But was that "feverish member" simply engaging in an expression of love or was it also wielded as a weapon of conquest? Could sexual assault, or at least coerced sex, have been a regular feature of early transatlantic "encounters," beginning with the voyages of Christopher Columbus in the 1490s? Should we not scrutinize the role of sexual domination in warfare and war's particularly repugnant expression, conquest, before we giddily salute the so-called civilization Europeans introduced into this hemisphere some five hundred years ago?[3] Rape has gained notoriety as a feature of conflicts as recent as the wars in Bosnia-Herzegovina and Rwanda and counterinsurgency efforts from Peru to the Middle East. For this reason, a critical examination of the topic has the potential not only for shedding light on the darker side of the Columbian legacy but for illuminating resolutions of social conflict in our modern, crime-ridden societies as we approach the turn of the millennium.[4]

There is no universally accepted definition of the highly charged term "rape," whether in law or in common usage. Because the topic is so loaded emotionally, "definitional consensus is difficult to attain," writes Linda Brookover Bourque in her preface to *Defining Rape*.[5] She finds a "wide variety of behaviors" that different people will identify as rape. The violence of sexual assault can be expressed in various forms, has a wide range of perceived gravity, and meets with varying degrees of acceptance by both men and women.[6]

For the purposes of this essay, which focuses on heterosexual relations, what is important is the possible sexual violation of a woman's physical and spiritual being, her integrity, dignity, self-possession, power, control, and choice. "Sexual violation" is defined in European terms, owing to our meager knowledge of corresponding concepts among the indigenous populations. Both short- and long-range effects on her person, her family, her community, and her nation are also important. Other issues of concern are the perpetrator's possible gender chauvinism, racism, classism, religious intolerance, or other forms of cultural prejudice, and the meaning this gives to the colonialism that took shape in the Americas.[7] The degradation and subjugation of native women by European men may have been part and parcel not only of conquest but of the imposition of a new, multilayered power structure.[8]

Sexual assault and coercion, all-too-often secret acts, defy quantification, neat historical synthesis, and easy answers. What was the exact nature of the act? What kinds of people committed these acts? At what times and in what kinds of places? What means were used? Why, and how often? Single incidents, which can be shocking and can seem larger than life, do not necessarily clarify the prevalence of sexual violation.[9] Although we have lately begun to broaden our definition of "text," the work of historians usually demands some kind of written documentation.[10] Unfortunately, our sources on sexual assault and coerced sex in the conquest of the Americas are both limited in number and dominated, almost exclusively, by the perspective of the European male.[11] Lamentably, all too often we have to approach other views, such as that of the indigenous male through the filter of European sources. Even more rarely do we find the perspective of native woman (object of most assaults) in these sources.

Dancing around sensitive moral and ethical issues, these records can be fraught with euphemism and metaphor or subterfuge and denial, particularly when directed toward an official or audience of mixed gender. Alternatively, authors also sought to intrigue, impress, and arouse their (typically, male) readers, employing fantasy, invention, exaggeration, bragging, and projection. As Gordon Sayre eloquently discusses elsewhere in this volume, Europeans also saw in Native American sexuality what they wanted to see.

The following account, left by Michele de Cuneo, an Italian noble on Columbus's second voyage to the Caribbean, is extremely rare for its detail and clarity:

> While I was in the boat, I captured a very beautiful Carib woman, whom the said Lord Admiral [Columbus] gave to me. When I had taken her to my cabin she was naked—as was their custom. I was filled with my desire to take my pleasure with her and attempted to satisfy my desire. She was unwilling, and so treated me with her nails that I wished I had never begun. But—to cut a long story short—I then took a piece of rope and whipped her soundly, and she let forth such incredible screams that you would not have believed your ears. Eventually we came to such terms, I assure you, that you would have thought she had been brought up in a school for whores.

Cuneo twists the rape into a scene of seduction, titillating his European male audience back home, knowing full well that the "Carib" woman's version of events would never come to the fore.[12] Her resistance—overcome—is central to the message of his own sexual prowess, and such resistance was apparently not unusual in the Caribbean experience.

Examples of women's particular resistance and fear provide important *indirect* evidence of sexual violation. On one of Columbus's voyages, ten women who had been captured and taken aboard ship jumped overboard at one point and tried to swim the half-league to safety on the island of Hispaniola (modern-day Haiti and the Dominican Republic).[13] In another incident, Cuneo reports that when Spanish conquerors released some surplus female slaves on the same island, they "left their infants anywhere on the ground and started to flee like desperate people." The scene suggests a considerable feeling of urgency on the part of the women to put distance between themselves and the Spaniards. Cuneo reported that some ran eight days "beyond mountains and across huge rivers."[14] If the story is true, the infants could have been the product of sexual assault at the time of capture or in the ensuing captivity period, and the women may have figured that the Spanish fathers should claim the infants and care for them, not wanting the sad burden themselves.[15]

We know from the experience at the first settlement Columbus left behind on Hispaniola, La Navidad, that the European men were coercing sexual relations with the local women. As one European of the period, Guillermo Coma, put it, "Bad feeling arose and broke out into warfare because of the licentious conduct of our men towards the Indian women, for each Spaniard had five women to minister to his pleasure," and "the husbands and relatives of the women, unable to take this, banded together to avenge this insult and eliminate this outrage." Columbus found the fort destroyed and all the men he had left behind dead when he returned on his second voyage.[16]

While Christopher Columbus regularly remarked about Caribbean women's nakedness, launching what has become a long tradition we might call ethnographic voyeurism,[17] his reports were fairly matter-of-fact and aimed at an official audience. In contrast, his contemporary Amerigo Vespucci felt free to elaborate a more literary image, loaded with sexual hyperbole.[18] Whereas other records remind us that "the women of the islands seem . . . to have been naturally resistant to European advances," Vespucci's accounts emphasize the women's sexual liberality and exaggerated lust, continuing a legend-making tradition launched at least as early as the reconquest of Spain, in descriptions of Moorish women.[19] He teases his male audiences with stories such as the one that made him famous, about how sexually voracious women encouraged venomous animals (insects?) to bite their indigenous mates' penises, enlarging them, apparently for the women's satisfaction but to the point that many men would "lose their virile organ and remain eunuchs."[20] The scene was thereby set for Europeans to take the native men's places and become the object of erotic tortures (and take control of the island, to boot) because, the story goes, the women were so fond of "Christians" that "they debauch and prostitute themselves." Still, European men were to proceed cautiously, for Vespucci reminds them of one man who complacently received the attentions of a group of indigenous women while another bludgeoned him from behind.[21]

Gonzalo Fernández de Oviedo remarked several times on the sensuality of indigenous women on Hispaniola. He continued to build the myth of their preference for European men over their own. Like Vespucci, he recounts an episode with a subtext of arousal: "an Indian woman took a bachelor called Herrera, who had fallen behind his companions and was left alone with her, and seized him by the genitals and made him very tired and exhausted."[22]

Figure 1.1. European depiction of a scene described by Amerigo Vespucci, in which an indigenous woman prepares to bludgeon a Spaniard in the Caribbean. Line-drawing copy by Gabriela Quiñones of a scene in the *Quatuor navigationes* (1509), as published in Tzvetan Todorov, *The Morals of History* (Minneapolis: University of Minnesota Press, 1995), 111.

Notwithstanding the fantasy of sexual paradise that European writers were forging, and the suggestions of coercion and resistance that sometimes temper it, we must also allow the possibility that indigenous cultures did have different perspectives on sex. According to Ramón Gutiérrez, among the precontact Pueblo peoples of what is now New Mexico, the women, especially, found sexual intercourse an activity of considerable "cultural import" and "essential for the peaceful continuation of life." He says these "libidinous" women were "empowered through their sexuality," which was "theirs to give and withhold." They did extend it to outsiders, but often expected "blankets, meat, salt, and hides" in return, or some "bond of obligation." Thus, when the Spanish "soldiers satisfied their lust with Indian women but gave nothing in return, the Indian men declared war."[23]

The women's willingness—possibly expressed under certain circumstances—vanished when confronted with the Spaniards' insatiable demands and failure to reciprocate. Neither a playful, intimate exchange nor the satisfaction of a biological need were the Spanish men's sole objectives; it seems, rather, that some or many saw sexual subjugation as an inherent feature of political and economic conquest.[24] During an investigation made in 1601 into the conquest of the Pueblos of 1598, Franciscan friar Francisco Zamora testified, "I know for certain that the soldiers have violated them [the women] often along the roads." Fray Joseph Manuel de Equía y Leronbe reported overhearing conquerors shouting: "Let us go to the pueblos to fornicate with the Indian women. . . . Only with lascivious treatment are Indian women conquered." But in this investigation the conquerors would not admit to assault, again insisting that the indigenous women were licentious and lustful and that their men did not care about faithfulness.[25]

In early Brazil, European men also rhapsodized about a land of insatiable, sexually welcoming native women. Jean de Parmentier reported that the young women of Brazil, given as gifts by their fathers to the Europeans, were like "colts who have never experienced a rein."[26] The reading of this metaphor is ambiguous: were they playful and frisky, or were they frightened and resisting, requiring that they be broken? Virgins, too, could be seen as needing to be "broken in," another element in male fantasy.

Pero Vaz de Caminha, a Portuguese invader of the early sixteenth century, went into raptures about the local Brazilian women's "privy parts" (described in intimate detail) and how, "even when we examined them very closely, they did not become embarrassed."[27] His mention of embarrassment is a clue that he, at least, felt this close examination was a kind of violation, or would have been if it had been conducted on European women. Were these indigenous women, in contrast, some kind of "other" against whom such abuses were freely committed?[28]

Another report from early Brazil tells how the women "have little resistance against those who assault them. In fact, instead of resisting, they go and seek them out in their houses."[29] But the phrase "those who assault them" raises a red flag. Is this an age-old example of the blame-the-victim mentality that claims "she asked for it?" Perhaps what some indigenous women sought was *peaceful* sexual intercourse with *some* of these Europeans in Brazil, hoping to derive a benefit from it. Jean de Léry, a French Protestant pastor traveling among the Tupinambá in the 1550s, said that the women "drove us crazy by following us about continually, saying, 'Frenchman, you are good, give me some of your bracelets or glass beads!'"[30]

When modern historian Magnus Mörner notes that prematrimonial virginity was not prized by all tribes and from this concludes that "Indian women very often docilely complied with the conquistadores' desires," the leap seems considerable.[31] If assault or coercion were regular features of early exchanges, particularly in conquest settings, we must not underestimate the native women's probable repulsion and fear on such initial meetings. We must make a greater effort to distinguish sexual violation from consensual intercourse.

Ecclesiastical chroniclers were more likely than other European men on the scene to make this distinction, and to make complaints about coerced sex.[32] It was the clergy's role to help reassert order and control during the Counter-Reformation and as the Iberian empire rapidly expanded and became more heterogeneous than ever.[33] Just as Franciscans protested abuses in New Mexico, their counterparts in California also complained regularly about the men of the presidios "molesting" the indigenous women.[34] In the mid-sixteenth-century conquest of Venezuela, Fray Pedro de Aguado charged that mixed-heritage recruits were imitating the Spanish, daring to "fornicate with the (Indian women) so shamelessly . . . because in front of the Indians themselves, husbands and fathers, they perpetrated this evil."[35]

On the Chilean frontier the clergy also denounced abuses committed by resentful men stationed at distant outposts among the Araucanians. But it was a secular chronicler who reported that in "one encampment where there were soldiers recently arrived from Spain, together with others whom the maestre de campo had under his command," during a single week sixty women gave birth to "illegitimate" babies of mixed heritage. Many women had been "carried off . . . for [these] more shameful purposes," creating a "deep-seated spirit of rebellion."[36]

Note the use of the adjective "shameful" even by a lay observer. By the early sixteenth century, European art indicates a growing repugnance for the act of rape, which, in medieval times, had often been seen as "heroic" and was generally "sanitized or eroticized," according to Diane Wolfthal. Economic crises in the 1480s and resulting migrations of rural poor to the cities frightened the urban middle class which responded by "formalizing and tightening up social control," probably contributing to these changing attitudes. While a few artists had occasionally shown some sympathy for the rape victim, the trend became one in which she was made into a woman of loose morals, responsible for her own fate.[37] These multiple views of sexual violence could have been influencing behaviors and attitudes expressed in the Iberian colonies of the Americas, entities emerging at precisely the time of the shift Wolfthal identifies in European art.

Those who felt concerned to establish permanent settlements and replicate European institutions of church and government were probably more likely to censure sexual assault and the protracted, coercive sex exacted from female slaves and servants. It can be hypothesized that greater offenses were committed with higher frequency earlier in the conquest phase and farther from center of society. In such settings, justice was more likely to be suspended, due to the relatively light representation of officials and courts and the weak, distant pull of social mores.

Frontier behaviors, which lasted into the nineteenth century in many parts of Latin America and the United States, were not terribly different from those of the conquest period in the more densely populated central areas, such as highland Mexico of the sixteenth century.[38] Bartolomé de las Casas, a conqueror-turned-priest who freed his indigenous slaves and began speaking out against the abuses of conquest, wrote a book (published in 1552) in which, among other things, he recalls an attempted rape in Jalisco, Mexico, in which a Spanish conqueror "took a maiden by force to commit the sin of the flesh with her, dragging her away from her mother, finally having to unsheathe his sword to cut off the woman's hands and when the damsel still resisted they [the conqueror's companions] stabbed her to death."[39] While rival Europeans anxious to discredit the Spanish style of colonization devoured Las Casas's accounts, forging the Black Legend, we cannot ignore his sometimes detailed descriptions, particularly when less inflammatory records largely substantiate this kind of activity in the conquest era.[40]

Bernal Díaz, a conqueror of Mexico, recalled how the men's primary concern after breaking "enemy ranks" had been "to look for a pretty woman or find some spoil." He also spoke of women as synonymous with spoil, noting how a Captain Sandoval brought to Texcoco "much spoil, especially of good-looking Indian women" from the conquest of another part of Mexico.[41]

Conquerors did not simply ravish women on the roads or in the fields; they increasingly seized them for long-term domestic service. These women would heal the conquerors of their battle wounds and gather and prepare food for them and their horses, eventually settling down into a domestic relationship in which they had to perform all kinds of duties, including sexual ones. Here, the nature of sexual relations probably varied along a continuum between assault and mutual agreement. One can imagine that some women resisted and continually faced assault; some became resigned and gave in to their powerful masters' demands, possibly still finding subtle ways to resist or take revenge; some came to accept the relationship as a form of marriage or concubinage, possibly striving to make it work to their advantage in some way; and others possibly welcomed the new unions. It is noteworthy, however, that protests about these long-term relationships continued to issue from both Spanish and indigenous observers on the scene.[42]

In choosing the candidates for this form of servitude, some conquerors may have been guided by their racism to seek out fair-skinned indigenous women. In the Florentine Codex, containing rare indigenous testimonies of the Conquest, citizens of Mexico City told how, after the capital fell, the Spaniards "took, picked out the beautiful women, with yellow bodies. And how some women got loose was that they covered their faces with mud and put on ragged blouses and skirts."[43] If the men looked upon their captive women as "beautiful," perhaps they tried to develop romantic views toward them, something that might have brought some affection and romance to the sexual relationship. But Cortés periodically ordered, coldly, that these commoner women, who were seized during the various expeditions of the Conquest, be branded and auctioned off, with one-fifth of the proceeds going to the crown and one-fifth to him. Some of Cortés's men allowed a few of the "sound and handsome Indian women" to escape these proceedings and then later hired them "as free servants," probably hoping to avoid the stiffer tax yet still have access to these women.[44] So, even when viewed as beautiful, these slave or servant women enjoyed little or no power in their relationships with the Spanish invaders and probably many had to endure regular unwanted sexual advances.

That sex was a clear expectation from the men's perspective is reflected in their concern to capture virgins. In the Ajusco manuscript, another one of the exceptional records made by indigenous males about the Spanish conquest of Mexico, we learn, "It is known how [the Spaniards] take away [the indigenous rulers'] pretty women and also their women [who are] girls, virgins."[45] In certain passages Bernal Díaz also emphasizes the women's virginity (while simultaneously conveying his racist impression that indigenous women, in general, were not attractive), as when he re-

Figure 1.2. Indigenous pictorial showing women of Tlaxcala, Mexico, presented to Spanish conquerors as gifts. Line-drawing copy by Gabriela Quiñones of a scene in the *Lienzo de Tlaxcala*, as published in Luis Reyes García, *La escritura pictográfica en Tlaxcala: Dos mil años de experiencia mesoamericana*, Colección Historia de Tlaxcala, no. 1 (Tlaxcala, Mexico: Universidad Autónoma de Tlaxcala, 1993), 280.

counts a gift of "five beautiful Indian maidens, all virgins. They were very handsome for Indian women."[46]

The gift to which he refers exemplified the many exchanges that solidified alliances between indigenous communities and the Spanish conquerors of Mexico. The famous "La Malinche," or doña Marina, was one of twenty women given to Cortés in Tabasco in 1519, along with presents of gold and handwoven clothing, as symbols of peace. (The people of Tabasco had attacked the Spaniards three times but were finally capitulating.) Through baptism, Bernal Díaz recalls, these twenty became "the first women in New Spain to become Christians," and Cortés quickly distributed them to his captains, just as Columbus had done in the Caribbean a generation before him. Doña Marina eventually became a hardworking interpreter for Cortés and had a child by him.[47] Although later in Mexican history she appears as a traitor to indigenous peoples, Frances Karttunen points out that "she had no people and nowhere to flee. Her best hope for survival was to accept whatever situation was assigned to her and to try to make herself useful and agreeable."[48]

One elite indigenous male perspective on the presentation of such gifts of women to the Spaniards can be detected in the chapter where Díaz discusses another "eight Indian girls," this time from Cempoala, who were also baptized and taken away by Cortés and seven of his men. The *caciques*, or chieftains, reportedly "told Cortés that as we were now their friends they would like to have us for brothers and to give us their daughters to bear us children." This statement, filtered through Díaz, quietly underlines the sexual and maternal role both sides apparently expected of the women. With their daughters (and subsequent grandchildren) in the European camp, both sides knew that this group of chiefs would not be sending their warriors to attack the Spaniards. Perhaps the women would also be expected to help influence the foreign invaders to maintain peace with their hometowns. The same caciques, Díaz claims, "were very well

Figure 1.3. Indigenous pictorial showing elite maidens being removed from the city at about the time of the arrival of conqueror Hernando Cortés to Mexico-Tenochtitlan. Line-drawing copy by Gabriela Quiñones of the *Azcatitlan Annals*, as published in Gordon Brotherston, *Painted Books from Mexico: Codices in the UK Collections and the World They Represent* (London: British Museum Press, 1995), 60 (plate 57).

disposed towards us from that time forward, and particularly so when they saw that Cortés accepted their daughters."[49]

If we had more direct testimony from the caciques, we might find that some saw the gifts of women as a necessary but reluctant sacrifice. The Ajusco document reads: "It is prudent that we give ourselves to the men of Castile, to see if that way they do not kill us."[50] To reduce sexual assault and possibly avoid putting themselves in this kind of dilemma about having to offer women as gifts, some communities helped the women hide from the approaching conquerors. In one indigenous city in Michoacán, Mexico, the Spaniards found that "there were no women in the city, all of them having run away."[51]

Returning to the example of the Cempoalan women given as gifts to Cortés's group, we note an additional feature worthy of comment. These women came with both golden jewelry and their own maids, and the one with the highest status was a "mistress of towns and vassals." The generosity of this gift, according to Díaz, brought a "gracious smile" to Cortés's lips.[52] These kinds of alliances gave the conquerors more than virtual wives. They sometimes brought the men wealth and power in the form of royal grants called *encomiendas*, or trusteeships over communities from which they could extract tribute in goods and labor. Many a conqueror hotly pursued these matches with the indigenous "ladies," or noblewomen.

Similarly, in Peru, writes historian Steve Stern, "To the Spanish elites, marriage to native women from influential or wealthy families brought social connections and dowries." He adds, "Spanish individuals and power groups . . . enhanced their authority and economic potential by cultivating a clientele of Indian allies and functionaries." For the indigenous peoples, these alliances brought protection and advancement.[53]

In Brazil, the native men "wanted [the foreigner] to be surrounded by their women," according to John Hemming, because they were "godlike figures who easily qualified for the many wives befitting their rank." He repeats the sixteenth-century European claim that the "women were ready partners," adding that "in the early days their men acquiesced because it was hospitable to offer women to strangers." He reports how one indigenous chief supposedly said that in early times the Europeans "freely slept with our daughters, which our women . . . considered a great honour."[54] These attitudes changed over time, as in New Mexico, when it became obvious that the invaders did not really behave as gods and did not regularly return the hospitality and honor some individuals tried to show them.

In most of these scenarios—of alliances being cemented on the backs of young indigenous women—the women appear as pawns without a voice, which is not only a commentary on the emerging colonial system but also reveals a possibly unequal gender dynamic within the indigenous societies themselves. The European interpreters, at least, saw the young women as the property of their indigenous fathers, to be distributed to the foreigners in these arrangements as the fathers saw fit. Even in the indigenous records, where the more forceful taking of the women by Spaniards is lamented upon occasion, the women's own testimonies are grievously lacking.[55]

A desire to strengthen their own wealth or status may have guided the Aztec women who were allegedly reluctant to return to their own people after being kidnaped by Spanish conquerors toward the end of the siege on Mexico City. Perhaps they saw the Spanish victory as inevitable. Perhaps there was some aspect of their new lives with the Europeans that appealed to them more than their old. If, like doña Marina, they had been slaves in the indigenous world, they may have had no homes to return to. At any rate, according to Bernal Díaz, when Cortés ordered that the daughters and wives of the elite be returned to their families, "there were many who did not wish to go . . . but preferred to remain with the soldiers with whom they were living. Some hid themselves, others said they did not wish to return to idolatry, and yet others were already pregnant."[56]

With the pending arrival of a child, one can imagine that the indigenous female attached for some time to a conqueror, whether as gift, hired servant, or slave, might adjust her view of the relationship. She might make concessions in order to secure a better future for her child. Some conquerors did provide for the offspring they produced with indigenous women, if not in a way that was equal to their provision for their "legitimate" heirs.[57] One conqueror of sixteenth-century Paraguay sired children with seven different indigenous women, six of whom were his own "servants," but he assisted the daughters of these unions, giving them dowries substantial enough to enable them to marry other Spanish conquerors.[58] In 1530, a Pedro de Vadillo left large monetary bequests in his will for the dowries of several indigenous women in his West Indian household and one *mestizo* (mixed-heritage) woman (his offspring?), plus

Figure 1.4. Indigenous depiction of a struggle in colonial Peru between a Spanish conqueror and an indigenous man over possession of the latter's daughter. Line-drawing copy by Gabriela Quiñones from a leaf of the *Nueva crónica y buen gobierno* of 1615, as published in Steve J. Stern, *Peru's Indian Peoples and the Challenge of Spanish Conquest: Huamanga to 1640* (Madison: University of Wisconsin Press, 1982), 172.

money for a "bastard" (probably mestizo) nephew, for "food, clothing, books, and education for ten years, so that he may become a lawyer."[59]

Just as pregnancy largely "served to move the story line forward" in Greek mythology about rape,[60] *mestizaje* (the production of mixed offspring) has captured the attention of some modern historians who may be uncomfortable studying the role of sexual violation in conquest and in the evolving colonies. Even people of the conquest era preferred to focus on the offspring rather than the method of conception. Francisco de Aguirre, governor of Tucumán, pronounced that "the service rendered to God in producing mestizos is greater than the sin committed by the same act."[61] This story line also appeals, understandably, to the modern descendants of the Spanish, Portuguese, indigenous, and African actors on the stage of conquest and colonization, descendants who now proudly point to their roots in two or more ancient civilizations. It is not easy to consider oneself a descendant of the "hijo de la chingada" (child of the violated woman).[62] The famous independence hero, Simón Bolívar, remarked acidly on this heritage of violation in order to stir emotions against colonialism: "The most impure origin is that of our being: all that has preceded us is wrapped with the black veil of the crime."[63]

The English, long-time rivals of the Spanish, relished making comparisons between the colonial practices of these two imperialist powers. Sir Walter Ralegh wrote, for example,[64]

> "I neither know nor beleeve, that any of our company . . . by violence or otherwise, ever knew any of their [the indigenous men's] women. . . . I suffered not any man . . . so much as to offer to touch any of their wives or daughters: which course so contrary to the Spaniards . . . drewe them to admire her Majestie [Queen Elizabeth], whose commaundement I tolde them it was."

Defenders of the Iberian conquerors will admit apologetically that some may have "known" indigenous women "by violence," but they showed less racism toward Native American women in their willingness (and eagerness in the case of elite women) to form lasting unions and raise families with them. English-American males, in contrast, with a different background and distinct colonial goals, largely shunned indigenous women.

The national-character angle has long been a favorite, for better or worse, in comparisons of colonial situations across the hemisphere. More aptly approached when viewed as a study of cause and effect rather than a process assigning moral blame for the perceived flaws of some stereo-typed ethnic personality, this methodology may have validity for examining Iberian patriarchy and its significance for patterns of sexual violation. The strongly patriarchal nature of Spanish and Portuguese societies could have affected gender power relations to the extent that sexual licentiousness was both a greater likelihood in conquest and a serious concern after colonization, when wives and daughters needed "protection." In sixteenth-century Spain, men wanted to enjoy their own "sexual privilege" but also sought to "protect the chastity" of women in their families. Still, it was women, not men, who were viewed as sexually dangerous. Sources indicate that women, in general, were thought to have the power to "lead men's souls to hell," and therefore required control.[65] In the so-called Justice paintings of Renaissance art, in which rape comes to be condemned but attributed to the woman's seductiveness and willingness, male behavior was excused, in much the same way that actual accused rapists tried to exculpate themselves, when they went before judges, by throwing blame on the victim.[66]

The circumstances of war, in the men's view, could provide further justification for their behavior. The view of sexual violation as a privilege of conquest in the Americas probably had roots in medieval Europe, where "to rape and loot were among the few advantages open" to foot soldiers, according to Susan Brownmiller.[67] In the main, the Spanish conquerors in this hemisphere were not trained, salaried soldiers in whose wake would follow civilian society; the conquerors would form the core of first settlers. They were investors in each expedition of "discovery" and conquest, called an *entrada*, and many would fight, expecting material rewards that would correspond to their investment and service.[68] As we have seen, women slaves and servants formed a part of the "reward" system.

The common fighter, if lucky, might receive a lump sum, from the captains' investment pool, with which to outfit himself. After that, booty was probably his principal payment.[69] This booty, or spoil, included indigenous women. Similarly, even when permanent settlement was not the objective, there was another form of enterprise engaged in by Iberians, especially the Portuguese, called *rescate* or *resgate*, which originated as "trading at an advantage" but evolved into the "direct taking of Indian slaves."[70] Often, again, these were indigenous women. We must remember, too, how the soldiers of both entradas and rescate enterprises saw the indigenous peoples as members of an "inferior race" of "savages."[71]

While the cultural, social, political, and economic context may have been ripe for sexual violation in Spanish and Portuguese conquest expeditions, it remains to be explored whether it was a conscious tool. The monarchs often advocated a race-conscious, biologically defined policy of "miscegenation,"[72] but nowhere did they recommend abuses, and, in fact, they legislated against them.[73] Nor did leaders such as Christopher Columbus, Hernando Cortés, and Francisco Pizarro specify rape as a military strategy in any known written records, although they personally distributed indigenous women to their captains, surely knowing that the men were forcing themselves upon their captives. The leaders must also have watched (if they did not participate in) the ravishment of women in their sieges of communities, yet were more likely to speak out against other abuses, such as the trading of worthless European trinkets for gold nuggets.[74] This, coupled with their silence upon witnessing the destructive retaliation their "sensual debauchery" could bring (in the words of a Jesuit in Brazil),[75] and the prolongation of conflict that postponed effective settlement and complicated trade, leads one to suspect that sexual assault had become at least a spontaneous tactic and sometimes a conscious strategy.[76] Europeans could have viewed rape apologetically as a necessary "release" that followed on the heels of battle. More cynically, it may have also represented the striking of a relatively easier target in the heat of a contest, and an indirect hit aimed not only at women but at their male partners and relatives and the integrity of native society as a whole. Finally, unwanted European advances against indigenous women could have served to pick the fight that would lead to a "just war," a full-scale invasion and occupation of indigenous territory, and an excuse for enslaving (and subsequently controlling in various other ways) the labor force on a more permanent basis.[77] The *membrus febrilis*, alongside sword and microbe, was indeed a deadly implement of war.[78]

NOTES

A shorter version of this essay appeared in 1992 as "Rape as a Tool of Conquest in Early Latin America," in the *CSWS Review* of the Center for the Study of Women in Society, University of Oregon.

1. R. C. Padden, *The Hummingbird and the Hawk: Conquest and Sovereignty in the Valley of Mexico, 1503–1541* (Columbus: Ohio State University Press, 1967), 229–31. He interprets this behavior as an emulation of the indigenous lords, deflecting any blame away from European culture. He also calls the

conquest "amorous." And, lest we mistake the conqueror for a rapist, he reminds us, "She sought that exquisite pain as avidly as He, and beneath the enveloping Christian heaven She also found guilt."

2. Ricardo Herren, *La conquista erótica de las Indias* (Barcelona: Planeta, 1991), 12.

3. Tzvetan Todorov captures the repugnant aspects of colonialism as "humiliation, shameless exploitation, and loss of liberty." *The Morals of History* (Minneapolis: University of Minnesota Press, 1995), 53–54. This is especially true of a colonialism imposed on an already inhabited land through conquest.

4. On the Bosnian conflict, see *Mass Rape: The War against Women in Bosnia-Herzegovina*, edited by Alexandra Stiglmayer (Lincoln: University of Nebraska Press, 1994). On Rwanda, see James C. McKinley, Jr., "The Legacy of Rwanda Violence," *New York Times*, September 23, 1996, A1:2. On rape as a tool of counterinsurgency in Peru, see the discussion of an *Americas Watch Report* in the *New York Times*, April 29, 1993, A4:3; in Argentina, see *Nunca más: informe de la Comisión Nacional sobre la Desaparición de Personas* (Buenos Aires: EUDEBA, 1994); and, in general, see the discussion of an Amnesty International report in *The Middle East* 210 (April 1992): 5–11.

5. Linda Brookover Bourque, *Defining Rape* (Durham, N.C.: Duke University Press, 1989), xv.

6. Bourque, *Defining Rape*, 286–91.

7. Albert L. Hurtado lists all these forms of chauvinism with the exception of sexism, which he recognizes implicitly. *Indian Survival on the California Frontier* (New Haven: Yale University Press, 1988), 185.

8. Elinor Burkett has astutely observed that "the rape of indigenous women must be seen as a type of violent behavior intended to subjugate and oppress." "Indian Women and White Society: The Case of Sixteenth-Century Peru," in *Latin American Women: Historical Perspectives*, edited by Asunción Lavrin (Westport, Conn.: Greenwood Press, 1978), 128.

9. See Bourque, *Defining Rape*, 296, for a reference to prevalence and incidence.

10. See Gordon Brotherston's discussion of American Indian literature in *Image of the New World: The American Continent Portrayed in Native Texts* (London: Thames and Hudson, 1979), 15–18; and Elizabeth Boone's introduction to *Writing without Words: Alternative Literacies in Mesoamerica and the Andes*, edited by Elizabeth Hill Boone and Walter Mignolo (Durham, N.C.: Duke University Press, 1994).

11. I sympathize with Louis Montrose's concern "that the trajectory of this essay courts the danger of reproducing what it purports to analyze: namely, the appropriation and effacement of the experience of both native Americans and women by the dominant discourse of European patriarchy." "The Work of Gender in the Discourse of Discovery," in *New World Encounters*, edited by Stephen

Greenblatt (Berkeley: University of California Press, 1993), 179. But I will also critique those sources and attempt to bring to light indigenous perspectives at every possible turn.

12. J. M. Cohen, *The Four Voyages of Christopher Columbus: Being His Own Log-Book, Letters and Dispatches with Connecting Narrative Drawn from the Life of the Admiral by His Son Hernando Colón and Other Contemporary Historians* (Harmondsworth, England: Penguin, 1969), 139. Cuneo may have called this woman a Carib with the intended meaning of "hostile Indian"; some Taínos were misrepresented this way, both intentionally and unintentionally. See Irving Rouse, *The Tainos: Rise and Decline of the People Who Greeted Columbus* (New Haven: Yale University Press, 1992), 146; and Kirkpatrick Sale, *The Conquest of Paradise: Christopher Columbus and the Columbian Legacy* (New York: Penguin, 1991), 130.

13. Hans Koning, *Columbus: His Enterprise* (New York: Monthly Review Press, 1976), 77.

14. Sale, *The Conquest of Paradise*, 138.

15. The thousands of offspring that resulted from rapes in the war in Rwanda in 1994 (see McKinley, "The Legacy of Rwanda Violence") are called "enfants mauvais souvenir," or children of bad memory, which may capture something of the sentiments, too, from the Caribbean. We also have this tragic account from the chronicler Girolamo Benzioni, quoted in Samuel M. Wilson, *Hispaniola: Caribbean Chiefdoms in the Age of Columbus* (Tuscaloosa: University of Alabama Press, 1990), 97, of the situation on Hispaniola in the late fifteenth century, which may shed light on the possible abandonment of infants witnessed by Cuneo: "The women, with the juice of a certain herb, dissipated their pregnancy, in order not to produce children, and then following the example of their husbands, hung themselves."

16. Quoted in Sale, *The Conquest of Paradise*, 139–40. As Sam Wilson, *Hispaniola*, 83–84, notes, the accounts of this period reflected some factional rivalry within the Spanish camp, which may have led to exaggerated descriptions of events at La Navidad, such as Peter Martyr's statement: "Incapable of moderation in their acts of injustice, they carried off the women of the islanders under the very eyes of their brothers and their husbands; given over to violence and thieving, they had profoundly vexed the natives"

17. See Michael Taussig's discussion of twentieth-century photographs of naked indigenous women of South America as a form of "cannibalism in another mode" in *Shamanism, Colonialism, and the Wild Man: A Study in Terror and Healing* (Chicago: University of Chicago Press, 1987), 114–15.

18. Todorov (*The Morals of History*, 103–7) contrasts the writings of these two men.

19. Sale, *The Conquest of Paradise*, 140. Iris M. Zavala recalls how the Muslims "had been frequently represented as licentious, lascivious, and having body

odors." "Representing the Colonial Subject," in *1492–1992: Re/Discovering Colonial Writing*, Hispanic Issues, no. 4, edited by René Jara and Nicholas Spadaccini (Minneapolis: University of Minnesota Press, 1989), 330. Magnus Mörner, in *Race Mixture in the History of Latin America* (Boston: Little, Brown and Company, 1976), 21, reminds us of efforts on the part of the indigenous men of the Antilles "to hide their women from the white strangers," suggesting that relations were unwanted.

20. Montrose ("The Work of Gender," 181) quotes the passage about the women's sexual torture of their husbands' penises. Todorov (*The Morals of History*, 105) quotes a French translator of 1855, who indicates how popular this story made Vespucci.

21. Todorov, *The Morals of History*, 105–9. Montrose ("The Work of Gender," 180) quotes in full the text from Vespucci's letter of 1504 that seems to describe this scene.

22. Antonello Gerbi, *Nature in the New World: From Christopher Columbus to Gonzalo Fernández de Oviedo* (Pittsburgh: University of Pittsburgh Press, 1985), 350–51.

23. Ramón Gutiérrez, *When Jesus Came, the Corn Mothers Went Away: Marriage, Sexuality, and Power in New Mexico, 1500–1846* (Stanford, Calif.: Stanford University Press, 1991), 17, 45. Gutiérrez's use of the term "libidinous" may reflect more of the European point of view than the indigenous. Many modern observers have been greatly influenced by European male writings on the sexuality of the indigenous women of this hemisphere. Even Hilde Krueger, a woman publishing in New York in the 1940s, shockingly calls the "young Indian women, so animal-like in their approach to sex" and suggests that they "looked upon the Spaniard as a kind of god." She adds that the "mutual feeling of strangeness . . . must have lent the erotic experience entirely new facets and an emotional aspect we can only faintly imagine." Quoted by Frances Karttunen, *Between Worlds: Interpreters, Guides, and Survivors* (New Brunswick, N.J.: Rutgers University Press, 1994), 3.

24. Many modern observers have apologized for sexual assault in the conquest of the Americas by saying that, after long voyages and with so few European women present in the early years, the invaders were inevitably scratching a sexual itch. Later, as colonial society began to resemble the metropolis and Iberian women came over in large numbers, rape diminished. However, the evolution from conquest to full-blown settlement entailed myriad social and political transformations, besides the growing presence of European women, that likely affected the frequency of sexual assault. Sex-ratio proponents slight the role of rape as a tool both for terrorizing initially and for maintaining control over time. Further, the results of recent sex-ratio research have diminished rather than strengthened its relationship to the frequency of rape. See Hartmann and Ross, "Comment on 'On Writing the History of Rape,'" 932–33. Peggy Reeves Sanday asserts flatly

that "Rape is not an instinct triggered by celibacy" in "The Socio-Cultural Context of Rape: A Cross-Cultural Study," *Journal of Social Issues* 37.4 (1981): 25.

25. Gutiérrez, *When Jesus Came*, 51.

26. Quoted in John Hemming, *Red Gold: The Conquest of the Brazilian Indians, 1500–1760* (Cambridge: Harvard University Press, 1978), 17.

27. Quoted in Hemming, *Red Gold*, 3–4.

28. Enrique Dussel interprets the relationship this way: "In satisfying a frequently sadistic voluptuousness, Spaniards vented their purely masculine libido through the erotic subjugation of the Other as Indian woman." *The Invention of the Americas: Eclipse of "the Other" and the Myth of Modernity*, translated by Michael D. Barber (New York: Continuum, 1995), 46.

29. Quoted in Hemming, *Red Gold*, 43–44.

30. Quoted in Hemming, *Red Gold*, 17.

31. See Claudio Esteva-Fabregat, *Mestizaje in Ibero-America* (Tucson: University of Arizona Press, 1995), 157. Of course, clergy were not guiltless of seducing indigenous women and siring mixed-heritage offspring. The indigenous critique of Spanish colonization in Peru, apparently written by Felipe Guamán Poma de Ayala, includes an illustration of children sired by priests (reproduced in Mörner, *Race Mixture*, xiv). In New Mexico, Fray Nicolás de Freitas noted that many friars had concubines and "all the pueblos are full of friars' children." Quoted in Gutiérrez, *When Jesus Came*, 123. Gutiérrez (124–25) elaborates on charges made by indigenous women against priests and various priests' admissions of guilt, including a case in which a friar had forcibly raped "a woman, splitting her throat, and burying her in his cell." In an indigenous petition to have a priest removed from a pueblo in Jalisco in 1611, Juan Vicente complained that the priest had tried to force himself on the man's daughter when she went to sweep the church one evening. "She would not let him," Juan Vicente wrote (but in his original language, Nahuatl), "and there inside the church he beat her." See *Beyond the Codices*, edited by Arthur J. O. Anderson, Frances Berdan, and James Lockhart (Los Angeles: UCLA Latin American Center, 1976), 170–74. See also Robert Haskett, "'Not a Pastor but a Wolf': Indigenous Clergy Relations in Early Cuernavaca and Taxco," *The Americas* 50.3 (1994): 318–22.

32. Mörner, *Race Mixture*, 23.

33. See Anne J. Cruz and Mary Elizabeth Perry, "Culture and Control in Counter-Reformation Spain," in *Culture and Control in Counter-Reformation Spain*, Hispanic Issues, no. 7, edited by Anne J. Cruz and Mary Elizabeth Perry (Minneapolis: University of Minnesota Press, 1992), ix–xxiii.

34. Hurtado, *Indian Survival on the California Frontier*, 25.

35. Quoted in Esteva-Fabregat, *Mestizaje in Ibero-America*, 157.

36. Eugene Korth, *The Spanish Policy in Colonial Chile: The Struggle for Justice, 1535–1700* (Stanford, Calif.: Stanford University Press, 1968), 217–19.

37. Diane Wolfthal, "'A Hue and a Cry': Medieval Rape Imagery and Its Transformation," *Art Bulletin* 75.1 (1993): 39–40.

38. One difference was that, over time, a greater number of permanent relationships between Spanish men and indigenous women would form in these central areas as the European presence increased.

39. Bartolomé de Las Casas, *The Devastation of the Indies: A Brief Account* (Baltimore: Johns Hopkins University Press, 1992), 2, 4, 77.

40. Tzvetan Todorov also reproduces passages from Las Casas which he sees as possibly realistic eyewitness accounts. In one, *The Conquest of America: The Question of the Other*, translated by Richard Howard (New York: Harper Torchbooks, 1987), 139, a Dominican ecclesiastic tells about some overseers in the gold mines in the Caribbean in 1519 who regularly violated married women and "maidens," while sending the indigenous men out to the fields, even going so far as to tie one man up and throw him "under the bed like a dog, before the foreman lay down, directly over him, with his wife."

41. Bernal Díaz, *The Conquest of New Spain* (Harmondsworth, England: Penguin, 1963), 330–31.

42. See Esteva-Fabregat, *Mestizaje in Ibero-America*, 157–58.

43. *We People Here: Nahuatl Accounts of the Conquest of Mexico*, Reportorium Columbianum, no. 1, edited and translated by James Lockhart (Berkeley: University of California Press, 1993), 248. A Spanish preference for fair skin seems also to be indicated by Gonzalo Fernández de Oviedo's reference to the efforts of indigenous women on Hispaniola in the sixteenth century to bleach their skin in order to attract alliances with colonists. See Kathleen A. Deagan, "Spanish-Indian Interaction in Sixteenth-Century Florida and Hispaniola," in *Cultures in Contact: The Impact of European Contacts on Native American Cultural Institutions, A.D. 1000–1800*, Anthropological Society of Washington Series, edited by William W. Fitzhugh (Washington, D.C.: Smithsonian Institution Press, 1985), 306.

44. Díaz, *The Conquest of New Spain*, 352.

45. Marcelo Díaz de Salas and Luis Reyes García, "Testimonio de la Fundación de Santo Tomás Ajusco," *Tlalocan* 6.3 (1970): 196.

46. Díaz, *The Conquest of New Spain*, 176. Elsewhere (125), Díaz also speaks of a doña Francisca as being "very beautiful, for an Indian."

47. Díaz, *The Conquest of New Spain*, 80–82.

48. Karttunen, *Between Worlds*, 22.

49. Díaz, *The Conquest of New Spain*, 121, 125. Díaz also quotes two caciques of Tlaxcala who speak of giving the Spaniards women "so that we may have kinship with their children" (154).

50. Díaz de Salas and Reyes, "Testimonio de la Fundación de Santo Tomás Ajusco," 199.

51. *Relación de las ceremonias y ritos y población y gobierno de los indios de la Provincia de Michoacán (1541), Reproducción facsímil del Ms. ç. IV. 5. del El Escorial*, edited by José Tudela, with a preliminary study by Paul Kirchoff (Madrid: Aguilar, 1956), 256.

52. Díaz, *The Conquest of New Spain*, 121.

53. Steve Stern suggests that, in colonial Peru, the indigenous women may have had little say in the decision that they be given by their fathers in alliances to Spanish men. He also considers the possibility that they may have found "marriage or informal conjugal relations with outsiders" attractive, in order to acquire property or escape taxation burdens in their communities. The indigenous writer Felipe Guamán Poma de Ayala complained in the early seventeenth century that indigenous women "no longer love Indians but rather Spaniards, and they become big whores." This shows resentment and exaggeration but still reflects what Steve Stern calls "a very real social pattern." See Steve J. Stern, *Peru's Indian Peoples and the Challenge of Spanish Conquest: Huamanga to 1640* (Madison: University of Wisconsin Press, 1982), 170.

54. Hemming, *Red Gold*, 43–44. There are other, occasional attestations of indigenous women's sometimes positive views on sexual relations with the foreigners, relations which their own leaders encouraged. For instance, in Florida in the 1560s an indigenous leader offered his sister to the Spanish conqueror Pedro Menéndez de Avilés and, after a supposed debate about what should be the appropriate action on Menéndez's part, the "captains" (his men or the indigenous leaders?) explained to her that it would be good for Menéndez to "sleep with her, for this would be a great beginning to their trusting him and the other Christians." Supposedly, "in the morning she arose very joyful and the Christian women who spoke to her said that she was very much pleased." Such a response on her part, if not a European invention or something she pretended, could mean that she was pleased with herself for fulfilling a role expected of her by either her own people, the new power holders, or both. See *New American World: A Documentary History of North America to 1612*, 5 vols., edited by David B. Quinn (New York: Arno Press and Hector Bye, 1979), 2:484.

55. Stern, *Peru's Indian Peoples*, 171–73.

56. Díaz, *The Conquest of New Spain*, 409. It was self-serving of Díaz to recount this story, but it may be true. He also tells how Cortés's interpreter doña Marina said that "she would rather serve her husband and Cortés than anything else in the world" (86).

57. Padden (*The Hummingbird and the Hawk*, 232) describes the "tragic origin" of the first mixed-heritage offspring from the Spanish conquest of Mexico, who faced considerable rejection and hostility and supposedly created such havoc that they caught the attention of the first bishop sent to the region.

58. Mörner, *Race Mixture*, 27.

59. *New Iberian World: A Documentary History of the Discovery and Settlement of Latin America to the Early 17th Century,* 5 vols., edited by John H. Parry and Robert G. Keith (New York: Times Books, 1984), 2:349–53.

60. Susan Brownmiller, *Against Our Will: Men, Women, and Rape* (New York: Bantam, 1975), 313.

61. Mörner, *Race Mixture,* 25.

62. See Octavio Paz's essay "Sons of La Malinche," in his book, *The Labyrinth of Solitude: Life and Thought in Mexico* (New York: Grove Press, 1961), for his exploration of the psychological trauma of being sons of "la chingada." Novelist Carlos Fuentes's narratives (quoted, for example, in Dussel, *The Invention of the Americas,* 47) also eloquently capture the struggle of the mestizo child.

63. Herren, *La conquista erótica,* 256 (the translation is mine).

64. Quoted in Montrose, "The Work of Gender," 187. Note how Ralegh, not unlike his Mediterranean counterparts, refers to the indigenous women as possessions of the indigenous men. Northern European men were not guiltless of behaviors they delighted in attributing to the Spanish. Captain John Sutter of New Helvetia colony in Mexican California allegedly had a special room next to his chambers where a "large number of Indian girls . . . were constantly at his beck and call," and he had sex with some as young as ten years old. In Oregon, when one of Jedediah Smith's men raped an Umpqua woman in the late 1820s, the tribe killed most of Smith's men and stole their horses and pelts in retaliation. See Hurtado, *Indian Survival on the California Frontier,* 63, 42. Susan Brownmiller (*Against Our Will,* 150) suspects that rape was "a casual by-product of the move westward and The Great Frontier," where the "rape of a 'squaw' by white men was not deemed important. The Indian woman gave her testimony to no one; it was never solicited, except perhaps orally within her tribe."

65. Cruz and Perry, "Culture and Control in Counter-Reformation Spain," xviii–xix.

66. Wolfthal, "'A Hue and a Cry,'" 57, 61–62.

67. *Against Our Will,* 35.

68. Bernal Díaz (*The Conquest of New Spain,* 140–41) discusses the disappointing calculation of the shares for the captains and soldiers after the entrada that gained the Spaniards control of Mexico.

69. James Lockhart, *Spanish Peru, 1532–1560: A Colonial Society* (Madison: University of Wisconsin Press, 1968), 138.

70. Lyle N. McAlister, *Spain and Portugal in the New World, 1492–1700,* Europe and the World in the Age of Expansion, no. 3 (Minneapolis: University of Minnesota Press, 1984), 91.

71. Zavala, "Representing the Colonial Subject," 326, 333.

72. The monarch declared intermarriage permissible in a pronouncement of 1501. The governor of Santo Domingo, Hispaniola, encouraged intermarriage in

1503 (Mörner, *Race Mixture*, 25–26). Pronouncements in favor of marriage were also included, for example, in the Laws of Burgos of 1512 (Deagan, "Spanish-Indian Interaction," 298). Still, only about 10 percent of Spanish men in Santo Domingo in 1514 were married to native women; concubinage was the norm (Mörner, *Race Mixture*, 25–26).

73. Note the instructions given Christopher Columbus in 1493, "that the Indians be treated with kindness," which, in the wake of abuses, evolved quickly into much more specific orders (*1492–1992: Re/Discovering Colonial Writing*, 387). In 1501, for instance, the instructions prohibited "Christians living in the Indies to take the wives or sons or daughters of the Indians or do any other harm or damage to their persons or their possessions" (*New Iberian World*, 2:261). Again, in 1510, Hernando Cortés was told to prevent "any of the Spanish Christians of your company [from engaging] in an excess or casual coitus with any woman outside of our law, because it is a very odious sin against God" and urging that "there should not be scandal . . . nor in any way or manner should they dare to enter their houses or trifle with their women nor should they take them, nor approach them, nor speak to them, nor say or do anything else that might be presumed to cause any annoyance" (*1492–1992: Re/Discovering Colonial Writing*, 402, 410). The persisting need for such pronouncements suggests the nightmare lived on, but it also shows an official effort to curb such behavior.

74. McAlister, *Spain and Portugal in the New World*, 91. King Ferdinand ordered that items given to indigenous peoples must have a least a third of the value of the item obtained from them: the trading advantage had to have limits. Rescate practices surely exceeded the limits, although some captains kept trying to remind their men of such rulings. Columbus objected to what he saw as unfair trading with the Taínos, for instance. See James Axtell, *Imagining the Other: First Encounters in North America* (Washington, D.C.: American Historical Association, 1991), 27.

75. Quoted in Hemming, *Red Gold*, 41.

76. Claudio Esteva-Fabregat (*Mestizaje in Ibero-America*, 120, 123) calls the seizure of women a "predatory excess," "a constant," and a "habitual process within the very strategy of war."

77. There was a formal ceremony in which a legal (in European terms) document, called a *requerimiento* (requirement), was read to the indigenous peoples about their pending colonization. If they resisted, the would lose their liberty and property. See Lewis Hanke, *The Spanish Struggle for Justice in the Conquest of America* (Boston: Little, Brown and Company, 1965), 31–36. On "just war" see also Padden, *The Hummingbird and the Hawk*, 136.

78. Venereal disease can be another vile legacy of sexual coercion and assault. "Syphilis was especially devastating" for the indigenous population of California, says Albert Hurtado (*Indian Survival on the California Frontier*, 25), "killing people outright or weakening their defenses so much that other diseases killed

them. It was particularly hard on women in childbirth, killing both mother and child." The men in the conquering expedition of Hernando Cortés in Mexico complained as they descended a pyramid that their "thighs pained them" because they were "suffering from pustules or running sores," a possible indication of venereal disease (Díaz, *The Conquest of New Spain*, 238). They called venereal disease "mal de mujeres" (illness from women), revealing their one-sided view. See Padden, *The Hummingbird and the Hawk*, 230.

Chapter 2

Native American Sexuality in the Eyes of the Beholders, 1535–1710

Gordon Sayre

Early explorers' accounts of the sexuality of Native American peoples are strongly influenced by the sexual overtones which imbued their perceptions of the continent as a whole. For sixteenth-century explorers the New World was charged with eroticism. Many engravings and paintings from the sixteenth through the eighteenth centuries portrayed a nude woman as an allegorical figure for the American continent. John Donne, in his well-known Elegy 19, uses America as a figure for the woman the poet is trying to undress, or "discover," and seduce, even though the poem has, on a literal level, nothing to do with exploration or colonialism. The name "America" is itself the feminine form of the first name of explorer Amerigo Vespucci. A well-known engraving made around 1600 by Jan van der Straet shows Vespucci dis-covering America naked in her hammock.[1] Many sixteenth-century explorers wrote narratives which dramatized their achievements as a sexual conquest of a virgin land, as in Sir Walter Ralegh's description of Guiana as "a country that hath yet her maidenhead, never sacked, turned, nor wrought."[2]

Therefore, representations of America and Native Americans written in the sixteenth and seventeenth centuries entered into a discourse that was highly eroticized. Even when explorers and missionaries tried to represent literally their eyewitness observations of native sexual or marriage customs, they were always responding to their own preconceptions, and frequently were writing of behavior in which they had been involved. The following analysis of accounts of indigenous Amerindian sexual practices will reveal how the position of the writer, as discoverer, missionary, fur

trader or colonial promoter, influenced the patterns of representations of
sexuality.

Giovanni da Verrazzano was the first European to explore the mid-Atlantic coast from the Carolinas north to Maine, in 1524. His brief report
to King Francis I of France, who employed him to make the trip, presents
a romantic, Arcadian image and can be read as a comedic tale of
courtship between two eager partners, each anxious for signs of willingness in the other, but unable to communicate by speech and inclined to
misinterpret the other's gestures. Verrazzano found the natives of Narragansett Bay (presumably the same described by Roger Williams 120 years
later) to be "the most beautiful and have the most civil customs that we
have found on this voyage. They are taller than we are . . . and their manner is sweet and gentle, very like the manner of the ancients. . . . Their
women are just as shapely and beautiful; very gracious, of attractive manner and pleasant appearance . . . they go nude except for a stag skin."[3]
Verrazzano also noted that they wore rich pelts, fancy hair arrangements,
and jewelry of copper, which they valued more than gold. After detailing
these ornaments, he added, "They are very generous and give away all
they have."[4] This image is not of a virgin land, innocently awaiting penetration by European men, but of a wealthy, comely, and civil partner
who is generous and willing to please. It is more courtly than the more famous lines of the courtier, Ralegh. Three brief encounters in Verrazzano's
narrative sketch a courtship process that is also quite different from the
John Smith/Pocahontas legend, which has been thoroughly mythologized
and, more recently, analyzed.[5]

In the first episode, on North Carolina's Outer Banks, Verrazzano
sends a sailor swimming ashore with gifts of trinkets. The sailor tries to
throw these onto the beach and return, but he is overcome by the surf and
swept up on the beach. The natives "took him up by the head, the legs,
and arms and carried him some distance away. Whereupon the youth, re-
alizing he was being carried away like this, was seized with terror, and
began to utter loud cries. . . . They took off his shirt and shoes and hose,
leaving him naked, then made a huge fire next to him."[6] Though both
sides have good intentions, the scene conveys anxiety about captivity,
rape, and cannibalism, for the observers on board the ship do not know
will happen the youth, but believe that he will be roasted and eaten. Yet
when he "showed them by signs that he wanted to return to the ship . . .
with the greatest kindness, they accompanied him to the sea, holding him
close and embracing him,"[7] like a kind lover reassuring a reluctant virgin.

In a second episode soon after, Verrazzano's men turn the tables. They meet an old woman who accepts their offer of food and a young woman with three children who angrily throws the food on the ground: "we wanted to take the young woman, who was very beautiful and tall, but it was impossible to take her because of the loud cries she uttered."[8] They are forced to settle for one of her sons as a captive. The third episode comes after an exchange of commodities, and suggests that the natives have set limits to the kinds of trade they will enter into. During Verrazzano's two-week stay, the Narragansetts every day "came to see us on the ship, bringing their womenfolk. They are very careful with them . . . and however many entreaties we made or offers of various gifts, we could not persuade them to let the women come on board ship."[9] This Arcadia is full of enticing things, but its women are elusive. Verrazzano from the start sees North American women as attractive, but his efforts to court them are spurned, and each side reveals great anxiety about being captured by, or surrendering to, the other. And because we have only Verrazzano's side of the story we cannot know for sure if the resistance of the young woman with the three children and the reticence of the "womenfolk" in general was customary or an impulsive reaction to alien aggression.

This is the difficulty of studying Amerindian life in early contact and colonial times. For the social customs where archeology offers no evidence, for the outlook of tribes which barely survive today, we are dependent on accounts by Europeans who didn't understand the cultures they described. These accounts are often laden with ethnocentrism, or project Europeans' cultural obsessions onto the Amerindian Other, as we see in the courtly assumptions of Verrazzano or in the figures of the Wild Man, Noble Savage, and Natural Man.[10] Nowhere is this more true than in descriptions of sexuality. Not because it was a taboo subject that explorers and colonists could not describe in frank or objective terms, but because nowhere, not even in war and trade, was the observer's relationship to the behavior he described more fraught with semiconscious desires and fears. It's easy to identify tropes referring to Arcadia or the Amazons, or phallocentrism as in Ralegh, but it is more difficult to determine what accurate ethnological information if any, lies behind the prejudices, and to do so one must take into account the particular position of each observer. Should an author's portrayal of modest and chaste young virgins in Canada, for instance, be accepted as accurate, or attributed to his own situation as a missionary sworn to chastity and the defense of the sacred vows of marriage? To his contempt for or envy of the colonists who solicit the attention of the local women? To his disgust with the licentious life of the upper classes in France? Examining accounts of northeastern North America from Verrazzano to 1710, one begins to see a fundamental contrast between the attitudes toward Indian sexuality characteristic of missionaries and those characteristic of explorers, traders, and colonial promoters. Missionaries grounded their representations in a need to maintain a separation between the Indians' behavior and that of the Europeans, themselves included. Behavior which showed a primitive innocence had to be protected from the corrupting influences of the whisky and wealth acquired through trade. Alternatively, behavior they considered lewd and lascivious had to be reproved and corrected, or there was a risk it would infect colonists.

In contrast, explorers' and promoters' accounts of Indian marriage and sex treat it almost as another resource of the land. Instead of anxiety about maintaining separation, there is a promise of engagement and participation. Sometimes it takes the form of a metaphorical male conquest of the land itself, as in Raleigh's portrayal of Guiana or Thomas Morton's description of New Canaan (New England) as: "Like a faire virgin, longing to be sped,/And meete her lover in a Nuptiall bed,/Deck'd in rich ornaments t'advance her state."[11] But sometimes it's more of a romantic farce, as in Verrazzano, or a bawdy comedy, as we shall see in Lawson, and by 1700 there emerged inklings of a rationalized utopian system of sexuality, as in Lahontan.

Both groups of men relied upon hospitable receptions from the Indians, but each sought a different kind of hospitality. A Jesuit missionary might live in a *cabane* and welcome adoption into a native family, but he would never marry a native woman. Traders, on the other hand, often married natives, and wrote with jocular delight of their hosts' custom of offering young women as bedfellows during their stay in a community. Virginia planter and promoter Robert Beverley leant an exotic seraglio atmosphere to this hospitality, this "remarkable way of entertaining Strangers of Condition."

he is regal'd till Bed time; when a Brace of young Beautiful Virgins are chosen, to wait upon him that night, for his particular refreshment. These Damsels are to Undress this happy Gentleman, and as soon as he is in Bed, they gently lay themselves down by him, one on one side of him, and the other on the other. They esteem it a breach of Hospitality, not to submit to every thing he desires of them.[12]

Although this treatment is reserved for "Men of great Distinction," the American setting broke down the class strata of Europe and offered a commoner the chance to acquire such "Distinction" through a wealth of trade goods. The contrast between this eroticism and the missionary attitude can be seen in a comment from Gabriel Sagard, a Recollet missionary among the Huron, who wrote in 1632: "One of the chief and most annoying embarrassments they caused us at the beginning of our visit to their country was their continual importunity and requests to marry us, or at least to make a family alliance with us."[13]

There was ample evidence in native customs to support both the theory that Indians were lustful and promiscuous and the view that they were chaste and reserved. Jesuit Paul LeJeune's *Relation* of 1639 described native courtship practices: "There is a most evil custom among the Savages. Those who seek a girl or a woman in marriage go to her to make love at night."[14] Because the woman reportedly would extinguish a small fire as a signal that her suitor was welcome, the baron de Lahontan called this custom *courir l'allumette*, "running the match."

Common evidence of chastity, on the other hand, included the custom of a sexual probation period for newlyweds. Lafitau, LeClercq, and Deliette all wrote of a six-month to one-year delay in consummating a marriage, "to do themselves honor, for when they have children immediately at the end of nine months it is a matter of reproach when they quarrel to say that they loved their husbands before marrying them."[15] A few texts reported on abortion techniques which could have ensured that newlyweds were childless. Missionaries, however, were generally more inclined to stress the chastity of the Indians, or at least of their converts, often as part of a melodrama of primitive innocence confronting the corruption of trade and rum. Thus, missionaries took the well-defined Christian separation between the chaste and the unchaste and used it as an analogy for the distinction between the converted and unconverted around their mission. LeJeune, who lived among the Huron in today's Ontario in the 1630s, reported on the chastity of his converts: "I have heard on good authority that some shameless women, who had approached some men at night and solicited them to do evil in secret, received for answer, only these words: 'I believe in God, I pray to him every day; he forbids such actions, I cannot commit them.'"[16] He added a parallel story about female converts who rejected the advances of unchaste men:

> Three young Algonquins from the Island [Ottawa], having come down to Kebec, and wishing to make love according to their custom, addressed themselves to Christian girls. They were greatly astonished when these girls told them to apply to us about the matter, and that they would decide nothing without our advice. These good people came to us and asked us if we governed the Savage girls.[17]

A later *Relation* tells of a Frenchman who "took the resolution to entice into sin as many Savages as he could, so as to ruin the country. . . . He cajoles some girls, and invites them to drink, on purpose to intoxicate them, in order to pass from one crime to another."[18] But when he attempts to seduce a Christian Indian girl, she upbraids him so effectively that he vows to change his ways and work for the conversion of Indians. The Canadian Jesuits had little success at fully Frenchifying the Indians, but in vignettes such as these, they could use sexuality, or rather chastity, as a sign that the natives were a docile and regenerate people with moral concepts familiar to Europeans, and denounce the dissolute morals of unregenerate colonial traders. It's hard to tell if the Hurons' traditional customs encouraged the chastity which the converts maintained, or if it was a product of Christian ideology.

For traders, assimilation took a different meaning. John Lawson explained how it was for more than sensual reasons that traders sought out native partners:

> The English Traders are seldom without an Indian Female for his Bed-fellow, alledging these Reasons as sufficient to allow of such a Familiarity. First, they being remote from any white People, that it preserves their Friendship with the Heathens, they esteeming a white Man's Child much above one of their getting, the Indian Mistress ever securing her white Friend Provisions whilst he stays amongst them. And lastly, This Correspondence makes them learn the Indian Tongue much the sooner.[19]

This process quickly became almost routine. Most Indian nations were accustomed to strengthening alliances through intermarriage or sexual exchange. The French fur traders, or *coureurs de bois*, used this practice to their advantage, maintaining wives or lovers in one or more villages as a means of securing a steady supply of pelts.[20] This was also common in the southern colonies, but forbidden in Puritan New England. William Byrd II, a wealthy Virginian with a cavalier jocularity even stronger than

Lawson's, extolled the advantages of intermarriage, describing the Indians as healthy and attractive, as Verrazzano had, and satirically contrasting religion with sex, the missionary's with the trader's style: "a sprightly Lover is the most prevailing Missionary that can be sent among these, or any other Infidels." Byrd also recognized that "The French, for their Parts, have not been so Squeamish in Canada, who upon Trial find abundance of Attraction in the Indians. Their late Grand Monarch thought it not below even the Dignity of a Frenchman to become one flesh with this People, and therefore Ordered 100 livres for any of his Subjects, Man or Woman, that would intermarry with a Native."[21]

Byrd believed that this gave the French colony, and Catholicism, an edge over the English. He was mostly accurate; in the earliest days of the colony, Québec founder Samuel de Champlain had encouraged marriages between French men and Christianized Indians. Officials had offered a grant of three thousand livres to any man who married a native woman.[22] This offer was never taken up, however, for the Church would marry only Christian Indians such as the girls sent to Québec convents. But these girls often refused to assimilate, or refused to abandon the chastity so firmly inculcated by the nuns. The Jesuits soon withdrew their support for intermarriage, and starting in 1684 colonial policy prohibited it. The major reason was that the sexual liaisons of traders and explorers had had the effect of easing the transition of Frenchmen into Indian life and away from the colony, rather then solidifying the Frenchification of the Indians. A 1709 letter from a Jesuit in Canada reports that "the experience we have had in this country is that all the Frenchmen who have married Indian women have become libertines . . . and that the children they have had are as idle as the Indians themselves; one must withhold permission for these sorts of marriages."[23] This judgment might be attributed to an antipathy between fur traders and missionaries, but at times the missionaries opposed not only fur traders' relations with the Indians but even settlers'. Explorer Pierre-Esprit Radisson suspected that this was because missionaries were themselves profiting from the fur trade: "The fathers Jesuits not willing to permitt French families to goe there, for to conserve the best to their profitt, houlding this pretext that yong men should frequent the wild women, so that the Christian religion by evil example could not be established."[24]

In stories told by John Lawson, the worst fears of missionaries seem to be borne out; the ethnographic account of native customs undisturbed by Europeans turns into a promotional tract offering sex for male colonists' exploitation: "The Girls at 12 or 13 Years of Age, as soon as Nature prompts them, freely bestow their Maidenheads on some Youth about the same Age, continuing her Favours on whom she most affects, changing her Mate very often . . . Multiplicity of Gallants never being a Stain to a Female's Reputation, or the least Hindrance of her Advancement, but the more Whorish, the more Honourable."[25] The innocence of "Nature" and "freedom" in this passage quickly shifts to a language specific to European masculinist sexuality. By the next page, the innocence of these girls becomes an excitatory ploy:

> They set apart their youngest and prettiest Faces for trading Girls; these are remarkable by their Hair, having a particular Tonsure by which they are known, and distinguish'd from those engag'd to Husbands. They are mercenary, and whoever makes Use of them, first hires them, the greatest Share of the Gain going to the King's Purse, who is the chief Bawd . . . and his own Cabin (very often) being the chiefest Brothel-House.[26]

The later chapter "An Account of the Indians of North Carolina" repeats much of this, going into more detail about the customs behind this sex trade: "every one of the Girl's Relations arguing the Advantage or Detriment that may ensue such a Night's Encounter; all which is done with as much Steadiness and Reality, as if it was the greatest Concern in the World . . . making no Difference betwixt an Agreement of this Nature, and a Bargain of any other."[27] Lawson also remarked that "The Trading Girls . . . have an Art to destroy the Conception, and she that brings a Child in this Station, is accounted a Fool."[28]

Lawson thus tears down the utopian isolation and innocence of Native American sexuality, the favorable image that prompted both to the lightly salacious charms in Verrazzano's narrative and the moralizing of the missionaries, in order to set up a colonial trading house for sexual resources. Yet like many prurient scenes, his have a comic side as well. Lawson tells a story of "Our Fellow Traveller" on his thousand-mile trek through Carolina, who, making camp in an Indian village, and "having a great Mind for an Indian Lass, for his Bed-Fellow that Night, spoke to our Guide, who soon got a Couple, reserving one for himself."[29] The system is presented as indigenous, a natural opportunity for lustful colonists. Lawson's friend goes through a farcical marriage, what he calls a "Winchester-Wedding," which seems contrived to amuse his English readers: "Every one of the Bride-Maids were as great Whores, as Mrs. Bride."[30] In the morning, however, Lawson finds that "Mr. Bridegroom, who in less than 12 Hours, was Batchelor, Husband, and Widdower"[31] has been rolled, relieved of all his trading goods and even his shoes. The veracity of Lawson's story is doubtful, but its objective truth is less the issue than the inappropriateness of the terms he uses. The whorehouse was alien to Native America, even if this particular trader did treat the women as whores, and was relieved of his goods.

Lawson's Indian bordello is just one trope used to twist representations of Indian sexuality into forms attractive to male European readers. Robert Beverley's *History and Present State of Virginia* (1705) was a promotional piece similar in goals and form to Lawson's (both Beverley and Lawson owned large tracts of land in their colony and stood to profit from immigration), yet Beverley chose to ennoble the Indians, to depict them as worthy company for tobacco planters with social pretensions. In the area of sexuality, this entailed the seraglio for "Strangers of Condition" quoted above, but Beverley insisted that this was not prostitution, "Tho the young Indian Women are said to prostitute their bodies for Wampom Peak, Runtees, Beads, and other such like fineries; yet I never could find any ground for the accusation, and believe it only to be an unjust scandal upon them."[32] The origin of accounts such as Lawson's, Beverley suggested, lay with the more vulgar male colonists, not with the girls whose sexual license was merely a "frolicksom" freedom in the disposition of their own bodies: "Indeed I believe this story to be an aspersion cast on those innocent Creatures, by reason of the freedom they take in Conversation, which uncharitable Christians interpret as Criminal, upon no other ground, than the guilt of their own Consciences."[33]

Beverley was one of a few early eighteenth-century writers who approached an understanding of sexuality which went beyond what Michel Foucault has called the "repressive hypothesis," a dynamic which imagines sexual freedom only as the transgression of restraint, and, conversely, social power as controlling sexuality through "prohibition, censorship, and denial."[34] Most colonial writers recognized that repression would not exist in a prelapsarian society, nor in that of the Deists' Natural Man. However, they couldn't quite figure out any other way to think about sexual behavior. For example, if marriages among the Indians were not indissoluble, and divorce was not accompanied by any stigma, did this mean that virtually all marriages ended in divorce, or that so few did that there was no need to control it? Did an apparent libertinism imply a high rate of adultery? What was the cause of such promiscuity?

The accounts of Roger Williams, in his annotated dictionary of the Algonquian language, are symptomatic of the confusion on these issues. With regard to adultery, he gave the word "Mammaûsu. *an adulterer*" and described the punishment: "commonly, if the Woman be false, the offended Husband will be solemnly revenged upon the offendor, before many witnesses, by many blowes and wounds."[35] Yet in the preceding chapter, "Of their Government and Justice," he suggested that the moral purity of the Indians greatly exceeded the English, that "although thay have not so much to restraine them (both in respect of knowledge of God and Lawes of men) as the English have, yet a man shall never heare of such crimes amongst them of robberies, murthers, adulteries, &c, as amongst the English."[36] If there was no adultery, how did he observe the punishment for it, and why would such a law be needed? Does the report of a harsh punishment for adultery contradict the claim that adultery was unheard of support it? The repressive hypothesis led to accounts of Indian behavior which seem scarcely credible in the context of European customs. For example, many colonial observers echoed Williams's remark that promiscuity among the unmarried Indians was not inconsistent with later fidelity: "Single fornication they count no sin, but after Mariage . . . then they count it hainous for either of them to be false."[37]

Since most European readers imagined the Indians to be "savages" living in a bestial anarchy without morals or restraints, colonial writers struggled to either affirm this view or to rebut it. However, the rebuttal sometimes consisted of a claim for an innocent absence of sin, at other times for a repression more effective than in Europe. The controversy over nakedness, modesty, and visual provocation was indicative of this conundrum. Williams's chapter "Of their nakednesse and clothing" described how "their Female they, in a modest blush cover with a little Apron of an hand breadth from their very birth," but that "Custome hath used their minds and bodies to it [nakedness], and in such a freedom from any wantonnesse, that I have never seen that wantonnesse amongst them, as, (with griefe) I have heard of in Europe."[38] If seeing others naked was really so routine, one would not expect the women to show a "modest blush." Marc Lescarbot, a French visitor to Acadia in the early seventeenth century, stated the problem more clearly, yet initiated a series of repetitions and corrections: "One might think that the nakedness of this people would make them more lecherous, but the contrary is the case. . . . I can say for our savages, that I never saw amongst them any immodest gesture or look, and I venture to affirm that they are far less given to that vice than we in these parts."[39] He explained this not by familiarity with the sight of the naked body but by reference to medical theories that the Americans' lack of salt, spices, meat, and even hats all suppressed the libido, as did the use of tobacco.

Lescarbot was a lawyer who went to Acadia in 1606–7 as a guest of the colonial commander de Poutrincourt. During his short stay, he studied the customs of the Souriquoi Indians around Port Royal in today's Nova Scotia. Gabriel Sagard, author of *Le Grand voyage du pays des Hurons* ("Long voyage to the country of the Hurons"), was a Recollet missionary and one of the first Frenchmen to live among the Hurons, along the south shore of Lake Huron, in 1623–24. These two men's eyewitness accounts of the native customs of two separate tribes might, one hopes, offer accurate ethnological information. Yet instead, the two texts weave a maze of misplaced repression hypotheses, plagiarism, and contradictions whose motives we can only guess at. In describing the continence of the Indians, Lescarbot used an analogy to a barbaric people of ancient times, which, from Herodotus to Tacitus, often inspired the same tropes of primitivism as the American Indians did in the Renaissance: "Caesar praises the Germans for having in their ancient savage life such continence that they reputed it a thing most vile for a young man to have the company of a woman or girl before he reached the age of twenty." Sagard began his chapter "Marriage and Concubinage" with the same allusion to the Germans, yet drew a contrast rather than a comparison: "It is the reverse with the boys and young men of Canada, and especially with those of the Huron country, who are at liberty to give themselves over to this wickedness as soon as they can, and the young girls to prostitute themselves as soon as they are capable of doing so. Nay even the parents are often procurers of their own daughters."[40] Lescarbot, the lawyer and classicist, saw the Souriquoi as emblematic of a primitive innocence and absence of lust, such as prevailed among the ancient Germans, while Sagard, the missionary, saw in the Huron a sinful license for youthful sex, altogether unlike the mores of the Germans. One might assume that this contrast was due to the customs of different tribes or the prejudices of different observers, if there were not evidence that both writers were expressing preconceived notions. In the following lines Sagard again reverses his ground: "the parents are often procurers of their own daughters; although I can truthfully say that I have never seen a single kiss given, or any immodest gesture or look, and for this reason I venture to assert that they are less prone to this vice than people here." These are almost the same lines as in Lescarbot! Sagard, like Lescarbot, claims that he saw no immodesty. He even offers the same reasons as Lescarbot: the absence of hats, spices, and wine, and the presence of tobacco (which was still a novelty in Europe). The authority of these exploration narratives was grounded on the eyewitness observations that few other Europeans could offer in the 1610s and 1620s. Yet can Sagard's claim for what he saw or didn't see be taken seriously if it is copied nearly verbatim from Lescarbot, who had seen a different tribe in a distant place? Although such plagiarism or repetitions are common in the colonial ethnographic sources on American Indian life, they are particularly instructive in regard to sexuality, because in sex, the truth, like desire itself, is so often believed to reside in what is hidden, although its promise is conveyed through a gaze upon a body.

It's not simply that Sagard copied Lescarbot. Both responded to a third, earlier colonial ethnographer, Jean de Léry, whose *History of a Voyage to the Land of Brazil* (1578) included a detailed account of the customs of the Tupi people of the Rio de Janiero area. At a time when the geography of America was vague, the great cultural and geographic distance between Canada and Brazil was less significant to these writers than the chance to generalize about "les sauvages américains." De Léry too praised the discretion of the natives, described harsh punishments for adultery, and the coexistence of premarital promiscuity with marital fidelity. His most precise echo of Sagard and Lescarbot, however, regards the so-called panders: "It is true that before they marry off their daughters, the fathers and relatives have no great scruples about prostituting them to the first comer."[41] I don't believe that this observation can be rejected simply because it appears to be plagiarized. Lescarbot does cite de Léry ("Jean de Léry praises the Brazilians for this continence")[42] and therefore refers to him obliquely also in this passage: "The maidens of Brazil have the same liberty of Canada to prostitute themselves as soon as they are able. Indeed the fathers act as their pandars, and think it an honour to give them to the men of these parts, in order to have children of their blood."[43] The issue might be clarified by separating what the three writers may have seen from the conclusions they drew. The "liberty" of the "maidens" corresponds to the freedom and agency attributed to native girls by many other observers, including Lahontan (see below). Sagard's version, by first claiming that the girls "prostitute" themselves, then shifting the agency to the fathers/panders, suggests that he may have assumed a patriarchal prerogative controlling the girls' behavior, where in fact there was none. Moreover, both Lescarbot and de Léry specify that the fathers acted as panders to the French colonists (de Léry added, "the Norman interpreters had already, before our arrival, taken advantage of them in several villages").[44] Significantly, it is the secular colonist, Lescarbot, who describes the involvement of the French in the natives' behavior, adding: "But to consent to this would be a thing unworthy of a Christian, and we see, to our great hurt, that God has severely punished this vice by the pox."[45] The pox was syphilis, thought to have been brought to Europe from America by the Spaniards. In his account, the Indians' sexual freedom, or rather the sexual hospitality which the colonists enjoyed and confused with a natural libertinism, is less a feature of their own culture than a temptation and a lesson to colonists. Such moral lessons were also drawn by missionary writers, but with the important difference that missionaries were not likely to include the involvement of Europeans (the succumbing to temptation) as part of the lesson. Sagard describes the wickedness of the girls prostituting themselves at the beginning of his chapter on "Marriage and Concubinage," and then tells in euphemistic language of the importunity of the girls toward him and his brother Recollects at the very end of the chapter, as if he feared the reader might connect the two and suspect that the missionaries consorted with the girls.

The opposing attitudes of the missionaries and the traders toward sex with and among the Indians frustrates efforts to understand what native sexuality was really like. Missionaries saw only innocence and corruption and anxiously tried to separate the two, while traders and promoters described sexual customs as if made for their own use and abuse. One French writer, however, offers a third position on native sexuality, an eagerness to engage, not in penetration, but in a comparison and philosophical examination of sexual customs in European and American Indian societies. This is the baron de Lahontan, a cultural and literary innovator in colonial writing. His *Nouveaux Voyages dans l'Amérique septentrionale* does more than merely narrate his experience or describe his observations, and therefore he needs to be read rhetorically, not literally.

As the third volume of his 1703 work, Lahontan wrote a dialogue between "Adario," a Huron Indian who has been to France, and "Lahontan," and used the native's voice to express radical ideas that the author had learned from living among the Indians. "Adario" describes Huron sexuality, law, and medicine in a manner which antipates Diderot and the

French Enlightment, while the "Lahontan" character defends Catholicism and the colonial policies which the author had by that time rejected.

By contrasting and comparing colonial and native societies, Lahontan begins to transcend the repressive hypothesis; he calls into question the common Enlightenment opposition between reason and passion, noting that the Indians "are altogether Strangers to that Blind Fury which we call Love"[46] and implying that reason is a natural faculty and passion a product of society. In the empiricist thinking of the Enlightenment, from Locke to Condillac and LaMettrie, sex was offered as proof of the causal relationship between sensory stimuli and physical responses. "What Man in the World can hear the Amorous Intrigues of the confessing Ladies, without being Transported, especially if he be one of those who injoy Health, Youth, and Strength?"[47] asks Adario of the priests. Since the Indians apparently do not have the same hard-wired patterns of stimulus and response, they are immune from the embarrassing inconsistencies of biology and morality that plague Europeans, such as the contradiction between the Jesuit vows of chastity and the natural imperative of reproduction. Adario goes on to accuse the priests of cavorting with young girls, of using the withdrawal method of contraception, and of lacking the power of resistance which, he claims, is natural to the Indians. Lahontan also reversed the Western pattern of the male as aggressor in sexual relations. We've seen that many writers observed a high degree of sexual liberty among Indian girls before marriage. Sagard even included an account of a healing ritual, whereby in accordance with a sick woman's dream, "all the girls in a town" assemble by the patient and "are all asked, one after another, which of the young men of the town they would like to sleep with them."[48] The chosen boys are notified, and the next night all the couples have sex in the presence of the ill woman. Lahontan transforms this provocative idea of female sexual initiative by theorizing it within a rationalized system of sexuality that contrasts with European mores. In his earlier ethnographic "Account of the Amours and Marriages of the Savages," Lahontan wrote that "the Men are as cold and indifferent as the Girls are passionate and warm. The former love nothing but War and Hunting, and their utmost ambition reaches no farther."[49] This leads to an eroticization of the Indian woman, and a corresponding promise of potency and penetration for the male colonist: "The Savage Women like the French better than their own Countrymen, by reason that the former are more prodigal of their Vigour, and mind a Woman's Business more closely."[50] In the *Dialogues*, Lahontan develops this point beyond a merely sensualist male fantasy, showing that such fantasies are as much about the male's loss of sexual control as they are about gaining control over females. The consequence of the "nakednesse" of the Indians upon modesty and excitability was addressed by Lescarbot, Williams, and others, as we've seen. Rather than consider the automatic physical response which such an unobstructed gaze would provoke, Lahontan reverses the question, considering the power of the female gaze over the male member: "the young Women taking a view of the Naked parts, make their choice by the Eye. . . . Some love a well shaped Man let a certain matter about him be never so little. Others make choice of an ill shap'd sorry like Fellow, by reason of the goodly size of I know not what."[51] Adario's fantasy of female choice leads to a critique of the double standards of European sexual mores: "You Christians have another impertinent Custom. . . . Your Men glory in the Debauching of Women, as if yielding to the Temptations of Love were not equally Criminal in either Sex. . . . Every body Censures the Lady, and cries up the Cavalier, whereas the former merits a Pardon, and the latter deserves to be Punish'd."[52]

The sexual and the political are entwined in Lahontan's text as in the feminism of the late 1960s: "A Young Woman, say they, is Master of her own Body, and by her Natural Right of Liberty is free to do what she pleases."[53] Adario provides a concrete instance of this when he speaks of his daughter, who has come to the interview with "Lahontan" and is about to marry a man her father disapproves of. Adario reminds us that he cannot prevent this liaison, because she would say to him, "What do you think Father! Am I your Slave? Shall I not enjoy my Liberty?"[54] The sexual freedom of the Indians in Lahontan is imbued with revolutionary and rational demands for freedom from restraint and for the natural power of reason over social custom. The Indians' practice of divorce and of marriage by contract for thirty years leads to an indictment of Europe: "they lay down this for a firm and unmovable truth, that we Europeans are born in Slavery."[55] Finally, when Adario invites the "Lahontan" character to repeat the transformation which Lahontan the author had in fact already accomplished, that is, to "turn Huron," Adario buttresses the invitation with the comment, "I am Master of my own Body."[56] Thus the Indian is feminized, yet the feminine becomes the position of reason and freedom of choice.

Lahontan's radical, utopian parable climaxes the story of how colonial writers' representations of Native American sexuality reflected their own positions and interests. Lahontan was perhaps the first to manipulate the material self-consciously, to be aware that the argument he was making had less to do with the innocence or corruption of Indian sexuality than it did with his own critique of European sexuality. Yet Lahontan is the beginning of another narrative, that of modern speculations about what is "natural" sexual behavior. Margaret Mead's *Coming of Age in Samoa* created a stir in 1950s America by presenting a favorable portrait of a society where sexual freedom and experimentation was encouraged among young people, where the impulses of hormones did not have to battle against social and moral restraints. George Devereux proposed a similar reading of the customs of an American Indian tribe, based on fieldwork done among the Mohave in the 1930s. Devereux wrote that "Mohave sex-life is entirely untrammeled by social restraint" and that children enjoyed sexual relations without adult reprisal. Most significant were Devereux's observations that "there is little or no objection to homosexuality among the Mohave."[57]

The sexual appetite of adolescents is no longer noteworthy in our society, but arguments about the naturalness of homosexuality are, and therefore it should be no surprise that recent scholarship on Native American sexuality has emphasized homosexuality. Many articles have addressed the phenomenon of the *berdache*, the term French seventeenth-century explorers applied to Indian men who adopted the clothing and social roles of women. The Jesuit Jacques Marquette, first European to explore the upper Mississippi valley, wrote,

> I know not through what superstition some Illinois, as well as some Nadouessi [Sioux], while still young, assume the garb of women, and retain it throughout their lives. There is some mystery in this, for they never marry and glory in demeaning themselves to do everything the women do. They go to war, however, but can use only clubs, and not bows and arrows . . . they pass for Manitous.[58]

Brief accounts of berdaches appear in many early explorers' writings, with varying degrees of homophobic scorn. Marquette's comment that "they pass for Manitous," spirits or signs of natural power, is significant for Walter L. Williams, whose *The Spirit and the Flesh* (1986) collects the observations of early colonists and combines them with his own fieldwork to propose a theory of the berdaches as spiritually inspired. By taking on women's roles, berdaches were not demeaning themselves, because women and women's work were not seen as inferior to men's. If berdaches' gender identity did not correspond with their physical sex, it was because they had received special spiritual messages. Williams emphasizes that berdache is not the same as gay identity, and that many Indian men engage in sex with other men or with berdaches, but do not become berdaches. He concludes that the berdache phenomenon is not a sexual behavior but a cross-gender identity inspired by spiritual impulses. Most recently, Jonathan Goldberg's *Sodometries* has entered the debate over Native American homosexuality by launching charges that Williams falls into ethnocentrism and "homogenize[s] all natives into the figure of the Indian," and that others who study the berdaches are insufficiently sensitive to contemporary gays or uncomprehending of Indian homosexuality.[59] As with the treatment of prostitution by Sagard and Lescarbot, Goldberg and Williams take the observations of earlier ethnographers and use them to support very different conclusions, revealing as much about their own positions as gay scholars as they do about the cultures they purport to describe. Because sexual identity is so culturally determined and determining, the berdaches are virtually impossible to understand or represent in any neutral or objective way. Native American sexuality continues to be seen through a lens which reflects the eye of the beholder.

NOTES

1. Two leading critics of colonial American literature have published provocative interpretations of van der Straet's engraving: see José Rabasa, *Inventing America: Spanish Historiography and the Formation of Eurocentrism* (Norman: University of Oklahoma Press, 1993), 27; and Peter Hulme, "Polytropic Man: Tropes of Sexuality and Mobility in Early Colonial Discourse," in *Europe and Its Others: Proceedings of the Essex Conference on the Sociology of Literature* (Essex: Essex University Press, 1984), ed. Francis Barker et al., 17–18. The hammock is an invention of the Arawak natives of the Caribbean, and the word was adopted from their language.

2. Sir Walter Ralegh, *Selected Writings,* ed. Gerald Hammond (Harmondsworth, England: Penguin, 1986), 120. A fine study of this trope in the exploration and conquest of America-as-woman is Annette Kolodny, *The Lay of the Land: Metaphor as Experience and History in American Life and Letters* (Chapel Hill: University of North Carolina Press, 1975).

3. Lawrence C. Wroth, ed., *The Voyages of Giovanni da Verrazzano* (New Haven: Yale University Press, 1970), 138.

4. Ibid., 138.

5. See Kolodny, *The Lay of the Land*, 5; Hulme, "Polytropic Man," 19–27; and Jeffrey Knapp, *An Empire Nowhere: England, America, and Literature from Utopia to* The Tempest (Berkeley: University of California Press, 1992), 210–18.

6. Wroth, *The Voyages of Giovanni da Verrazzano*, 135.

7. Ibid., 135.

8. Ibid., 136.

9. Ibid., 138.

10. A great number of scholarly studies could be listed here. Among the best are Olive Patricia Dickinson, *The Myth of the Savage and the Beginnings of French Colonialism in the Americas* (Edmonton: University of Alberta Press, 1984); Edward Dudley and Maximilian Novak, eds., *The Wild Man Within: An Image in Western Thought from Renaissance to Romanticism* (Pittsburgh: University of Pittsburgh Press, 1973); Hoxie Fairchild, *The Noble Savage: A Study in Romantic Naturalism* (New York: Russell and Russell, 1961).

11. Thomas Morton, *New English Canaan* (New York: Arno Press, 1972), 10.

12. Robert Beverley, *The History and Present State of Virginia* (Chapel Hill: University of North Carolina Press, 1947), 188–89.

13. Gabriel Sagard, *The Long Journey to the Country of the Hurons*, trans. H. H. Langton (Toronto: Champlain Society, 1939), 125.

14. Reuben G. Thwaites, ed., *The Jesuit Relations and Allied Documents*, 73 vols. (Cleveland: Burrows Bros., 1896–1901), 16: 63.

15. Quotation from Pierre Deliette, "Memoir of De Gannes Concerning the Illinois Country," in *The Western Country in the 17th Century* ed., Milo M. Quaife (Chicago: Lakeside Press, 1947), 116–17. See also Chrestien LeClercq, *New Relation of Gaspesia with the Customs and Religion of the Gaspesian Indians*, trans. William F. Ganong (Toronto: Champlain Society, 1910), 259; Joseph-François Lafitau, *Moeurs des sauvages américains comparées aux moeurs des premiers temps* (Paris: Maspero/La Découverte, 1983), 156–57.

16. Thwaites, *Jesuit Relations*, 16:61.

17. Ibid., 16:63

18. Ibid., 29:185.

19. John Lawson, *A New Voyage to Carolina, containing the exact description and Natural History of that Country, together with the present state thereof and a Journal of a Thousand Miles Travel'd thro; several Nations of Indians, Giving a particular Account of their Customs, Manners, etc.* (London, 1709; reprint Chapel Hill: University of North Carolina Press, 1967), 35–36.

20. French historian Philippe Jacquin has described the blending of native custom and colonial desire: "The European saw the Indian as a seductress, fanatic with desire, a dream which fascinated the colonists and pushed them toward Indian society; a dream which became reality through the willingness of the Indians not only to allow their women to couple with the newcomers, but to encourage

these liaisons. In fact, the Indians could not imagine commercial or political relations without the exchange of women, without proposing a young woman for the stranger." *Les indiens blancs: Français et indiens en Amérique du nord, XVIième–XVIIIième Siècle* (Paris: Payot, 1987), 190; my translation.

21. William Byrd, *Histories of the Dividing Line betwixt Virginia and North Carolina* (New York, Dover, 1967), 4.

22. See Jacquin, *Les Indiens Blancs*, 192.

23. Ibid., 193; my translation. Quoted by Jacquin from document C11a in the French Archives de la Marine.

24. Pierre-Esprit Radisson, *Voyages of Peter Esprit Radisson, being an account of his Travels and Experience among the North American Indians from 1652 to 1684*, ed. Gideon Scull (New York: P. Smith, 1943), 93.

25. Lawson, *A New Voyage to Carolina*, 40.

26. Ibid., 41.

27. Ibid., 190.

28. Ibid., 194.

29. Ibid., 46.

30. Ibid., 47.

31. Ibid.

32. Beverley, *History and Present State of Virginia*, 170.

33. Ibid., 171.

34. Michel Foucault, *The History of Sexuality: An Introduction*, trans. Robert Hurley (New York: Vintage Books, 1990), 10.

35. Roger Williams, *A Key into the Language of America*, ed. John J. Teunissen and Evelyn J. Hinz (Detroit: Wayne State University Press, 1973), 205.

36. Ibid., 203.

37. Ibid., 205.

38. Ibid., 185.

39. Marc Lescarbot, *The History of New France*, 3 vols., trans. W. L. Grant (Toronto: Champlain Society, 1907–14.), 3:163.

40. Gabriel Sagard-Theodat, *The Long Journey to the Country of the Hurons,* ed. George M. Wrong, trans. H. H. Langton (Toronto: Champlain Society, 1939), 121.

41. Jean de Léry, *History of a Voyage to the Land of Brazil,* trans. Janet Whateley (Berkeley: University of California Press, 1990), 153.

42. Lescarbot, *The History of New France*, 3:164.

43. Ibid., 3:163.

44. de Léry, *History of a Voyage to the Land of Brazil*, 153.

45. Lescarbot, *The History of New France*, 3:163.

46. Louis Armand de lom d'Arce, baron de Lahontan, *New Voyages to North America*, ed. Reuben Gold Thwaites (Chicago: A. C. McClurg, 1905), 452.

47. Ibid., 544.

48. Sagard-Theodat, *Long Journey to the Country of the Hurons*, 120.

49. Lahontan, *New Voyages to North America*, 451.

50. Ibid., 455.

51. Ibid., 609.

52. Ibid., 610–11.

53. Ibid., 453.

54. Ibid., 605.

55. Ibid., 456.

56. Ibid., 554.

57. George Devereux, "Institutional Homosexuality of the Mohave Indians," *Human Biology* 9 (1937): 518, 498–99.

58. Thwaites, *Jesuit Relations,* 59:129.

59. Jonathan Goldberg, *Sodometries: Renaissance Texts, Modern Sexualities* (Stanford, Calif.: Stanford University Press, 1992), 189–92. Goldberg criticizes Ramon Gutierrez, *When Jesus Came, the Corn Mothers Went Away* (Stanford, Calif.: Stanford University Press, 1991); Harriet Whitehead, "The Bow and the Burden Strap," in *Sexual Meanings*, ed. Sherry B. Ortner and Harriet Whitehead (Cambridge: Cambridge University Press, 1981), 80–115; Pierre Clastres, *Society against the State*, trans. Robert Hurley and Abe Stein (New York: Zone, 1987); and Devereux's article cited above.

Chapter 3

Her Master's Voice

Gender, Speech, and Gendered Speech in the Narrative of the Captivity of Mary White Rowlandson

Steven Neuwirth

The captivity narrative of Mary White Rowlandson, long a staple of American literature anthologies, has come under new scrutiny of late.[1] More than a horripilating tale of Indian captivity, Rowlandson's chronicle tells us much about New England's Puritan culture and the inferior status of women in colonial America. Rowlandson's narrative, in point of fact, is nothing less than a commentary on gender and gender politics in Puritan New England and reveals, albeit subtly, Rowlandson's quarrel with her male superiors—be they white or Indian.[2] Although, at almost every turn in her story, Mary presents herself as the exemplar of Puritan womanhood, at certain moments, when the mask of perfection drops, we are greeted with a different Mary Rowlandson: a woman speaking in her own voice against (not in support of) a male-constructed vision of womanhood. For this reason, I shall argue, there are two Mary Rowlandsons in the narrative, literary creations who not only represent and speak for the male-dominated Puritan culture, but who (on rare occasions) give voice to the woman who authored the narrative. In other words, while there may be only one historical Mary Rowlandson (the author of the text), she (as author) has constructed several female narrators who offer different (and sometimes opposing) insights into the author's sense of self and sense of place within white as well as Indian culture.[3]

Given the presence of multiple narrators, perhaps our discussion of voice and gender in Rowlandson's text would best be served by introducing the reader to the historical Mary Rowlandson first. In brief, Mary Rowlandson was born Mary White, in Somerset, England, in 1637, and came to America with her parents (Joan and John White) in 1638, settling in Salem, Massachusetts. From Salem, Mary and her parents moved to Lancaster, Massachusetts, in 1653. Three years later, at the age of nineteen, Mary White wed Joseph Rowlandson (1631–1678), the town's minister. The Rowlandsons lived in Lancaster in relative peace and comfort for more than twenty years. That peace and tranquility was shattered by Indian attack, however, on the morning of February 10, 1675/76.[4] The confederated Nipmunk and Narragansett Indians burned the town to the ground, taking Mary Rowlandson and her three children (Joseph, age fourteen; Mary, age eighteen; and Sarah, age six) hostage. Joseph Rowlandson, Mary's husband, escaped capture because he was en route to Boston at the time, raising troops for the town's protection. (Lancaster had already been raided once before, during the opening forays of King Philip's War.)[5]

In the course of her narrative, Mary Rowlandson tells us about her children: Sara, her youngest, was wounded during the Indian assault and died in captivity in her mother's arms. Her two surviving children, Joseph and Mary, were released near Boston soon after Mary's rescue, which occurred eleven weeks and five days after she was taken captive (May 2, 1676). Mary joined her husband in Boston (Lancaster was in ashes), where they lived for about a year, aided by the generosity of friends.

Then the Rowlandsons moved to Wethersfield, Connecticut, where Joseph had accepted a position as minister. Mary's remaining years in Connecticut were spent in relative anonymity. Joseph Rowlandson died in 1678, and a year later Mary married Samuel Talcott. Thirteen years later, in 1691, Sam Talcott died. Mary Rowlandson Talcott, then fifty-four, outlived her husband by twenty years, dying in Wethersfield in 1710/11 at the age of seventy-four.[6]

The narrative of the captivity of Mary Rowlandson was published in 1682, six years after her release. Of the twenty-four settlers taken hostage during the Indian raid on Lancaster, Mary Rowlandson (as far as we can tell) is the only one who left a record. The exceptionality of Mary's chronicle needs to be underscored, for our perception of the Indian raid on Lancaster, as well as Rowlandson's own captivity experience comes to us filtered through the experience of one and only one chronicler, who was the wife of the town's Puritan minister, Lancaster's highest-ranking and wealthiest citizen.[7]

Although Mary Rowlandson continues to be of interest to historians and genealogists, the historical Mary Rowlandson is less important to our study than the Mary Rowlandsons who grace the chronicle's pages. Mary Rowlandson, the woman who actually lived the experience, is external to the tale and does not exist within the text. She is not to be confused with the narrators who speak to us from within the text. An lest there be any doubt, we meet and hear from several different narrators during the course of Mary's narrative. Most interesting, each narrator adds to our knowledge of women's roles and responsibilities in Puritan culture—a culture where men not only dictated the terms of the discourse—be it religious, social, or political—but also stipulated the circumstances under which a woman could publish her narrative. In other words, the many Mary Rowlandsons whom we encounter (and who speak on behalf of the author) tend to be male constructions—speakers who identify themselves as female, but who have so internalized the Puritans' male ideology that the narrative serves to silence the woman's voice while it affirms male primacy as well as the male-centered Puritan ethos.[8]

The most conspicuous example of the masculine voice's speaking through the narrator is evidenced by Rowlandson's use of biblical quotation. Whenever Rowlandson wants us to understand the moral and spiritual significance of her captivity, she portrays herself as a latter-day Job or David or Joshua or Daniel and speaks to us in the lofty phrases of Old Testament heroes, as opposed to heroines. On these occasions (and there are many such occasions), we are in the presence of the male-constructed narrator, Mary Rowlandson qua spokesperson and apologist for the Puritan Way. Even when she is not elevating her experience to the level of sacred drama, Mary Rowlandson continues to draw on male constructions of virtuous femininity to describe and define herself, presenting us with Mary Rowlandson the submissive gentlewoman, Mary Rowlandson the virtuous female captive, Mary Rowlandson the obedient servant, Mary Rowlandson the patient helpmate, and Mary Rowlandson the sorrowful, mother.

On the other hand, we seem to be in the presence of a female-constructed narrator when we hear the narrator deploring (rather than accepting) her condition and complaining about (rather than condoning) her masters' treatment of her. On the occasions, we can hear a woman speaking, in a woman's voice, attempting to articulate a woman's vision of womanhood, a woman attempting to come to terms with male oppression. In other words, the Mary Rowlandson who takes issue with male rule and male authority, while she may also be a rhetorical figure, fights against the male construction of womanhood. Rowlandson qua termagant does have literary antecedents, to be sure; yet, in the context of the narrative, the assertive Rowlandson strikes us as a real person in real time. Indeed, when she is most independent of male authority, she strikes us as a spokesperson for oppressed women everywhere and serves to remind us what it meant to be female in male-dominated, Puritan New England.

The differences between the ameliorative, male-constructed narrators and the narrators who speak for the besieged woman are as different in *kind*, as they are different in *degree*. The narrator who challenges male domination is sui generis—unmistakable and irreplaceable; she is assertive, strident, frustrated, sarcastic, and far more critical of men who govern her life than is the male-constructed, compliant narrator who defends male-primacy and Puritan hegemony. The male-constructed narrator reminds us of Homer's Penelope (*The Odyssey*), Milton's Lady (*Comus*), Shakespeare's Miranda (*The Tempest*), and Bunyon's Christiana (*The Pilgrim's Progress*).[9]

Consciously or unconsciously, Mary Rowlandson has fashioned her narrator (at least in part) after virtuous women of classical and Christian antiquity, women rediscovered by Renaissance artists and writers. Indeed, when Rowlandson is true to the Renaissance ideal, she embodies the male vision of perfected womanhood: submissive, passive, obedient, patient, quiet, and chaste.[10]

When she speaks to us as suffering woman (the paragon of virtue), we are in the presence of a male construction of femininity. When she speaks to us in the indignant, outraged voice of the female captive, on the other hand, we seem to be in the presence of a more authentic, original narrator—a narrator who speaks out of a feminine sensibility—the sensibility of the oppressed, the disadvantaged, the silenced. The grumbling Mary Rowlandson may be no less a literary construct than her compliant co-narrator, but as termagant, Mary Rowlandson seems genuine. The narrator in rebellion, unlike her Bible-touting sister does not suffer in silence, nor does she approve of the men who have kept her captive and subordinate, men who have silenced her mind, body, and tongue. This figure of oppressed womanhood makes rare appearances in the course of the narrative and has relatively few lines, and not without reason. In seventeenth-century New England it was rare (and dangerous) for women to speak in public, even more to publish or critique the male establish-ment.[11]

Mary Rowlandson was a woman rooted in her time and place, in sev-enteenth-century Puritan Massachusetts. She was the wife of a Puritan minister who was the principle magistrate of the town. Mary derived her sense of Self (wife, mother, sister, neighbor, and Indian captive) from the men and male institutions that framed her life: God, husband, colonial magistrates, Puritan ministers, and Quinnapin (Indian master).[12] The point is worth emphasizing: Mary Rowlandson could not have published her narrative in Puritan New England without permission from the Puri-tan governors: it just wasn't possible.[13] The consequences of nonconfor-mity effectively silenced most women, at least in public venues.[14] Con-versely, women, especially Puritan women, readily accepted their subor-dinate status as established by Scripture, by custom, and by local law. If the Puritan elders were going to allow Mrs. Rowlandson to step out of character and publish her narrative, assuredly they would have to defend her (and themselves) against the charge of immodesty that was sure to fol-low. To avoid public ignominy—theirs and hers—Increase Mather (the Bay Colony's foremost preacher and personal friend of the Rowlandsons) provided a "Preface" to the narrative (signing it Ter Amicam,[15] "thy threefold friend"):

> though this gentlewoman's modesty would not thrust it into the press, yet her gratitude unto God made her not hardly persuadable to let it pass, that God might have his due glory, and others benefit by it as well as herself. I hope by this time none will cast any reflection [i.e., aspersions] upon this gentlewoman, on the score of this publication of her affliction and deliver-ance. . . . No serious spirit then (especially knowing anything of this gen-tlewoman's piety) can imagine but that the vows of God are upon her. Ex-cuse her then if she come thus into public, to pay those vows, come and hear what she hath to say.[16]

Part introduction and part apology, the author of the preface defends Mary's publication on the grounds that it affords her the opportunity to fulfill promises she made to God while she was in captivity.[17] Of course, Mary did not have to publish her account to keep her vows. Daily private prayer would have fulfilled her holy obligations. Sensing a flaw in his ar-gument, perhaps, Increase Mather offers a second explanation: Mary's husband. Mary's text warrants a public audience, Mather tells us, be-cause she is married to a prominent Puritan minister, and his grief has made Mary somewhat famous, drawing attention to her captivity, making it "of public note and universal concernment."[18] In other words, the husband's status in the community is what legitimates his wife's transgression into print.

Given the rules prohibiting women from speaking in public, one can appreciate the need for a prefatory note. But the preface, interestingly, is Mary's (as well as Mather's) second line of defense. The wording of the title deemphasizes the gender of the author because it places her name in a subordinate position:

The Soveraignty & Goodness of God, Together With the Faithfulness of His Promises Displayed; Being a Narrative Of the Captivity and Restauration of Mrs. Mary Rowlandson. Commended by her to all that Desire to Know the Lord's Doings to, and Dealings with Her. Especially to Her Dear Children and Relations.

Written by Her Own Hand for Her Private Use, and Now Made Public at the Earnest Desire of Some Friends, and for the Benefit of the Afflicted.

Deut. 32.[3]9. See Now that I, Even I am He, and There Is No God with Me; I Kill and I Make Alive, I Wound and I Heal, Neither Is There Any [who] Can Deliver Out of My Hand.

From the opening phrase of the title to its closing Biblical epithet, we are meant to know that Mary's narrative has more to do with Mary's God than it has to do with Mary. The syntax of the opening sentence speaks to the point. Note how the second half of the sentence, the half that contains the author's name—"Being a Narrative Of the Captivity and Restauration of Mrs. Mary Rowlandson"—is a dependent, adverbial clause modifying the introductory phrase that contains the sentence's true subject: "The Soveraignty & Goodness of God, Together With the Faithfulness of His Promises Displayed." Mary's narrative, we are to understand, tells the story of God's dealings with His people, particularly with God's commitment to the covenant He has made with Mary Rowlandson: as long as Mary is faithful to Him, He will remain faithful to her, keep her safe in His care. The phrase, "Captivity and Restauration," as her friends, family, and neighbors knew, refers to her spiritual as well as physical condition. And since the title omits any reference to her Indian captors, an anagogical reading is surely encouraged. Mary's wilderness ordeal refers to the captivity and restoration of Mary's soul, not just of Mary's body.[19] Read anagogically, the opening section places Mary's secular experience in the context of sacred drama: the Christian soul first bound in, and then freed from, the Devil's snares.

Of course, the title's opening section does more than contextualize Mary's wilderness drama in the framework of sacred experience. It also focuses our attention on Mary's sex and her various roles in her community.[20] The name Mary, the use of the possessive pronoun "Her," the appellation "Mrs.," and the reference to her "Children and Relations" identify Mary as female and place the captive in a sociocultural construct. The secular and social dimensions of the narrative are featured in the title's second section:

Written by Her Own Hand for Her Private Use, and Now Made Public at the Earnest Desire of Some Friends, and for the Benefit of the Afflicted.

The scope of the title has narrowed from the divine to the human, and the rhetoric has taken on a personal rather than a sermonic tone. In place of God's divine attributes, moreover, we are introduced to Mary's gifts and virtues. She is a literate, modest, and community-minded woman. With regard to her literacy, we are to understand that Mary and no one else authored her text. With regard to her modesty, we are informed that the author intended her chronicle for her "Private Use," not for public consumption. Indeed, had it not been for the "Earnest Desire of Some Friends," Mary never would have ventured into the public arena and so draw unwanted attention to herself. Finally, Mary's narrative is meant to bring comfort to fellow sufferers: the narrative was written for the "Benefit of the Afflicted."

But if the second section of the title focuses on secular matters, the title's third and concluding section, returns us to the realm of the sacred:

Deut. 32.[3]9. See Now that I, Even I am He, and There Is No God with Me; I Kill and I Make Alive, I Wound and I Heal, Neither Is There Any [who] Can Deliver Out of My Hand.

God is the speaker in the title page's closing epigram, but the God of Deuteronomy is not the mild, beneficent God of the title. The "Good" Sovereign of the title was the God who restored Mary to family and friends. The punishing God of Deuteronomy then, is the same God who afflicts Mary Rowlandson. And, in fact, the Deutoronomic citation does not serve to elevate Mary Rowlandson in her readers' eyes, inviting us to see Mary as the object of God's divine attention. It is Mary Rowlandson whom God has wounded, as it is Mary whom he has healed.

The closing quotation from Deuteronomy, then, serves multiple purposes: it not only presents Mary Rowlandson's Indian captivity as sacred drama but also elevates Mary to symbol: from humble, female citizen of Lancaster to sacred antitype. She stands for God's chosen people. Her history, in fact, is Israel's history: when Mary, like Israel, was faithful to her God, He blessed her house. However, when Mary requited God's love with forgetfulness and unfaithfulness, He chastened her, as He chastened Israel, by setting her enemies over her. In the context of sacred history, Mary's captivity is a constant reminder that she is totally dependent on God, that there is no one who "Can Deliver [her] Out of [His] Hand."

The experience of captivity, then, affords Mary an opportunity to mend her ways, but also to celebrate her election; for affliction, as every Puritan knew, is the sign of salvation: "How evident is it that the Lord hath made this gentlewoman a gainer by all this *affliction*, that she can say, 'tis good for her[,] yea better that she hath been, than that she should not have been thus *afflicted*" (emphasis mine).[21] God has inscribed his message to Mary on her body, and Mary presents her body to us in the body of her narrative. Indeed, we are reading text within text. And when read rightly, both texts teach the same lesson: "whom the Lord loveth he chasteneth" (Hebrews 12:6).[22] But providential affliction was also a sign of God's displeasure. The attack on Lancaster (like the war with King Philip of which it was a part) was meant as a rebuke to Mary (and to the Puritans), reminding them that they had fallen away from the path of righteousness.[23]

Though the Bay Puritans co-opted Mary's story to serve their own ideological ends, her publication had the potential to embarrass them, as well as bring shame upon herself. After all, it was decidedly inappropriate for women to enter the arena of public discourse. How could the author present her uniquely female experience without offending her readership who, assuredly, would have been offended by her impertinent act of authorship? One solution was to mute (as much as possible) the narrator's female voice and female nature. Toward that end, Rowlandson invokes the stories of Old Testament heroes whenever she wants to emphasize the sacred nature of her captivity experience. The effect is quite dramatic. In lieu of a woman's voice intoning a woman's sorrow, Mary defers to the male experience: "I hope it is not too much to say with Job, Have pity upon me, have pity upon me, O ye my friends, for the hand of the Lord has touched me" (Job 19:21). Or Mary will pose as the contrite prodigal son: "Father I have sinned against heaven and in thy sight [and am no more worthy to be called thy son]" (Luke 15:21). Stated conversely, neither the names nor the stories of Sarah, Ruth, Rachel, Leah, Esther, Rebeccah, Hannah, Dinah, Deborah, Mary, Martha, and Elizabeth are invoked. In their stead, the reader is invited to reflect upon the sufferings of Joshua, Daniel, Samson, David, Jesus, and, of course, Job.[24] What Mary has learned—the lesson that her narrative teaches—is that men are more closely aligned with the sacred than are women, that male suffering is holier than female suffering: "For whom the Lord loveth he chasteneth, and scourgeth every *son* whom he receiveth" (Hebrews 12:6; emphasis mine)."[25]

To appreciate the devalued status of women in Rowlandson's world, one has but to consider Mary's reference to Lot's wife, the woman with whom she can best identify: "I went along that day mourning and lamenting, leaving farther my own country, and travelling into the vast and howling wilderness, and I understood something of Lot's wife's temptation, when she looked back."[26] At the very least, Mary's reference to Lot's wife is self-condemning, for Lot's wife, as we know, was turned into a pillar of salt for disobeying God's command, for turning around and looking upon His destruction of Sodom and Gomorrah (Genesis 19:26). Mary's readers—especially her Puritan readers—would have approved the narrator's self-effacing gesture, for they, too, saw Mary Rowlandson, and all women, as aligned with the world, the flesh, and the devil.[27] Like Lot's wife, Rowlandson presents herself as spiritually weak, preferring to cling to the things of the world.

That Mary Rowlandson never alludes to another biblical woman in the course of her narrative speaks volumes about her perception of herself as a woman. Because of her sex, Mary Rowlandson must present herself as inferior, unworthy, as the weaker vessel, subject to the onslaughts of temptation. Nowhere is the male/female, sacred/profane, spirit/flesh dichotomy more in evidence than in Mary's celebration of her chastity, the preservation of which she attributes to God's goodness:

> And I cannot but admire at the wonderful power and goodness of God to
> me, in that, though I was gone from home, and met with all sorts of Indi-
> ans, and those I had no knowledge of, and there being no Christian soul
> near me; yet not one of them offered the least imaginable miscarriage to
> me.[28]

The word *miscarriage* according to the Oxford English Dictionary, means "misconduct" or "misbehavior."[29] But clearly the semantic yield of "miscarriage," as Mary uses it, extends beyond mild censure. Mary's readers would have understood "miscarriage" to be a polite term for "sexual misconduct"—and for obvious reasons. First, Mary's captivity narrative is a chronicle of native abuses during King Philip's War, from their slaughter of pregnant women to their cannibalism.[30]

In fact, rape is the only offense which the Indians do not commit. Since Mary is not squeamish about detailing all other native "miscarriages," her vagueness here suggests that the offense is greater than she, speaking as a woman, can name—a crime great enough, in fact, to require God's protection. Only the crime of rape carries such weight.[31]

And Mary's readers would have read "rape" for "miscarriage" because Increase Mather had invoked the figure of the sex-crazed savage in his preface to the narrative, using it to underscore God's sovereignty and goodness to Mary. Nowhere is God's glory made more manifest, Mather would have us believe, than in his ability to control the Indians' "savage" lust:

> God is indeed the supreme Lord of the world, ruling the most unruly, weakening the most cruel and savage, granting His people mercy in the sight of the unmerciful, curbing the lusts of the most filthy, holding the hands of the violent, delivering the prey from the mighty, and gathering together the outcasts of Israel.[32]

Of course, Mary's readers did not need Mather's say-so to think the worst of the Indians. The Indian-qua-savage stereotype, after all, had been in vogue for centuries. That stereotype, in its most horrific form, depicted indigenous people of America as a subhuman species, brute beasts ruled by appetite rather than human beings governed by reason.[33]

Mary's polite euphemisms for rape and the defense of her chastity may also be her way of responding to charges that she had "gone savage," for one of her contemporaries reported that she had been forced to marry "one-eyed" John Monoco, a Nashaway chief who had been one of the leaders of the raid on Lancaster.[34] Even if rumor proved false, Mary Rowlandson's claims of sexual purity, placed in a Freudian context, can be read as a projection of her desire to commit sexual "miscarriages" with her Indian master.[35] Whether Mary was repulsed or attracted by her male captors is moot. The fact that Mary was a woman, "cursed" with a woman's body, made her suspect:

> Puritans believed that Satan attacked the soul by assaulting the body, and that because women's bodies were weaker, the devil could reach women's

souls more easily, breaching these "weaker vessels" with greater frequency. . . . A woman's feminine soul, jeopardized in a woman's feminine body, was frail, submissive, and passive—qualities that most New Englanders thought would allow her to become either a wife to Christ or a drudge to Satan.[36]

Mary's celebration of her chastity is warranted, if only because her readers expect her to succumb to the chaos of the wilderness. Given the misogyny of her age, one can certainly understand why the narrator takes such pains to portray herself as sexually inviolate.

A Freudian critic, on the other hand, might link Mary's claim of chastity (which might be read as repressed sexual appetite) to her unsuppressed appetite for nourishment. The link between engaging in illicit sex and eating forbidden food is a staple of Freudian psychology and certainly plausible given the connection between illicit sex and the ingestion of forbidden food that we can infer from Mary's text.

Mary takes great pains to remind us that she was forced to eat foodstuffs that she considered inedible, "filthy trash": the intestines and feet of a horse, the flesh and bones of an unborn fawn, rotten corn, moldy bread crumbs, blood of deer, frozen, raw wheat.[37] Notwithstanding her revulsion at her diet, starvation ultimately prevailed over palate and preference, for Mary makes a complete about-face later in her narrative and openly admits to liking that which she claimed "was enough to turn the stomach of a brute creature":

> There came an Indian . . . with a basket of horse liver. I asked him to give me a piece: what, says he, can you eat horse liver? I told him, I would try, if he would give a piece, which he did, and I laid it on the coals to roast; but before it was half ready they got half of it away from me, so that I was fain to take the rest and eat it as it was, with the blood about my mouth, and yet a savory bit it was to me: for the hungry soul, every bitter thing is sweet.[38]

The invocation of Proverbs 27:7 ("for the hungry soul, every bitter thing is sweet") certainly allows Mary to explain why she was able to eat "savage" fare. Only God, we are led to believe, could have converted Indian "swill" into edible food. But how does Mary explain the "savage" gusto with which she attacks her food or her delight in turning "savage" herself? She doesn't. She can't.

What she can do—and tries to do further on in the narrative—is to present herself as a woman who has conquered her body's appetite; hence her claim of chastity. Mary's claim to chastity (denial of sexual appetite)

Sex and food

may actually be Rowlandson's attempt to expiate her guilt for eating foods that were an abomination. Mary's reference to her receptive mouth smeared with blood, I would argue, charges the scene with sexual energy. Keeping this passage (and other references to her ravenous appetite) in mind, one can appreciate her sense of guilt and why she would claim sexual purity. Clearly, Mary feels impure.

Had the issue of Mary's chastity been limited to her veiled reference, our reading of "miscarriage" as "rape" or as "inappropriate sexual conduct" could certainly be challenged. But Mary returns to the issue later in her chronicle, suggesting her deep-seated need to allay her readers' suspicions:

> O the wonderful power of God that I have seen, and the experience that I have had: I have been in the midst of those roaring lions, and savage bears, that feared neither God, nor man, nor the devil, by night and day, alone and in company: *sleeping all sorts together, and yet not one of them ever offered me the least abuse of unchastity to me in word or action.* (Emphasis mine)[39]

If we did not see the Indians as promiscuous before, we surely see them as promiscuous now, for "unchastity" means exactly what we think it means: "sexual impurity, lasciviousness."[40] Once again, God intervenes on Mary's behalf, protecting her from sexual assault.

Mary's insistence on her chastity quite obviously—and quite deliberately—draws attention to her sexuality, highlighting for us the narrator's concern with her readers' perception of her sexual conduct. Given the time, the place, the circumstance of Indian captivity, and given her Puritan readership, one can certainly appreciate Rowlandson's desire to present her body as chaste. Mary may have been of God's elect, one of the chosen, but her election cannot dispel the seductive charms her readers have come to associate with the female body. Mary, after all, has inherited Eve's curse. It is Mary's female body that has put her in harm's way. And since no Christian men were present to check native lechery, Mary was bound to be ravished by her male captors—unless a miracle occurred, something that would curb the natives' savage lust. And a miracle did occur; at least, Mary would have us believe so. So Mary is glorified—glorifies herself, actually. And yet, given the sexual taboos associated with her body, she can only elevate herself by self-denigration, by admitting that her body is the agent of her potential ruin, by acknowledging that it would take an act of God to protect her from her body's seductive charms. Indeed, Mary has all but admitted that she, qua woman, is slave to the sinful powers of her own body, that because she is female, she (em)bodies, literally and figuratively, that which all Puritan men and women are taught to despise, the "sins" of the flesh.

Did Mary believe what she wrote? Did she really see herself as a temptress needing God's intervention to protect her body from the rape it seemed to provoke? We don't really know. What we do know is that Mary and her readership—Puritan and non-Puritan alike—had come to associate women with the sins of the body, especially sex, and to see women as provocateurs. That Mary sees herself from the male perspective, that she adopts the male view of her own body, is not so surprising. Mary Rowlandson, after all, is a product of her time and her place. Then, too, Mary's primary readers are the male Puritans who have endorsed her publication—who have given her permission to speak. Not only must Mary affirm the Puritan view of the captive woman, she must assure her fellow Puritans (as well as her husband) that their worst fears are not warranted: she has remained inviolate despite her sojourn in the wilderness among the beasts of the wilderness.

Though Rowlandson affirms the Puritan ethos, promotes the culture's male ideology, adopts male standards to evaluate her conduct, the narrator does not accept, wholesale, men's claims to superiority. In fact, at discrete moments in her chronicle, men come in for their share of criticism. Granted, Mary usually subscribes to the male perception of women and writes a phallologic discourse. And yet, now and then, particularly near the end of her narrative, the speaker does seem to adopt a woman's point of view and seems to speak in a woman's voice. It is as if Mary Rowlandson, female author, grew weary of her male-constructed narrator, grew weary of inscribing the male script and promoting the Puritan ethos. On such occasions, when Mary views her world from a woman's perspective, documenting a woman's experience in a woman's idiom, we encounter a social critic and a burgeoning frontier feminist. On such occasions, Mary Rowlandson becomes the true subject (as opposed to the true object) of her narrative. Moreover, when Mary surveys the phallocentric world she inhabits, her captivity narrative becomes a feminist manifesto of sorts, wherein she rails against the men and male institutions that have held (and continue to hold) her hostage. Her Indian master, Quinnapin, the colonial militia, her husband, her Puritan friends, even the Old Testament Jehovah, are scrutinized and found wanting.

To appreciate the narrator's ability to break free of male paradigms and phallologic discourse, one need but recall Mary's description of her master and mistress preparing for their evening's entertainment:

> He was dressed in his holland shirt, with great laces sewed at the tail of it, he had his silver buttons, his white stockings, his garters were hung round with shillings, and he had girdles of wampum upon his head and shoulders. She had a kersey coat, and [was] covered with girdles of wampum from the loins upward: her arms from her elbows to her hands were covered with bracelets; there were handfuls of necklaces about her neck, and several sorts of jewels in her ears. She had fine red stockings, and white shoes, her hair powdered and face painted red, that was always before black. And all the dancers were after the same manner.[41]

The shift in focus and tone is as radical as it is unorthodox. No longer are we listening to Mary Rowlandson, the submissive, self-effacing Puritan spokesperson, the pious narrator bearing witness to God's sacred truths. Rather, we are invited to read social satire and to watch Mary's captors make a spectacle of themselves. The radical nature of the shift in focus cannot be overstated. Bear in mind, the Indian dancers are the enemy—enemy of the Puritans and of the Puritans' God. Satan's emissaries on earth, these natives have been portrayed in the course of Mary's narrative as the wilderness's savage spirit incarnate. And the narrator has taken great pains to show them at their savage worst: stripping dead and dying Lancastrians (men, women, and children) of their clothes, leaving them naked and bleeding to death. Given the visual imprint of these earlier, violent scenes, the image of Mary's master and mistress donning English attire is not only unconventional but calculated to offend.[42] More to our purposes, however, is the way in which Mary has her master and mistress occupy the middle ground between wildness and sophistication. They are savages, true, but they seem to have an understanding of propriety and a degree of civility about them—albeit misplaced. They are, in essence, liminal characters, not unlike their captive, Mary Rowlandson. Indeed, Mary Rowlandson, captive and narrator, has presented herself in similar terms, occupying the middle ground between savagery and civility.[43] The above scene, in fact, is the twin to an earlier scene, where Rowlandson and her Indian mistress rejoin their master after several days of traveling by themselves. We come upon the two women when they enter camp. Mary appears before Quinnapin. Mary, quite clearly, is offensive to his eye, if not his nose. "After many weary steps we came to Wachusett, where he was: and glad I was to see him. He asked me, When I washed me? I told him not this month, then he fetched me some water himself, and bid me wash, and gave me the glass to see how I looked and bid his squaw give me something to eat."[44]

How interesting that Mary Rowlandson would cast herself in the role of squaw and spouse, attending to her toilette in order to "please her man." Will Quinnapin find her attractive and keep her, or will he sell her at a bargain price to a less civil Indian? The woman looking at the woman in the "glass" sees herself through her master's eyes—as property.[45]

Notwithstanding the cleaned-up face, Mary, like her master and mistress, has made accommodations to her captivity and has to some degree assimilated to Algonquian culture, and consequently may be more "savage" than she appears (or than her readers realize). Alternatively, Rowlandson, for all her savage appearance, may be more civilized than she looks. It's impossible to opt for one reading over the other, for both are equally plausible. Rowlandson has placed herself in the middle ground where there are no clear-cut distinctions between savagism and civilization.

While Mary Rowlandson will reassume her role as spokesperson for male rule and Puritan hegemony at the close of her narrative, she does occupy the middle ground and does sustain the liminal persona for longer than we might realize. For example, following the comic vignette about the natives' "dance," Mary Rowlandson introduces the topic of sexuality—male sexuality versus female sexuality; Indian licentiousness versus Puritan restraint; Quinnapins's lechery versus her own chastity. Ostensibly, the subject of Mary's chastity is prompted by Quinnapin's untoward (but perhaps not unwanted) sexual advances toward his female captive. Mr. John Hoar, agent for the New England Council (and sent by the council to negotiate Mary's release) has arrived in camp with liquor, cloth, and other goods, hoping to effect a trade.

Hoar enters the narrative immediately following the comic description of Mary's Indian master and mistress, Quinnapin and Weetamoo, dressing for their victory celebration.[46] Quinnapin, having exhausted himself in revel, hears of Hoar's arrival and offers to sell Mary back to him for a pint of liquor. Hoar agrees to the sale, but not trusting Quinnapin, the English emissary "called his own Indians, Tom and Peter, and bid them go and see whether he [Quinnapin] would promise before them three: and if he would, he [Quinnapin] should have it [the liquor]; which he did, and he had it."[47] Quinnapin downs the pint of liquor, and its effects are im-

mediate and predictable: his savage nature manifests itself in all its lasciviousness:

> My master after he had his drink, quickly came ranting into the wigwam
> . . . and called for Mr. Hoar, drinking to him, and saying, He was a good
> man: and then again he would say, Hang him [Mr. Hoar] rogue: being al-
> most drunk, he would drink to him, and yet presently [my master would]
> say he [Hoar] should be hanged. Then he [my master] called for me. I trem-
> bled to hear him, yet I was fain to go to him, and [so] he drank to me, show-
> ing no incivility. . . . At last his squaw ran out [of the wigwam], and he after
> her, [chasing her] around the wigwam, with his money jingling at his knees:
> but she escaped him: but having an old squaw he ran to her: and so through
> the Lord's mercy, we were no more troubled that night.[48]

The image of the drunken, lascivious male lunging for the "girl" (with his
pants around his ankles) is such a familiar trope we are likely to ignore
Rowlandson's subtext: that women (be they Indian or white) are victims
of male oppression.

Once again, Mary introduces the subject of her chastity. Only now the
captive is in real danger of being raped. But if the narrator's outrage seems
genuine, we should realize that her author (the flesh and blood Mary
Rowlandson) places the captive in a liminal position. The liminal position
here, however, is not bracketed by wildness and sophistication. In the
above episode, the middle ground is the difficult and destabilizing world
of sexual attraction. Mary teeters on the edge of sexual misconduct. Will
she (or won't she) succumb to her captor's sexual overtures?

As noted, the figure of the besotted male in breeches or loincloth in
pursuit of the hapless maiden is a familiar trope in literature. But what
makes Mary's version of the trope so interesting is the subtle (and perhaps
unconscious) pleasure she, as narrator, takes in being a sex object—the
unwilling recipient of Quinnapin's untoward advances. (The narrator, of
course, would deny any such feeling. Indeed, she would rebuke us
soundly for mistaking her words.) And yet, her text is somewhat ambiguous and makes us wonder if she really is as offended as she says she
is.

The key to reading Mary's reactions rests on her use of the word
"fain," as in her sentence, "I was fain to go with him." The first meaning
of the word fain is "glad, well pleased, disposed, inclined, willing or
eager." So, if we read Mary's statement with the first definition in mind,
she sounds pleased and willing to go to Quinnapin when he calls for her:

"I trembled to hear him, yet I was fain to go to him." Mary, of course, would deny she was pleased or eager to go to Quinnapin. She wants us to understand the exact opposite was true: she was most reluctant to go to him, especially since he was drunk. And the dictionary supports her denial, for the second definition of fain is "glad under the circumstances; glad or content to take a course [of action] in default of opportunity for anything better, or as the lesser of two evils." Given the narrative context, the second definition of fain certainly seems more applicable. As the second definition implies, Mary chooses the lesser of two evils. She can step forward and suffer verbal abuse (and risk being raped), or she can refuse to step forward and be chased around the wigwam. But that course of action doesn't bode well either. First, she has no place to run except out of the wigwam and into the night and wilderness. Second, she is thirty-nine years old, weak, and exhausted from her three-month ordeal. She is not condition to run away. Besides, if Rowlandson is caught, and being caught is a likely scenario, she will be raped: witness the fate of Quinnapin's older, slower squaw. The second meaning of "fain" is assuredly the more applicable and obvious meaning.

Having proven the case for the second definition, how do we defend our assertion that the first definition of "fain" is also a possibility? The answer lies in the ambiguity of the word. Notwithstanding Mary's intention, the positive connotation of fain is attached to both the first and second definitions. Mary may have been trembling in fear, but she uses a word that says she was glad or delighted. The second definition only qualifies the first definition; it doesn't mean its opposite: loath, disgusted, or outraged. Also worth noting is the narrators's use of the word "yet" to link her independent clauses: "Then he called for me. I trembled to hear him, *yet* I was fain to go to him."

The word "yet," like the word "but," is a coordinating conjunction, the function of which is to reverse the direction of the introductory clause or sentence. These words tell us to get ready for a qualification or an outright denial of the previous thought. Mary's placement of "yet" is most curious, for it suggests Mary was pleased to go to Quinnapin: "Then he [Quinnapin] called for me. I trembled to hear him, yet I was fain to go to him." She trembled in fear, yet she was delighted to be called. Grammatically speaking, the word "yet" qualifies her fear and reverses the negative flow of the sentence. Mary's sentence says the exact opposite of what she means, or does it? The word "yet" pulls the narrator (at least grammatically) toward the beckoning Quinnapin. Had Mary wanted to be unambiguous, or at least less ambiguous, she would have omitted the second phrase and written: "Then he called for me . . . yet I was fain to go to him." Here the words "yet" and "fain" convey reluctance and work together to give us a sense of the captive's discomfort. But Mary does not write this grammatically correct sentence; she qualifies her negative reaction, allowing us to "misread" her intentions and actions. In other words, Mary is in a liminal place, occupying the middle ground between chastity and sexual adventure.

But if the female narrator is torn between the sexual freedom of the Indians and the sexual restraints of the Puritans, she is not torn for long. The narrator knows her readership, and thus, closes her vignette with Mary's remaining inviolate. Rowlandson stands her ground. As for Quinnapin, he seems vanquished. Mary has him play the gentleman to her role as "lady virtue": [Quinnapin] drank to me, showing me no incivility." It's as if Quinnapin's savage lust were subdued by the power of Mary's chastity—a popular and conventional outcome of Christian allegory. But lust is still lust, and a savage is still a savage, so Mary wants her readers to know. And in Mary's mind, male sexual aggression must spend itself, and spend itself it does, not on Mary (symbol of staunch Christian virtue), but on Quinnapin's own Indian squaw.

Though thwarted by Rowlandson's virtue, Quinnapin needs to vent his sexual appetite. He turns to his youngest squaw for satisfaction. But the young woman will have none of him and evades his lunges with relative ease. Foiled a second time, Quinnapin turns his attention to his old squaw; she chooses not to escape. His "savage" appetite sated, Rowlandson and the other women are safe from harm.

What are we to make of this scene, and how does it illuminate Mary's attempts to fashion a feminine character who tells a woman's story in a woman's voice? Surely there is nothing remarkable in Mary's portrayal of a debauched Indian, for the figure of the lecherous "savage" was a stock character in colonial belles lettres. Surely Mary's readers would not have been surprised by the episode. They might even have expected it. Its true significance lies in the manner of the telling more than the matter of the tale. By focusing our attention on her master's sexual appetite, Mary not only reverses the conventional male:head::female:body association but also effectively reverses the sexual dynamics of her discourse, making Quinnapin (and all men by extension) the object of the female gaze rather than vice versa. This is no minor shift in stylistics. Renaissance scholar

Patricia Simons offers us this insight into the dynamics of the male gaze and its relation to the social construction of gender:

> To be a woman in the world was/is to be the object of the male gaze: to "appear in public" is "to be looked upon" wrote Giovanni Boccaccio. The Dominican nun Clare Gambacorta (d. 1419) wished to avoid such scrutiny and establish[ed] a convent "beyond the gaze of men and free from worldly distractions." The gaze, then, a metaphor for worldliness and virility, made of Renaissance woman an object of public discourse, exposed to scrutiny and framed by the parameters of propriety, display and "impression management." Put simply, why else paint a woman except as an object of display within male discourse?[49]

Though Simons's comments refer, specifically, to the pictorial representation of women in Quattrocento Tuscany, her insight into the power of the male gaze is applicable to our discussion of sexual politics in Puritan New England and to Mary Rowlandson's attempts to fashion a feminine Self independent of the female Self fashioned for her by a male-dominated society.

As the Quattrocento artists of Tuscany placed their female clients on display, so the Puritan leader of the Bay Colony have placed Mary Rowlandson on display, exposing her to the male gaze. It is this exploitation that may have inspired Mary's vilification of her Indian master. She wants to be free of Quinnapin's (and all men's) gazing. Toward that end, Rowlandson rethinks her narrative voice and changes it on the spot. In lieu of the pious, Bible-spouting Puritan spokeswoman, Rowlandson ushers in a female narrator, a symbol of insulted womanhood. It is she, the outraged woman, who steps forward and casts her (and our) eyes upon Quinnapin, subjecting his body to her gaze, making him the unwilling captive of her (and her readers') eyes.

But the virtue of the passage extends beyond Mary's denigrating portrayal of Quinnapin. By standing her ground and by refusing to respond to her master's voice, Mary Rowlandson, symbolically at least, openly rejects her assigned role as the passive, compliant female servant. Her body may be held in bondage, but she assuredly will not surrender her virtue to a "savage." And the risk of rape is a real possibility given Quinnapin's aroused state: witness Quinnapin's sexual advances toward his two wives. Mary's decision to stand her ground, however, has symbolic, as well as pragmatic value. Her refusal to yield to Quinnapin's supremacy

can be read symbolically as a definitive "no" to male power and male rule
in general. In other words, Quinnapin is a stand-in for all the masters in
Mary's life: God, the Puritan ministry, as well as her preacher husband.
Of course, Mary is on safe ground when she refuses to go to Quinnapin.
After all, he epitomizes the drunken lecherous, "savage." Mary's readers
would want her to refuse male authority in this situation, especially since
Mary presents herself as the model of chastity. Her role as the chaste wife
means she must protect her sex from the onslaught of the lecherous male.
What makes the scene interesting, of course, is that Quinnapin is not just
an Indian. He is Mary's legal master for as long as she is his captive. Indeed, Mary calls Quinnapin "Master" throughout her narrative. Thus,
her refusal of her Indian master, drunk or sober, can be read symbolically
as a refusal of all men who presume to lord over her.

Mary's denial of Quinnapin's authority has startling consequences. It
is as if the female narrator had discovered a latent self—a female self—
that finds fault with men and their presumptive right to rule and decide
the fate of women. The Mary at the narrative's close is a critical Mary,
critical of her Indian master for being drunk and disorderly, and critical
of the colonial militia for being tardy in their pursuit of the enemy and for
missing several opportunities to rescue her when they has the chance:

> But before I go any further, I would take leave to mention a few remark-
> able passages of providence, which I took special notice of in my afflicted
> time.
> 1. Of the fair opportunity lost in the [militia's] long march, a little after
> the fort fight, when our English army was so numerous, and in pursuit of
> the enemy, and so near as to take several and destroy them: and the enemy
> in such distress for food, that our men might track them by their [the Indi-
> ans'] rooting in the earth for ground nuts whilst they were flying for their
> lives.
> 2. I cannot but remember how the Indians derided the slowness, and
> dullness of the English army, in its setting out. For after the desolations at
> Lancaster and Medfield . . . they asked me when I thought the English army
> would come after them? I told them I could not tell: It may be they will
> come in May, said they. Thus did they scoff at us, as if the English would
> be a quarter of a year getting ready.
> 3. . . . I can but admire to see the wonderful providence of God in pre-
> serving the heathen for further affliction to our poor country. They could
> go in great numbers over [rivers] but the English must stop: God had an
> overruling hand in all those things.[50]

Though seemingly a separate issue, Mary's rebuke of the colonial militia is closely connected to her censure of her Indian master, Quinnapin: both symbolize male inadequacy of the first rank. Quinnapin, we may recall, was too drunk to seize upon either Mary Rowlandson or his young wife and had to settle for his old squaw. The militia's failure to capture the enemy when they had the chance is also a sign of male impotence. The English army, like the Indian warrior, was too slow and too dull to wreak havoc on a bedraggled, fleeing enemy. True, Mary's rebuke of the militia is couched in the language of Christian deference: their tardiness was God's will. And yet, one can hear an edge in Mary's voice as she wonders at God's "preserving the heathen for further affliction to our poor country." Mary herself is that "poor country," laid waste and bare by Indians—or so she sees herself. Having been held hostage by Indians for three months, Mary is ready to be rescued, but her God fails her. Of course, Mary dare not presume to question God's actions. Nevertheless, her perfunctory "God's will be done" suggests resignation born of disappointment.[51]

Though delightfully iconoclastic, refreshingly unorthodox, and seemingly invincible, Mary's heroic pose proves to be short-lived. Having had her say, Mary Rowlandson, self-authorizing writer, retreats into her text and resumes the role and voice her Puritan authors have assigned her: defender of the Puritan faith, champion of the male prerogative.

But if we feel sorry for the author, be assured our sympathy would be misplaced. Mary Rowlandson is not the least bit sad or sorry for herself. Quite the contrary, her concluding remarks reveal a woman who is perfectly content with her prescribed narrative pose and expresses unfeigned joy in representing the ideal Puritan female, the pious, dutiful, submissive, dependent, self-effacing, obedient, servant of man and God, she who revels in pain and sorrow:

> Affliction I wanted, and affliction I had, full measure. . . . yet I see, when God calls a person to anything, and through never so many difficulties, yet He is fully able to carry them through and make them see, and say they have been gainers thereby. And I hope I can say in some measure, as David did, It is good for me that I have been afflicted (Psalm 119:71). . . . I have learned to look beyond present and smaller troubles, and to be quieted under them, as Moses said, Exodus 14.13 Stand still and see the salvation of the Lord.[52]

Mary's reference to Exodus 14:13, we need to point out, is a partial quotation and, in its biblical context, is spoken as a rebuke, not as a joyous outburst. The Israelites, having just followed Moses out of Egypt and through the Red Sea (which God had parted for their easy passage), are now camped on the Red Sea's far shore. Though free, the Israelites can see the Egyptians making their way through the very breach in the water God had cut for his chosen people. Their faith in Moses begins to falter: "It had been better for us to serve the Egyptians," they complain, "than that we should die in the wilderness" (Exodus 14:12). In response to their short-sightedness, their unfounded doubts, and fears, Moses utters his injunction: "Fear ye not, stand still and see the salvation of the Lord, which he will shew to you to day: for the Egyptians whom ye have seen to day, ye shall see them again no more for ever." Here, at the close of her text, Mary chooses a passage from Scripture that resolves the issues of voice, gender, and power that have been at the center of her captivity narrative and postcaptivity life.

Extrapolating from biblical drama to her life in Puritan New England, Rowlandson aligns herself with the complaining Israelites, which means her Puritan sponsors are stand-ins for Moshe Rabbenu ("Moses our Master"). Moses' rebuke of the Israelites, then, translates into the Puritans' rebuke of Mary—if not Mary's rebuke of herself (chastising herself with the "inner voice" of her Puritan masters). As Moses stood in relation to the Israelites—their leader and lawgiver—so the Puritan patriarchs stand in relation to Mary Rowlandson, synecdoche for all New Englanders.

Mary's invocation of Exodus 14:13, moreover, seems to be an iteration of the feminine virtues of patience, obedience, passivity, submission, silence, and stillness that Mary's narrator has espoused from the very beginning of her narrative. To appreciate the extent of Mary's commitment to the male construction of the ideal woman, one has but to recall the sad fate of Goodwife Joslin, a woman who refused to "stand still" and suffered God's wrath for her impatience.[53]

Goodwife Joslin, who was taken captive with Mary Rowlandson, was so overwhelmed by her predicament that she suggested to Mary that they run away. But escape, Mary knew, was a foolish idea. First, it was winter and they were thirty miles from any English town. With no roads to follow and no way to navigate home, they would die. Second, Mrs. Joslin was in no condition to make the journey. As Mary notes, Mrs. Joslin was "very big with child, and had but one week to reckon: and [was carrying] another child in her arms, two years old."[54] Backing up her arguments with sacred text, Rowlandson opens her Bible and reads to Joslin from Psalm 2:14: "Wait on the Lord, Be of good courage, and he shall strengthen thine heart, wait I say on the Lord."[55] The lesson is clear: be patient, be still; let God provide. But Goodwife Joslin could not be consoled and importuned her Indian captors over and over again to take her home. The Indians, impatient with Joslin's constant complaining, decided to kill her and her unborn child.

The lesson of Joslin's impatience obviously imprinted itself on Mary's memory and allowed her to wait out a time of extreme stress. One Sabbath morning, Mary asks her master, Quinnapin, if he is going to sell her back to her husband. Quinnapin says, "Yes." Mary was delighted, and Quinnapin's "Yes," is, in fact, confirmed by the natives' new line of march—back toward Lancaster. But just when things seem to be getting better, Mary's mistress, Weetamoo (Quinnapin's squaw), refuses to go any further and says Mary must go to camp with her.[56] Mary's disappointment and frustration is almost too much to bear:

> My spirit was upon this, I confess, very *impatient* and almost outrageous. I thought I could as well have died as went back: I cannot declare the trouble that I was in about it; but yet back again I must go. As soon as I had an opportunity, I took my Bible to read, and that quieting scripture came to my hand, Psalms 46.10. Be still, and know that I am God. Which stilled my spirit for the present. [Emphasis mine][57]

Mary perseveres, and God has the natives spare her life, unlike the fate that befell Goodwife Joslin. Since Joslin was impatient (restless) and outspoken (complaining), God—according to Mary—allowed the Indians to destroy her. That Mary would return to these particular female virtues at the end of her chronicle is significant. Most significant is the fact that Rowlandson finds three different biblical passages that teach very much the same lesson.

Clearly, Mary wants her readers to see her as the exemplary woman, patient, quiet, and obedient, the woman of virtue par excellence. True, we cannot lose sight of the religious thrust of her narrative. But Mary's chronicle, for all its religiosity, is more than an exercise in piety, more than an argument for the Puritan view of the world. The "Narrative of the Captivity and Restauration of Mrs. Mary Rowlandson" is a domestic novel of sorts and tells us much about what it meant to be female in a world dominated by men. Read as a domestic tale (as opposed to a religious tract), Rowlandson's chronicle offers us true insight into gender roles and the prescribed dynamics of male and female sexuality in colonial New England.

Mary's celebration of feminine virtues, moreover, allows the speaker to reclaim her known self and to place it before her readers. Or, as the postmodernist would say, Mary Rowlandson, at the end of her narrative, attempts to (re)construct herself in accordance with the male vision of the ideal Puritan woman. And she succeeds. Indeed, author as well as narrator succeed, for the real Mary Rowlandson disappeared from public view after she published her chronicle, living out her life in relative obscurity (she wrote no more), exemplifying—one might assume—the virtues of patience, silence, stillness that she promoted in her chronicle.

NOTES

I am most pleased to acknowledge the scholarly contributions of my colleague Professor Ingrid Pruss and the editorial assistance of my wife, Dr. Margaret Solomon. This chapter bears witness to their intelligence, encouragement, and support.

1. For recent examinations of Rowlandson's captivity narrative, see Gary L. Ebersole, *Captured by Texts: Puritan to Postmodern Images of Indian Captivity* (Charlottesville: University of Virginia, 1995); Michelle Burnham, "The Journey Between: Liminality and Dialogism in Mary White Rowlandson's Captivity Narrative," *Early American Literature* 28.1 (1993): 60–75; Lisa Logan, "Mary Rowlandson's Captivity and the 'Place' of the Woman Subject," *Early American Literature* 28.3 (1993): 255–77; Margaret H. Davis, "Mary White Rowlandson's Self-Fashioning as Puritan Goodwife," *Early American Literature* 27.1 (1992): 49–60; Teresa A. Toulouse, "'My Own Credit': Strategies of (E)Valuation in Mary Rowlandson's Captivity Narrative," *American Literature* 64.4 (1992): 655–76; Tara Fitzpatrick, "The Figure of Captivity: The Cultural Work of the Puritan Captivity Narrative," *American Literary History* 3 (1991): 1–26; Mitchell R. Breitwieser, *American Puritanism and the Defense of Mourning: Religion, Grief, and Ethnology in Mary White Rowlandson's Captivity Narrative* (Madison: Univ. of Wisconsin Press, 1990); Capt. Greg Sieminski, "The Puritan Captivity Narrative and the Politics of the American Revolution," *American Quarterly* 42 (1990): 35–56; Kathryn Zabelle Derounian, "Puritan Orthodoxy and the 'Survivor Syndrome' in Mary Rowlandson's Indian Captivity Narrative," *Early American Literature* 22.1 (1987): 82–93.

2. For earlier (but equally valid) studies of Rowlandson's text, readers might consider Edward M. Griffin, "Women in Trouble: The Predicament of Captivity and the Narratives of Mary Rowlandson, Mary Jemison, and Hannah Dustan,"

in *Für eine offene Literaturwissenschaft: Erkundungen und Erprobungen am Beispiel US-Amerikanischer Texte* (Opening Up Literary Criticism: Essays on American Prose and Poetry), ed. Leo Truchlar (Salzburg: Wolfgang Neugebauer, 1986), 41–51; Susan Howe, "The Captivity and Restoration of Mrs. Mary Rowlandson," *Temblor* 2 (1985): 113–21; Annette Kolodny, *The Land before Her: Fantasy and Experience of the American Frontiers 1630–1860* (Chapel Hill: University of North Carolina Press, 1984), 17–34; David Downing, "'Streams of Scripture Comfort': Mary Rowlandson's Typological Use of the Bible," *Early American Literature* 15.3 (1981): 252–59; Alden Vaughan and Edward W. Clark, "Cups of Common Calamity: Puritan Captivity Narratives as Literature and History," in *Puritans among the Indians: Accounts of Captivity and Redemption, 1676–1724*, ed. Alden T. Vaughan and Edward W. Clark (Cambridge: Belknap Press of Harvard University Press, 1981), 1–28; Ann Stanford, "Mary Rowlandson's Journey to Redemption," *Ariel: A Review of International English Literature* 7.3 (1976): 27–37; David Minter, "By Dens of Lions: Notes on Stylization in Early Puritan Captivity Narratives," *American Literature* 45.3 (November 1973): 335–47; Richard Slotkin, *Regeneration through Violence: The Mythology of the American Frontier, 1600–1860* (Middletown, Conn.: Wesleyan University Press, 1973), 101–14; Douglas Edward Leach, "The 'Whens' of Mary Rowlandson's Captivity," *New England Quarterly* 34.3 (1961): 352–63; Henry Nourse, "Mrs. Mary Rowlandson's Removes," *Proceedings of the American Antiquarian Society*, 2d ser., 12 (1898): 401–9.

3. My reading of Rowlandson has been especially influenced by Lisa Logan's insightful essay "Mary Rowlandson's Captivity and the 'Place' of the Woman Subject," *Early American Literature* 28.3 (1993): 255–77. Like Logan, I am interested in the issue of gender and Rowlandson's perception of herself as woman in a male-dominated culture. Where Logan focuses on literal and figurative spaces (body, text, home, wilderness) and how the narrative is about the physical, ideological, social, and discursive places Rowlandson occupies, I focus on narrative voice and the disjunction between masculine and feminine voices (and the masculine and feminine ideologies they express) within the narrative.

4. Until the eighteenth century, the new year began on March 25, that celebrates the feast of the Annunciation, when Christ was conceived. Dates preceding March 25 are conventionally noted in both years as, in this case, 1675/76.

5. For book-length studies regarding the causes and consequences of King Philip's War, see Alden T. Vaughan, *New England Frontier: Puritans and Indians, 1620–1675* (Boston: Little Brown, 1965); Douglas Edward Leach, *Flintlock and Tomahawk: New England in King Philip's War* (New York: Norton, 1966); Charles T. Burke, *Puritans at Bay: The War against King Philip and the Squaw Sachems* (New York: Exposition Press, 1967); Francis Jennings, *The Invasion of America: Indians, Colonialism, and the Cant of Conquest* (Chapel Hill: University of North Carolina Press, 1975); Russell Bourne, *The Red King's Rebellion:*

Racial Politics in New England, 1675–1678 (New York: Atheneum, 1990). In her narrative, Rowlandson reports Lancaster's casualties as twelve killed and twenty-four taken captive.

6. Mary Rowlandson gave birth to a daughter in 1660, but that daughter (also named Mary) died in 1661 before she was a year old. Biographical information on Mary Rowlandson has been gleaned from various sources. See, in particular, Robert K. Diebold, "Mary Rowlandson," in *American Writers before 1800: A Biographical and Critical Dictionary*, ed. James A. Levernier and Douglas R. Wilmes (Westport, Conn.: Greenwood Press); Robert K. Diebold, "A Critical Edition of Mrs. Mary Rowlandson's Captivity Narrative" (Ph.D. diss., Yale University, 1972).

7. Rowlandson's chronicle is the first captivity narrative published in North America and the first such narrative written by a woman. It has appeared in over thirty editions since its initial publication. For history of the publication of Rowlandson's narrative and explanations for its wide appeal, see Kathryn Zabelle Derounian, "The Publication, Promotion, and Distribution of Mary Rowlandson's Indian Captivity Narrative in the Seventeenth-Century," *Early American Literature* 23.3 (1988): 239–61; David L. Greene, "New Light on Mary Rowlandson," *Early American Literature* 20 (Spring 1985): 24–38.

8. In his study of documents generated by the trials of Anne Hutchinson, Lad Tobin applies the theories of the French feminists (most notably Julia Kristeva, Hélène Cixous, and Luce Irigaray) to his analysis of the debate between Anne Hutchinson and her Puritan judges. Summing up the French feminists, Tobin notes that "speech layered with multiple meanings, speech intended to disrupt institutional discourse, speech which seeks to open up rather than to resolve, is more female, while rules-conscious, 'sense of an ending' speech, is more clearly male." I have applied Tobin's examination of masculine and feminine discourse to Rowlandson's text. See Lad Tobin, "A Radically Different Voice: Gender and Language in the Trials of Anne Hutchinson," *Early American Literature* 25.3 (1990): 263–64.

9. The image of women in Renaissance literature has received much critical attention in the past decade. Some of the works that I found useful include Margaret W. Ferguson, Maureen Quilligan, and Nancy J. Vikers, eds., *Rewriting the Renaissance: The Discourses of Sexual Difference in Early Modern Europe* (Chicago: University of Chicago Press, 1980); Margaret Olofson Thickstun, *Fictions of the Feminine: Puritan Doctrine and the Representation of Women* (Ithaca, N.Y.: Cornell University Press, 1988), 1–53; Caroline Walker Bynum, "'. . . And Woman His Humanity': Female Imagery in the Religious Writing of the Later Middle Ages," in *Gender and Religion: On the Complexity of Symbols*, ed. Caroline Walker Bynum, Stevan Harrel, and Paula Richman (Boston: Beacon Press, 1985), 257–88; Margaret L. King, *Women of the Renaissance* (Chicago: University of Chicago Press, 1991); Marie B. Rowlands, "Recusant Women

1540–1640," in *Women in English Society 1500–1800*, ed. Margaret Prior (London: Methuen, 1985), 149–80; Philippa Berry, *Of Chastity and Power: Elizabethan Literature and the Unmarried Queen* (London: Routledge, 1989); Flora Alexander, "Women as Lovers in Early English Romance," in *Women and Literature in Britain, 1150–1500* (Cambridge: Cambridge University Press, 1993), 24–40; Doris Mary Stenton, *The Englishwoman in History* (New York: Schocken Books, 1957); Philip Mirabelli, "Silence, Wit, and Wisdom in The Silent Woman," *Studies in English Literature 1500–1900* 29.2 (1989): 309–36; Patricia Simons, "Women in Frames: The Gaze, the Eye, the Profile in Renaissance Portraiture," *History Workshop Journal* 25 (1988): 4–30.

10. Peter Stallybrass discusses the feminine virtues celebrated during the Renaissance in "Patriarchal Territories: The Body Enclosed," in *Rewriting the Renaissance: The Discourses of Sexual Difference in Early Modern Europe*, ed. Margaret W. Ferguson, Maureen Quilligan, and Nancy J. Vickers (Chicago and London: University of Chicago Press, 1986), 123–42. According to Stallybrass, "Silence, the closed mouth, is made a sign of chastity. And silence and chastity are, in turn, homologous to woman's enclosure within the house" (127). Using Stallybrass's paradigm, Rowlandson's journey into the wilderness (outside the house) and her decision to write about that experience (externalizing internal thought) are, by definition, violations of the female virtues of chastity and silence.

11. Margaret H. Davis notes that for the entire seventeenth century, only four examples of women's writing are listed in Charles Evans's *American Bibliography*: Anne Bradstreet's *Several Poems* (1678); Sarah Goodhue's *A Valedictory and Monitory Writing* (1681); Rowlandson's *The Soveraignty and Goodness of God . . .; Being a Narrative of the Captivity and Restauration of Mrs. Mary Rowlandson* (1682); and M. Hooper's "Lamentations for Her Sons Poisoned by Eating Mushrooms" (1694), cited in Davis, "Mary White Rowlandson's Self-Fashioning," 59. The social construction of gender in Puritan New England placed the pen in men's hands, thereby effectively denying women an opportunity to develop an authorial and self-authorizing feminine voice. Notwithstanding their subordinate status, however, women were integral to social, political, and religious life in colonial New England. For discussion of women's roles in male-dominated Puritan New England, see Emory Elliott, *Power and the Pulpit in Puritan New England* (Princeton: Princeton University Press, 1975); Ivy Schweitzer, *The Work of Self-Representation: Lyric Poetry in Colonial New England* (Chapel Hill: University of North Carolina Press, 1974); Elizabeth Abel, ed., *Writing and Sexual Difference* (Chicago: University of Chicago Press, 1982); Laurel Thatcher Ulrich, *Good Wives: Image and Reality in the Lives of Women in Northern New England 1650–1750* (New York: Alfred Knopf, 1982); Edmund S. Morgan, *The Puritan Family: Religion and Domestic Relations in Seventeenth-Century New England* (New York: Harper & Row, 1966).

12. Quinnapin (Quinapin) was a Narraganset sachem allied with King Philip

during King Philip's War. He was married to Weetamoo, sachem (chief) of Pocasset village of the Wampanoag confederacy. See *Native American Women: A Biographical Dictionary*, ed. Gretchen M. Bataille (New York: Garland Publishing), 275–76. See separate entry under Weetamoo for more information.

13. Women rarely spoke in public in colonial New England, not even to confess their sins. Indeed, the history of women's silence is a familiar one. For studies on the subject, see Davis, "Mary White Rowlandson's Self-Fashioning," 49–60; Ivy Schweitzer, "Anne Bradstreet Wrestles with the Renaissance," *Early American Literature* 23.3 (1988): 291–312; Frank Shuffelton, "In Different Voices: Gender in the American Republic of Letters," *Early American Literature* 25.3 (1990): 289–303; Lad Tobin, "A Radically Different Voice: Gender and Language in the Trials of Anne Hutchinson," *Early American Literature* 25.3 (1990): 253–70. As Lyle Koehler reminds us, "From parent, husband, and pulpit, Puritan women learned that they were supposed to submit to male rule. If a wife tried to exercise much self-government, she had to confront the fact that her own expression of freedom threatened to destroy the God-created hierarchy of her own family and Puritan society." Lyle Koehler, *A Search for Power: The "Weaker Sex" in Seventeenth-Century New England* (Urbana: University of Illinois Press, 1080), 22.

14. Since no copies of the first edition of Rowlandson's captivity narrative are extant, scholars assume the chronicle had a wide circulation and was an immediate best-seller. The first edition may have been read to shreds, but I would argue for a small first printing, distributed to family, friends, and intimates. The chronicle's popularity and wider distribution began, I would argue, after it was advertised in the first American edition of Bunyan's *The Pilgrim's Progress* (1681). For discussion of the history of the narrative and its growing popularity over time, readers should see Derounian, "The Publication, Promotion, and Distribution of Mary Rowlandson's . . . Narrative," 239–61; and Richard Slotkin and James K. Folsom, *So Dreadfull a Judgment: Puritan Responses to King Philip's War, 1676–1677* (Middletown, Conn.: Wesleyan University Press, 1978), 301–14.

15. That "Ter Amicam" (identified as Increase Mather) finds it necessary to defend Mrs. Rowlandson against charges of immodesty speaks to this point particularly well. Of the many works treating the subject of men silencing women in colonial New England, the essay that best bears upon my discussion is Davis's, "Mary White Rowlandson's Self-Fashioning," 49–60. See also, Koehler, *A Search for Power*, 54.

16. Slotkin and Folsom, *So Dreadfull a Judgment*, 320. All subsequent citations from Rowlandson's captivity narrative refer to the Slotkin-Folsom edition.

17. The author of the preface, Ter Amicam, has been variously identified as Increase Mather, Nathaniel Saltonstall, and Joseph Rowlandson. I follow Slotkin and Folsom's lead and attribute the preface to Increase Mather.

18. Slotkin and Folsom, *So Dreadfull a Judgment*, 320. This point is also made by Davis in "Mary White Rowlandson's Self-Fashioning," 58.

19. Images of captivity and redemption were central to the Puritans' self-definition. Drawing on Old Testament types, especially bondage of the Jews in Egypt and the Babylonian Captivity, the Puritans of New England read their wilderness experience through the lens of historical typology. On the Puritans' use of historical typology, see Sacvan Bercovitch, *Typology and Early American Literature* (Amherst: University of Massachusetts Press, 1972); Mason I. Lowance, Jr., *The Language of Canaan: Metaphor and Symbol in New England from the Puritans to the Transcendentalists* (Cambridge: Harvard University Press, 1980); Slotkin, *Regeneration Through Violence*, 94–115; Downing, "'Streams of Scripture Comfort,'" 252–59; Ursula Brumm, *American Thought and Religious Typology* (New Brunswick, N.J.: Rutgers University Press, 1970).

20. By "sex," I mean Mary's genetic makeup, and the fact that she is anatomically female. By "gender," I mean the various roles she plays within her community (spouse, mother, sister, etc.).

21. Slotkin and Folsom, *So Dreadfull a Judgment*, 322.

22. Ibid., 365.

23. She enjoyed tobacco, and failed to keep the Sabbath on occasion. She had even been jealous of those who suffered, believing they had been favored by God: "whom the Lord loveth he chasteneth" (Hebrews 12:6).

24. Slotkin and Folsom, *So Dreadfull a Judgment*, 342, 346, 365. Rowlandson's preference for male (rather than female) examples of suffering may seem a small point. After all, references to Job, Hezekiah, Jonah, David, and the Prodigal Son would have been appreciated for their symbolic value. These biblical heroes, after all, are recognized as types of suffering. Besides, Mary's allusions to Job, Daniel, Joshua, and David do not conjure up images of actual men undergoing actual suffering. Since they are rhetorical figures, one might argue that gender is irrelevant here. But such is not the case. Mary avoids any and all allusions to women's suffering because such references would only have elevated her status as author. Mary might have written, "I hope it is not too much to say with Sarah," or "I have suffered as Ruth suffered." Such comparisons, however, would have made more of her sex than was meet: it would have violated the decorum of female silence and diffidence. For a complete listing of Rowlandson's scriptural references, see Downing, "'Streams of Scripture Comfort,'" 257–59.

25. Slotkin and Folsom, *So Dreadfull a Judgment*, 365. Though contemporary readers might assume that Mary uses "he" as the generic pronoun reference for all humanity, the "son" cited in Hebrews 12:6 refers, specifically, to Jesus Christ; thus, "he" refers to Christ, specifically. Rowlandson may consider herself a true daughter of Zion, but she clearly wants her readers to think of her in masculine terms and to see her relationship with God as a father-son, rather than a father-daughter, relationship.

26. Ibid., 334. Mary is recollecting the events of Monday, November 16, 1675. The Indians break camp, set fire to their makeshift wigwams, and head deeper into the woods.

27. For discussion of the male/female, spirit/flesh dichotomy and the Puritan "logic" that associated womanhood with evil and sin, see Elizabeth Reis, "The Devil, the Body, and the Feminine Soul in Puritan New England," *Journal of American History*, June 1995, 16.

28. Slotkin and Folsom, *So Dreadfull a Judgment*, 338–39.

29. *Oxford English Dictionary*, compact ed., vol. 1 (Oxford: Oxford University Press, 1971), 1809.

30. Mary not only refers to the Indians as liars, thieves, and cheats but she labels them "wild beasts," "ravenous wolves," "inhuman creatures," savages prone to "devilish cruelty." See Slotkin and Folsom, *So Dreadfull a Judgment*, 332, 358, 327, 360, passim.

31. Mary's fear of being raped by an Indian is a rhetorical pose. Northeastern woodland Indians, Rowlandson and her readers knew, did not rape women, white or Indian—ever. In fact, more than one of Mary's contemporaries, conscious of the pernicious effects of the Old World stereotype, attempted to clear the Indians of the charge. See, for example, Daniel Gookin, *A Narrative of the Troubles with the Indians in New England, From the First Planting thereof to the present Time*, 2 vols. (Roxbury, Mass.: S. G. Drake, 1865), passim.

32. Slotkin and Folsom, *So Dreadfull a Judgment*, 321.

33. The image of the lascivious Indian, though fraudulent, served to justify—albeit after the fact—the settlers' war against the Algonquian people. Since warring natives were perceived as unredeemable "savages," their complete annihilation was sanctioned. The literature on the ignoble savage stereotype and his/her appetites is legion. See Richard Bernheimer, *Wild Men in the Middle Ages* (Cambridge: Harvard University Press, 1952); W. Arens, *The Man-Eating Myth: Anthropology and Anthropophagy* (New York: Oxford University Press, 1979); and Margaret Hodgen, *Early Anthropology in the Sixteenth and Seventeenth Centuries* (Philadelphia: University of Pennsylvania Press, 1964); Louise K. Barnett, *The Ignoble Savage: American Literary Racism, 1790–1890* (Westport, Conn.: Greenwood Press, 1975). These seminal studies trace the persistence of the negative stereotype throughout the Renaissance and into the modern era. In his preface to Rowlandson's chronicle, Increase Mather provides his own list of epithets. Mary's captors are "atheistical, proud, wild, cruel, barbarous, brutish (in one word) diabolical creatures . . . the worst of the heathens" (Slotkin and Folsom, *So Dreadfull a Judgment*, 321). See also Diebold, *A Critical Edition of . . . Rowlandson's Narrative*, cxxi–cxlii.

34. Diebold, *A Critical Edition of . . . Rowlandson's Narrative*, viii.

35. As critics have long recognized, sexual "misconduct" is a familiar trope in women's captivity narratives and may very well reflect the chronicler's own sex-

ual longings. The sexual lure of the wilderness and the female captive's desire for sexual contact with her Indian captors is the focus of June Namias's study *White Captives: Gender and Ethnicity on the American Frontier* (Chapel Hill: University of North Carolina Press, 1993).

36. Reis, "The Devil, the Body, and the Feminine Soul," 15–16.

37. Slotkin and Folsom, *So Dreadfull a Judgment*, 333, 347, 349.

38. Ibid., 335.

39. Ibid., 360–61.

40. *Oxford English Dictionary*, compact ed., vol. 2 (Oxford: Oxford University Press, 1971), 3477.

41. Slotkin and Folsom, *So Dreadfull a Judgment*, 356–57.

42. And the offense goes deeper. By donning English finery (as opposed to "everyday" English attire), Mary portrays her Indian captors as criminals in violation of the colony's sumptuary laws. Excesses in attire (including the wearing of powdered wigs) was commonly pointed to as one of the reasons why God had set the Indians upon New England. See Perry Miller, *The New England Mind: The Seventeenth Century* (Boston: Beacon Press, 1954), 463–91.

43. Liminality, I would argue, not only speaks to Mary's difficulty in maintaining her cultural identity (civilized, Christian, Puritan, female) during her captivity in the Indian wilderness, but also reveals her difficulty in speaking a prescribed male discourse. As she pens her narrative, Mary reflects on her experience. And as she reflects, she seems to appreciate the validity of her grievance against male hegemony. Her liminality, then, refers to the shift in her tone of voice (from compliant to outraged) as well as the shift in her image of herself. For an interesting discussion of liminality in Rowlandson's captivity narrative, see Burnham, "The Journey Between," 60–75. Liminality, for Burnham, refers to Mary's ability to cross the metaphysical border of Puritan theology, thus enabling her to recognize the Indians as a people in their own right rather than as abstract types. Mary's liminal position as captive, Burnham correctly notes, is reflected in the chronicle's conflicting narrative styles.

44. Slotkin and Folsom, *So Dreadfull a Judgment*, 351.

45. Mary Rowlandson was redeemed by the English for twenty pounds. The conditions of her return are presented in Slotkin and Folsom, *So Dreadfull a Judgment*, 352.

46. Weetamoo (also known as Namumpam, Tatatanum, Tatapanum, Squaw sachem of the Pocasset, Wetamoo, Wetemoo, Wetamou, Wetamoe, Weetamou, Weetamoe, Weetammo, Weetamore, Queen Wetamoo) (1635? 1650?–1676) was born near the Fall River in present-day Rhode Island and was an Algonquian leader during King Philip's War. Weetamoo was married several times, most notably to Alexander (Wamsutta), grand sachem of the Wampanoag confederacy and brother of King Philip (Metacom). When Alexander died, Weetamoo married Quequequamanchet, whom she left because he sided with the colonists at the be-

ginning of King Philip's War. She then married Quinnapin, a Narraganset. See *Native American Women: A Biographical Dictionary*, 275–76. No one knows how Weetamoo died. According to Increase Mather, Indians allied with the English found Weetamoo's dead body in the woods surrounding Taunton, Rhode Island, sometime between August 6 and August 10, 1676. These Indians decapitated her body and brought the head to the English (in Taunton) who set it upon a pole. See Increase Mather, *A Brief History of the Warr with the Indians in New-England* (Boston: John Foster, 1676), cited in Slotkin and Folsom, *So Dreadfull a Judgment*, 138–39.

47. Ibid., 357.

48. Ibid., 357. Definitions of "fain" are from the *Oxford English Dictionary*, compact ed., 950.

49. Patricia Simons, "Women in Frames," 8.

50. Slotkin and Folsom, *So Dreadfull a Judgment*, 358.

51. Mary rebukes the colonial militia on two occasions. Here is the earlier incident:

> And here I cannot but take notice of the strange providence of God in preserving the heathen. . . . Monday they set their wigwams on fire, and away they went: on that very day came the English army after them. . . . and saw the smoke of their wigwams, and yet this river [i.e. the Baquag river], put a stop to them. God did not give them courage or activity to go over after us; we were not ready for so great a mercy as victory and deliverance. (333–34)

In this earlier account, Mary tempers her criticism of the militia by focusing on the captives. In a later episode, the continued enslavement of the captives becomes the fault of the colonial militia. Had the colonial militia been alert and swift, Mary could have been restored to civilization sooner—so she would have us believe.

52. Slotkin and Folsom, *So Dreadfull a Judgment*, 366–67.

53. My reading of the Joslin episode follows Mitchell Breitwieser's. See Breitwieser, *American Puritanism and the Defense of Mourning* 111–12.

54. Slotkin and Folsom, *So Dreadfull a Judgment*, 331.

55. Ibid., 331.

56. Ibid., 341.

57. Ibid., 341.

Part II

Regulating Sex and Sexuality in Colonial New England

Puritan New England took moral offenses very seriously. Any threat to the virtue of its citizens jeopardized the survival of their New Zion, "City upon a Hill." Key to this survival was the family, consisting of a father, a mother, children, and other dependents. Through the family, order was maintained, values instilled, and property transferred. Any disturbance of family stability posed a threat to the society. Thus, moral transgressions were prosecuted as crimes and included any sexual activity outside of marriage.

Else L. Hambleton traces the evolution of these laws in her study of the fornication trial of Samuel Appleton and Priscilla Willson. Through the examination of the records and people involved, Hambleton concludes that Appleton received privileged treatment because of his class and past associations with the judges. Moreover, Appleton may have escaped a rape charge due to beliefs about sexuality and conception existing at that time. Hambleton's essay also explores gender roles and the nature and extent of extramarital sexual activity in seventeenth-century Massachusetts.

Just as sexual activity prior to marriage threatened the stability of colonial New England society, so did an absence of marital sexual activity. The issue of marital sex is at the crux of Erik R. Seeman's essay. Sarah Prentice's celibacy threatened her society because it threatened family stability. By ending her role as a childbearer, she was ignoring her duty as a wife. Since the ideal Puritan woman was a wife and a mother, Prentice disturbed her community's values. Seeman demonstrates that questions of sexuality, purity, and the body were central to understanding the positions of those influenced by the Great Awakening, as well as the opposition of the Old Lights. Both Hambleton's and Seeman's essays give readers a greater understanding of gender roles and sexuality in colonial New England.

87

The Regulation of Sex in Seventeenth-Century Massachusetts
The Quarterly Court of Essex County vs. Priscilla Willson and Mr. Samuel Appleton

Else L. Hambleton

> Mr. Samll. Appleton, jr., and Priscilla Willson were presented for fornication, and the said Samuel denying it was dismissed, paying half the costs. Priscilla was fined. The child died, and Appleton was ordered to pay half the costs to Mr. Purchis.[1]

This terse entry in the Essex County Quarterly Court Record Book for June 28, 1683, conceals a complex series of events that had broad social and economic ramifications extending beyond the bare statement that Priscilla Willson, a sixteen-year-old orphan, was convicted of fornication and Samuel Appleton, a twenty-nine-year-old married man, was not. A study of the evidence presented in this trial, the verdict, and the outcomes of contemporary fornication trials make it possible to draw some conclusions about the nature and extent of sexual activity among unmarried persons in Essex County, Massachusetts, between 1641 and 1685.

Women who bore illegitimate children, their sexual partners, and couples whose first child arrived within eight months of marriage were prosecuted for fornication in the Quarterly Courts of the Massachusetts Bay Colony. A quantitative analysis of bastardy and premarital fornication cases indicates that sexual activity outside of marriage was rare. The ratio of fornication cases relative to the population increased in the last thirty years of the seventeenth century. The proportion of unwed mothers and pregnant brides remained even. In Essex County, Massachusetts, between 1641 and 1685, 135 married women and 131 unmarried women were cited for fornication. However, there is a significant difference between these two groups of women. While pregnant brides fall into the same age group as their peers who married prior to the conception of their first child, 62 percent of the women who bore illegitimate children are younger, between the ages of fifteen and twenty.

The Appleton-Willson fornication trial is a particularly apt subject for analysis, because this case has similarities to other contemporary fornication trials as well as important differences that help to clarify Puritan sexual mores, gender ideology, and cultural values in seventeenth-century Massachusetts. Gentlemen like Appleton did not normally find themselves in court charged with fornication. The dismissal of the charges by the judges, with the concomitant assignment of court costs and child support payments, is unique. The experience of his codefendant, Priscilla Willson, on the other hand, represents that of many women in seventeenth-century Essex County, Massachusetts, who were tried and convicted of fornication. Evidence of coerced sexual activity was presented, but Appleton was not charged with rape. Additionally, this fornication trial was encased in an economic dispute over the ownership of one of the first iron foundries in America, the Saugus Ironworks.

Documentary Evidence

The trial began June 27, 1683. The first two witnesses testified that Appleton had had the opportunity to father Willson's illegitimate baby. Hester Witt, Willson's eighteen-year-old friend, said that

> one night when I the deponant lived at the old Ironworks with my father stocker, in ye roome yt my father stocker lived there was a bed on wch priscilla wilson lay downe saying shee was not well & Mr. Samuel Appleton came into the roome & went & lay down upon the bed & drew the Curtaines & the said priscilla desired him severall times to let her goe forth, but he kept her inn when she desired to Come away & soe he hindered her & they tarried there a Considerable tyme.[2]

Naomy Flanders, a twenty-four-year-old servant, presented even more damaging testimony. She claimed to have questioned Appleton about his treatment of Willson and to have been rebuked by him.

> Mr. Samuell Appleton of Lynn came into the Roome & went & lay downe upon the bed where shee was. And the said priscilla wilson desired him to lett her goe forth: but he kept her inn until Mrs purchis Came & Called for her & then in a little time after hee lett her goe: and a little while after this deponant asked Mr. Appleton why he did soe: viz: stopp her & keepe her at that time: when shee was so desirous to goe away. And Mr. Appleton told mee I was a foole and knew nothing.[3]

More witnesses followed the next day. Both Sarah Hathorne, the fifty-eight-year-old midwife who had presided at the birth of Willson's baby, and Experience Tarbox, a neighbor whose husband had delivered all the warrants in the case, testified that Willson, after much persuasion, had named Appleton during labor as the father. Sarah Hathorne deposed that

> by the providence of god it was her lott to be midwife to priscilla wilson of Lyn when the time of her travell came; before I entered upon performance of anything, though her paynes came upon her, this deponant said priscilla deal truly & playnly with mee & tell mee truly whoe is the father of the child & doe noe body any wrong, shee the said priscilla answered noe more shee would not. In the instant of tyme, her grandfather purchis came into the roome & said to this purpose oh my child, thou hast not gods feare before thee when thou didst this evill but now lett the feare of god be upon thee & doe no person any wrong but as thou knowest not but thou maist dy. I charge thee in gods feare deal truly & declare truly whoe is the father of ye child & so spake to this purpose—left the room. Immediately her pangs came upon her & still this deponant & the rest present pressed her to tell truly & in her extremity shee said shee did & Mr. Appleton of Lyn was the father of it & that there was never noe other man had to do with her.[4]

The testimony of Experience Tarbox corroborated Sarah Hathorne's. She further testified that "to her best Judgment the child was the Image of Mr. Samuell Appleton from the Crowne to the foote."[5]

The final piece of evidence was a statement signed by fourteen residents of Lynn attesting to Priscilla Willson's good character. While they did not condone her behavior, they laid the blame explicitly at Samuel Appleton's door, saying that they had been

the neerest neighbors unto Priscilla Wilson of Lyn, whoe hath greatly dis-
honord god and her relations together with her selfe by Committing Fornication: yet wee make bold to signifie to the Honord Court: That it was a
matter of great admiration to us to heare of it: because from her childhood
shee behaved herselfe soe modestly and Civilly all her time before this transgression as that none of us ever saw or heard of any Immodest or Uncivill
behavior or wantonnesse and that wee beleeve she was overcome by some
subtill slights and temptations of one that beguiled her to yeeld to his lust
and wee are all perswaded that shee doth not wrongly accuse him whoe she
doth lay the charge upon: and so much wee present to the Honord Court
hoping god will returne her by repentance and help her to deal truly in the
case.[6]

This was the evidence the judges considered before dismissing the fornication charge against Samuel Appleton. Priscilla Willson was convicted;
the birth of her daughter provided irrefutable evidence that she had engaged in sexual activity.

Background Information

Priscilla Willson was born March 28, 1666 in the close-knit community
of Hammersmith, the site of the Saugus Ironworks, located in Lynn,
Massachusetts. She was the second child and first daughter of William
and Priscilla Willson. Her father, William Willson, worked for his father-
in-law, Oliver Purchis, the superintendent of the Saugus Ironworks. The
births of another son and daughter followed. On October 21, 1671, Willson's mother and grandmother died and her father seems to have disappeared from Lynn.[7] Fifty-nine-year-old Oliver Purchis became responsible for four grandchildren, ranging in age from one to seven, and within
a year he married twenty-one-year-old Mary Perkins.[8]

The Saugus Ironworks, perennially undercapitalized, had been beset
by stockholder lawsuits, deteriorating equipment, and limited production
runs as early as 1658, when Purchis had been appointed works manager
and assumed responsibility for its day-to-day management.[9] He kept the
ironworks labor force busy—a disparate group, composed of skilled iron-
workers from Hammersmith, England, Scottish prisoners-of-war who
had been deported to Massachusetts Bay, and locally recruited workers—
maintained the physical plant, and made production decisions. Between

1658 and 1663, Purchis produced three hundred tons of iron at the Saugus Ironworks.[10]

In 1660, William Paine, the majority shareholder, died, leaving his interest in the ironworks to his son, John, who lacked his father's financial acumen. By 1664, the ironworks was in serious financial trouble and Major Samuel Appleton of Ipswich, William Paine's son-in-law, sued Purchis and the Saugus Ironworks to secure an inheritance of fifteen hundred pounds that had been left by Paine to Appleton's children, Samuel, Jr., Hannah, and Judith. Twelve years later, in 1676, the Essex County Quarterly Court issued Purchis an ultimatum: he was to pay Samuel Appleton, Jr., and his sisters, their fifteen-hundred-pound inheritance out of the assets of the Saugus Ironworks or turn it over to the Appleton family. Purchis was forced to allow Samuel Appleton, Jr., twenty-two at the time, to take possession of the ironmaster's house in partial settlement of the fifteen-hundred-pound debt.[11] Priscilla Willson was a child of ten when Samuel Appleton took possession of the ironmaster's house and established himself at the operating center of the ironworks.

Six years later the situation in the small village of Hammersmith was tense, as competing interests sought to control the ironworks' land. Oliver Purchis, now seventy, had a thirty-two-year-old wife and four dependents, two male and two female, between the ages of twelve and eighteen. Legal title to the Saugus Ironworks was entangled in a morass of lawsuits and countersuits. The Appletons were still pursuing Purchis through the Essex County Quarterly Court for title to the Saugus Ironworks, in order to develop the land. In addition, local farmers complained that water contained by the ironworks dam was encroaching on their fields, and fishermen petitioned the Essex County Quarterly Court to destroy the ironworks dam so that alewives could return to their natural spawning ground up the Saugus River.

That May the ironworks dam was sabotaged. The resulting flood washed away two bridges and some stone fences, deposited debris downstream on previously productive farmland, ended any possibility of iron production on the site, and produced a new crop of lawsuits.[12] Purchis had become adept through long experience at stalling creditors and placating local farmers, but as he absorbed the inevitable loss of hope for resumption of iron production, he received a personal blow. Purchis learned that his sixteen-year-old granddaughter, Priscilla, was pregnant.

Samuel Appleton's background was very different from that of the orphaned Willson. Born in Ipswich in 1654, he was heir to considerable economic power and prestige. The Appleton family had long been prominent in the financial and governmental affairs of the Massachusetts Bay Colony. His grandfather and great-uncle, Samuel and John Appleton, had become freedmen in Ipswich, on May 25, 1636. While sixty-two men were sworn in that day, only four of them, including Samuel and John Appleton, qualified for the gentleman's appellation of "Mr." A second generation of Samuels and Johns had consolidated the position of the Appleton family. The third generation, Samuel Appleton, Jr., and his brother, John, as well as his cousins, Samuel and John Appleton, were the beneficiaries, possessing considerable material assets along with an intangible, but no less important, asset: their status as gentlemen.

Appleton attended the Reverend Thomas Parker's school in Newbury, where one of his fellow students was Samuel Sewall.[13] He received an education steeped in religious values and at nineteen was received into full membership in the Ipswich Congregational Church.[14] During Metacomet's War he served in the militia under his father, who was charged with the defense of western Massachusetts. The leadership ability that Appleton, Sr., evinced at that time cemented his position, and that of his sons, in the upper ranks of Massachusetts society. In 1676, at the conclusion of his military service, Appleton moved into the ironmaster's house, as the Essex County Quarterly Court had ordered. By 1682, Thomas Savage of Boston, another creditor, pressed his claim against the ironworks by putting his agent, Samuel Stocker, into a room in Appleton's house, and Appleton and Savage joined forces in a series of lawsuits against local claimants to parts of the ironworks land. It was in Stocker's room in the ironmaster's house, while visiting her friend Hester Witt, that Priscilla Willson alleged that she and Appleton had sexual intercourse.

On June 19, 1682, Appleton married Elizabeth Whittingham, the fifteen-year-old daughter of a prosperous merchant, William Whittingham, formerly of Ipswich, who had returned to England.[15] Nine months later their first daughter, Mary, was born in the ironmaster's house. Three weeks after Mary's birth, Appleton was charged with fornication, when Priscilla Willson claimed that he had fathered her daughter as well. It was not an auspicious start to Appleton's marriage.[16]

More auspicious for Appleton was the composition of the court. Unless there was a specific request for a jury, fornication cases were decided by the sitting judges. Of the six judges who served at this session of the

Essex County Quarterly Court, at least four had a direct relationship with Samuel Appleton. One was his father, another was a relative by marriage, and two more were close political allies of his father. Furthermore, it took only three of these judges to constitute a quorum. Priscilla Willson did not lack influence. Her grandfather, Oliver Purchis, had been a representative to the General Court and the town clerk of Lynn for many years, and it is likely that his local prestige provided the leverage to bring charges against Appleton in the first place. In the courtroom, though, however loyal her friends and however assiduous they were in her defense, their eyewitness testimony and statement of character were not enough to outweigh the Appleton family influence.

A breakdown of the trial participants by class and occupation, where it is known, is illustrative. The judges were the elite of Massachusetts Bay Colony. Willson's supporters, with the exception of Oliver Purchis and one of the petition signers, Captain Thomas Marshall, who was related to an ironworks employee and was himself involved in a separate dispute with Appleton over the ownership of land in Lynn, were all of more humble status, had a connection with the ironworks, and lived in the Hammersmith area of Lynn.

It is clear that the judges had social, economic, and familial connections to Appleton. For this reason the fornication charge was dismissed, although Appleton called no witnesses on his behalf. There was a second reason for the dismissal: Appleton had made a public denial of paternity, and gentlemen did not lie. A conviction would have branded him as a liar as well as a fornicator. By dismissing the charges against Appleton, the judges sidestepped the issue of his guilt or innocence, thus preserving his honor.

However, even as the judges gave, they took away. Appleton was required to pay one-half of Willson's childbirth expenses and the expenses incurred by the female child during her brief existence, including the midwife's fee, two weeks' pay for a nurse, and burial expenses. Appleton was also required to pay one-half of the court charges, money to the constable for summoning the witnesses, and, ironically, the witness fees due to Purchis and to Willson's neighbors.

Each party got something out of the court's verdict. Appleton had been able to get his fornication charge dismissed by denying that he had had sexual intercourse with Priscilla Willson. Willson was granted a tacit vindication of her claim that Appleton had fathered her child. Purchis was reimbursed for half of what he had laid out for the baby's expenses and the costs of bringing charges against Appleton. The judges had reached a clever compromise which salvaged Appleton's honor even as he was required to assume financial responsibility for Willson's daughter. Such a verdict would have been impossible had the infant not died. There was nothing in the court's verdict, however, that addressed the testimony of Hester Witt and Naomy Flanders, which suggested that Appleton had raped Willson. The judges were not willfully ignoring evidence that was damaging to Appleton; they considered the testimony irrelevant.

The Issue of Rape

The issue of rape was never raised at the trial, despite testimony that Appleton had forced his way into a curtained bed in which Willson lay ill and refused her requests to let her leave. Willson's friend, Hester Witt, testified that Willson had asked Appleton several times to let her go, but "he hindered her & they tarried there a Considerable tyme."[17] Naomi Flanders had said that "he kept her inn until Mrs. purchis Came & Called for her & then in a little time after hee let her goe," and that when Flanders questioned Appleton's behavior, he told Flanders that she was a fool and knew nothing.[18] However, even the fourteen neighbors who attested to her good character and expressed their surprise at her pregnancy, assumed that she had consented to intercourse with Appleton. Based on their prior knowledge of her character, they believed that Willson had been "overcome by some subtill slights and temptations of one that beguiled her to yield to his lust."[19]

It does appear that coercion was used, but a rape charge was never considered. One reason, of course, was Appleton's status as a gentleman, but there was another, more important, issue. Appleton was not charged with rape because Willson had conceived. This, in itself, was an indication to her contemporaries that she had been a willing participant. A scientific authority had stated in 1583 that "unwilling copulation for the most part is vain and barren: for love causeth conception."[20] A hundred years later this belief was encoded in the legal system of Massachusetts Bay Colony. A widely used English manual for justices of the peace stated that in any case where conception had occurred, "consent must be inferred."[21]

Priscilla Willson had conceived; therefore she could not have been raped. In all probability Willson shared the popular belief of her contemporaries and assumed that she would not become pregnant. As well, she would have been keenly aware that to accuse Appleton of rape would mean that her loss of virginity would become public knowledge. By the time that she realized that she was pregnant, it would have been too late to accuse Appleton of rape with any credibility. Her youth, the deferent attitude that would have been inculcated in her toward her seniors and betters, and her own perception of the relationship between rape and conception may have led her to internalize a sense of her own complicity.

Testimony provided by a midwife in the 1669 fornication case involving a young Salisbury servant, Ann Chase, indicates the pervasiveness of the belief that rape was essentially a sterile act. The midwife's interrogation during labor elicited the information from Chase that her employer's brother, John Allen, had accosted her one evening as she went from her workplace to her lodging, held her against a fence rail, covered her mouth with her hand to prevent her from crying out, and forced intercourse upon her. The midwife chided Chase for lying: "I often told her that her pains continued the longer because she had not spoken the truth." Chase answered that, "if she died for it she had spoken the truth and nothing else."[22] After six days of labor, with a disbelieving midwife at her side urging her to recant, Chase delivered her child.

The midwife was not insensitive. Ann Chase had been her servant for two years previously, and the midwife testified that she had never seen "any light or unseemly carriage in all that time."[23] However, so strong was the Puritan rape ideology that the midwife, despite her personal knowledge of Chase's character, was unable to accept her story. The court did not believe Chase either: not only was Allen never charged with rape or fornication, he was not assessed for child support payments.

Legal Background to Fornication Prosecutions

A fornication charge was the most common cause of legal action against women in seventeenth-century New England.[24] Fornication prosecutions had become increasingly common as the century progressed, as can be seen in table 4.1. The arrival of Constable Tarbox at Appleton's house, bearing a summons, made the recently married Appleton the object of neighborhood censure and the topic of alehouse gossip.[25] For Appleton, it involved a tangible but temporary loss of status, since Puritans construed male extramarital sexual activity as one facet of a larger pattern of

TABLE 4.1
Analysis of Fornication Cases for Unmarried
and Married Women in Essex County,
Massachusetts (1641–1685)

	Cited for Fornication	
Year	Unmarried Women (N=131)	Married Women (N=135)
1641–45	3	1
1646–50	3	2
1651–55	7	3
1656–60	10	7
1661–65	6	8
1666–70	14	12
1671–75	23	35
1676–80	31	35
1681–85	29	29

identity.[26] For Priscilla Willson, however, it was a social and economic calamity.

Willson, and any other young woman who had to answer such a charge without a husband at her side when she appeared in court, faced an uncertain future. Marriage was the only viable career option for women in seventeenth-century Massachusetts, and a fornication conviction presented an almost insuperable bar to marriage. Chastity before marriage and faithfulness within marriage were at the core of female honor: virtue and worth were defined, for women, in sexual terms.[27] Marriageability was determined through a weighing of three factors: sexual reputation, adherence to female societal norms, and material circumstances.[28] Seventy-three per cent of the unmarried women convicted of fornication in Essex County between 1681 and 1685, including Priscilla Willson, did not marry. Their pregnancies and subsequent fornication convictions had offended Puritan notions of appropriate feminine behavior.

The idea that sexual activity among unmarried persons could be controlled through criminal prosecution of those who bore illegitimate children and those whose first child arrived before eight months of marriage did not originate in Puritan Massachusetts. English authorities had used the ecclesiastical courts to control sexual activity for centuries. However, in England the primary purpose had become the reduction of public welfare costs, and in consequence the courts selectively targeted the poorest members of the community for prosecution. English Puritans had pressed for a uniform application of the fornication laws and harsher penalties and had tried unsuccessfully to use their parliamentary clout to transfer jurisdiction over sexual irregularities to the civil courts.[29] The New World offered Puritans a chance to create a civil court system in which moral offenses could be prosecuted as crimes.

There were four reasons for wanting to repress sexual activity between unmarried persons in the seventeenth century. First, female chastity prior to marriage and female fidelity within marriage were essential to the orderly transmission of property. Second, illegitimacy represented the production of incomplete families. A family headed by a single mother could not be incorporated into a social order predicated on patriarchal authority. Third, and specific to the Puritans of Massachusetts Bay Colony, was religious ideology. The survival of their "City upon a Hill," hedged in by dark and threatening forests populated by Indians described by Puritan ministers as "God's principle rod of chastisement" required a citizenry attuned to any deviance from societal norms.[30] Their lives, both temporal and spiritual, depended on the virtue of the community in general. Fornication was a sin, and a community that harbored fornicators exposed itself to the wrath of God. Fourth, Puritans desperately needed to control their source of labor, their children, and sexual activity between unmarried persons threatened that control. A pregnancy could be used to wrest a disbursement of land for the establishment of a separate household or to force an unequal or premature distribution of family resources. Of even greater concern, was the potential withdrawal of labor from two parental households.

Consequently, the Puritans of Massachusetts Bay Colony established very specific laws for sexual offenses. In the 1630s, men were held responsible for initiating illegitimate sexual activity. Their female partners were not named in the court records until 1642, when, in response to a rising number of illegitimate pregnancies, an ordinance was passed stating that fornicators should be strongly encouraged to marry. If marriage was not feasible, because of unfinished indentures or a lack of financial resources, the law provided for the payment of a five-pound fine, the equivalent of a year's wages for a female servant, or a public whipping.

In 1665, an additional clause stated that a man with freeman status could be disenfranchised as the result of a fornication conviction. The threat of disenfranchisement was not a sufficient deterrent, for in 1668 the court amended the law yet again. It had become increasingly difficult to get the putative father to confess, and unless he confessed he could not be convicted of fornication or assessed for child support payments. In order to relieve local communities from the burden of supporting a rapidly increasing number of bastards, it was necessary to find a legal way to assign paternity in cases where there was no confession. The amendment of 1668 stated that a woman's declaration during childbirth would sustain a finding of paternity, and midwives were ordered to ferret out the father's identity before delivering the baby. Male premarital fornicators continued to be assessed five-pound fines in addition to their wives' five-pound fines. Now, however, single men who did not confess but who were named during childbirth testimonies were assessed for child support payments without the concomitant fornication fine.

Men found that an obdurate refusal to confess to the act of intercourse spared them a fornication conviction.[31] But, in each instance, except for Appleton, even when the supposed father denied paternity, while he might escape a fornication conviction, he was judged to be the father, treated to a tongue-lashing from the bench, and assessed for child support payments. Denial of paternity had become the norm. In the less religiously charged atmosphere that prevailed in the final third of the seventeenth century, confession was no longer considered good for the soul, and the loss of honor implicit in a fornication conviction became the paramount reason for the denial of paternity.

When Samuel Appleton denied that he was the father of Priscilla Willson's baby, he was acting in the same manner as other male defendants. However, none of them were influential enough to secure a dismissal and leave the court with honor intact. Judges in the Essex County Quarterly Courts regularly stated that they did not believe the denials of the male defendants. In the 1684 case of Mary Sterling of Haverhill and Timothy Osgood of Andover, "[h]e denied the charges, but the court judged him the reputed father of the child, which is now dead."[32] In 1686, Joseph Burnam, like Samuel Appleton, denied paternity in a similar situation but the court did not believe him, and he was assessed for child support payments.[33]

Lesser sexual offenses were also punished by the courts. Puritan authorities sought to repress potential youthful sexual activity through the selective prosecution of young women who violated social norms. In March 1674, Hannah Gray was convicted of lascivious behavior for "laughing and giggling at the boys bed which was in the same room." She was sentenced to stand at the meetinghouses in Salem and Beverly with a paper pinned to her forehead stating, "I STAND HEERE FOR MY LAS-

CIVIOUS AND WANTON CARRIAGES."[34] This punishment would have served to deter not only Hannah Gray but all the adolescent females in Salem and Beverley who passed her on their way into church. In the same way, the effect of even a limited number of fornication trials was to inhibit sexual activity among unmarried persons.

The Extent of Sexual Activity among Unmarried Persons

Fifty-eight women, including Priscilla Willson, were charged with fornication by the Essex County Quarterly Court between 1681 and 1685. One woman died in childbirth before she could be tried, but the remaining fifty-seven, whether married or single at the time of their court appearances, were convicted.[35] Twenty-nine of the women, or 50 percent, were married at the time of their court appearances. Both they and their husbands were fined or whipped for fornication. The twenty-eight women who bore illegitimate children were also fined or whipped for fornication. Six of them did not name a father during childbirth, and five were unable to sustain their childbirth accusations. Two of the pregnancies had occurred outside the jurisdiction of the Essex County Quarterly Court, so the men were not presented, and two more putative fathers fled. Only three of the twenty-three men who had been named by unwed mothers during childbirth were actually convicted of fornication as the law required. They were convicted because they admitted paternity. The remaining eleven, of whom six, including Samuel Appleton, were already married, denied paternity. None of them were convicted of fornication, although all were assessed for child support payments.

In the five-year period between 1681 and 1685, then, it can be documented that at least fifty-eight unmarried couples engaged in sexual activity in Essex County, Massachusetts. Over a longer time period, between 1641 and 1670, there had been only forty-three illegitimate births, or 1.4 per year. During the same time period, only one couple per year was cited for premarital fornication. As illustrated in table 4.1, sexual activity between unmarried persons increased between 1671 and 1685, with 5.5 illegitimate pregnancies per year and 6.5 premarital pregnancies per year. However, when the population increase is factored in, it is apparent that the level of extramarital sexual activity in Essex County remained low throughout the seventeenth century. In adjoining Middlesex County, Roger Thompson observed the same low level of extramarital

sexual activity, as well as the assiduity with which the community moni-
tored its young people. He found ninety-six fornication trials involving
unmarried persons and sixty-six premarital fornication trials between
1649 and 1699. Despite his quantitative data, Thompson theorized that
unmarried Puritans were fascinated by sex. They read and talked about
sex and used various means, up to and including intercourse, to relieve
their sexual tensions.[36]

Other scholars have made similar assumptions about sexuality in New
England. Edmund Morgan suggested that Puritans were "inured to sexual offenses because there were so many."[37] He commented that "early
New Englanders possessed a high degree of virility and very few inhibi-
tions."[38] David Flaherty accepted Morgan's view that illicit sexual activity was common. He commented on the dissonance between the popular
conception of the Puritan as joyless and repressive and the high frequency
with which sexual offenses appeared in the court records. He cited as well
the general agreement among scholars as to the existence of widespread
sexual irregularities among the Puritans.[39] However, the work of historical demographers, as well as the evidence presented here on Essex
County, supports the conclusion that the rates of illegitimacy and premarital pregnancy were relatively low.[40]

Puritan Sexual Attitudes

Puritans were not inexorably opposed to all sexual activity. Frequent and
mutually satisfying sexual activity was not just a right but a duty for both
partners in a marriage.[41] The authors of Puritan marriage manuals
stressed the importance of marital sexual activity in binding the affections
of husband and wife together.[42] Regular orgasm promoted good health,
although too much sexual activity could be debilitating and shorten life.[43]
Moreover, while the only legitimate object of marital sexual activity was
procreation, conception required a mutual orgasm. This allowed Puritan
married couples considerable latitude in the conduct of their sexuality.
Medical texts advised that good food, wine, a relaxed atmosphere, and
foreplay encouraged conception.[44] This is perhaps where the confusion
arises concerning the Puritan attitudes toward sex. Within marriage, pleasurable sexual activity was expected, even mandated. However, while Puritans embraced marital sexual activity with enthusiasm, they were im-
placable in their opposition to any expression of sexuality outside of mar-

riage. A wide range of heterosexual activities, ranging from lewd or promiscuous behavior to intercourse, were illegal, as was sexual activity that did not promote conception, such as homosexuality, masturbation, sodomy, and bestiality, which were capital crimes.[45] Therefore, when assessing Puritan sexual attitudes, it is necessary to distinguish between marital and extramarital sexuality. Another important factor that needs to be considered is gender ideology.

It was commonly believed in the early modern world that women were inferior to men.[46] God had ordained this inferiority when He created Eve from Adam's body, to be his helpmeet, not his equal. John Milton summed up the Puritan view aptly in *Paradise Lost*: "he for God only, she for God in him."[47] It was assumed that God had created women as lesser individuals, skilled in the housekeeping arts and happiest within the four walls of their homes. Men were equipped by their greater physical and intellectual strength to be the dominant sex. Female inferiority was also predicated on a scientific model. Men's bodies contained more heat than women's bodies, and this heat made men more intelligent, more capable of reason, and physically stronger.[48] Women, as they grew older, especially if they were the wives or wealthy widows of influential men, gained authority in Puritan society, but it was their age and marital status, not their gender, that conferred power on them.[49]

The ideal young woman, as defined by Cotton Mather in 1692, was pious, chaste, silent, industrious, educated, and modest.[50] She was not assertive; she was submissive. Willson's neighbors, in attesting to their "surprise" upon learning of her pregnancy, indicate that Willson had previously displayed Mather's expected attributes. Willson had been "beguiled," and "overcome," to "yield" to Appleton's "subtill slights and temptations."[51] Their words, suggesting as they do, Willson's submissiveness and Appleton's ability to manipulate her, indicate that her neighbors interpreted Willson's sexual activity in light of contemporary gender ideology. However, their interpretation was undoubtedly influenced as well by Appleton's age and superior status, their respect for Purchis, and their opinion on the ironworks dispute.

Willson and her unmarried contemporaries, both male and female, were warned to avoid even the mental expression of sensuality as the precursor to sexual activity. One young man, Nicholas Gilman, listed in his diary methods he had developed to repress vagrant sexual thoughts: hard physical labor, prayer, and a focus on a heavenly, not earthly, reward. When tempted to masturbate, he counseled himself to seek out other people rather than to remain alone. Refraining from sexual intercourse required the exercise of all of the above, as well as ensuring that those he sought out were equally committed to chastity.[52] Ideally, both partners would enter a marriage as virgins, and most Puritans probably did. However, as mentioned above, sexual reputation comprised only one aspect of a man's character, while a woman's identity was wholly defined in terms of her sexual integrity. A recent study of slander suits in early modern England has shown that while women were most concerned about the loss of sexual reputation, men were most likely to go to court when they felt their honor had been impugned.[53]

Women had good reason to protect their sexual reputations. The assumption of female inferiority led to the belief that women lacked self-control and good judgment. In turn this led inevitably to the popular belief that women possessed voracious sexual appetites that, once awakened, could not be governed. The simultaneous existence of two very dissimilar belief systems about women, one that promoted female submissiveness and one that acknowledged female promiscuity, placed great pressure on Puritan society to regulate sexual activity between unmarried persons, because the consequences of uncontrolled female sexuality were so frightening. The emphasis placed on submissiveness as a desired female characteristic can be construed as an attempt to counteract the potential threat to patriarchal authority posed by sexually active women living outside family government. The fallen woman, the virgin transformed into a whore, became a potent symbol for everything that was rotten in Puritan society. Priscilla Willson embodied their fears. Her neighbors could only hope that God would "return her by repentance."[54]

Willson was catapulted into adulthood at the age of sixteen when she became pregnant. In the normal course of events she would have married between the ages of twenty-two and twenty-five and borne her first child within a year of her marriage. That the majority of young people abstained from sexual intercourse during this period of prolonged adolescence is apparent from the low incidence of fornication trials. While it has been argued that "love and affection played an important part in adolescent relationships," and that youthful sexual activity was common, the fornication trial statistics do not bear this out.[55] Depositions in which single women indicate that an avowal of affection or an offer of marriage had preceded their sexual activity must be regarded with a degree of skepticism. While affection was undoubtedly a factor in many illegitimate pregnancies, the very fact that these relationships did not culminate in

TABLE 4.2
*Age at Which Unmarried Women Became
Pregnant in Essex County,
Massachusetts (1641–1685)[1]*

Age	Number of Unmarried Women
15–17	10
18–20	15
21–23	10
24–26	1
27–29	4

[1]40 cases found

TABLE 4.3
*Age at Which Men Fathered Illegitimate
Children in Essex County,
Massachusetts (1641–1685)[1]*

Age	Number of Men
18–20	4
21–23	3
24–26	4
27–29	5
30–32	3
33–35	2
36–38	2
39 and over	3

[1]25 cases found

marriage leads to the conclusion that some women made exculpatory statements to justify their sexual activity and that some men made false promises. Marriage required the financial resources to establish an independent household. In Essex County 62 percent of the women who became pregnant out of wedlock were twenty years of age or less (see table 4.2). It is unlikely that they would have already accumulated sufficient savings to contribute to the establishment of a household. Their very youth and lack of experience made them vulnerable to male approaches. Moreover, while the women involved were usually adolescents, their partners were not. Sixty percent of the men assessed for child support payments between 1641 and 1685 in Essex County were older than twenty-seven (see table 4.3). This is evidence not of an affective bond but a predatory relationship.[56] Priscilla Willson was sixteen; Samuel Appleton twenty-nine. Their relationship clearly falls into this category. As well, at least 50 percent of the men who were assessed for child support payments for illegitimate children between 1681 and 1685 were married already. This evidence does not support the view that adolescents were engaging in mutual sexual exploration with other adolescents.

The belief that women were ruled by their passions virtually guaranteed that they would receive a disproportionate share of blame in cases of illicit sexual activity. The assiduity with which male sexual offenders had been prosecuted in the initial phase of Puritan settlement is evidence of the strength of the Puritan commitment to controlling extramarital sexual activity rather than their rejection of a sexual double standard. For example, the adultery laws contained an explicit double standard. Samuel Appleton was married, but he and Willson were not charged with adultery. If Willson had been married, an adultery charge would have followed. A sexual double standard also emerges when the status of defendants is considered. Gentlemen, like Appleton, received more lenient treatment at the hands of the law than men of lower degree.[57] But elite women were held to a *higher* moral standard than other women. In 1678, Dionysia Savage, the daughter of Thomas Savage, another ironworks creditor, was fined fifteen pounds, treble the usual fine for fornication, in the Suffolk County Quarterly Court.[58]

The Role of the Women's Community in Repressing Female Sexual Activity

Laurel Thatcher Ulrich has explored the role of the women's community in restricting female sexual activity.[59] She has discovered that older women functioned as monitors to prevent young women from engaging in unduly provocative behavior which might lead to sexual activity. Older women also protected young women, who, because of their sex-role conditioning, often lacked assertiveness when it came to dealing with sexual predators. In one example Ulrich discusses a Puritan matron who used her moral authority to prod Puritan officials into action against a gentleman whom she suspected of attempting to seduce a young, married woman while her husband was at sea. The selectmen had been unwilling to act because of his elite status.

Similar behavior can be observed in Essex County, where women played a variety of roles in the Willson-Appleton fornication case. The testimony of Hester Witt and Naomy Flanders provided evidence that

Samuel Appleton had had the opportunity to father Willson's baby, as well as exculpatory evidence on behalf of Willson. Naomy Flanders questioned Appleton's behavior and met with the rebuke that she was a fool. Her behavior and Appleton's response is evidence of the limits of female authority. That Witt and Flanders did not intervene or that Willson was unable to leave the bed despite her protests could be construed as evidence of sex role conditioning in the face of male aggression. However, a skeptic might ask, if Willson was unwilling, why wasn't the opposition more vigorous?

The older women appear to fit neatly into the protector role defined by Ulrich. Unable to protect Willson's virtue, they tried to preserve her character by signing a joint statement with their husbands, naming Appleton as the initiator of sexual activity. As required, the midwife urged Appleton to name the baby's father, "before I entered upon performance of anything, although her paynes came upon her."[60] The women then backed up Willson's allegations by noting a physical resemblance between Appleton and the baby.

Conclusions

In the final analysis there is no definitive answer to the question of who fathered Priscilla Willson's infant daughter and the circumstances under which conception occurred. The first and most plausible interpretation is that Appleton raped Willson, as the first two witnesses indirectly testified. The arrival of Willson's step-grandmother is telling. Had she come because she had been told Willson was sick, or because someone had run over to the Purchis house to tell her that Samuel Appleton had forced his way into her young step-granddaughter's bed? Willson was in her own neighborhood and in the general course of events would not have required assistance returning home. Also, the midwife's testimony suggests that she was waiting for more than the rote naming of a previously identified man to satisfy the court's requirement for an assignment of paternity during labor. Willson's apparent reluctance to name Appleton can be interpreted in many ways. She was very young and was probably very frightened and confused. From the moment her pregnancy had became noticeable her life had been irretrievably altered. She had dishonored her family and lost her good character in the neighborhood. Her grandfather, who had raised her from the age of seven, told her during her labor that

she had committed a great evil. It was probably not the first time he had
made that pronouncement, and he was probably only telling her what she
believed herself.

We can only speculate about the events surrounding Willson's pregnancy. Her age, and Appleton's age, status, and adversarial relationship
with Purchis, coupled with the evidence, make an inference of rape plausible. Possibly she was the victim of a predatory sexual relationship. Appleton, like his contemporaries, believed that rape and conception were
antithetical; in other words, he might have thought he could proceed with
impunity. However, it could be argued that Willson lied and that the court
acted correctly when it dismissed the charges against Appleton. Willson's
reluctance to name Appleton until her grandfather added his plea to that
of the midwife's could be viewed in a sinister light. Was Purchis reminding her that she had agreed to name Appleton as the father in order to
blacken Appleton's name? That Appleton had been charged with fornication in the first place was a tribute to Purchis's local influence.

Another scenario is that Willson was a calculating young woman who
sought to divert the attention of her grandfather and the midwife from
the actual culprit, whoever he was, and to protect him from Purchis's
wrath, by naming Appleton. After all, Appleton was a wealthy man, and
one against whom her grandfather would believe the most despicable
charges. However, while one would like to show that the Puritan court,
in all cases, acted with remarkable sagacity and sensitivity, and that the
truth always "outed," there are serious problems with this scenario. First,
Willson was endangering her immortal soul if she was lying when she told
the midwife, Mrs. Hathorne, and the assembled women that Appleton
was the only man who could have fathered her child. A convincing lie
would have required great fortitude. Too, what motive would she have
had for lying? It is not likely that her grandfather, knowing she was pregnant, would have restrained her from marrying any single man in the
neighborhood who might have been the father. Additionally, very few
women who appeared in court charged with fornication were able to
bring with them a statement, signed by fourteen of her neighbors, attesting to her virtue.

Willson's neighbors believed her when she said that Appleton was her
baby's father and therefore believed that Appleton had seduced her. While
this was the only possible conclusion in the seventeenth century, it seems
less likely to us now. During the approximate time that Willson conceived, Appleton was either newly married or engaged in marriage nego-

tiations with a young heiress, Elizabeth Whittingham, and his efforts would have been focused in that direction. He would not have wanted his negotiations imperiled by gossip that he was also courting Priscilla Willson. However, if he had wanted to seduce Willson, he would not have been deterred by her youth, for Elizabeth Whittingham, his wife was even younger, barely fifteen.

We know nothing of Priscilla Willson's subsequent life. The only recorded fact about her, apart from the birth notice in the Lynn Vital Records, is her fornication trial. That her family continued to regard her with affection is evidenced by the fact that her brother, William, named one of his daughters Priscilla. Public opinion may be inferred from Purchis's election to the Court of Assistants in 1685, at the same time that Samuel Appleton, Sr., was reelected. Purchis was the only man in seventeenth-century Massachusetts to decline to serve, possibly because of a disinclination to serve with judges who had convicted his grandaughter but not Samuel Appleton. He settled in Concord with the remaining Willson children in 1691, where he had a financial interest in another iron foundry.

Samuel Appleton had come out of the trial with his reputation legally intact. He and his family left Lynn in 1688, as soon as the titles to the ironworks and his other properties in Lynn were clear and he could sell them. He had been unable to convince a jury to grant him sole possession of the ironworks, so he had had the jury attainted. This was a legal procedure through which Appleton claimed that no jury would be able to render a fair decision in this matter, and so jurisdiction was granted to the Court of Assistants, where Appleton, as we have noted, had many friends.

He may have settled briefly in Boston but had returned to Ipswich by 1692, where he continued to combine business and public service, serving on the Governor's Council regularly between 1703 and 1714, as his father had done before him between 1681 and 1692. In 1706, Appleton was sent as a commissioner to Quebec to redeem the Deerfield captives, and in 1707 he commanded a regiment in the abortive Port Royal expedition. He suffered a stroke in 1724; Samuel Sewall recorded in his diary on May 22, 1724, "I visited my old school-fellow Col. Samuel Appleton, who lies without motion but as he is mov'd by others; yet he discours'd with me; will be 70 if he live to 9r. Gave Madam Appleton Mr. Colman and Coopers Sermons to read to him."[61] He died the following year, and a sign of the esteem in which he was held was the range of courtesy titles he was accorded by the public at his death: Samuel Appleton, Hon., Col., Esq., October 30, 1725.

An examination of the circumstances surrounding this and other contemporary fornication trials has made possible some conclusions about the extent of fully consumated sexual activity between unmarried persons, the nature of this activity, and the attitudes of both the community and the participants. It is clear that few unmarried Puritans were engaging in sexual intercourse. Prior to 1670 only one couple per year in Essex County was convicted of premarital fornication, and only 1.4 women per year had illegitimate children. While the numbers had increased fivefold by the period from 1671 to 1685, so had the population. Sexual activity that resulted in a pregnancy (which is the only type of sexual activity that can be credibly considered at this distance) can be divided into two categories. The first category includes couples who engaged in sexual intercourse prior to marriage. The second category includes couples who had sexual intercourse without intent to marry. Women who engaged in premarital sexual activity appear to have been in the same age group as their peers who married before conception, and they could be reintegrated into the community, along with their husbands, after the observance of certain rituals of penitence, such as appearing before the congregation wrapped in white sheets, confessing their premarital sexual activity and begging for forgiveness, and paying fornication fines. The women convicted of fornication in Essex County between 1641 and 1685 who bore illegitimate children were younger than the women who married: 62 percent were twenty years of age or less, while 60 percent of their partners were twenty-seven years of age or older. Some of these women were engaged in affective relationships that were broken off because of insufficient financial resources, parental opposition, or the death of the male partner. However, a substantial portion of the partners were married, which suggests a predatory relationship. Given the prevalent rape ideology that equated conception and consent, some women, like Ann Chase and Priscilla Willson, were probably convicted of fornication when they were in fact the victims of coerced sexual activity. Willson and Appleton represented the prevalent pattern: she was sixteen and single; he, twenty-nine and married.

Puritan gender ideology guaranteed that single women who had been convicted of fornication would pay a higher price than their partners. The idea that women, once aroused, possessed voracious sexual appetites, limited their reintegration into the Puritan community, with its opposition to sexual activity among unmarried persons. Marriage, which would have served a rehabilitative function, and which was, moreover, a woman's only "career option" in the seventeenth century, became difficult for women branded as sexual transgressors. Of the single women prosecuted for fornication whose cases were examined for this study three-quarters did not marry. The remaining 25 percent married later than their peers, and less advantageously. Again, Willson and Appleton were representative. Willson disappeared into obscurity after the trial: Appleton, after encountering initial public disapproval from the residents of Lynn, flourished.

The religious fervor and high ideals of the first generation of Puritan settlers were unsustainable. Prior to the 1660s, both men and women, having been detected in fornication, had confessed. Later, while an untimely pregnancy led inevitably to a fornication conviction for single women and married couples, men were able to escape the consequences of their sexual activity by denying, as Samuel Appleton had done, that they had committed fornication. Retaining their honor among their earthly peers became more important than securing a place in heaven. However, the judges were not reluctant to accuse men of lesser status of lying and to require child support payments from them. The leniency with which Appleton was treated stands out, therefore, all the more conspicuously. The judges recognized the importance of reinforcing Appleton's status, because they shared his economic and social identity. Their decision to dismiss the fornication charge against Appleton illuminates both the value placed on honor and the role of class in Puritan Massachusetts.

NOTES

1. M. G. Thresher, ed., *Records and Files of the Quarterly Court of Essex County, Massachusetts*, vol. 9 (Salem, Mass.: Essex Institute, 1975), 64.

2. From the WPA transcription of the records of the Essex County Quarterly Court, June 1683, property of the Supreme Judicial Court, Division of Archives and Records Preservation, on deposit at the Peabody Essex Museum, Salem, Massachusetts, 39–140–4. I have changed the "j"s to "i"s, "f"s to "s"s, "v"s to "u"s, and brought superscripts down, but otherwise have retained the original spelling in these quotations.

3. Ibid., 39–140–4.

4. Ibid., 39–140–3.

5. Ibid., 39–140–1.

6. Thresher, *Records and Files*, 9:64.

7. The death of a young nephew two weeks later may indicate that a household disaster, such as a fire or epidemic disease, claimed mother and daughter. William Willson had made frequent court appearances with his father-in-law, Oliver Purchis, on ironworks business. His name does not appear after his wife's death, and it appears likely that Mrs. Willson had already returned home to live with her parents. Her death is entered in the Lynn Vital Statistics under her maiden name.

8. Although only twenty-one when she married Purchis, the couple did not have any children, and it appears to have been a marriage of convenience.

9. E. N. Hartley, *Ironworks on the Saugus* (Norman: University of Oklahoma Press, 1957). The Saugus Ironworks, including the ironmaster's house, were reconstructed in the 1950s and can be visited today as the Ironworks National Historic Park in Saugus, Massachusetts.

10. First Ironworks Association, *The Saugus Ironworks Restoration* (New York: American Iron and Steel Institute, 1955), 1.

11. I am unable to establish whether the ironmaster's house had been, up to this date, occupied by Purchis or the Paine family.

12. Thresher, *Records and Files*, 9:41.

13. Ola Elizabeth Winslow, *Samuel Sewall of Boston* (New York: Macmillan Company, 1964).

14. Abraham Hammatt, *The Hammatt Papers: Early Inhabitants of Ipswich, Massachusetts, 1633–1700* (Baltimore: Genealogical Publishing Company, 1980), 21. Samuel Appleton was one of a large number of young men who "got religion" at this time. During a four-month period in the winter of 1673–74, ninety people joined the church. Sixty-three were men.

15. There seems to have been a general dissolution of the Whittingham family at this time, with at least two daughters marrying and Appleton assuming guardianship of Elizabeth's younger brother, Richard. The marriage was a very good match for Appleton.

16. Their daughter, Mary, was born March 30, 1683, and Samuel Appleton was summoned April 22, 1683. Like Priscilla Willson's daughter, Elizabeth Appleton's first daughter likely died young. A second daughter, Hannah, was born November 1, 1684, indicating that Appleton was no longer breastfeeding Mary. There is no further record of Mary after the notice of her birth.

17. From the records of Essex County Quarterly Court, June 1683, 39–140–2.

18. Ibid., 39–139–3

19. Thresher, *Records and Files*, 9:64.

20. Angus McLaren, *Reproductive Rituals: The Perception of Fertility in England from the Sixteenth Century to the Nineteenth Century* (London: Methuen & Co., 1984), 20.

21. Michael Dalton, *The Countrey Justice*, (London: Company of Stationers, 1655), 350–51. The Massachusetts Court of Assistants ordered two copies of Dalton's book and relied on it for their preparation of the 1641 law code.

22. Thresher, *Records and Files*, 4:243–44.

23. Ibid.

24. Lyle Koehler, *A Search for Power: The "Weaker Sex" in Seventeenth-Century New England* (Urbana: University of Illinois Press, 1980), 193. To put the number of women convicted of fornication in context, it is helpful to note that the next largest category of offenders is the 431 women charged with Sabbath violations. This hardly suggests that sexual activity was rampant among the Puritan settlers given a population estimate at 20,000 by 1640, perhaps reaching 90,000 in Massachusetts by 1700.

25. The feelings of the Appleton household can be extrapolated from those of Cotton Mather when a woman accused his son, Increase, of fathering her child. Mather wrote in his journal, "Oh! Dreadful Case! Oh! Sorrow beyond any that I have met withal! What shall I do now for the Foolish Youth! What for my afflicted and abased family!" He protected his son by keeping him "confined and retired with me until the Storm shall be blown over." He plied his son with sermons and prayed for him. Increase was not charged with fornication. Kenneth Silverman, *The Life and Times of Cotton Mather* (New York, Harper & Row, 1984), 308.

26. Laurel Thatcher Ulrich, *Good Wives: Image and Reality in the Lives of Women in Northern New England, 1650–1750* (New York: Oxford University Press, 1980), 97.

27. Lyle Koehler (*A Search for Power*, 77) states that "the loss of virginity was such a blemish that a father could sue the man who deflowered his daughter, collecting as much as fifteen pounds in damages.

28. Anthony Fletcher, *Gender, Sex and Subordination in England, 1500–1800* (New Haven: Yale University Press, 1995), 102.

29. Martin Ingram, *Church Courts, Sex and Marriage in England, 1570–1640* (New York: Cambridge University Press, 1987), chapter 1.

30. Alden T. Vaughn and Edwin W. Clark, *Puritans among the Indians: Accounts of Captivity and Redemption, 1676–1724* (Cambridge: Harvard University Press, 1981), 9.

31. Carol F. Karlsen, *The Devil in the Shape of a Woman: Witchcraft in Colonial New England* (New York: Random House, 1987), 200.

32. Thresher, *Records and Files*, 9:328.

33. Ibid., 9:531.

34. Thresher, *Records and Files*, 5:290–91.

35. The fifty-eighth woman, Mary Williams, died in childbirth. She was married, but her husband had disavowed the child. Her lover, Jonathan Gatchell, fled. The case still came to court, because provision had to be made

for the infant. The Gatchell family agreed to pay child support on behalf of their absent relative.

36. Roger Thompson, *Sex in Middlesex: Popular Mores in a Massachusetts County, 1649–1699* (Amherst: University of Massachusetts Press, 1986), 33, 195.

37. Edmund S. Morgan, "The Puritans and Sex," *New England Quarterly*, December 1942, 595. This is the seminal paper on Puritan sexual attitudes, but Morgan is talking almost exclusively about male sexuality. He blames the "abundance of sexual offenses" on the fact that many of the men left their wives behind in England.

38. Ibid., 596.

39. David H. Flaherty, "Law and the Enforcement of Morals in Early America," in *Perspectives in American History*, ed. Donald Fleming and Bernard Baylin, Vol. 5 (Cambridge: Harvard University for the Charles Warren Center for Studies in American History, 1971), 225. The testimony provided in fornication cases is colorful, bawdy, and very readable. It is easy to forget the dry details of debt litigation, land disputes, and probate proceedings that take up the majority of the court's time and to overestimate the frequency with which fornication cases occur.

40. Daniel Scott Smith and Michael Hindus, "Premarital Pregnancy in America 1640–1971: An Overview and Interpretation," *Journal of Interdisciplinary History 5* (Spring 1975): 537–70.

41. Morgan, "The Puritans and Sex," 592–93.

42. Fletcher, *Gender, Sex and Subordination*, 54.

43. Ibid., 45.

44. Ibid., 55.

45. Richard Godbeer, "'The Cry of Sodom' Discourse: Intercourse and Desire in Colonial New England," *William and Mary Quarterly*, 3d ser., 52.2 (1995): 259–86.

46. Margaret R. Somerville, *Sex and Subjection: Attitudes to Women in Early Modern Society* (London: Arnold, 1995), 25.

47. Ibid., 27

48. Fletcher, *Gender, Sex and Subordination*, 34.

49. Ulrich, *Good Wives*, 9–10.

50. Cotton Mather, *Ornaments for the Daughters of Zion*, 3d ed. (Boston: S. Kneeland and T. Green, 1741), 80–85.

51. Thresher, *Records and Files*, 9:64.

52. Philip Greven, *The Protestant Temperament: Patterns of Child-Rearing, Religious Experience, and the Self in Early America* (Chicago: University of Chicago Press, 1977), 129.

53. Laura Gowing, "Gender and the Language of Insult in Early Modern London," *History Workshop Journal*, 35 (1993): 1–21.

54. Thresher, *Records and Files*, 9:64.

55. Thompson, *Sex in Middlesex*, 39.

56. A 1994 study of ten thousand teenage pregnancies conducted by the National Center for Health Statistics reported that "teen pregnancy is not just a matter of kids getting each other into trouble, but also of grown men taking advantage of girls." In half of the cases, the fathers were age twenty or older.

57. Flaherty, "Law and the Enforcement of Morals," 231.

58. Colonial Society of Massachusetts, *Records of the Suffolk County Court, 1671–1680*, part 2 (Boston: The University Press, 1933).

59. Ulrich, *Good Wives*, 89–125.

60. From the records of the Essex County Quarterly Court, June 1683 39–140–3.

61. M. Halsey Thomas, *The Diary of Samuel Sewall*, vol. 2, (New York: Farrar, Strauss & Giroux, 1973), 1017–18.

Chapter 5

Sarah Prentice and the Immortalists

Sexuality, Piety, and the Body in Eighteenth-Century New England

Erik R. Seeman

Sarah Prentice lived a life in the eighteenth century that in today's world of tabloid journalism would garner a great deal of media attention. Prentice came from a wealthy New England family and married a prominent minister, but the rumors that swirled about her were nothing less than salacious. Some claimed that Prentice participated in group sex; others suggested that she committed adultery with a local religious extremist. Even leaving aside these unfounded accounts, the details of Prentice's life were remarkable: she spent many years traveling and preaching in an era when women were enjoined from both activities; she challenged her husband's authority and eventually got him fired from his ministerial post; and she contradicted the dominant religious and sexual beliefs of her day by embracing celibacy and claiming that she was immortal.

Given the occasionally lurid details of her life, one would think that historians would have paid her a great deal of attention, but Prentice has not played an important role in studies of eighteenth-century religion and society. Although partly the result of a dearth of sources, this inattention seems mostly due to a sense that Prentice was too atypical to be worthy of study. But despite her unusual beliefs and practices, Prentice's story tells us a great deal about the relationship between religion and sexuality in New England after the Great Awakening. By inversion, Prentice's advocacy of celibacy demonstrates the importance of marital sex to orthodox Protestantism. In addition, Prentice and her fellow religious radicals reveal that questions of sexuality and purity, lying just below the surface of mainstream evangelical belief, were in fact central to the radical possibilities of the Great Awakening. These individuals formulated heterodox beliefs in a culture where the dominant religious and sexual ideologies were powerful but nonetheless open to contest and negotiation.

Finally, the example of Prentice and the Immortalists may be used to make a historiographical point. Recent historians of Christian celibacy have generally seen sexual renunciation as a way for women to avoid the "sexual servitude" that was entailed in marital sexual relations.[1] According to this view, women used religious vows of celibacy to fend off predatory male sexual desire and to gain physical autonomy.[2] This interpretation may have some validity for the nineteenth century, when middle-class white women were considered "passionless."[3] Nineteenth-century women, who were typically represented as being victims of male sexuality, occasionally used celibacy to reclaim some degree of sexual autonomy. But this analysis has less relevance to the period up to and including the eighteenth century, when women were represented in sermons and medical literature as the more lustful sex.[4] In other words, early modern women did not use celibacy only or even primarily to gain sexual autonomy, as women were already seen to be sexually powerful. Furthermore, it is difficult to explain the attraction of men to the doctrine of celibacy espoused by the Immortalists if one sees sexual renunciation only as a strategy that women employed to avoid sexual servitude.[5]

This essay will argue that the challenge represented by Sarah Prentice and the Immortalists was more complex than these historians have allowed. In addition to using celibacy to counter aggressive male sexuality, the Immortalists' celibacy represented a break with ministerial dictates about marital sexuality providing more soldiers for Christ's army. Even more significantly, their sexual renunciation was an attempt to make the body holy and incorruptible, in opposition to the orthodox duality between corrupt flesh and immortal soul. While New England ministers saw the body and the soul representing incommensurable poles of corruption and purity, the Immortalists sought to efface this stark distinction. Hence, the Immortalists' beliefs were a direct challenge to ministerial ideas about the proper relationship between the body and piety.

Sarah Prentice was born in 1716 to the wealthy Sartell family in Groton, Massachusetts.[6] At age sixteen she married Solomon Prentice, a minister eleven years her senior. The following year, in 1733, Sarah had a conversion experience, joined Solomon's church in Grafton, and proceeded over the next eight years to bear five children.[7] By 1742 the people of Grafton were experiencing the Great Awakening in all its power, under the direction of Solomon, their radical New Light minister.

At this point religious passions were running so high in Grafton that Sarah had a second conversion experience, even though she had joined the church almost ten years before.[8] Her reconversion experience, as narrated by her husband, was a typical, if somewhat more explosive than ordinary, tale of spiritual distress followed by spiritual emancipation. For about a full month in early 1742, Sarah's soul was in such distress that it "Much Effected her Body to that Degree that She was Scarce able to Stirr hand or foot for some few Minuits." Finally, she experienced the delightful release of the conversion moment:

> And Now, her Nerves and Sinews are contracted, and her Tongue Stiff in her head: her Own Phrase was, it felt like an Iron bar in her Mouth, She begged of the Lord She might have the Liberty of her Tongue, that there with She Might Shew forth the Wondras work of the Lord. . . . At length her Stomack heaved, and, She broke forth—*its Lovely! its Lovely!*"[9]

Even at an early stage of the Awakening, and in this fairly conventional experience of conversion, the connection between evangelical spirituality and the body is evident. In the throes of her conversion Sarah's nerves, sinews, tongue, mouth, and stomach mirrored her own experience of paralysis and release. In fact, Old Light opponents of the revival seized on the bodily manifestations of New Light piety as evidence that the Awakening was the result of little more than overheated passions. According to the staunch revival opponent Charles Chauncy, the "*bodily agitations*" of New Lights demonstrated that their piety was guided "not by a rational Conviction of Truth, but a sudden and strong Impression on the *animal Oeconomy.*"[10] For Old Lights and other guardians of religious orthodoxy, the body was a site of corruption and should not play such a prominent role in religious experience; to link the body with religious experience was to risk descending from rational man to irrational animal.

Despite such warnings from opponents of the revival, events in Grafton quickly moved from the ordinary to the uncommon. Solomon found himself isolated: too radical for the many Old Lights in his congregation, too conservative for his wife and others of a like mind. Nor was Solomon Prentice's reputation aided by the "very terrible storys," which proved to be true, that he was beating his wife ever more severely.[11] But most of the local concern was generated by religious events, as nearby ministers reported unusual occurrences among the awakened in Grafton. In 1744 Ebenezer Parkman, the pastor of neighboring West- borough, received a report from a moderate New Light woman from Grafton of the "many things which she finds among her Neibours— [with] regard to Dreams, and holding most sensible Communion with God in sleep, etc."[12] Apparently those in Sarah Prentice's circle had been having visions of God in their dreams and considering their nocturnal communications to be authentic and not just metaphorical. More dis- turbing yet were accounts in 1747 of spiritually inspired free love in Grafton. In February of that year Parkman cryptically noted that he had learned that Sarah Prentice's group "Vindicated the Doctrine of Knowl- edge of one another by the union of Love etc. etc."[13] Three months later Parkman confronted Sarah Prentice with these reports. During a long af- ternoon of discussions, Parkman "endeavour'd also to warn her against . . . giving occasion to others to suspect criminal Freedoms with the other sex, under the splendid Guise of Spiritual Love and Friendship."[14] It is easy to see why Parkman viewed such "freedoms" as a threat to the standing order. If in fact Sarah Prentice and those in her circle were hav- ing sex with one another on the grounds that they were all spiritually "spouses," this obviously represented a disruption of traditional ideas about marriage. But the reality, at least a few years later, would turn out to be the very opposite of these early reports: Sarah had opted for a strategy of sexual renunciation.

The reports of heterodoxy in the 1740s were not limited to Grafton. In this period a number of communities throughout southeastern New Eng- land had residents who maintained such heterodoxies as Immortalism, whose proponents held that they had experienced a change that would render their bodies incorruptible and hence not subject to death. There was a group of Immortalists in Windham County, Connecticut, and at least one of them declared himself to be Christ.[15] Likewise, Sarah Pren- tice was sometimes associated in the late 1740s with Nat Smith of Hop- kinton, Massachusetts, who along with his four brothers considered him- self to have achieved eternal life.[16] In 1751 the Baptist minister Isaac Backus described the views of a group of Immortalists in Norton and Taunton:

> They hold that the union between two Persons when rightly married to- gether is A Spiritual Union whereas God Says they Twain shall be one flesh:—they deny The Civil Authoritys Power in Marriage:—and they hold that they are Getting into a state of Perfection in this World so as to be free

from all Sicknings And trouble, and so that they Shall Never Die, and many other corrupt things.[17]

This belief in spiritual union was expressed by Molly Bennet of Cumberland, Rhode Island, in 1749, when she stated "that Solomon Finney and she was man and wife Enternally [internally] but not Externally," that is, that they were spiritual spouses who did not engage in sexual intercourse. Although Bennet and Finney were not legally married, "she said that they was man and wife in the sight of the Lord and it was made known to them that it was so."[18] While the exact relationship between Sarah Prentice and these groups, or among the groups themselves, is not clear, they were united at least by a relatively uniform set of beliefs, namely, that marriage should be a "spiritual union" not involving sexual relations, and that they were (or were approaching) bodily incorruptibility. These beliefs were considered so threatening to the standing order that in 1749 the Rhode Island general assembly passed a law clarifying the illegality of "Adultery, Polygamy, and unlawfully marrying Persons."[19]

If the uniformity of beliefs among Immortalist groups separated by dozens of miles suggests proselytizers who spread the word, there were probably two people responsible. One was Sarah Prentice, who moved to Easton with her husband in 1747 when he was made pastor there. The other was Shadrack Ireland, a pipe maker and leading Immortalist from Charlestown, Massachusetts, who was Sarah Prentice's spiritual partner. Ezra Stiles, writing in 1793 about the death of Immortalist Nat Smith, declared that "he was one of Old Ireland's Men & of the Company of a dozen or 15 wild Enthusiasts who about 50 years ago lived in & about Medford, Sutton, Uxbridge, & declared themselves *Immortals:* of which Rev. Mr. Prentice's Wife of Grafton was one. She used to lie with Ireland as her spiritual Husband."[20] It seems, however, that Stiles's report of Ireland and Prentice lying together was based more on rumor than anything else, for in 1748 and 1751 Sarah bore two children by Solomon. Furthermore, Sarah had not yet fully embraced Immortalism for herself. But it appears that in the late 1740s and early 1750s Ireland and Sarah Prentice were spiritual confederates in Easton, working to gain converts to their heterodox religiosity. It may even have been the case that Ireland baptized Prentice; in 1751 Solomon wrote in Latin in the Easton church records that "she is an Anabaptist. She was immersed by a most despicable layman, namely ____ ____, December 5, 1750, her husband being absent."[21] Whether it was Ireland or someone else who baptized Sarah Prentice, this step represented her further rejection of orthodoxy: she not only signaled that her infant baptism was invalid but that a layman could effectively baptize.

In 1753 Sarah Prentice removed herself even further from the orthodox fold: she embraced celibacy and the related belief that she had become immortal. In June 1753 she told Isaac Backus "that this night 2 months ago She passed thro' a change in her Body equivalent to Death, so that She had ben intirely free from any disorder in her Body or Corruption in her soul ever Since; and expected she ever should be So: and that her Body would never see Corruption, but would Live here 'till Christs personal coming."[22] Prentice recounted her decision to become celibate to Ebenezer Parkman in 1773:

> She speaks of her Husband under the name of Brother Solomon: she gave me some account of the wonderful Change in her Body, her Sanctification, that God had shewn to her His mind & Will, she was taught henceforth to know no man after the Flesh, that she had not for above 20 years, not so much as shook Hands with any Man, &c. Then came in Mr Benjamin Leland & Mr Samuel Cooper whom she call'd Brother Benjamin & Brother Samuel, &c.[23]

According to Sarah Prentice, her celibacy was not merely a whim but the very will of God, revealed directly to her.

Prentice and those of similar religious propensities maintained their beliefs for the next twenty-five or thirty years, occasionally appearing in the historical record. In 1756 Isaac Backus preached in Grafton and ran across some who still remained Immortalists.[24] Likewise, Backus reported in 1764 that there were still some people in Norton and Easton who believed in "spiritual union" and had left their lawful wives "for a great while."[25] Shadrack Ireland continued living in Harvard, Massachusetts, among his followers until 1778, when his death caused a crisis of faith for those who had believed him to be immortal.[26] Sarah Prentice, who would live until 1792, maintained her convictions until at least 1773 and probably for the rest of her life, as Ebenezer Parkman noted in 1782 that "Madam Prentice of Grafton has been with the *Shakers*."[27] Unfortunately there survives no context for this tantalizingly cryptic remark, and it is unknown exactly what Prentice had been doing with the Shakers. Did she merely visit them to survey another group favoring celibacy, or had she become a follower of Mother Ann Lee? It seems more likely that Prentice was merely visiting the Shakers, as she lived her last years in the house of her son John Prentice in Ward, Massachusetts, and membership in the Shaker community usually entailed taking up residence in the Shaker settlement in Harvard.[28]

Whatever the case, Sarah Prentice and the Immortalists renounced ordinary sexual relations in favor of celibacy. Why? Although it is impossible to plumb the psyches of the members of this heterodox group with complete confidence, several explanations may be offered. Celibacy would have been seen as having powerful effects for this group. A long—though contested—Christian tradition saw celibacy as a way to clear the mind of earthly interference, allowing for heightened powers of spiritual perception. This was exactly the reason why Shakers later demanded celibacy of their members: they saw it as a way to better communicate with God. For the Shakers, this was a gendered construct: celibate women were seen to be particularly ready conduits for revelation.[29] This gender distinction was based on the long-standing opposition, going back to Aristotle, that connected women with the spirit and men with the mind. As the contact between Prentice and the Shakers suggests, this belief that celibacy enhanced receptivity to divine messages was probably held by the eighteenth-century Immortalists as well. Furthermore, for a group trying to hasten the coming of the millennium, celibacy was one way to escape earthly temporality for a more spiritual temporality. Much Christian literature has portrayed the ability of the body to reproduce itself as a form of decay, and celibacy as a way to gain a sort of immortality. As Caroline Walker Bynum argues, "to medieval theorists, fertility was also decay; the threat lodged in the body was change itself."[30] Of course, the Immortalists were not medieval Catholics, but they got many of their ideas about sexuality and the body from the same source: the Christian Bible.

The Bible is one of the most multivocal texts one can find, written by dozens of authors over many centuries. It is the key to understanding where the Immortalists got their ideas, and as such it is the key to understanding the flexible nature of religious culture in early New England. The Bible contains ideas about sexuality that are open to multiple and conflicting interpretations, and it is possible to demonstrate that the Immortalists relied on a reading of the Bible that was radically different from that advocated by orthodox ministers in eighteenth-century New England. Based on their reading of multivocal texts like the Bible, and on their own creativity, laypeople were able to add ideas to the matrix of beliefs and practices that made up religious culture.

The Bible includes numerous prescriptions and injunctions about sexuality. Famously, the Old Testament command to "be fruitful and multiply" (Genesis 1:28) seems to be contradicted by the New Testament teachings of St. Paul (especially 1 Corinthians 7).[31] Whereas the Old Testament puts reproduction in a positive light, Paul casts doubt on the worthiness of conjugal relations. Though Paul clearly says, "if you marry, you do not sin" (1 Corinthians 7:28), he also says that married people are distracted by worldly affairs, and he seems to exalt perpetual virginity.[32] It is important to note that Paul's advice was offered in the context of anxious millennial expectations; he explains his views by saying that "the appointed time has grown very short" (1 Corinthians 7:29). But these were precisely the concerns that animated the Immortalists in the eighteenth century, as well as other religious groups that embraced celibacy throughout the Christian era. Thus, it is not surprising that the Immortalists adopted Paul's attitude toward marriage and celibacy.

From the beginning of the Christian era some radicals sought to remove themselves from the ordinary workings of time by becoming celibate. Starting in the second century and following the logic first elucidated by Paul, certain Christian groups believed that sexual renunciation might allow them to transform their bodies and escape corporeal corruptibility. As Peter Brown writes, these people believed that "By renouncing all sexual activity the human body could join in Christ's victory: it could turn back the inexorable."[33] In other words, because society was continued through sexual reproduction, individuals who renounced sex simultaneously announced their desire to abandon the continuation of society.[34] In addition to turning back nature's clock, celibacy served to gain these groups a great deal of notoriety, for observers were impressed that the followers of this new religion were willing to forego sex. Celibacy was also able to unite various second-century Christian groups in a period when commonality among believers was sometimes hard to establish.[35]

But as Christianity became more institutionalized, the groups that renounced sex increasingly found themselves in conflict with the priestly caste. By the third century, priests tried to distinguish themselves from the laity through celibacy. Although the Catholic Church was not able to assert full jurisdiction over matters of marriage and sexuality until the tenth or eleventh century, clerical continence basically became a prerequisite starting in the fifth century.[36] Thus, as priests increasingly defined themselves in terms of their renunciation of sex, it became ever more important that the laity not renounce it.[37] In this climate, those lay Christians who sought to avoid sexual contact were defined by the priests as heretics. For example, in 1028 near Milan a group was defined as heretical for practicing celibacy. A statement made by one of the members of this group to the bishop of Milan reveals parallels with the eighteenth-century Immortalists: "We esteem virginity above all else, although we have wives," said this heretic under questioning. "He who is virgin keeps his virginity, but he who has lost it, after receiving permission from our elder, may observe perpetual chastity. No one knows his wife carnally, but carefully treats her as his mother or sister."[38] Though this testimony was given by a man, the leader of these celibates was allegedly a woman, the countess of Monforte.

One would think that this conflict between priests and laity over the issue of celibacy would cease among Protestants after the Reformation, since ministers of that faith were allowed to get married and therefore did not define themselves in opposition to a procreating laity. But Protestant ministers continued the tradition of wariness toward lay celibacy. Some based their concerns on the fact that marital sex provided a legitimate outlet for irrepressible sexual urges: pastors worried that vows of celibacy could lead people into a variety of sexual sins. The first Protestant attack on celibacy came in 1521, when Andreas Bodenstein von Karlstadt wrote that sexual renunciation promoted homosexuality and, even worse in von Karlstadt's eyes, masturbation.[39] The following year Martin Luther followed von Karlstadt's lead and argued vividly that conjugal relations helped prevent the sin of masturbation: "Nature never lets up . . . we are all driven to the secret sin. To say it crudely but honestly, if it doesn't go into a woman, it goes into your shirt."[40]

This tradition of exalting marital sexuality and combating the allure of celibacy was inherited by Protestants in England and New England. In 1622 the English Puritan William Gouge admitted that virginity "may be of good use" in the proper circumstances.[41] But Gouge cautioned that "not one to a million of those that have come to ripenesse of yeares" is able to remain celibate their entire lives.[42] Gouge went on to criticize celibacy as being an unnatural yoke that people were not meant to bear.[43] This stance was not limited to Puritans: the Westminster Larger Catechism of 1647, which sought to standardize Anglican teachings, cautioned against "intangling vows of single life" and "undue delay of marriage."[44] Likewise, Anglican minister William Secker condemned celibacy because it prevented propagation, and this deprived the church of the soldiers it needed.[45] Even more to the point, Secker, like Luther before him, worried that celibates would be unable to suppress their sexual urges. As Secker graphically put it, "Some indeed force themselves to a Single Life, meerly to avoid the Charges of a Married state: They had rather fry in the grease of their own Sensuality, then [sic] extinguish those Flames with an allowed Remedy: 'It is better to Marry than to Burn': To be lawfully Coupled, than to be lustfully Scorched."[46]

In eighteenth-century New England, this sort of rhetoric continued and even intensified, as ministers there were even more strident in viewing celibacy as a threat to the social order. While English Puritans like Gouge claimed that a celibate life had value (even if it was not the preferred course), New England Puritans moved away from any exaltation of celibacy and held procreative marital sex in the highest esteem.[47] This was the direct result of the Puritan celebration of the family—children and procreating parents—as the source of societal stability and the center of daily religious experience. Cotton Mather told women that virginity was not necessary to please God. Rather, the virtuous woman pleases God by pleasing her husband through moderate sexual relations.[48] Likewise, in the early eighteenth century Samuel Willard made the case that celibacy was contrary to nature, while marital sexuality was the natural result of God's design. Willard argued that the "the *Conjugal* Relation" was based upon "the natural Inclinations of Men, of which [God] Himself is the Author."[49] How could something instituted by God be sinful? Willard asked. In fact, Willard asserted, throughout history celibates had been among the most unchaste people: "too often, there are none more *Unchast[e]*, than such as boast themselves in *Cœlabacy*, who in the mean while nourish in them *Unclean* Lusts."[50] Rehashing the standard Protestant propaganda that Catholics constrained by vows of celibacy were among the greatest sinners and hypocrites, Willard declared that celibacy had been the cause of "horrendous *Whoredoms*, and bloody *Murders*."[51] Thus, ministers in seventeenth- and eighteenth-century New England were steadfast in their denunciation of vows of celibacy as unnatural and dangerous, which is why Ebenezer Parkman, on a visit to the Prentices in 1755, "enquir'd strictly into their Sentiments and Practices respecting their Conjugal Covenant."[52] Ministers like Parkman could not countenance celibacy.

In this context of clerical condemnation, the views of Prentice and the Immortalists represented a stark challenge to ministerial ideas about sexuality and the body. In two ways these challenges were gender specific.

That is, the fact that Prentice was a woman and a leader of this heterodox religious group made her advocacy of sexual renunciation particularly threatening. First, Prentice's conversion to celibacy at age thirty-six, when she was most likely still fertile, meant that she was consciously rejecting further motherhood, in a society where procreation was considered a woman's greatest and holiest duty. As Laurel Thatcher Ulrich has suggested, "through motherhood Eve became an instrument of redemption."[53] In other words, at least in the sermons of ministers in colonial New England, women were able to overcome their sinful natures, and specifically their tendency to become sexual temptresses, by channeling their sexuality into reproduction through legitimate marital intercourse. By rejecting procreation, Prentice upset traditional notions of what a woman's proper role was.

Second, Prentice's celibacy not only allowed her to remove herself from the cycle of perpetual childbearing but also formed the central theme in her itinerant ministry. For at least two decades Prentice traveled around much of New England, looking for converts to her radical piety. In an era when women were not expected to speak their mind in public, Prentice traveled from town to town, telling all listeners (including ministers) of her heterodox beliefs. Clifford K. Shipton sums up the local reputation of Prentice by noting that she "was a genius who knew most of the Bible by heart and could, it was said, preach as good a sermon as any man."[54] It is not surprising, given her abilities and her rejection of traditionally female roles, that Sarah Prentice's powers were compared to those of a man by her contemporaries.

These two gender-based concerns about the threat of celibacy to women's traditional roles are corroborated by attacks on the Shakers that were published about twenty years after the Immortalists were most active. The similarities between these two groups of celibates allow the historian to understand contemporary fears about the meaning of celibacy. The minister Valentine Rathbun focused on the negative effects that the Shaker doctrine of celibacy had on families. Rathbun wrote, "the effect of this scheme is such, that men and their wives have parted, children ran away from their parents, and society entirely broke up in neighbourhoods."[55] Rathbun also compared Mother Ann Lee to Eve, noting that "as [God] first deceived the woman, and made use of her to delude the man; so he is playing his old prank over again."[56] It is reasonable to assume that many people felt the same way about Sarah Prentice, seeing her advocacy of celibacy as a delusion that threatened the order of family and society. Two years after Rathbun wrote, Benjamin West, another critic of the Shakers, made clear the threat he envisioned from a female-headed religious sect. Because the doctrine of celibacy demanded that husbands leave their wives and vice versa, not only were families destroyed, but "women become monsters, and men worse than infidels in this new and strange religion."[57] The cause of all this subversion of order, West argued, could be found in the fact that a woman was the head of this group: "when we consider from whence these new laws and rules originate, and who stands at the head of their discipline, the wonder may abate in some degree, for God placed the man next to himself in the creation, between the woman and himself, and enjoined the womans obedience to the man, and said the man should rule over her."[58] Thus, because among the Shakers "the men hold themselves in intire subjection to the woman,"[59] it was hardly a surprise to West and his orthodox contemporaries that a female-headed religious group would have the effect of destroying families and society by inverting the "natural" supremacy of men over women.

Although these were important concerns voiced by writers in the second half of the eighteenth century, the challenges of Prentice and the Immortalists were not only gender based. After all, the men who were attracted to this small band also were celibate. Most importantly, male and female celibacy was a fundamental challenge to ministerial ideas about the connection between the body and religion. Ministers were wary about the body, comfortable with sexuality only when it was turned toward the legitimate function of reproduction, as this was the process through which the church gained more adherents. In addition, the attitudes of New England ministers were dualistic, seeing a strong distinction between the corrupt body and the immortal soul. But through celibacy Prentice and the Immortalists were saying that the body could indeed be a site of holiness and incorruptibility. As opposed to a distinction between a corrupt body and an immortal soul, the Immortalists hoped to fuse both into a holy and immortal body. There had long been a strong bodily component to this group's ecstatic form of worship. Going back to Sarah Prentice's second conversion in 1742, continuing through the visions and trances among the awakened in her circle in the late 1740s, and including the "spiritual unions" of a number of members, Immortalist piety was notable for its bodily outlets. Like the medieval fasting women studied by Caroline Walker Bynum, the Immortalists did not hate their bodies.[60] Rather, the Immortalists were forced to deal more palpably than most with their bodies, for they could not find a legitimate or sanctioned outlet for their sexual desires, as ordinary Protestants could through marital sexual activity. Instead, they grappled with their sexuality on a daily basis, seeking to channel it into their piety in their quest for bodily purity. Thus, contrary to what some historians have argued about sexual renunciation in the premodern world, for the Immortalists celibacy was much more than a strategy whereby women avoided the "sexual servitude" of marriage.

Of course, the Immortalists never numbered more than a few dozen adherents, but their significance is not to be measured numerically. For though their beliefs were extreme, they represented the logical end of the ideas held by more orthodox New Lights coming out of the Great Awakening. The vast majority of New Lights in New England did not claim to have been immortal, nor did they embrace celibacy. But above all New Lights were seeking purity, in their worship and in themselves. And as the conversion experiences of Sarah Prentice and others during the Awakening demonstrate, New Lights found bodily outlets for their piety. The Immortalists merely took this desire for purity and its connection to the body to its logical conclusion. Ultimately, it is important simply to recognize that Prentice and the Immortalists were a significant phenomenon and were able to gain converts across southeastern New England. Although their numbers remained small throughout thirty years of existence, they represented the potential for heterodox beliefs and practices in a culture where the dominant religious and sexual ideologies were strong but never uncontested. Taking advantage of the corporeal religiosity that came into favor during the Great Awakening, the Immortalists' message of bodily purity resonated with women and men who were not satisfied with the attempts of orthodox ministers to separate the body from manifestations of piety.

NOTES

1. Dyan Elliott, *Spiritual Marriage: Sexual Abstinence in Medieval Wedlock* (Princeton: Princeton University Press, 1993), 300; see also 5, 264.

2. Sally L. Kitch, *Chaste Liberation: Celibacy and Female Cultural Status* (Urbana: University of Illinois Press, 1989), 43, 48, 202.

3. Nancy F. Cott, "Passionlessness: An Interpretation of Victorian Sexual Ideology, 1790–1850," *Signs* 4.2 (1978): 219–36.

4. Thomas Laqueur, *Making Sex: Body and Gender from the Greeks to Freud* (Cambridge: Harvard University Press, 1990).

5. For an interpretation of sexual renunciation closer to my own, see Jo Ann Kay McNamara, *Sisters in Arms: Catholic Nuns through Two Millennia* (Cambridge: Harvard University Press, 1996), especially 1–33.

6. Sarah's father, Nathaniel, was wealthy indeed: when he died in 1740 he owned £1120 in warehouses and land in Charlestown and £3848 in property in Groton. "Brief Memoirs and Notices of Prince's Subscribers," *New England Historic Genealogical Register* 6.3 (1852): 275.

7. Information on Sarah Prentice's early life is from Ross W. Beales, Jr., "The Ecstasy of Sarah Prentice: Death, Re-Birth, and the Great Awakening in Grafton, Massachusetts" *Historical Journal of Massachusetts* 26 (summer 1997): 101–23. I am extremely grateful to Prof. Beales for sharing his manuscript with me. See also C. J. F. Binney, *The History and Genealogy of the Prentice or Prentiss Family, in New England, from 1631 to 1852* (Boston: published by the author, 1852), 20–32.

8. This conversion narrative is part of Ross W. Beales, Jr., "Solomon Prentice's Narrative of the Great Awakening," *Massachusetts Historical Society Proceedings* 83 (1971): 130–47. Although Sarah Prentice is not mentioned as the subject of the conversion story on pages 134–36, Beales convincingly argues that the demographics of the subject indicate that it could be no one else. Beales, "Ecstasy," 30, n. 21.

9. Beales, "Solomon Prentice's Narrative," 135.

10. Charles Chauncy, *Seasonable Thoughts on the State of Religion in New-England* (Boston: Rogers and Fowle, 1743), 78, 80; see also "Extracts from the Interleaved Almanacs of Nathan Bowen, Marblehead, 1742–1799," *Essex Institute Historical Collections* 91.2 (1955): 163–90.

11. Francis G. Walett, ed., *The Diary of Ebenezer Parkman, 1703–1782* (Worcester, Mass.: American Antiquarian Society, 1974), 157; also 156.

12. Ibid., 101.

13. Ibid., 150.

14. Ibid., 154. Parkman did not describe Sarah Prentice's reaction to these warnings.

15. Francis G. Walett, "Shadrack Ireland and the 'Immortals' of Colonial New England," in *Sibley's Heir: A Volume in Memory of Clifford Kenyon Shipton* (Boston: Colonial Society of Massachusetts, 1982): 543. See also Isaac Backus, *A History of New England with Particular Reference to the Denomination of Christians Called Baptists*, 2d ed. (Newton, Mass.: Backus Historical Society, 1871), 2:88.

16. Walett, "Shadrack Ireland," 545–46.

17. William G. McLoughlin, ed., *The Diary of Isaac Backus* (Providence, R.I.: Brown University Press, 1979), 141.

18. Quoted in William G. McLoughlin, "Free Love, Immortalism, and Perfectionism in Cumberland, Rhode Island, 1748–1768," *Rhode Island History* 33.3–4 (1974): 75.

19. Rhode Island Colony, *Acts and Resolves, March 1749* (Newport, R.I.: James Franklin, 1749), 53.

20. Franklin Bowditch Dexter, ed., *The Literary Diary of Ezra Stiles* (New York: C. Scribner's Sons, 1901), 1:418.

21. Solomon Prentice originally wrote, "Ipsa Anna baptista; Immersa Indignissimo Laico, Viz., ____ ____, December 5, 1750, absente marito." William L. Chaffin, *History of the Town of Easton, Massachusetts* (Cambridge, Mass.: John Wilson and Son, 1886), 136. The translation is by Chaffin.

22. McLoughlin, *Diary of Isaac Backus*, 294. Backus's report was corroborated by Ebenezer Parkman in 1755. Walett, *Diary of Ebenezer Parkman*, 292.

23. Diary of Ebenezer Parkman, manuscript in Massachusetts Historical Society (hereafter cited as MHS), entry of 23 February 1773. Shadrack Ireland also urged his followers in Harvard to be celibate: "Ireland forbade them to marry, or to lodge with each other, if they were married." Backus, *History of New England*, 2:462.

24. McLoughlin, *Diary of Isaac Backus*, 430.

25. Ibid., 570–71.

26. Backus, *History of New England*, 2:462.

27. Diary of Ebenezer Parkman, entry of 11 October 1782. Quoted in Beales, "Ecstasy," 1.

28. Binney, *History of the Prentice Family*, 29.

29. Kitch, *Chaste Liberation*, 168. For the same dynamic in the second century, see Peter Brown, *The Body and Society: Men, Women, and Sexual Renunciation in Early Christianity* (New York: Columbia University Press, 1988), 67.

30. Caroline Walker Bynum, *The Resurrection of the Body in Western Christianity, 200–1336* (New York: Columbia University Press, 1995), xviii.

31. Will Deming convincingly argues that Paul did not exalt celibacy to the degree that people have claimed. But for the purposes of this essay, more important than what Paul was really arguing is how his words have been interpreted throughout history. Deming, *Paul on Marriage and Celibacy: The Hellenistic Background of 1 Corinthians 7* (Cambridge: Cambridge University Press, 1995).

32. See also Romans 8:1–17 and Galatians 5:13–26.

33. Brown, *Body and Society*, 32.

34. Ibid., 64.

35. Ibid., 60.

36. Elliott, *Spiritual Marriage*, 32, 77–87.

37. Ibid., 98.

38. Quoted in Ibid., 96.

39. Steven Ozment, "Marriage and the Ministry in the Protestant Churches,"

in *Celibacy in the Church*, edited by William Bassett and Peter Huizing (New York: Herder and Herder, 1972), 40.

40. Quoted in Joel F. Harrington, *Reordering Marriage and Society in Reformation Germany* (New York: Cambridge University Press, 1995), 63.

41. William Gouge, *Of Domesticall Duties* (London: W. Bladen, 1622), 212.

42. Ibid., 210.

43. Ibid., 184.

44. *The Humble Advice of the Assembly of Divines . . . Concerning a Larger Catechism* (London: Evan Tyler, 1647), 39.

45. William Secker, *A Wedding Ring, Fit for the Finger* (Boston: T. Green, 1705), 25, 29.

46. Ibid., 24–25.

47. Kathleen Verduin, in "'Our Cursed Natures': Sexuality and the Puritan Conscience," *New England Quarterly* 56.2 (1983): 220–37, argues that Puritans were wary about marital sexuality, seeing it as unclean. I agree that ministers saw conjugal relations as *potentially* licentious, but I would argue that they did exalt what they called "chaste," that is, moderate, marital sexuality.

48. Cotton Mather, *Ornaments for the Daughters of Zion* (Cambridge, Mass.: Samuel Green and Bartholomew Green, 1692), 77.

49. Samuel Willard, *A Compleat Body of Divinity* (Boston: B. Green and S. Kneeland, 1726), 675. This sermon was originally delivered in 1704.

50. Ibid., 674.

51. Ibid.

52. Walett, *Diary of Ebenezer Parkman*, 292.

53. Laurel Thatcher Ulrich, *Good Wives: Image and Reality in the Lives of Women in Northern New England, 1650–1750* (New York: Vintage, 1980), 153. In this quote Ulrich is specifically referring to a 1713 sermon by Cotton Mather, but the point is more broadly applicable as well.

54. Clifford K. Shipton, *Sibley's Harvard Graduates*, vol. 8 (Boston: Massachusetts Historical Society, 1951), 249.

55. Valentine Rathbun, *An Account of the Matter, Form, and Manner of a New and Strange Religion* (Providence, R.I.: Bennett Wheeler, 1781), 12.

56. Ibid., 20.

57. Benjamin West, *Scriptural Cautions Against Embracing a Religious Scheme* (Hartford: Bavil Webster, 1783), 7.

58. Ibid.

59. Ibid.

60. Caroline Walker Bynum, *Holy Feast and Holy Fast: The Religious Significance of Food to Medieval Women* (Berkeley and Los Angeles: University of California Press, 1987), 218, 250, 294.

Part III

Race, Sex, and Social Control in the Chesapeake and Caribbean in the Eighteenth Century

Unlike Puritan New England, the southern colonies and the Caribbean Islands of the eighteenth century did not control premarital and extramarital sexual activity so strictly. For white men, especially the rich and powerful, there were frequent opportunities for sexual encounters, especially with servants and slaves. This activity, if not condoned, was accepted by most of the white population.

Richard Godbeer's essay concerns the sexual exploits and inner musings of William Byrd. Based upon Byrd's diaries, correspondence, and commonplace book, this study draws upon one of the first-person accounts we have of sexual behavior in the southern colonies. Godbeer paints a portrait of a man whose sex life embodied his view of himself as both a confident, cosmopolitan planter and an insecure failure.

Similarly, Trevor Burnard bases his study on the private diaries of an eighteenth-century man. Despite a lack of self-scrutiny, Thomas Thistlewood, an overseer, kept a remarkable record of his life in Jamaica. Burnard's essay gives readers an insight into both the prolific sexual exploits of Thistlewood and, more broadly, into the interactions between free white men and black slave women. These sexual encounters enabled the white society to solidify its hold over the larger, but fragmented, overworked, and brutalized black population. Nevertheless, this molestation of black women ruptured white society, as white men became jealous over the attention their sexual partners received from others. As Burnard notes, the sexual adventures and promiscuity of white and black Jamaicans makes Thistlewood's diary read like a soap opera.

Natalie A. Zacek challenges the idea that society in the English West Indies was unregulated by moral standards. Although she concurs that certain practices, such as sexual relations between white men and black women, were overlooked, she argues that islanders punished sexual transgressions that challenged the patriarchal ideals of colonial British America. When Daniel Parke, the appointed governor of the Leeward Islands, was murdered by an angry crowd of Antiguans, many back in England viewed it as an example of the lawlessness prevalent in the islands. Zacek, however, observes that Parke's repeated assaults on other men's wives led the Antiguans to turn to violence in order "to enforce the local norms of sexual behavior."

Chapter 6

William Byrd's "Flourish"
The Sexual Cosmos of a Southern Planter

Richard Godbeer

In a letter dated 21 February 1723, forty-eight-year-old Virginian planter William Byrd included a self-portrait entitled "Inamorato L'Oiseaux" ("The Enamored Bird"), which he began as follows:

> Never did the sun shine upon a swain who had more combustible matter in his constitution than the unfortunate Inamorato. Love broke out upon him before his beard, and he could distinguish sexes long before he could the difference betwixt good and evil. Tis well he had not a twin-sister as Osyris did, for without doubt like him he would have had an amourette with her in his mother's belly.

Byrd claimed in his self-portrait that he had always aspired to a rational and virtuous life but had been constantly hampered by "the lively movement of his passions." Byrd's "hot" disposition had proven troublesome, he averred, in public and private life, but particularly so when it came to sexual self-control. He characterized the struggle between his "principles" and "inclinations" as an unresolved "civil war": "sometimes grace would be uppermost and sometimes love, [but] neither would yield and neither could conquer."[1]

Byrd's other writings leave no room for doubt that he was a passionate and lustful man. In scores of diary entries and in dozens of letters, he recorded his sexual escapades, which included marital cavorting on the billiard table, amorous advances to a string of servants and slaves, an ongoing relationship with one maidservant, and multifarious encounters with prostitutes in London. The passages that describe these incidents are

135

so arresting that they can give an impression of frenetic sexual activity. Yet that impression is misguided: Byrd was not as highly sexed as his reputation among early Americanists would suggest. What made him unusual was the extent to which he wrote about sex and revealed the place that it occupied in his mental world.

Gaining access to the interior life of early Americans is no easy matter, given the dearth of private, self-contemplative sources. The challenge is less severe when dealing with New England, since members of the godly elite left behind journals and other confessional writings in which they recorded their inner responses to the world around them and their experiences in it, while depositions from court records provide glimpses of popular culture. But the further south one travels, the more elusive become the personal thoughts and attitudes of early Americans. William Byrd's writings are a startling exception: three lengthy and secret diaries written in code have survived (1709–12, 1717–21, and 1739–41), as well as a voluminous private correspondence, a commonplace book compiled in the early 1720s, and several travel journals. Together these sources give a detailed and intimate impression of Byrd's world. Particularly striking is the sheer range of themes addressed by the author, from dietary fads and exercise routines to political machinations and social rituals, from spiritual contemplation and reading regimens to militia gatherings and slave relations, from botany and scientific innovation to the trials of married life and the pleasures of the flesh.[2]

Byrd's writings provide by far the most revealing commentary on sex that survives from the early South and so constitute an extraordinary opportunity for the historian of sexuality.[3] In two recent books, Kenneth Lockridge has underscored the significance of these sources for our understanding of southern gender relations and sexuality. *The Diary, and Life, of William Byrd II* explores the dynamic between Byrd's inner life and the evolving culture of colonial Virginia. In a second essay, *On The Sources of Patriarchal Rage*, Lockridge analyzes the commonplace books of Byrd and Thomas Jefferson, focusing on their misogynist outbursts. Lockridge argues that Byrd's and Jefferson's tirades against women reveal a fragile self-worth and chronic fear of emasculation that was generated not only by their personal experiences with women but also by the general insecurities that afflicted eighteenth-century Virginian patriarchs.[4]

This essay seeks, not to contradict Lockridge's reading of Byrd's commonplace book, but to show how misleading it is to privilege that particular source at the expense of Byrd's other writings. Lockridge's focus on that one text results in an incomplete and distorted impression of William Byrd and eighteenth-century Virginia. Drawing on the entire range of Byrd's literary output complicates our understanding of his sexuality and also the sexual culture in which he lived. It enables us to reconstruct the self-affirming, potent sexual persona that Byrd crafted for himself and through which he sought to integrate his personal with his public identity. That more confident persona operated in conjunction with the self-doubts that Lockridge has explored. The very range of sexual experience and commentary included in Byrd's writings reflects his status and success as a member of the elite in early eighteenth-century transatlantic society.

Byrd's discussions of sex fall into two broad categories. In his diaries, he entered tellingly framed descriptions of his sexual activities. These passages are laconic but nonetheless revealing: the language that Byrd deployed in them reflects his conceptualization of sex as an expression of his gentility and power. Some of his escapades he presented in a manner highly flattering to himself; others, in a tone of self-condemnation, as they evidently caused him considerable moral discomfort. In his correspondence and commonplace book, on the other hand, Byrd explored at length what he saw as the seamy and alarming realm of sexual politics, sometimes in generalized terms and sometimes in a more personal context. These two trains of thought, one in which he conversed with himself through the medium of his diaries and the other in which he engaged with an outer world that consisted of his correspondents and the authors whose words he copied into his commonplace book, provide an important counterpoint to each other. Together they reveal Byrd's profoundly ambivalent attitude toward sex and women. They also demonstrate that his sexual ethos was tightly bound up with his social identity: the sense of entitlement that it inspired, the insecurities that it engendered, and the preoccupation with control of self and others that it fostered. Byrd's writings bear eloquent testimony to the importance of treating sex as a cultural production, contingent upon the context in which it takes place and effectually an agent of that culture.

William Byrd was born in Virginia and also died there, but he lived almost half of his life in England. Although he inherited his father's Virginian estate in 1704, it was not until 1726 that he settled permanently in Virginia as a planter. Byrd saw himself as an English gentleman who resided for much of his life in Virginia, not as a Virginian who spent many years in England. In residence at Westover plantation, he surrounded himself with the trappings of English gentility and sought to behave in all regards like an English gentleman, an obsession that many of his fellow planters would pursue with dire financial consequences.[5] Byrd had always been politically ambitious, spent much of his time in London pursuing political advancement, and hoped to become governor of Virginia. That office eluded him, but Byrd did become one of the most influential public figures in the colony and eventually secured the second highest office in Virginia, the presidency of the governor's council. As we will see, Byrd's aspirations to gentility and power are crucial in understanding his conceptualization of sex.

Byrd's private life, like his public career, was shadowed by disappointment. He married for the first time in 1706, to Lucy Parke; his diary for 1709–12 depicts a stormy, albeit passionate, relationship. Although his father-in-law's position as governor of the Leeward Islands in the West Indies made him a promising political connection, Lucy brought to the marriage no substantial fortune. In fact, her marriage portion of one thousand pounds never arrived, and all that Byrd was able to secure after his father-in-law's death was a debt-ridden estate.[6] After Lucy's death from smallpox in 1716, he embarked on a number of ambitious courtships in London, none of which were successful. These rejections testified to the limited appeal of a Virginian planter as a potential husband in London's polite society, however wealthy and studiously genteel he might be. Byrd eventually secured the respectable, but by no means socially dazzling, hand of Maria Taylor, whom he married in 1724. His diary has little to say about that second marriage, either in its sexual aspect or any other.

Byrd's sex life was by no means limited to marital relations. He dallied with women of equal rank during his first marriage and committed adultery during the second. All three diaries describe his sexual advances toward servants and slaves; the diary for 1717–21, which covers a portion of his widower years, reveals his regular use of prostitutes in London. As the leading member of a commission to investigate the boundary between Virginia and North Carolina in 1728, Byrd witnessed the sexual escapades between his colleagues and Indians whom they encountered in the backcountry; his account of the expedition makes clear his own attraction toward native women. Byrd's libido was, then, remarkably comprehensive in its racial and social scope, underscoring the importance of erotic activity as a form of communication between people of different status and race in the colonial South. As we will see, such communications could range from gestures of courtly sensibility to brutal and violent demonstrations of power, although Byrd himself neither condoned nor (apparently) engaged in coerced sex.

Byrd was determined that all his relationships, public and private, should serve to fulfil his image of himself as a gracious yet masterful gentleman.[7] The significance he ascribed to sex as an extension of that persona was never clearer than in the language he used to describe sex with his first wife. Unfortunately, there is no surviving account of their physical relationship from her perspective. William and Lucy had a lively but irregular physical relationship that was often suspended due to Byrd's absences from Westover, their frequent marital quarrels, and physical ailments on either side.[8] In the entries that catalogued their moments of intimacy, Byrd usually wrote either that he "gave [his] wife a flourish" or that he "rogered" her. "I gave my wife a flourish in which she had a great deal of pleasure." "In the afternoon my wife and I played at billiards and I laid her down and rogered her on the trestle."[9] Each phrase deserves careful attention. The word "flourish" was used in early modern English to describe an elaborate physical gesture or rhetorical expression, a mark of one's social grace and sophistication. Byrd thus described sex with Lucy as an expression of cultured panache, as a stylish parade of his ability to perform as an accomplished gentleman. In a similar vein, he sometimes referred to sex in his correspondence as "gallantry," describing prostitutes sardonically as "ladies of universal gallantry."[10]

The significance of sex for Byrd's identity as a gentleman was sometimes enhanced in his mind by the setting in which it took place. "It is to be observed," he wrote, "that the flourish was performed on the billiard table." In another entry, he and Lucy had sex "on the couch in the library."[11] Byrd drew attention to these particular articles of furniture (he never thought to mention that he had sex on his bed or the floor) because they were ideal props for his genteel performances. Byrd, who considered himself to be an Englishman rather than a Virginian, lived in a region increasingly obsessed with the trappings of English culture and fashion. Furniture in the rooms at Westover intended for social interactions would have been modeled after English trends and indeed many household items had been imported from England.[12] In writing that he gave his wife "a flourish" on the couch or billiard table, Byrd quite literally inscribed his sexuality onto his material credentials as a gentleman. The library in which Byrd gave his wife "a flourish" bore testimony to his education and provided a backdrop for many of his gentlemanly conversations with neighbors and guests. That intimate encounters between husband and wife occurred in a public space (albeit in the absence of other people) rendered them more explicitly performative. Sex functioned for Byrd, then, as a highly dramaturgical component of his gentility: in having sex, especially if it took place on elegant furniture that embodied his status, Byrd demonstrated to himself (perhaps also to his wife) that cultured polish to which southern planters in general and Byrd in particular so earnestly aspired.

Sex as an expression of gentility was closely allied in Byrd's mind to sex as an act of aggressive and domineering masculinity. In writing that he "rogered" Lucy, Byrd took a colloquialism for penis, a "roger," and turned it into a verb, in effect portraying sex as an extension of his own penis and so endorsing a phallic view of intercourse in which his member became, like the verb itself, the active force that defined sex. In "roger[ing]" his wife, Byrd presented himself as an aggressively potent figure. He enhanced this impression of phallocratic mastery by noting that he bestowed "a powerful flourish" or "rogered" his wife "with vigor."[13]

But Byrd's physical relationship with Lucy was much more than a display of his gentlemanly bravado. A few of his diary entries leave traces of the gentle affection that William and Lucy had for each other. "About ten o'clock we went to bed," he wrote in April 1709, "where I lay in my wife's arms." "I rose at eight o'clock," he noted later that year, "because I couldn't leave my wife sooner."[14] Byrd's love for his wife is evident throughout the diary, notwithstanding their frequent arguments.[15] He was not an entirely selfish lover and certainly expected that Lucy would derive pleasure from their intercourse; he made sure, for example, to record on 30 April 1711 that his "powerful flourish" gave her "great ecstasy and refreshment."[16] He also recognized that his spouse had an appetite of her own: "my wife made me lie in bed and I rogered her."[17]

Nonetheless, Byrd expected his wife to acknowledge his mastery over her and the primacy of his will. When Lucy was "much indisposed" from one of her pregnancies, he still went ahead with a sexual encounter from which, he admitted, "she took but little pleasure."[18] There was an exact symmetry between Byrd's sexual and nonsexual expectations for his relationship with Lucy: he sought to establish a gentlemanly but self-consciously potent dominion over her. Yet Byrd's ascendancy in their marriage and his control over the Westover household were far from secure. Lucy often made decisions regarding domestic affairs with which he disagreed and over which she refused to compromise. Byrd noted approvingly when their arguments ended with Lucy's "submission" or "begg[ing]" his "pardon," but this does not seem to have happened very often.[19] He wrote with a hint of relief on 5 February 1711 that he "got the better of her, and maintained [his] authority." That he felt the need to articulate his success is itself telling.[20] The contested nature of Byrd's authority over his wife may have made assertions of sexual mastery seem all the more necessary to him. In Byrd's mind, sex may well have functioned to reinforce an otherwise rather shaky interpretation of their relationship.

Almost no information survives about Byrd's relationship with his second wife, Maria. They clearly had sex, for Maria bore William four children during the late 1720s. Indeed, Byrd complained in 1729 to his brother-in-law's widow, Jane Pratt Taylor, that he knew "nothing but a rabbit that breeds faster." Maria had been "delivered of a huge boy in September last" and was already "so unconscionable as to be breeding again." In that letter, which is the only surviving discussion of their physical relationship, Byrd went on to remark that "[i]t would [be] ungallant in a husband to dissuade her from it [i.e., reproduction]" but asked his correspondent to "preach" Maria "upon that chapter as a friend." He suggested, ostensibly in jest, that his wife "procreate[d] so fast" because she wanted to prevent his remarrying in the event of her death, by leaving him "too great an encumbrance." Byrd's letter gives no hint of emotional attachment, and his third diary is devoid of any reference to sexual relations or affection between them.[21]

Even during his marriage to Lucy, Byrd was often attracted sexually to other women: neighbors and acquaintances, servants and slaves. He often made comments in his diary about women being "pretty" or "very pretty."[22] Byrd's appreciation of the women around him was not purely aesthetic: while visiting his sister's house in 1711, Byrd noted, he "had wicked inclinations to Mistress Taylor."[23] At a dance in Williamsburg, Byrd "got some kisses" from the ladies in attendance; when out for an afternoon walk, he "met a pretty girl and kissed her and so returned." Then as now, kissing was multipotential in its significance: Byrd kissed the hand of the governor as a sign of respect, whereas his "kisses among the ladies" probably combined social greeting with flirtation; his encounter with the "pretty girl" was clearly at least flirtatious.[24] On one occasion the erotic implications of kissing became unpleasantly clear to Byrd's wife and the woman receiving his attentions: in November 1709, when Lucy had joined her husband in Williamsburg, they invited some friends back to their room; he played cards with Mrs Chiswell "and kissed her on the bed till she was angry and [his] wife also was uneasy about it, and cried as soon as the company was gone." The remorseful comment that completed this entry related to the illicit nature of his desire and the proprietary rights of Mrs. Chiswell's husband, not the two ladies' discomfort: "I neglected to say my prayers," he wrote, "which I should not have done, because I aught to beg pardon for the lust I had for another man's wife."[25]

Byrd never mentioned actually committing adultery during his first marriage, but later, as a widower in London, he ventured much further in his intimacies with both social equals and inferiors.[26] In 1718, he had an affair with "Mrs. A-l-c," which he ended when a female acquaintance confided that the lady in question was seeing another man and produced several letters as proof. A few days later, he wrote that he "saw Mrs. A-l-c for the last time because she had played the whore."[27] During his infatuation with Mary Smith, the daughter of a wealthy excise commissioner, Byrd's imagination ran riot: "I dreamed that Miss Smith called me dear and was in bed with me. . . . I dreamed that I saw Miss Smith almost naked and drew her to me." His sexual fantasies did not stop even after she married another man: in an adulterous dream, he "rogered my Lady Des Bouverie." Byrd later recalled fondly the "many a close hug and tender squeeze" he enjoyed with "Charmante," a lady whom he courted assiduously in 1722.[28] Byrd rarely focused his attention on one woman to the complete exclusion of others: his affair with Mrs. A-l-c overlapped with his pursuit of Miss Smith, and he had sex with prostitutes throughout the former liason and the latter courtship.

Byrd's London diary contains dozens of references to sex with prostitutes.[29] During the portion of his stay covered by the diary, he was resorting to prostitutes on average three times per month. He met most of them on the streets, either making his way home from social functions ("about twelve o'clock walked home and met a woman by the way and committed uncleanness") or on strolls specifically intended for that purpose ("then I took a walk to pick up a woman").[30] He sometimes met them at the theatre: on 25 March 1718, he went with Lord Orrery to the opera, where they "saw two handsome women in the gallery and went to them upon their invitation," although on that occasion they "went away without coming to any business."[31] Once contact had been made, sex took place in a variety of locales. On 4 August 1718, Byrd went for a walk in the park and ended up "lay[ing] with a woman on the grass."[32]

But usually he would either procure a coach in which to have sex or accompany the woman to her home, a tavern, or a "bagnio." The latter was a commercial establishment that served as both a bathing facility and a brothel. Sometimes Byrd would mention cleaning himself before having sex: "about ten o'clock we carried them to the bagnio, where we bathed and lay with them all night and I rogered mine twice."[33]

Whether or not Byrd and his friends made any connection between hygiene and disease is not clear, but they were evidently worried by the possibility of venereal infection. When Byrd had dinner with Sir Wilfred Lawson and Mr B-r-t-n on 13 June 1718, they not only told him that they "were clapped" but also let him know which prostitute they believed had given them the disease. In a later entry, he mentioned having had a nightmare about becoming "clapped."[34] Byrd noted down in his commonplace book several potions that would prevent or cure venereal infection (e.g., two quarts of epsom water). Those who consumed such concoctions "feared no ill consequence in the world, tho [the] nymph was never so common or dangerous."[35] Another response to the anxieties aroused by using prostitutes was to develop a trusting relationship with one of the brothel madams; these women seem to have deliberately cultivated a reassuring, even maternal, image. Byrd became genuinely fond of "my kind Mrs. Smith," the owner of a brothel on Queen Street which Byrd visited on many occasions in 1718–19; he referred to her as "my mother."[36]

Byrd's experience of prostitution was limited for the most part to his years in London. After returning from England to Virginia in 1719, Byrd "endeavoured to pick up a whore" during one of his stays in Williamsburg, "but could not find one."[37] If there were prostitutes available in Williamsburg, they would have been far fewer than in London. But the master of a plantation household had other options, and Byrd certainly availed himself of them. Throughout the British American colonies, servants were vulnerable to sexual abuse by their masters, although their rights as free men and women offered at least the possibility of legal recourse against such abuse.[38] In the southern colonies, where the increasingly pervasive institution of slavery encouraged a much more absolute sense of possession and entitlement on the part of masters, the potential for sexual exploitation was correspondingly greater.

Each of Byrd's diaries record sexual aggression toward servants and slaves, although the dynamic changes dramatically from one diary to the next. During the period covered by the 1709–12 diary, Byrd appears to have gone no further than a little kissing and groping, perhaps because he was fulfilled by his sexual relationship with his wife. These extramarital encounters usually took place during his visits to Williamsburg. "I sent for the wench," he wrote in 1709, "to clean my room and when she came I kissed her and felt her." On another occasion, he "asked a negro girl to kiss" him.[39] The second diary reveals him as a widower, exploring more fully the sexual possibilities of his position as a master and privileged gentleman. While in London, Byrd frequently "kissed the maid till [he] polluted [him]self," on one occasion feeling her privates, and on another forcing her to "feel [his] roger."[40] He also kissed Lord Orrery's housekeeper, and "the fruit girl," when she arrived one evening with a delivery.[41]

After his return to Virginia at the beginning of 1720, still wifeless, Byrd focused his sexual energies on "Annie," probably a white servant whom he had engaged in London.[42] Sometimes he "only kissed her" or toyed with a part of her body ("I felt Annie's belly this morning"), but on other occasions he "spent" (i.e., ejaculated).[43] There were weeks when Byrd would record intimacies with Annie on an almost daily basis, but over the entire period between his journey back to Virginia and the end of the second diary their encounters averaged roughly three times per month, as did his use of prostitutes in London. Although Byrd's libido was concentrated on Annie, there are no suggestions in the diary of emotional intimacy between maid and master. His interest in Annie was certainly not exclusive. In March 1721, he kissed Jenny P-r-s "and felt her breasts for about two hours" when she came to collect some medicine. (Byrd was an amateur doctor and often dispensed medicines to his dependents and neighbors.)[44] During a visit to Williamsburg in the fall of 1720, Byrd took a white maid "by the cunt." She managed to stop him from going any further by telling him that "she was out of order, else she would not mind it" (probably a reference to menstruation). A week later, "the maid of the house" came into his room after he had retired for the night: "I felt her and committed uncleanness but did not roger her." The following week, he "felt the breasts" of a "negro girl, which she resisted a little."[45]

The objects of Byrd's lust could and did resist his advances, although slaves presumably felt less able to do so. Take Annie as an example. Byrd's comment in one entry that he "made Annie feel about [his] person" implies an element of coercion, yet she does not seem to have been defenseless. On 9 August 1720, Byrd urged Annie "to come to bed but she would not consent." On 4 September 1720, he wrote that she would not let him "feel her," and on 9 March 1721 that "she would not be prevailed with."[46] It is not clear from the diary whether Annie was sexually attracted to Byrd: perhaps she was testing the limits of permissible resistance to unwanted advances, or, alternatively, seeking to ensure that encounters she enjoyed took place on her terms. In any case, she was not alone in refusing to cooperate with Byrd's libido. Jenny P-r-s, probably a dependent neighbor, also disappointed him: two days after the breast-fondling incident, Byrd "walked to the old plantation" to meet with her, presumably hoping to take their intimacy further, but she did not turn up.[47] As in London, Byrd consoled himself with dreams of romantic conquest for his failure to control women. One night he "dreamed the king's daughter was in love with [him]," the next that he "made love to a young sister and made her in love with [him], while [he] intended to get the older."[48]

Back in London a few years later, Byrd finally acquired a second wife, Maria Taylor. It is not possible to gauge the immediate effect of their marriage on his sex life since the only other surviving diary dates from 1739–41, near the end of his life. That diary contains far fewer references to sex than its predecessors. Byrd was by now in his sixties; he had admitted to his friend John Custis as early as 1723 that he was less in thrall to his lusts than before, although he stressed rather defensively that this was due to the triumph of "reason" over "inclination" and not the decline of his "constitution."[49] He made no reference in the diary to sexual relations with his second wife but did record having committed "folly with Caton," either Mrs. Caton De Wert, a gentlewoman recently arrived in Virginia whom Byrd befriended in misfortune, or her daughter Caton.[50] He also "committed folly" and "played the fool" with four slaves: Sally (four times), F-r-b-y (twice), Sarah (twice), and Marjorie (once). None of these women appear to have preoccupied him sexually as Annie did twenty years before and the frequency of sexual encounters was modest compared with the earlier diaries (on average once in two months).[51] Byrd's characterization of his later sexual encounters with slaves as "play[ing] the fool" and "committ[ing] folly" suggests a sense of his behavior as buffoonlike and undignified. There is none of the bravado that characterizes his earlier records of sexual adventure.

Eighteenth-century Virginians' interest in non-Europeans as sexual partners included Native Americans as well as Africans, although the context was quite different, given that planters in Virginia had not enslaved Indians. Byrd's account of the 1728 expedition along the boundary between Virginia and North Carolina made no attempt to conceal that he and his fellow travelers were much taken with Indian women whom they encountered along the frontier. That Byrd found Indian women attractive is evident from his description of "a dark angel" whom he met on a stroll in the woods with a fellow commissioner during the boundary expedition of 1728. "Her complexion," he wrote, "was a deep copper, so that her fine shape and regular features made her appear like a statue in bronze done by a masterly hand." Byrd claimed that his companion "was smitten at the first glance," but it seems fairly clear that so was Byrd himself. His colleague, discreetly nicknamed "Shoebrush" in the account, "examined all her neat proportions with a critical exactness." According to Byrd, she "struggled just enough to make her admirer more eager, so that if I had not been there, he would have been in danger of carrying his joke a little too far."[52]

Byrd reported that native women had "very straight and well proportioned" bodies as well as "an air of innocence and bashfulness that with a little less dirt would not fail to make them desireable." When the commissioners stayed overnight as the guests of an Indian tribe, Byrd commented with a hint of pique that their hosts "offered them no bedfellows, according to the good Indian fashion, which we had reason to take unkindly."[53] Although dirt was so "crusted on their skins" that "it required a strong appetite to accost them," that did not prevent William Dandrige and several other "gentlemen" from "hunting" the "sad-coloured ladies" through the night and staining their linen not only with dirt but also the red dye with which the native women decorated themselves.[54] Byrd sought to explain away Dandrige's behavior by suggesting that "curiosity made him try the difference between them and other women." He was less concerned that their subordinates had been frolicking with the native women since these men were, after all, "not quite so nice [i.e., particular]." The next day Byrd and Dandrige visited "most of the princesses at their own apartments" in hope of a close inspection, "but the smoke was so great there, the fire being made in the middle of the cabins, that [they] were not able to see their charms."[55]

A recurring theme in Byrd's narrative of the expedition was sexual aggression toward European as well as Indian women by the commissioners and their subordinates. On 9 March, some of the commissioners "broke the rules of hospitality by several gross freedoms they offered to take with our landlord's sister," prompting Byrd "to send her out of harm's way."[56] A week later, William Little, the attorney general of North Carolina, took their host's daughter to see the tent in which most of the men would be sleeping, "and might have made her free of it, had not we come seasonably to save the damsel's chastity."[57] This predatory behavior characterized auxiliary members as well as the leaders of the expedition. Richard FitzWilliams's servant made "boisterous" overtures toward a young woman "and employed force, when he could not succeed by fair means." Fortunately, "one of the men rescued the poor girl from this violent lover," although he was "so much his friend as to keep the shameful secret from those whose duty it would have been to punish such violations of hospitality."[58] On 20 September, some of the men became "too loving" from brandy, "[s]o that a damsel who came to assist in the kitchen would certainly have been ravished, if her timely consent had not prevented the violence." Meanwhile, their landlady barricaded herself in her bedchamber lest she also fall prey to "such furious lovers."[59] These incidents were symptomatic of a generally aggressive and maverick sexual ethos within the male culture to which Byrd belonged and which he himself exhibited in a number of contexts. Yet Byrd's criticism of the "unhandsome behaviour" and "outrage[s]" that local women suffered at the hands of his fellow commissioners and their servants was not entirely hypocritical: when servants and slaves resisted his advances at Westover and in Williamsburg, he did not force himself upon them; in Byrd's mind, this doubtless set him apart from those who attempted to assault women during the boundary expedition.[60]

Byrd was as anxious to control himself as he was to control others. In both these respects he was probably not unusual within his cadre: chronic tension within the Chesapeake's white population during the seventeenth century and the fragility of planters' mastery over the African slaves on whose labor they depended by the early eighteenth century had fostered an obsession with control in colonial southern society, while the elite's emulation of English gentry culture necessitated an intense self-consciousness and careful scrutiny of one's personal behavior.[61] Byrd's preoccupation with mastery and control, both of which he found elusive, has already been alluded to. His relentless surveillance of his reading, exercising, dietary, and spiritual regimens expresses a parallel concern for self-control.[62] Although Byrd was frequently in thrall to "the lively movement of his passions" and lusted to establish sexual empire over Indians, Africans, and European subordinates, he nonetheless also sought to colonize himself by subordinating his "inclinations" to his "principles." Byrd tried, though he often failed, to restrain his sexual appetite whenever it strayed outside the bounds of marriage. He did so because his errant lusts threatened his sense of identity as a rational, self-disciplined, and virtuous man.[63]

It was usually in a spiritual context that Byrd confided to his diary qualms about his sexual behavior. After most of his nonmarital encounters, Byrd asked that God forgive him. In London, for example:

> I walked home and picked up two women and committed uncleanness with the last of them because the first would not. I gave the last a mutton cutlet and some Rhenish wine. About eleven I went home and repented of what I had done and begged pardon of God almighty.

> I kissed the maid and my seed came from me, and neglected my prayers, for all which God forgive me.[64]

One evening in London, Byrd thanked God when he "endeavoured to pick up a woman, but could not."[65] He resolved in December 1720 "to forbear Annie by God's grace," although the resolution lasted only until the following February. When Annie refused his advances, Byrd wrote that it was an action "for which she is to be commended and for which God be praised."[66] On several occasions he claimed that his failure to pray was responsible for his masturbating, although at other times he bemoaned that he had "said a short prayer, but notwithstanding" committed "manual uncleanness."[67] Given the almost daily references in Byrd's diary to prayer, his constant examination of his spiritual condition, and his frequent reading of religious literature, there seems to be no good reason for distrusting his expressions of regret about extramarital lust and autoerotic activity.[68] His sense of guilt did not prevent him from entertaining what he considered to be illicit impulses, but he did see them as such. Byrd cared deeply about spiritual as well as social grace. His diary bears testimony to a genuine struggle between the spirit and the flesh, substantiating the assertion in his self-portrait that "neither would yield and neither could conquer."[69]

Byrd's diaries and journals reveal a sexual persona that combined gentility, control (of self as well as of others), and an often ineffective but nonetheless embedded spiritual conscience. Intrinsic to that persona was ambivalence: not only were Byrd's "inclinations" often offensive to his "principles," but the ways in which he conceived of himself as a sexual performer were sometimes antagonistic to each other. Gentility and mastery could work together, as in his bestowal of "a powerful flourish" upon Lucy, but his aggressive and proprietary instincts sometimes overpowered his courtly manner even within his marital relationship. Not surprisingly, a sense of entitlement and power were more visibly to the fore in his sexual encounters with subordinates, although even here Byrd aspired to a genteel restraint and (at least apparently) respected their right to refuse him access to their bodies. Byrd's letters and commonplace book reveal another aspect of the ambivalence that pervaded his sexuality: they testify, on the one hand, to his fascination by sex and, on the other, to his deep-seated distrust of women and the power of sexual attraction, as well as his lack of self-confidence as a player in the game of sexual politics. Byrd expressed these sentiments throughout his adult life, and so they cannot be dismissed as the callowness of youth.[70] His mordant attitude toward women was clearly intensified by the troubles of his first marriage and his unsuccessful courtships, for none of which difficulties he was willing to take responsibility. Lurking behind the facade of a potent and self-assured phallocrat was a frightened and insecure man who worried about male vulnerability to female predators and the threat of emasculation.

Byrd's attitude toward marriage in general was profoundly cynical. He wrote as a young man that he was drawn by "the convenience, the tenderness, the society of that condition," but finding a woman "of good sense, whose understanding forsooth might keep under all the impertinent starts of a woman's temper" was, in his opinion, no easy matter.[71] Byrd characterized his first wife as an unpredictable, irrational creature who constantly challenged his authority and disrupted the order of his household. In correspondence that ranged from 1703 to 1740, Byrd described marriage as a "galling yoke," a "contagion," a "distemper," and "a troublesome sea." So many were "shipwrecked in that sea" that it had "quite lost the name of the Pacific Ocean" and, in truth, resembled more closely "the Bay of Biscay, where the sea is perpetually disturbed, and the waves run mountain-high, making everybody sick that comes near it."[72]

That marriage so often became miserable and embittered owed a great deal, in Byrd's opinion, to sexual disillusionment. Despite his determined efforts to secure for himself marital alliances that would be socially advantageous, he remained convinced throughout his life that a marriage could not work without personal compatibility based on physical attraction. The promise of erotic fulfillment was for him a crucial factor in the choice of a spouse. He referred in a 1740 letter to the marrying off of young women as "put[ting] them to bed to agreeable husbands."[73] Yet Byrd himself stressed repeatedly in his writings that viewing marriage as intrinsically sexual and judging its success at least partly in terms of sexual gratification was problematic in two regards. First, sexual attraction usually declined as time passed by; and second, the physical allure that women used to attract men was more often than not a carefully prepared artifice, the exposure of which after marriage usually led to disappointment and alienation. Both problems resulted in male infidelity and both, Byrd argued, were primarily the fault of the wives concerned, not their husbands.

Sexual boredom, Byrd contended, often dulled the charms of a wife and sent the husband in search of new pleasures. He wrote in his commonplace book: "The two things in the world that the soonest grow stale upon our hands are a kindness received and a wedded wife."[74] There were, of course, exceptions. In a letter to Edward Southwell, written soon after the latter's marriage in 1703, Byrd expressed optimism that his friend's "joys" would "outlive the common term of conjugal happiness," since his wife had "variety enough [to] satisfy the inconstancy of any man living." She "comprehend[ed] all the agre[e]able qualities of her sex" and so would give Southwell "neither provocation [nor] excuse to go abroad for change." This unusually blessed husband, Byrd predicted, would encounter "none of [the] cloying every-day sameness that usually gives the men such a surfeit of their [wives]." Byrd implied that women who failed to "satisfy" their husbands, subjecting them to "cloying every-day sameness," were themselves responsible for their husbands' adultery.[75]

The other danger of choosing a wife largely on the basis of her "charms" was that the charms themselves often proved illusory. In 1737, Byrd defined love as "a longing desire to enjoy any person, whom we imagine to have more perfections than she really has." Once men fell in love, they became "idolaters" and "fondly fanc[ied] a kind of divinity in their mistresses." According to an entry in Byrd's commonplace book, women understood and exploited this tendency: "When a mistress wishes her gallant every thing that is good, she excepts always good sense, which might open his eyes and make him despise charms which owe their being to imagination only." Byrd portrayed courtship as a game of deception, even fraud, in which women held the trump cards. Women, he wrote, were more skilled than men in "the arts of dress and disguise." They knew "how to place their perfections in the fairest light, and cast all their blemishes in shade, so that the poor men who know no better take them to be cherubins and gems without flaw."[76]

But once the male victim of a woman's skillful deception gained "better acquaintance" as a husband and began "to judge a little by sense and not altogether by fancy," the woman's physical "irregularities" and "failings" became clear. The man's "vast expectations" were dashed, and disappointment led him to seek satisfaction elsewhere: "the appetite will naturally pall, and after we have missed of paradise in one place, we are apt to look for it in another." The ultimate responsibility for this pattern of behavior, Byrd wrote, lay with wives, not their errant husbands: "the inconstancy of our sex is owing to the disappointments it meets from yours, who are too solicitous to hide their blemishes before they throw themselves into a man's arms and too little afterwards."[77] In a 1729 letter, Byrd suggested in jest that when a couple was contemplating marriage, "the parties should view each other stark naked through an iron gate for the space of half an hour." This would prevent them from "concealing their personal defects" and so would "hinder their being surprised after marriage with any deformities and disproportions which they did by no means expect."[78] Beneath the superficial playfulness of this passage lurked a distrust of women's apparent beauty that pervades Byrd's writings. In his mind, male naivete and yearning for an idealized female body combined with feminine deceit to make a heady but dangerous potion with which men were drugged and duped into marriage.

Fortunately, Byrd wrote in a 1730 letter to his English friend John Boyle, the women of Virginia had fewer opportunities than their counterparts across the Atlantic to mislead their suitors. There were "no masquerades to conceal their frailties," and many social functions began before sundown, so that they were "forced to produce their beauties to fair daylight, which is not so friendly to their blemishes as candles." English ladies, on the other hand, "like bats turn[ed] night into day," preferring artificial light as an effective ally in schemes of seduction.[79] But women everywhere, in Byrd's opinion, were utterly unscrupulous. Even reproduction could become a tool of female manipulation, as evinced by his second wife's rapid production of children in what Byrd portrayed, tongue planted nervously in cheek, as a plot to burden him financially and so prevent a remarriage if she died.[80] Byrd's distrust of women was usually camouflaged in his correspondence by a coating of humor and counterbalanced in his letters to women by a tone of solicitous gentility. In the privacy of his commonplace book, however, he allowed himself to express more overtly and maliciously his fear of female beauty and sexuality; the humor deployed in these passages was more spiteful than in his letters and so deepened instead of lightening the overall vituperative tone.

Byrd entered into this volume a series of anecdotes and aphorisms that together constitute a bitter and paranoid commentary on sex and marriage. The entries described in lurid detail the insatiable nature of female lust, so potent that one woman in love with a social inferior could overcome her incommodious "concupiscence" only by "drinking the blood of her beloved," and so unrelenting in its demands that male victims faced utter prostration and sometimes actual annihilation. Women could dispense with men altogether either by becoming pregnant "without losing their maidenhood, when neither the hymen nor nymphae have been in the least torn or injured, that pregnancy has appeared miraculous," or by rejecting male love in favor of "Lesbian" pleasures ("an inclination not altogether unknown to the females of this island"). In entry after entry and page after page, Byrd built up a nightmarish collage of vampiric women, their voracious appetites, and the predatory wiles that trapped men in a destructive and debilitating cycle of helpless desire and humiliation. The extracts expressed profound fear of male sexual inadequacy, relating how one man, "finding his vigour begin to abate," had one of his legs cut off "so that the blood and spirits which used to nourish that limb might add strength to those which remained, and increase his abilities with the alluring sex." They dwelt on insecurities about penis size and the ability to get erect, lamenting that "poor men" fell far short of many animals that could ejaculate dozens of times in one session.[81]

Byrd's preoccupation with the threat of emasculation may have been encouraged by his particular response to the one-sex model of anatomy that still predominated in the early eighteenth century and posited a basic biological commonality between men and women. According to this model, female sexual organs constituted not a distinct apparatus but merely an inversion of male genitalia.[82] Byrd was alert to the possibility that male and female sexual organs, being fundamentally similar in design, might change in either direction under certain circumstances. He claimed in his "History of the Dividing Line" that "French women use to ride astraddle, not so much to make them sit firmer in the saddle as from the hopes the same thing might peradventure befall them that once happened to the nun of Orleans, who, escaping out of a nunnery, took post 'en cavalier' and in ten miles' hard riding had the good fortune to have all the tokens of a man break out upon her."[83] On the other hand, he recorded in his commonplace book the claim that male organs "grow less and dwindle away by excessive abstinence, of which St. Martin is reported to be a remarkable instance, who observed such strict rules of abstinence, and exercised such austerities upon himself, that when the women came to lay him out after he was dead, they could hardly find out any penis at all, at most not larger than a moderate clitoris."[84] Thus, while women, once firmly in the saddle, might actually be transformed into men, men had to choose between the prostration that resulted from meeting the sexual demands of women and the possibility of genital diminution that attended self-protective abstinence.

The tone of Byrd's commonplace book seems far removed from his exuberant "flourishes" atop the Westover billiard table. As Kenneth Lockridge points out, it is doubtless no coincidence that the commonplace book was compiled in the early 1720s. Lockridge argues that the book functioned for Byrd as a "confessional tirade," in which he vented his fury over "years of failure and frustration, much of it with women." Byrd's first wife had constantly challenged and sometimes usurped his authority over the Westover household and its budget; more recently, his attempts to improve his social and economic status through remarriage had resulted in repeated humiliation at the hands of women who were to have functioned as the means of reinforcing his patriarchal authority. In his commonplace book, Byrd expressed the rage that had grown out of his failure to exercise "power over women" or access "power through women."[85] Yet his correspondence shows a distrust of women that began in early manhood and lasted through old age.[86] His insecurities may have become more pronounced over the years in response to his romantic disappointments, but his assertive flamboyance on the one hand and his self-doubt on the other are perhaps best understood as ongoing counterpoints in his sexual personality. For example, Byrd referred in the London diary not only to his failed erections ("my roger would not stand with all she could do") but also the more triumphant moments in his sex life ("I rogered her three times with vigor, twice at night and once in the morning").[87] These passages coincide chronologically with romantic pursuits that were just as often hopeful as they were despairing. Despite his misgivings about women, he also appreciated their charms and enjoyed their company. Throughout his life, Byrd's attitude toward women in general and in particular was profoundly and consistently ambivalent.

Byrd's sex life, the ways in which he described sexual desire, and his attitudes toward sexual politics carry a significance that far transcends the personal. In a society that conceived of all relationships and authority in personal and familial terms, the shaping of public and private identity had profound mutual implications. According to Lockridge, Byrd's misogynistic tirade in the commonplace book was generated not only by his own personal experiences but also by the fragility of patriarchal power in eighteenth-century southern culture. It expressed in a gendered context the insecurities of planters whose apparent hegemony was "under pressure from all sides."[88] Lockridge criticizes historians of patriarchy in early modern Anglo-American culture for paying insufficient attention to the ways in which patriarchal authority was contested.[89] Yet southern planters survived pre-Revolutionary challenges to their power, produced many of the new nation's founding fathers, and successfully co-opted Revolutionary rhetoric in ways that enabled them to preserve largely unscathed their hegemony within southern society.

In this broader context, as well as for the purposes of individual biography, Lockridge's concentration on the "chamber of horrors" in Byrd's commonplace book is misleading. Not only, as Lockridge himself admits, are Byrd's and Jefferson's expressions of "patriachal rage" anomalous,[90] but the other writings that Byrd left behind him reveal his successes, as well as failures, in embodying the masterful gentility of a southern planter. The sheer range of his sexual experiences and observations was made possible by his status as a powerful, privileged, and cosmopolitan landowner. His sexual world included his wives and members of the workforce at Westover; maidservants at work in Williamsburg, the site of Virginia's colonial government, in which Byrd was so closely involved; native and European women whom he and his fellow commissioners encountered during the boundary expedition; the prostitutes over whom he exercised his proprietary rights as a consumer; and the ladies with whom he flirted in the London salons, to which he had ready access. If Byrd was not always successful in exerting control over women whose bodies he desired, such disappointments were surely unexceptional.

The very language that Byrd used to depict his sexual activities—the language of gentility and mastery—speaks to his incorporation of the most basic physical impulses into the discourse of genteel power that ruled his life and that of the eighteenth-century Chesapeake. That tight linkage between sexuality and cultural identity could prove dangerous if one or both became troubled. Lockridge has shown how different forms of insecurity fed on each other in Byrd's mind. But sexual and nonsexual identities could work together in a more constructive symbiosis, and that was also Byrd's experience: his sex life embodied the confident, even triumphalist, "flourish" of gentry culture as well as the self-doubts and fears that haunted the southern phallocracy. The relationship between the erotic and the nonerotic in Byrd's life and mind was double-edged in its implications. For Byrd, sex, power, and cultural legitimacy were utterly inseparable, blending physical and psychological needs, private and public personas, personal self-worth and political esteem. Given what he described as "the lively movement of his passions," as well as the perils that attend any political, romantic, or erotic venture, this was a volatile brew . . . which helps to explain the rich complexity of Byrd's sexual cosmos, as it percolates down to us through his writings.

NOTES

The research for this essay was made possible by support from the Academic Senate of the University of California, Riverside. I owe a special debt of thanks to my fellow fellows at UCR's Center for Ideas and Society in the spring quarter of 1996—Carole Fabricant, Lora Geriguis, George Haggerty, Stephanie Hammer, John Jordan, Askley Stockstill, and Linda Tomko—for their lively, constructive, and insightful discussion of my work-in-progress. I am also grateful to members of the Bay Area Seminar in Early American History for their helpful comments, and to Merril Smith for her sage editorial advice. John Phillips and Charles Wetherell in the History Department at UCR have been, as always, generous and astute readers.

1. William Byrd, "Inamorato L'Oiseaux," in *Another Secret Diary of William Byrd of Westover, 1739–41: With Letters and Literary Exercises, 1696–1726*, ed. Maude H. Woodfin, trans. Marion Tinling (Richmond, Va.: Dietz Press, 1942), 276–77.

2. *The Secret Diary of William Byrd of Westover, 1709–12*, ed. Louis B. Wright and Marion Tinling (Richmond, Va.: Dietz Press, 1941), hereafter *Secret Diary*; *William Byrd of Virginia: The London Diary (1717–1721) and Other Writings*, ed. Louis B. Wright and Marion Tinling (New York: Oxford University Press, 1958), hereafter *London Diary*; *Another Secret Diary of William Byrd of Westover, 1739–41*, hereafter *Another Secret Diary*; *The Correspondence of the Three William Byrds of Westover, Virginia, 1684–1776*, ed. Marion Tinling, 2 vols. (Charlottesville: Virginia Historical Society, 1977), hereafter *Correspondence*; Byrd Commonplace Book, MS, Virginia Historical Society (Richmond), hereafter Commonplace Book; "The Secret History of the Line," in *Colonial American Travel Narratives*, ed. Wendy Martin (New York: Penguin, 1994); "History of the Dividing Line," in *The Prose Works of William Byrd of Westover*, ed. Louis B. Wright (Cambridge: Harvard University Press, 1966); "A Progress to the Mines in the Year 1732," in *The Prose Works*; "A Journey to the Land of

Eden Anno 1733," in *The Prose Works*. I am grateful to Jan Gilliam and Kenneth Lockridge for sharing with me their transcription of the commonplace book, which I have used in conjunction with the manuscript.

3. By "sexuality" I mean the ways in which men and women ascribe meaning and value to sexual attraction and sexual activity. See Richard Godbeer, "'The Cry of Sodom': Discourse, Intercourse, and Desire in Colonial New England," *William and Mary Quarterly* 52 (1995): 260–61.

4. Kenneth A. Lockridge, *The Diary, and Life, of William Byrd II of Virginia, 1674–1744* (Chapel Hill: University of North Carolina Press, 1987); *On the Sources of Patriarchal Rage: The Commonplace Books of William Byrd and Thomas Jefferson and the Gendering of Power in the Eighteenth Century* (New York: New York University Press, 1992). Although my overall reading of Byrd differs from Lockridge's, this essay owes a substantial debt to his work.

5. Lockridge argues that Byrd used his diary as a "mirror" to "check his pose, as it were, and to reassure himself" of his success in performing as "the perfect gentleman" (*The Diary, and Life, of William Byrd*, 48). T. H. Breen discusses the Anglophiliac consumer craze in *Tobacco Culture: The Mentality of the Great Tidewater Planters on the Eve of the Revolution* (Princeton: Princeton University Press, 1985) and "An Empire of Goods: The Anglicization of Colonial America, 1690–1776," *Journal of British Studies* 25 (1986): 467–99. See also Cary Carson, Ronald Hoffman, and Peter J. Albert, eds., *Of Consuming Interests: The Style of Life in the Eighteenth Century* (Charlottesville: University Press of Virginia, 1994).

6. Lockridge, *The Diary, and Life, of William Byrd*, 75–76.

7. Lockridge discusses Byrd's general preoccupation with mastery in *The Diary, and Life, of William Byrd*, 66–73.

8. The 1709–12 diary contains fifty-six references to sex between the Byrds. This averages as roughly one and a quarter encounters per month, but the irregularity of their intercourse makes that figure rather misleading; in December 1710, for example, they had intercourse six times. Given the frankness of the secret diaries, which record failures as well as successes and moments of self-doubt as well as of confidence, I have decided to assume that Byrd's accounting of his sexual activity is fairly reliable.

9. *Secret Diary*, 253, 275. For other entries that describe Byrd as giving Lucy "a flourish," see 118, 125, 173, 202, 209, 210–11, 228, 235, 265, 266, 272, 308, 337, 338, 339, 361, 533; for other examples of Byrd "roger[ing]" Lucy, see 272, 278, 293, 345, 403, 411, 413, 430, 431, 437, 446, 459, 460, 463, 465, 481, 498, 510, 518, 521, 524, 525, 530, 541, 543, 546, 558, 575, 583.

10. *Correspondence*, 1:227; see also 370. The word "flourish" could also suggest spontaneous, even hasty, sexual intercourse. Francis Grose, *A Classical Dictionary of the Vulgar Tongue* (1785; New York: Barnes and Noble, 1963), 149;

John S. Farmer and W. E. Henley, *Slang and Its Analogues* (London, 1890–1909), 3:33.

11. *Secret Diary*, 93, 210–11, 275, 293.

12. See *Secret Diary*, 48, 53, and 202 for references to items arriving from England.

13. *Secret Diary*, 337, 446, 583. This colloquialism apparently originated with the common practice of giving the name Roger to bulls (Grose, *A Classical Dictionary*, 289; Farmer and Henley, *Slang and Its Analogues*, 6:44).

14. *Secret Diary*, 27, 101.

15. Byrd clearly enjoyed his wife's companionship: they often read, walked, and applied themselves to plantain chores together. Byrd appreciated his wife's ability to play the role of a lady and commented on the "respect" that she inspired during her stay in London from "many persons of distinction, who all pronounced her an honour to Virginia" (*Correspondence*, 296).

My impression of William and Lucy Byrd's relationship is quite different from that offered by Daniel Blake Smith's *Inside the Great House: Planter Family Life in Eighteenth-Century Chesapeake Society* (Ithaca, N.Y.: Cornell University Press, 1980). Smith describes Byrd as ruling over his household "with unchallenged authority" and muting his emotional attachment to family members in obedience to the ideals of "moderation and self-restraint" (21). Although it is abundantly clear from his diaries that Byrd aspired to authority and a reasoned restraint, I would argue that they also reveal a man whose position as patriach was often challenged by his wife and whose marriage was both companionate and passionate. Smith may be confusing emotional standards with emotional behavior; see Peter N. Stearns and Carol Z. Stearns, "Emotionology: Clarifying the History of Emotions and Emotional Standards," *American Historical Review* 90 (1985), esp. 824, and idem, eds., *Emotion and Social Change: Toward a New Psychohistory* (New York: Holmes and Meier, 1988), 7–8.

16. *Secret Diary*, 337; see also 253.

17. *Secret Diary*, 465; see also 481.

18. *Secret Diary*, 344–45.

19. *Secret Diary*, 18, 19.

20. *Secret Diary*, 296.

21. *Correspondence*, 391.

22. See, for example, *Secret Diary*, 450, 451, 454.

23. *Secret Diary*, 337.

24. *Secret Diary*, 26, 436. Byrd was also clearly flirting when he kissed Mrs. Hunt "several times" at a social gathering in 1721; he noted that "she was not very unwilling" (*London Diary*, 516).

25. *Secret Diary*, 101.

26. For discussion of sexual mores in eighteenth-century English society, see

A. D. Harvey, *Sex in Georgian England: Attitudes and Prejudices from the 1720s to the 1820s* (New York: St. Martin's Press, 1994); G. S. Rousseau and Roy Porter, eds., *Sexual Underworlds of the Enlightenment* (Manchester: Manchester University Press, 1987), esp. the introduction; Peter Wagner, *Eros Revived: Erotica in the Age of Enlightenment* (London: Secker and Warburg, 1988); Terry Castle, "Eros and Liberty at the English Masquerade, 1710–1790," *Eighteenth-Century Studies* 17 (1983/84): 156–76; Roy Porter, "Mixed Feelings: The Enlightenment and Sexuality in Eighteenth-Century Britain," in *Sexuality in Eighteenth-Century Britain*, ed. Paul-Gabriel Boucé, (Manchester: Manchester University Press, 1982), 1–27; and Paul-Gabriel Boucé, "Aspects of Sexual Tolerance and Intolerance in Eighteenth-Century England," *British Journal for Eighteenth-Century Studies* 3 (1980): 173–91.

27. *London Diary*, 134, 135. Mrs A-l-c's identity and status are unknown; it is not even clear whether she was still married or had been widowed. However, Byrd described himself as giving her "a flourish," language that he never used in passages clearly describing sex with social inferiors *London Diary*.

28. *London Diary*, 69, 95, 160; *Correspondence*, 332.

29. For discussion of prostitution in London, see Roy Porter, *London: A Social History* (Cambridge: Harvard University Press, 1995), 171–72, and Vern L. Bullough, "Prostitution and Reform in Eighteenth-Century England," in *'Tis Nature's Fault: Unauthorized Sexuality during the Enlightenment*, ed. Robert Purks Maccubbin (New York: Cambridge University Press, 1987), 61–74.

30. *London Diary*, 124, 146.

31. *London Diary*, 97.

32. *London Diary*, 157.

33. *London Diary*, 140; for other visits to the "bagnio," see 143, 146, 151, 219, 221, 239, 241, 275, 285, 289, 298, 318.

34. *London Diary*, 134, 356.

35. Commonplace Book. In "Amorato L'Oiseaux," he claimed to have been attracted to marriage in part by "the inconveniences that attend accidental and promiscuous gallantry," presumably a reference to venereal disease (*Another Secret Diary*, 278).

36. *London Diary*, 269, 272; for other entries describing visits to Mrs Smith's establishment, see 224, 226, 227, 229, 231, 233, 236, 243, 250, 280, 315, 317, 321, 327, 329, 331. Although Mrs. Smith's was the brothel with which he had the most lasting connection, Byrd also mentioned going with friends to visit "Mrs. W-d-l-n-t-n, a decent bawd." He doubtless found it emotionally and culturally reassuring that Mrs. W-d-l-n-t-n was "decent" (*London Diary* 130).

37. *London Diary*, 476.

38. For a detailed examination of sexual assault in early colonial America, see Sharon Block, "Coerced Sex in British North America, 1700–1820" (Ph.D. diss., Princeton University, 1995).

39. *Secret Diary*, 90, 425; see also 168–69.

40. *London Diary*, 71, 72, 77, 83, 85, 87, 346, 347, 348, 350.

41. *London Diary*, 197, 309.

42. Lockridge, *The Diary, and Life, of William Byrd*, 101.

43. *London Diary*, 374, 382, 506.

44. *London Diary*, 505.

45. *London Diary*, 479, 482, 484.

46. *London Diary*, 409, 437, 447, 505.

47. *London Diary*, 505.

48. *London Diary*, 444.

49. *Correspondence*, 346–47.

50. *Another Secret Diary*, 3.

51. *Another Secret Diary*, 31, 70, 93, 137, 155, 157, 166, 168, 174.

52. "Secret History of the Line," 96.

53. "Secret History of the Line," 113.

54. "History of the Dividing Line," 222; "Secret History of the Line," 113–14.

55. "Secret History of the Line," 113. Byrd's interest in Indian women far pre-dated the boundary expedition. On military exercise in 1711, he and his fellow officers "took a walk about the town to see some Indian girls, with whom we played the wag." Two days later he wrote that "Jenny, an Indian girl, had got drunk and made us good sport" (*Secret Diary*, 423, 425).

56. "Secret History of the Line," 95.

57. "Secret History of the Line," 100.

58. "Secret History of the Line," 106.

59. "Secret History of the Line," 124. See also 96, 97; and "History of the Dividing Line," 224.

60. Byrd's perspective on his fellow commissioners' behavior may also have been influenced by the recent change in his own circumstances. He had remarried a few years previously and was in the midst of siring four children by his second wife. Their procreative activities, combined with the onset of middle age, may have taken the edge off his own predatory appetite.

61. For another example of this twin preoccupation, see Jack P. Greene, ed., *The Diary of Colonel Landon Carter of Sabine Hall, 1752–1778*, 2 vols. (Charlottesville: University Press of Virginia, 1965), passim.

62. Lockridge examines this aspect of Byrd's diaries in *The Diary, and Life, of William Byrd*, esp. 6–9.

63. For a discussion of this psychological dynamic in the specific context of miscegenation, see Winthrop Jordan, *White over Black: American Attitudes Toward the Negro, 1550–1812* (Chapel Hill: University of North Carolina Press, 1968), 144.

64. *London Diary*, 71, 157.

65. *London Diary*, 133.

66. *London Diary*, 447, 491.

67. *Secret Diary*, 97, 169, 247, 336, 509; see also 250, 429, 442, 477, 500, 572.

68. Byrd did not see marital sex as spiritually problematic: he never mentioned the need for God's forgiveness after bestowing a "flourish" on Lucy.

69. Byrd took seriously not only his own sexual foibles but also those of his servants and slaves. In 1709, he threatened to whip Anaka, an African-American slave, unless she told him about the affair that he suspected was going on between Daniel and Nurse, both white servants. When Anaka preempted the beating by admitting that she had seen them together on a bed, Byrd "chided Nurse severely about it," although Nurse denied any impropriety. The following year, Byrd "caused L-s-n to be whipped for beating his wife, and Jenny was whipped for being his whore" (*Secret Diary*, 7, 192). But Byrd was not inflexibly righteous when dealing with the sexual lapses of others: in April 1721, he joined some friends in intervening "to save a poor girl from whipping that had a bastard" (*London Diary*, 514).

70. Lockridge argues that Byrd's emotional maturation was delayed for several decades (*The Diary, and Life, of William Byrd*, esp. nn. 25, 173, 177, 235) He also suggests that Byrd's despatch to England at the age of seven to acquire education and gentility constituted "twin burdens of responsibility and rejection." Having been rejected as a boy by his father, he was later rejected as a colonial by London society. That "twin burden" would manifest itself repeatedly in his dealings with women(155–66). Lockridge has accurately described Byrd's personality whether or not one accepts Lockridge's explanation of how it was formed.

71. *Another Secret Diary*, 277–78.

72. *Correspondence*, 230 (1703), 392 (1728), 432 (1730), 564 (1740); *Another Secret Diary*, 250 (undated). Even when he invoked the possibility of marital happiness, he ended up doing so in the context of the wretchedness that generally accompanied marriage. In a 1722 love letter to an English lady whom he addressed only as "Charmante," Byrd expressed the hope that he and she would "give matrimony as many charms as it had in paradise," thus redeeming "a state which has been made miserable by vile interest, perverse humour, and ungoverned passion" (*Correspondence*, 334; for discussion of this lady's identity, see 333). In 1729, he wrote to congratulate John Boyle on his recent marriage and wished him "all the joys of matrimony without any of the sorrow and satiety that but too frequently attend that state" (*Correspondence*, 393).

73. *Correspondence*, 564. See also "Journey to the Land of Eden," 381.

74. Commonplace Book. See also "Progress to the Mines," 343.

75. *Another Secret Diary*, 191.

76. *Correspondence*, 505; Commonplace Book.

77. *Correspondence*, 505.

78. *Correspondence*, 401.

79. *Correspondence*, 432.

80. *Correspondence*, 391.

81. Byrd admitted in his diary that his physical performance did not always match his appetite (*London Diary*, 182, 226). For a more detailed discussion of the commonplace book, see Lockridge, *On The Sources of Patriarchal Rage*, chapter 1. The passages relating to women and sex are complemented by Byrd's essay "The Female Creed," written around 1725, in which he portrayed women as insatiable in their appetite for food, sex, and power; physically debased and even revolting in their inability to control their bodily functions; superstitious; and the embodiment of moral and physical disorder. Lockridge discusses "The Female Creed" in chapter 2 of *On the Sources of Patriarchal Rage*.

82. "The clitoris in a woman," Byrd noted in his commonplace book, "is in many things like a man's penis, it has a nut and prepuse like that, and swells very much in the act and desire of copulation." Thomas Laqueur examines this model in *Making Sex: Body and Gender from the Greeks to Freud* (Cambridge: Harvard University Press, 1990). See also Mary Beth Norton's helpful discussion of the Thomas/Thomasine Hall case in *Founding Mothers and Fathers: Gendered Power and the Forming of American Society* (New York: Knopf, 1996), esp. 188.

83. *History of the Dividing Line*, 316. Byrd sought to bolster the credibility of this "piece of history" by informing his readers that the bishop of Burnet described two Italian nuns undergoing "the same happy metamorphosis, probably by some other violent exercise."

84. Commonplace Book.

85. Lockridge, *On the Sources of Patriarchal Rage*, 24, 75. Byrd's comments about women, sex, and marriage became somewhat less vitriolic after the late 1720s, as he forged for himself a more successful and mature identity as patriarch, planter, and public figure, a process described by Lockridge in *The Diary, and Life, of William Byrd*.

86. Byrd's self-portrait, written when he was a young man, testifies to a lack of self-confidence, especially with regard to women, that would prove lasting over the years. The essay was originally composed some two decades before Byrd redrafted it for inclusion in the 1723 letter. Lockridge discusses the dating of this composition in *The Diary, and Life, of William Byrd*, 27. According to "Inamorato L'Oiseaux," "when he was in love, no man ever made so disingaging a figure. . . . Venus and all the graces would leave him in the lurch in the critical time when they should have assisted him most." He would become "dismal," "all form and constraint when he should have the most freedom and spirit" (*Another Secret Diary*, 277–78).

87. *London Diary*, 182, 275. For other examples of self-congratulatory accounts of sexual activity, see 151, 221, 225, 318.

88. Lockridge, *On the Sources of Patriarchal Rage*, 91.

89. Lockridge, *On the Sources of Patriarchal Rage*, 116, n. 6. Lockridge refers to Lawrence Stone's *The Family, Sex, and Marriage in England* (New York: Harper and Row, 1977) and Daniel Blake Smith's *Inside the Great House*. Carole Shammas emphasizes the strength of patriarchal authority over eighteenth-century colonial households in "Anglo-American Household Government in Comparative Perspective," *William and Mary Quarterly* 52 (1995): 104–44.

90. Lockridge, *On the Sources of Patriarchal Rage*, 90.1.

Chapter 7

The Sexual Life of an Eighteenth-Century Jamaican Slave Overseer

Trevor Burnard

Thomas Thistlewood, a twenty-nine-year old man from Lincolnshire, England, arrived in Jamaica on 24 April 1750, determined to establish a new life for himself in Britain's most flourishing colony. Moving to Westmoreland Parish, in the far west of the island, he lived out the rest of his life in the tropics, dying in 1786 in his sixty-sixth year on his small agricultural property called Breadnut Island. Although on his own terms he achieved considerable success, establishing himself as an independent landowner and as a man of some local consequence, his life would have attracted little notice if he had not assiduously kept an extraordinary diary that has been fortuitously preserved in the Lincolnshire Archives.[1] This diary, running to perhaps half a million words, chronicles Thistlewood's life in rural Jamaica in the mid-eighteenth century, a life lived mainly among black African slaves in one of the most complete slave societies ever established. It offers valuable insights into a host of matters of central importance in the history of plantation societies and of slavery and it is particularly valuable for delineating the complex interactions that marked the relationship between white masters and black slaves in a mature eighteenth-century slave society. Among the most important of these interactions were sexual encounters between white men and black women.[2] Through his extensive diaries Thistlewood gives us a glimpse of this extremely important point of contact. He was something of a sexual athlete and meticulously recorded his sexual exploits. To my knowledge, his cataloguing of his extensive sexual experiences in Jamaica is the fullest surviving account of sexual activity between blacks and whites under a slave regime. His diary, despite being a problematic source, allows great insight into how sexual relations between blacks and whites were ordered and into the role of interracial sex in preserving and disrupting order in the slave system. In this essay, I wish to use Thistlewood's text to explore the meaning of interracial sex in a slave society. I hope to show how sexual encounters between black women and white men were both a rupture in the supposedly impregnable edifice of white solidarity and a means whereby the dominant minority of whites solidified its hold over the majority African population.

Sexual encounters between black women and white men ruptured white solidarity in several ways. First, they provoked disputes between fiercely independent white men. White men were extremely predatory in their attention to black women, and their predations often led to competition and quarrels when the same woman was desired by several men. Sexual jealousy was rife. Thomas Thistlewood's diaries read like an eighteenth-century soap opera, in which both blacks and whites were rampantly promiscuous. One constant refrain within this soap opera was disputes between whites, accustomed to unlimited power, over access to the sexual services of slave women. These problems were compounded by the havoc that such casual couplings caused within slave communities. Disputes between whites occurred when sexual access to female slaves conflicted with white property rights over the bodies of those slaves. What constituted ownership of a slave's body, including access to the sexual services of slaves, was highly contestable in a slave society. Having sex with a female slave, when that slave was owned by another white, was, from the perspective of white society, a violation of a slaveowner's property rights. Such a violation could have serious consequences for white harmony: respecting a slaveowner's absolute right to control and use his or her slaves was a sacrosanct ideological imperative.

Second, sexual relations between white men and black women made the relations between white men and white women particularly fraught. The evolution of plantation society in Jamaica, as I have argued elsewhere, allowed little place for white women.[3] The majority of the white population—perhaps 80 percent—were men, a large percentage of whom resembled Thomas Thistlewood in preferring black women to white. White men had full sexual license and suffered little or no social opprobrium as the result of their propensity to "riot in goatish embraces," as the historian Edward Long so vividly put it.[4] The sexuality of white women, on the other hand, was firmly regulated, especially from the mideighteenth century onward, as hopes that Jamaica would become a settler society full of Europeans faded and as relations between white men and black women increased in frequency. The rapid growth from mid-century on of the freed black population, the declining rates of marriage between white men and white women, and the increasing latitude given to moral dereliction by patriarchal males confirmed white women's lack of power in eighteenth-century Jamaica.[5] Native-born white women were extravagantly praised but in ways that emphasized their importance in what Hilary Beckles calls "the reproduction of freedom." They were progenitors of future generations of white patriarchs and were upholders of moral values and sensibilities.[6] Respectable mothers and matrons, white women were valued for domestic formality and respectability. As Barbara Bush notes, after the middle of the eighteenth century, "the now leisured white women became the embodiment of modesty and respectability, but also the victims of a rigid double-standard of morality."[7] It was upon black and colored women that white male sexual fantasies lingered, not upon white women.

Finally, sexual connections between white men and black women fractured relationships within all segments of Jamaican society. Their effects were particularly traumatic within slave communities, already in travail. Historians have viewed Afro-American and Afro-Caribbean slave behavior in diametrically opposed ways. Some historians have emphasized slave resilience, noting their solidarity against planter oppression and stressing their ability to maintain family relationships and a measure of cultural autonomy under adverse conditions. Other historians have highlighted the savageries of slavery and how they led to significant dehumanization, as masters sought, with considerable success, to obliterate slaves' personal histories.[8]

I incline to the latter interpretation. Slaveowners not only tormented their slaves physically but also subjected them to intolerable psychological stress. Jamaican slaves lived in a world of radical uncertainty, always vulnerable to the depredations of whites and fellow slaves. Unprotected by law, subject to a harsh work discipline, and forced to submit to the wills of often unpredictable masters or else suffer horrific punishments, slaves were cast adrift in a hostile and uncertain sea. This uncertainty was heightened when, as in eighteenth-century Jamaica, slaves were unseasoned migrants from Africa; when the membership of slave communities was ever fluctuating; when individual slaves had little in common with other slaves; and when the only shared experiences that slaves had were those gained through suffering. Instability in eighteenth-century Jamaican slave communities was also pronounced. Disease and malnutrition were rife; the work regime was debilitating; and planters were unconstrained by social opinion inside and outside Jamaica as to how they treated their slaves. That white society was also highly fluid and unstable also accentuated the instability of slave households.

Thistlewood's diaries provide graphic evidence of the radical instability of the slave world. The slaves who populate Thistlewood's diaries are brutalized and psychologically damaged. They lived in slave communities always under threat of attack from whites and from slaves on neighboring plantations. Moreover, they were paralyzed by internal depredations—from Thistlewood, from other resident whites, and from fellow slaves. Slaves were seldom safe. They had little protection from troublemakers within their own community, and even less protection from their white owners and rulers. As Philip Morgan has argued in an exploratory essay on Thistlewood and his slaves, the paternalistic ethos that operated, albeit imperfectly, in the North American plantation colonies, and that afforded slaves some small measure of protection and predictability, was mostly absent from eighteenth-century Jamaica.[9] Whites were free to act as they pleased, without concern for the welfare of their slaves; and they did so, but with purpose. A dominant minority, perpetually fearful of their perilous position in a country where they were vastly outnumbered by slaves (slaves who displayed on several occasions their antagonism to white rule), white men deliberately used terror as a strategy to intimidate slaves, to force slave obedience to their every whim, and to shore up a precarious white dominance.[10]

White men in Jamaica established a highly patriarchal society, but their patriarchy was not an ideology of metaphoric fatherhood in which protection to subordinates was given in return for automatic obedience to the patriarch's will. The patriarchy of Jamaican white men was the patriarchy of dominant males determined to express their dominance through the subjugation of inferiors. Part of that dominance involved the physical repression of other males, especially black males. Thistlewood whipped and punished slaves frequently, savagely, and with little provocation. Moreover, he went to great lengths to devise sadistic punishments that were intended to humiliate and shame slaves. One such punishment Thistlewood named for a slave, calling it "Derby's dose." It involved having a slave defecate in the mouth of a delinquent slave, after which the offending slave's mouth was wired shut.[11] Thistlewood needed to construct such punishments in order to demonstrate that his power to control his slaves was absolute and that slave challenges to such assertions of power would be strongly resisted.[12]

White men's need to show their dominance was also demonstrated in their continual molestations of slave women. The institutional dominance of white men in Jamaica needed to be translated into the personal dominance of strong, violent, and virile men. What better way was there for white men to show the dangerous and feared black man of whites' imagination who was in control than for white men to have the pick of black women whenever they chose? How black men and black women felt about these transgressions can only be guessed at, but it cannot be imagined that they took such violations of their sexual autonomy with equanimity. Undoubtedly, however, white men's continual sexual exploits with slave women considerably weakened the already strife-torn fabric of slave community life. Sexual relations between black women and white men must have complicated existing relationships between black men and black women and must have made dramatically clear blacks' powerlessness against white dominance. They also surely added to the atmosphere of violence that pervaded slaves' lives. Violence was a notable feature of slaves' interactions with each other as well as an essential ingredient in the strained and contentious relations between whites and blacks. Sexual violence no doubt contributed to and accentuated the physical violence that marked the Jamaican slave system.

The effects on slaves' psyches of whites' relentless sexual assaults on slave women are extremely difficult to determine. We are hindered in understanding the innermost world of eighteenth-century Jamaican slaves by the absence of any direct evidence from slaves themselves. Slaves' feelings, thoughts, and worldview can be guessed at only through sources that were neither written by slaves nor constructed with slaves' interests at heart. We are forced to view sexual relations between whites and blacks through the prism of sources left by white observers who made little attempt to understand a people whom they feared. The sorts of issues that most concern contemporary historians are not those that concerned eighteenth-century white Jamaicans. In regard to interracial sex, even an extraordinarily rich source like Thomas Thistlewood's diaries is inadequate. Thistlewood wrote for himself rather than for us and in so doing omitted much of what most interests us. Before we can evaluate the information about sexual relations between Thistlewood and slave women available in his diaries, we need to take stock of what type of evidence is presented in the diaries and ponder how we might best read these texts.

The diaries are problematic. Thistlewood included some things and excluded others in his cataloguing of each day's activities. More importantly, he wrote the diary for purposes that satisfied various needs arising from his particular personality. Thistlewood does not tell us why he kept a diary so assiduously. Nor did he discuss why he wrote his diaries in the form that he did, although the form is quite distinctive. The diaries themselves are small quarto notebooks, each one covering a single year. The entries are regular in form and consistent in the type of activities mentioned. Each evening, Thistlewood wrote down details of his and his slaves' work routines, punishments meted out, monies expended or acquired, people he met and details of his interactions with those people, activities engaged in during the day, illnesses he experienced, books that he read and items of curiosity that he found especially interesting. Included in these bare summaries of the day's events were notes about Thistlewood's couplings, written in an easily translated pig Latin. The principal features of the diary are its regularity—Thistlewood seldom missed an entry over thirty-eight years in Jamaica and seldom deviated from his customary format, in which the day's events were recorded in a flat, serviceable manner—and its singular lack of self-consciousness. The regularity and consistency of the entries indicates how addicted to routine Thistlewood was and how important his diary was to maintaining that routine. Thistlewood's diaries were part of a system of record keeping that also included a daily weather journal and several commonplace books, in which Thistlewood copied out passages of interest from the books that he read. Thistlewood was above all an inveterate list maker and collector of facts. His diaries were one way in which his passion for collecting facts could be advanced and through which his life could be made more orderly and systematic. Thistlewood wrote in order to improve himself, but this passion for self-improvement was entirely intellectual. Thistlewood showed virtually no interest in moral self-reform. A deeply conservative man (as far as it is possible to tell from the very few expressions of opinion noted in the diaries), Thistlewood accepted the world as it was and himself as he was, envisioning his quest for self-improvement as an entirely practical matter.[13]

Thistlewood's lack of introspection is both a virtue and a liability for the historian. On the one hand, his unself-consciousness about how he presented himself in his diaries suggests that the diaries are remarkably honest and accurate. Writing, it appears, solely for himself, obsessed with the recording of facts as they occurred, interested in those facts as facts alone, and incapable or uninterested in using his diary as a means of self-reflection about his behavior, Thistlewood exercised little self-censorship (witness his casual retelling of his sadistic behavior toward Derby) and made no attempt to conceal from future readers any aspect of his life. Most notably, he detailed his sexual activities in an extremely matter-of-fact way. His honesty about the extent of his sexual predations and lack of concern about what these sexual acts implied about his life and character are both extremely uncommon among writers of diaries.[14]

Thistlewood chronicled his sexual conquests in an evenhanded, regular, and consistent way. He described each sexual encounter as an event, concentrating on time, place, and person, rather than on emotions. He always identified his partner either by name, ethnic origin, or (in the case of slaves) owner. He invariably mentioned the time at which the coupling took place, and noted, often very precisely, where it occurred. The only variations in this formula were when the sexual position was unusual (he might note "stans! [standing] backward," for example) or the experience disappointing, at least from his perspective ("Sed non bene" was an occasional laconic remark). He also noted whether other people observed the sexual acts. Thus, on Sunday, 19 August 1750, after one of his first sexual engagements in Jamaica, he noted that he had sex "cum Marina" on his bed, with "Juba there." Finally, Thistlewood noted what payment, if any, he made to his sexual partner. He frequently gave gifts of food or clothing to his regular sexual partners and small sums of money to other slave women. Thus, having had sex with Rosanna ("Sup. Terr: hill Negroe gd"), he gave Rosanna a "Bitt" as payment.[15]

But if Thistlewood's descriptions of his sexual actions can be relied upon as to time, place, and person, his account of his sexual life is still far from complete. The problem here is less with representativeness—Thistlewood's comments on the sexual behavior of other white men suggest that his sexual athleticism was typical rather than extraordinary—than with balance. Thistlewood presented his sexual acts solely as "acts," without attention to the emotional context within which such acts occurred. Moreover, he presented his many couplings solely from his own point of view. He never once indicated any interest in the feelings of his partner about the sex that both had engaged in. Thus, it is impossible to determine when slave women had sex with Thistlewood willingly and when it was forced upon them. The wealth of data provided by Thistlewood's diaries should not blind us, therefore, to the deficiencies inherent in his mode of presentation.

Thistlewood demonstrated in his diaries that he had virtually no capacity for abstract thinking or self-analysis. He made no attempt to stand back from his relentless compiling of facts and events in order to draw patterns of meaning from such minutiae. His lack of concern about the wider meaning of his and others' lives is most apparent in the coldly dispassionate way in which he wrote about his relationship with Phibbah, his long-term mistress and the person to whom he had the strongest emotional attachment. Only once does he give a hint about his true feelings toward Phibbah. In 1757, Thistlewood changed estates and briefly parted company with Phibbah. He noted that his mistress "grieved much" for him and went so far as to write that he pitied Phibbah, as she was a "Poor girl" who was "in Miserable Slavery."[16] But this expression of feeling is singular. The moments of reflection in the diary are so rare as to be remarkable, and they only occur in the context of transformative events in Thistlewood's life: his parting from Phibbah, a major slave revolt, and the deaths of his nephew in 1765 and his mulatto son, John, in 1780.

What we miss as a result of Thistlewood's emotional distance can be partly guessed at through examining the sexual references in a fragmentary diary left by his young nephew. John Thistlewood arrived in Jamaica in 1763 and spent eighteen months working under his uncle before dying in a boating accident in 1765. Unlike his uncle, John was reticent about his sexual experiences. For example, John does not mention keeping a slave mistress, although his uncle notes this fact. But John's diary contains much fuller descriptions of how sexual encounters between white men and black women occurred than in Thomas's diaries. John's diary crackles with sexual tension as he debates whether he should or should not enter into a sexual attachment. His diary counterposes the amorous adventure of a fellow bookkeeper, who first slept with a "mustee, named Sally" and then entertained two white prostitutes, with his own experiences. One of the prostitutes offered herself to John, but he refused her, stating that "I much prefered a Negro wench to either of them." The offer clearly concentrated his mind, for five days later John commented, obliquely, that "this was the first time that I had with my mistress." John provides some reasons why black women might want to sleep with white men. He related on 3 February 1765 how a "negro wench came to persuade me if possible to lay with her." The woman wanted to do so because "she wanted to have a child for a master" but was sure that "she should never have one by him [her own master]." The two agreed to meet "on Monday nite," when it was John's spell to supervise the making of sugar, John noting that the woman was named Lettice and that she "was a very likely wench of the Mandingo Countrey but speaks good English." In a society where whiteness was the key mark of status, a black woman could advance herself through producing a child with white blood. Producing a mulatto child was also a way for Lettice to retain her privileged position as the mistress of a white man.[17]

What would be ideal for a comprehensive examination of white male sexuality in early Jamaica would be a text that combined John Thistlewood's insights into how sexual relations between white men and black women operated with Thomas Thistlewood's wealth of detail about his numerous sexual encounters. This is not to suggest, however, that the historical interest of Thistlewood's diaries is not enormous. One reason why Thistlewood's diaries are so valuable is the sheer number of sexual encounters that he detailed. Thistlewood was not sexually inexperienced before arriving in Jamaica. While in England, Thistlewood carefully numbered the women he slept with, by starting with *A* and proceeding through the alphabet. By 1750, when he left for Jamaica, he had completed a round of the alphabet. His sexual encounters included casual liaisons with "muliers" or prostitutes, an affair with the recently married wife of a friend and employer in his home village of Tupholme, and a relationship with a Lincolnshire woman, Bett Mitchell, that Thistlewood thought would end in matrimony.[18]

Thistlewood did not have sex in Jamaica for four months after his arrival, although he quickly learned that a white man's sexual access to black women was considerable and was socially acceptable.[19] But following his first experience of sex in Jamaica, on 10 August 1750, Thistlewood embarked upon an extremely active sexual life. Between 1751 and 1764, while he was an overseer on Egypt estate, Thistlewood engaged in 1,774 acts of sexual intercourse with 109 women. In other words, to reduce these intimate acts to the banality of statistics, in an average year Thistlewood coupled 126.7 times and had 7.8 different partners.

Yet within these impressive totals of sexual activity significant patterns can be traced. First, sex was a form of physical release for Thistlewood. He had sex on a regular basis with a large number of different partners, many of whom he never had sex with again. Of his 109 partners up to 1764, 69 had sex with him just once while only 18 had sex with him more than ten times. From Thistlewood's perspective, we can call him a sexual opportunist or sexual enthusiast; from the viewpoint of the female slaves under his care, Thistlewood was the quintessential sexual predator, continually exploiting his slaves' bodies and disrupting their lives in an extremely objectionable way. Slave women under Thistlewood's control, in particular, were constantly vulnerable to Thistlewood's predations. He had some form of sexual contact with every woman on the estates that he had care of, save for the very young and the old and infirm.

But while Thistlewood craved sexual release, he also wanted emotional attachment. Although he had many sexual partners, the majority of his sexual congresses were with a principal partner who served as his "wife," and this partner received an overwhelming proportion of his emotional attention as well. From August 1750 until September 1751, when he left his first post, he lived with Marina. Coming to Egypt estate, a sugar plantation owned by William Dorrill and then by Dorrill's son-in-law, John Cope, he took up with Jenny, a Nago slave woman. His relationship with Jenny proved stormy, and Jenny was replaced in his bed by a creole woman named Phibbah. Phibbah lived with Thistlewood from early in 1754 until Thistlewood's death in 1786. In his will, Thistlewood gave orders for his estate to purchase her and then for her to be manumitted.[20] Thistlewood and Phibbah's long involvement, ended only by Thistlewood's death, may not be a conventional love story, but they seem to have had considerable affection for each other, despite philandering on both sides.

Thistlewood operated within a particular sexual culture, influenced by a number of assumptions about the sexual character of white men, white women, and black women. The shared sexual assumptions of white men greatly influenced the type of sexual conduct that they engaged in. The sexual atmosphere of Jamaica, for example, was not the sexual atmosphere of colonial New England. New England towns had remarkably high standards of public morality. Although "ordinary people appear to have followed the devices and desires of their own hearts," with the unmarried, in particular, being "far from . . . erotically repressed," sexual deviations from customary community standards were rare. A pervasive Puritanism made New Englanders fear the spiritual consequences of such deviations, while highly effective community controls within a remarkably consensual society meant that sexual immorality was identified as an affront to the community as much as to God.[21]

Jamaica's sexual culture more closely resembled that of eighteenth-century Britain than that of New England. London's sexual license, in

particular, was notorious. As Lawrence Stone has argued, the period between 1670 and 1810 was sexually permissive, with much celebration of
frank and hedonistic eroticism.[22] Men from all social classes, from gentlemen like James Boswell to Thistlewood himself, in his brief sojourn in
London in the late 1740s, were enthusiastic patrons of the many prostitutes who traversed London's streets. Moreover, they were not deterred
by social opprobrium or twinges of conscience from embarking on numerous other sexual liaisons. Thistlewood's sexual encounters in England
confirms Roy Porter's contention that the sexual culture of eighteenth-
century England was remarkably easygoing and tolerated a good deal of
promiscuous behavior.[23]

Tolerance of white male licentiousness was an even more prominent
feature of eighteenth-century Jamaican society, even if that tolerance was
forced on the part of all except white men. The key fact about Jamaica's
sexual culture was that it allowed extreme latitude to white men, who
acted virtually as they pleased, without needing to fear that they would
suffer any social consequences for their persistent philandering. As a
white man, Thistlewood never had to explain or even hide his sexual behavior in order to fit into respectable white society. Despite openly living
with a slave concubine, he was welcomed at the homes of white planters
and their wives and was not barred from becoming a vestryman or justice
of the peace. Occasionally, moralists lamented white men's lack of sexual
restraint. Planter leaders such as Edward Long and British visitors like
Maria Nugent fulminated against the tendency of whites to luxuriate in
the "goatish" embraces of black or colored women rather than in the
bosom of a white family. Nevertheless, interracial sexual contact was frequent and socially condoned. Lady Nugent's friend, the fabulously
wealthy Simon Taylor, openly paraded his mulatto mistress and his
quadroon children in front of her without any fear of social opprobrium.[24] Indeed, white sexual access to black or colored women appears
to have been a principal reason why white men moved to Jamaica. Sexual opportunity may have helped keep them in the island. The dramatic
growth of a free colored class from the first third of the eighteenth century onward is tangible proof of the extensiveness of the sexual links between white men and their black concubines. The high proportion of mu-
lattoes within the slave population is evidence of the frequency of more
casual sexual contacts.[25]

White men explained their licentiousness and their "infatuation" with
black and colored women as resulting from the lasciviousness of black

women and the passivity of white women rather than arising from their own passionate urges and lack of self-control. White male sexual behavior was greatly shaped by their assumptions about female sexual propensities. Color and climate, they argued, combined to loosen social mores and encourage sexual libidinism. Observers noted that Europeans seemed overpowered by a tropical climate that stirred their nervous systems "to sudden and violent emotions of the mind." The climate, one author noted, "so changes the Constitution of its Inhabitants that if a woman land there as chaste as a Vestal, she becomes in forty eight Hours a perfect Messalina." As this quote suggests, initially white women were not exempted from the infidelity-inducing effects of the tropical sun. But they gradually lost their reputation for being, as John Taylor put it in 1688, "vile strumpets and common prostitutes." As the plantation economy matured and as women's participation in that economy receded in importance, the seventeenth-century characterization of white women as sexually avaricious gave way to a discourse in which all but the poorest women were seen as icons of propriety. This virtue was achieved, however, less by intrinsic goodness, than by an all-enveloping proscription on female infidelity, especially infidelity with black men. John Stedman, an adventurer in late eighteenth-century Surinam, summed up the Caribbean double standard: "Should it be known that any European female had an intercourse with a slave . . . [the woman] is forever detested and the slave loses his life without mercy—such are the despotic laws of men over the weaker sex."[26]

The lascivious white woman was replaced in white men's imagination by the sexually insatiable black woman. The stereotype of "hot constitution'd" black women, unburdened by restrictive moral codes, who "refused to confine themselves to a single connexion with the other sex" and who "made no scruple to prostitute themselves to the Europeans for a very slender profit" was easily accepted by white men eager for sexual adventure. As J. B. Moreton argued, white "children of the sun" found African manners and customs so "native and congenial to their hearts" that they became "eternal votaries to the revels of Bacchus and Venus" and "luxuriously and voluptuously" spent their nights in "dissipations dear delightful downy lap." The black woman was so eager for sensual delight that commentators argued that white men were powerless to resist her. Edward Long imagined the powers of black "quashebas" to be almost superhuman, exclaiming that "in her well-dissembled affection, in her tricks, cajolements and infidelities," the black woman "is far more perfectly versed than any adept of the Drury." Black women were described as heavily eroticized "sable queens," who bestowed "unbought raptures" on their fortunate partners.[27]

Thistlewood shared these assumptions about the sexual characters of white and black women. Blacks, he thought, were insatiable, sensual. Soon after arrival, for example, he commented that a female slave wanted to borrow his razor to shave her belly. "Many Creol men and women shave their affairs," he noted, observing also that "In Jamaica some are so sensual as to desire to have jiggers for ye pleasure of allaying ye itching."[28] In the same vein, he noted that negro women who ate too much sugar-cane became "loose and open as tho' [they] had just been concern'd with men" and asserted that "negro youths take unclarified hogs lard to make [their] Member larger."[29]

By contrast, white women were not eroticized in his texts. Thistlewood had few dealings with white women and, for reasons that he did not explain, sought neither to marry or have sex with any white women. In July 1753, he excitedly related how his former shipmate, Dianah Jones, came to visit him, inviting him to come over to where she had set up with a migrant bookkeeper. Thistlewood related that at dinner he "was Mightily Made." Jones told Thistlewood "Many off her Secrets etc.," and Thistlewood enthused about her domestic attainments, commenting that Dianah was "a Suitable Woman" who "Shew'd me a rug off her Working, in imitation off dresden Wash, admirable."[30] Even though Jones and Adams were not married, the qualities that Thistlewood praised in Jones were those of married domesticity: cooking, motherhood, home manufacture. Sexual adventurism, which Thistlewood praised in men (he was particularly impressed with the lurid tales told by his rich but uncouth creole neighbor, "Old Tom Williams")[31] was unacceptable in women. In 1753, he noted a conversation he had had with a man who had lived at Salt River eight years previously and who "told me enough off Mrs Anderson's tricks with a Scotch doctor."[32] Thistlewood clearly disapproved of such "tricks" when undertaken by women, even if he admired similar male infidelities.[33] When he heard a tale about a white woman consorting with a black man, he reported it as an extraordinary and scandalous event: "Mr Mordiner says, reported, Mrs Cocker made free with one of Michigan's Negro fellows! Strange, if true, but scarce to be doubted."[34]

White men, by contrast, had complete freedom of action, unimpeded by any moral scruples about the nature of their sexual behavior. The openness of white men's sexual interactions with black women demonstrated how much power white men exercised within the slave system, a system that was consciously shaped to accommodate white men's interests. Power relations within both white society and black communities were heavily skewed toward maintaining the power of white men. The inequality of power relations in Jamaica complicate and confuse our understanding of Thistlewood's sexual history. It is almost impossible, for example, to discern which of Thistlewood's sexual encounters were the result of mutual, consensual passion; which were rapes; which were alternatives to other forms of punishment; and which were regarded by slave women as either a disagreeable duty that they were expected to provide for white supervisors or a calculated act that might bring them tangible benefits. The point in any event is moot. The powerlessness of the black woman in sexual relations with white men meant that violent rape and coercive mechanisms of sexual manipulation were little different in reality: the social reality of plantation life made rape, in Orlando Patterson's words, "unnecessary since the slave negress soon gave in to the overwhelming pressures and made the best of its rewards."[35]

Power relations between blacks and whites were so unequal that to talk of the possibility of truly consensual sexual relations may be fanciful.[36] Indeed, some commentators, looking at the unequal power relations between slaves and masters, have considered all interracial sexual relations within slavery to be forms of rape.[37] Clearly, Thistlewood's female slaves lived in a world of systematic sexual coercion, where at any time they were potential victims of sexual exploitation. Female slaves suffered, through their presumed sexual availability, from frequent acts of sexual violence, whose consequences were seldom addressed.

Thistlewood was probably a rapist in deed and certainly in thought. He harbored attitudes toward the sexual exploitation of black women that were deplorable, even for men of his time and place. One story he relates speaks volumes about his attitude toward violent sex. A Mr. Banton told Thistlewood "of ye Barb[ados] woman that was rap'd by three of them (at Kingston) in a short space, he ye Middle one yet she laid ye Bastard Child to him and how he made her explain herself."[38] A gang rape of a black woman was only cause for comment when there was a story attached to it. Sex and violence were intimately linked in Thistlewood's mind, even if in his diaries he never describes his sexual actions as violent. But the threat of violence was always there. Thistlewood made clear to female slaves caught transgressing, for example, that they could have sex with him in lieu of other forms of punishment. In February 1753 Clara was absent, "wanting," all one afternoon. On her arrival home, Thistlewood promptly had sex with her "by the Coffee Tree."[39] In September of the same year Thistlewood had sex with "Waadah in the Still House sup floor," having "found her hid there, runaway I suppose."[40] Refusing to have sex with Thistlewood was not an option that was realistically open to any slave woman save Phibbah, whose relationship with Thistlewood was sufficiently well established to allow her to have some say in their sexual interactions. Clara and Waadah, however, knew that they needed to submit to Thistlewood's sexual demands or else receive physical punishment—punishment that may have been all the more severe as a result of their refusals.

Black women's capacity to resist the sexual advances of white men accustomed to having near-absolute power over their slaves was extremely limited, as the following two accounts show. On 12 March 1755, Thistlewood noted that his employer, John Cope, brought a party of six men to Egypt estate, where they caroused. Late in the evening "all except Cope and one other, after being heartily drunk, haw'led Eve separately into the Water Room and were Concern'd with her [.] Weech 2ce [twice] First and last."[41] Thistlewood's tone suggests that he disapproved of this gang rape of an innocent house slave. That he did not punish Eve when she ran away following her ordeal confirms his disapproval of the men's treatment of her. But he did nothing to stop the rape—it was hardly possible for him to do so considering that Cope was his employer—and continued to associate with the men involved in it. Two years previously, however, he had intervened in what was an attempted rape: "At Night Mr Paul Stevens and Thomas Adams going to tear old Sarah to pieces in her hutt, had a quarrel with them. They burnt her and would fire the hutt Note they both drunk."[42] But Thistlewood was not so much concerned at the attack on Sarah as alarmed by the white men's presumption in interfering with his charges and disturbed that Stevens and Adams had attempted to damage estate property. This episode demonstrates how perilous it was for slaves to resist white advances: Sarah got burnt for trying.

The costs of resistance could be high. John Cope, in 1756, following a drinking session with a Mr. McDonald ("who had Eve to whom he gave 6 bitts"), made "Tom fetch Beck from the Negroe's house for himself with whom he was with till morning." Beck, nevertheless, was not his first choice, as events on Monday proved, when Cope ordered "Egypt Susannah and Mazerine whipped for refusal."[43] Significantly, Cope's actions so outraged plantation slaves that they exacted revenge on their abusive

owner. Thistlewood tells that "Little Phibbah told Mrs Cope last Satur-
day night's affair. Mrs Cope also examined the sheets and found them
amiss."[44] What is most interesting here is that the slaves' sense of moral
economy had been sufficiently disturbed by the whipping of two slaves
for refusing sexual advances that one slave chose to inform on her master to her master's wife. Slaves had little power, but they did have sources
of information which they could use to their advantage. On occasion, the
private transcript of what slaves actually thought about their master's behavior was made public and countered the master's sense of his total
power and complete impunity from slave retaliation.[45] Nevertheless, the
slaves' ability to punish Cope for his transgressions against their sense of
moral order was minimal. Cope was able to continue his nocturnal visits
to the slave quarters, and the whipped slaves received no recompense for
what their peers believed was wrongful punishment. Moreover, John
Cope's young wife, Molly, was forced to turn a blind eye to her husband's
continuing infidelities. He suffered no harm from the discovery of his nocturnal activities. Indeed, he became in the 1770s an assemblyman and the
chief magistrate of the parish.

Thistlewood's diaries offer more than just quantification of his sexual
encounters. The diaries demonstrate how complex were the sexual relations between white men and black women. White men gained pleasure
and power from their relations with black women. But, in so doing, they
blurred the distinctions between white and black, disrupting the fiction
that the black world and the white world were entirely separate. Interracial relations gave black women entree into a white world supposedly
closed to them. It was for this reason that moralists and committed white
supremacists such as Edward Long condemned white men's "infatuated
attachments to black women."[46] Slave women often achieved power
within the slave community as a result of their entanglement with masters and were not averse to exploiting their connections with white men
to their own advantage. Conversely, white men's "infatuated attachments" to slave women meant that the ordinary rules governing black
and white interaction were discarded, when white men wished to bestow
favors on slave mistresses. White men's ability to form connections with
slave women resulted from their power within the slave community and
was a demonstration of that power, but their control over the power they
exercised was lessened by their ensuing emotional dependence on slave
women. Women's agency within these relationships caused some slippage
in the all-encompassing structures of white male dominance and allowed

a minority of women to create a space for themselves within these structures where they could exercise a limited but measurable power of their own. The strict lines demarcating white from black, male from female, propertied from nonpropertied thus became blurred by the social and sexual relationships white men and black women formed with each other. Occasionally, white men's emotional attachment to black women led them to betray their unconditional allegiance to the absolute dominance of white over black.

An examination of Thistlewood's acerbic comments on the contentious relationship that his subordinate, William Crookshanks, had with his slave lover, Myrtilla, sheds some light on how a slave could obtain advantages from concubinage with white men. Crookshanks arrived on Egypt estate early in 1754 and was soon having sex with his female charges. In May "Bess became William's bedfellow," and in June he suffered the usual consequence of sex in Jamaica, for Thistlewood notes that William was "afraid he has got the Clap."[47] In January 1755, William was enamored with Myrtilla, whom, in Thistlewood's opinion, quickly had Crookshanks wrapped around her little finger. On 13 February Thistlewood noted with derision, "Myrtilla very ill, it is thought she is going to miscarry. William Cry's sadly, the more fool he, as it is probably is for Salt River Quaw." Crookshanks was infatuated with Myrtilla, visiting her constantly, and agreeing, seemingly at her insistence, to hire her from her owner, Mrs. Mould. Myrtilla's hire cost £20, but it was not a good bargain: in a full year she worked 244 days and earned for Crookshanks only £15.2.6. As far as Thistlewood was concerned, Myrtilla was a malingerer, willing to pretend sickness in order "to put William to a needless Charge through Spite." The hiring arrangement failed, and Mrs. Mould resolved to take Myrtilla back to her estate. This removal precipitated a crisis for the besotted William, who went to the Moulds' house and abused Myrtilla's owners "in an extraordinary manner." William realized at this juncture that he had gone too far and, crying, begged the Moulds' forgiveness. Crookshanks's questioning how the Moulds' treated their slaves and his verbal abuse of the Moulds led to a reprimand from his employer, Mr. Cope, much to Thistlewood's satisfaction.[48] William's conduct can be explained by the fact that Myrtilla was heavily pregnant, giving birth to a "mulattoe girl" on 15 March. His lenient treatment of Myrtilla, however, continued to cause comment: in 1756 Thistlewood observed that there were "Many reports about Mr William Crookshanks, particularly in regard to his humouring Myrtilla."[49]

This case is revealing in two respects, even if our understanding of it is clouded by Thistlewood's evident distaste for both Myrtilla and Crookshanks. First, Myrtilla made the most of her involvement with a white man, even a white man of low status. Being Crookshanks's mistress was a means whereby Myrtilla could escape work. She gained other benefits, as Crookshanks occasionally gave her gifts and clearly doted on her, even if on one occasion, at least, he beat her. Having Crookshanks's child was tangible proof of their involvement but also may have helped persuade Mrs. Mould to allow her to stay near William, in the reasonably good conditions at Egypt, rather than return to field labor on the savanna.[50]

Second, Crookshanks's weakness for Myrtilla weakened his standing within white society. In Thistlewood's view, Crookshanks had made a fool of himself by his leniency to Myrtilla. Hiring her had only encouraged Myrtilla to shirk work and had cost him money. More seriously, his "extraordinary" abuse toward fellow whites and his questioning of the Moulds' treatment of slaves had breached one of the fundamental principles undergirding Jamaican social relations: slaveholders' control of their slaves as absolute and sacrosanct. William was out of order in not recognizing the absolute property rights of owners over slaves, especially as he himself did not own slaves. Cope's rebuke to his employee was consequently entirely justified: Crookshanks had betrayed tribal mores.

As this account illustrates, sexual relations between blacks and whites complicated the seemingly rigid but actually fluid etiquette surrounding slavery, property rights, and white supremacy. Whites gained much through their sexual connections with blacks: sexual pleasure, information about slave habits and customs, and a conduit into the slave community. But interracial sex was a fissure in the brick wall of white dominance. It allowed slaves entry into the white world; it occasionally caused whites to side with their black paramours rather than with their fellow whites; it could conflict with property rights; and it could sour relations between white men who were supposed to stick together. Moreover, when sexual attraction led to affection, and then to the granting of special privileges, or even freedom to a black mistress, or when a sexual union resulted in children who were neither properly white nor properly black, then the strict lines demarcating black from white, slave from free, became clouded. Sexual contact, therefore, was an important area in which the public transcript, to use James C. Scott's phrase, of what relations between white and black should be did not match the hidden transcripts of the real relationships between blacks and whites created in the privacy of bedroom, curing house, and cane field.[51] What was negotiated in these private encounters modified and cut across the strict ideological divide between black and white, a divide that in theory separated whites and blacks into two distinct castes.

A minority of black women tried to make the best of their uneasy situation as the sexual playthings of white men. Having sex with Thistlewood could be turned to a woman's advantage. As noted above, Thistlewood often gave his regular partners money or produce as a reward for having sex with him. Such sums of money could be considerable. In 1760, two of Thistlewood's partners, Egypt Susannah and Mazerine, earned money from their sexual encounters that was the equivalent of the amount needed to buy either food to feed themselves for half a year or to purchase half a pig each. Slave women were active participants in a dynamic internal commerce, and earnings from prostitution was one means whereby slave women could kick-start their entrepreneurial activities and enhance their likelihood of someday owning property.[52] Slave mistresses of white men were particularly adept in turning their liaisons into commercial gain. Partly through her connection with Thistlewood and partly through her own hard work and astute business sense, Thistlewood's mistress, Phibbah, became a woman of considerable property, by slave standards. By the mid–1760s, she owned livestock and household utensils and was wealthy enough to lend Thistlewood money. At his death, Thistlewood was still in debt to Phibbah: the last entry made by the appraisers of his estate concerned a cow that was claimed "by the old woman that lives with Mr Thistlewood."[53]

Nevertheless, if a few slave women achieved measurable benefits from their association with white men, the overall effects of white men's sexual exploitation of black women on slave communities seem to have been mostly detrimental. In part, this conclusion rests on a reading of Thistlewood's diaries: his sexual opportunism must have reinforced for slaves their already strong sense of helplessness against white domination and must have encouraged in them feelings of shame and self-loathing. These feelings in turn probably induced among slaves self-destructive and antisocial behavior.[54] But this conclusion also derives from an evaluation of the evidence in the diaries about slaves' interactions with each other. The psychological damage suffered by slaves living under traumatizing conditions and in a radically unstable society was especially apparent in slaves' sexual interactions. The tyranny that slaveholders exercised over their slaves, the constant dehumanization that slaves experienced under that tyranny, and the extreme instability and violence that marked slave plantations brutalized slaves. Subjected to constant violence themselves, they were quick to resort to violence against each other. The result was that slaves found it very difficult to maintain order in their own communities, especially since they emulated their masters in giving little respect to the integrity of established slave relationships. Consequently, the slaves under Thistlewood's care experienced marked domestic discord. Monogamy was as unfashionable among blacks as among whites, and slaves changed partners with at times dizzying rapidity. In some respect, slaves, in their tolerance of promiscuity, merely followed sexual customs inherited from West Africa, where polygamy was an established practice. But whereas in Africa polygamy operated within a secure social context and served to reduce domestic friction, in Jamaica African rules governing polygamous relationships no longer worked.[55] Male slaves, in particular, found it difficult to cope with the radically changed sexual climate of Jamaica, where traditional African assumptions about the proper relationship of men and women no longer held. A skewed sex ratio, combined with the propensity of some slave women to reserve themselves for white men, meant that many black men were left without partners. Competition for women was thus keen and disputes often arose when men found their "rights" to sexual access frustrated or challenged. Thistlewood's diaries are full of references to slave infidelities: on 16 March 1752, for example, he noted that "Sancho found Morris sleeping with Quasheba his wife," while on 2 April 1757 he heard that "Cobbena catchd London and Rosanna (Cobbena's wife) at work upon London's bed."[56] Sexual tension within slave communities was heightened by changes in sexual mores. As Michael Mullin has perceptively argued, women had considerably more say, more power, and more independence in domestic arrangements in Jamaica than they did in Africa. Slave men were dominant within slave communities, but their authority was precarious and was shaken by the ability of some slave women to insist on their own sexual independence.[57] The peculiar conditions of slavery rendered black men's attempts to control the sexuality of black women problematic. Changed gender expectations may have increased demoralization among slave men.[58] This topic warrants more detailed investigation than is possible here, but it seems that the social and sexual relationships that slaves formed with each other had their own dynamics and that these dynamics were greatly affected, first, by the radical uncertainty that marked the lives of slaves and, second, by predatory white men's continual disruptions of their lives.

Thistlewood used such a sexual climate to advance his management of the estate. Slaves often needed to refer disputes involving sexual infidelity to Thistlewood, an outside intermediary who had the power to adjudicate and punish. Sometimes he interfered; sometimes he punished transgressors; sometimes he left slaves to mete out justice themselves. Thistlewood found out about the infidelity of Sancho's wife because Sancho complained to him. Thistlewood "advised them to part, which they accordingly did." When London molested Hannah in 1755, Thistlewood, "upon Hannah's complaint Whipp'd London, he went to complain to his Master and Mistress, but they wld not hear him then he Absconded." In the case of Cobbena, however, he let Cobbena act the part of the master, not punishing her when she gave London "a good thumping."[59] To a limited extent, Thistlewood did recognize slave relationships and honored slave rights in these relationships. Although he did not hesitate to have sex with whomever he pleased, disregarding other claims on a woman's sexuality, he did recognize slave familial arrangements to the extent of never engaging in sex in the slave quarters. He also tried to prevent whites under his control from interfering too blatantly with what he considered to be the rights of male slaves (especially high-status male slaves, such as slavedrivers) over their partners. In 1765, for example, he reprimanded his nephew for sleeping with Little Mimber, the partner of Johnnie, a slavedriver. The fact that his nephew John had to be reprimanded, however, demonstrates how difficult it was for slaves to stop whites from intruding into their domestic affairs.[60] Moreover, the fact that the most important slave within the slave community had to resort to Thistlewood's authority to secure his sexual "rights" and thus demonstrate his willingness to recognize Thistlewood's power on the plantation shows how Thistlewood could exploit the chaotic conditions that characterized slave life—chaos that he, through his sexual opportunism and ready resort to violence, in large measure helped create—to solidify his hold over a harassed, tormented, and brutalized slave population.

Thistlewood died in 1786, two years before the abolitionist movement began to make serious inroads against the Jamaican plantocracy. His sexual practices had little effect on his social standing in his local community. White male sexual adventuring with black women was both commonplace and socially acceptable. Some commentators did criticize white men such as Thistlewood for their unwillingness to marry white women and propagate white children. But such criticism focused on how white men's "infatuated attachments" to women who were not of their race impeded

TREVOR BURNARD

colonization and prevented Jamaica from emulating more fully the parent civilization of Britain.[61] Abolitionists, however, attacked the licentiousness of white Jamaican men from a different angle, an angle, moreover, that attacked the beliefs of white Jamaicans at their very core. For abolitionists, firmly attached to the developing culture of sensibility and middle-class bourgeois propriety of late eighteenth- and early nineteenth-century Britain,[62] white men's sexual immorality was damning proof that a society based on slavery promoted godlessness. Evangelicals interpreted white men's fondness for "fornication and adultery" as sins and condemned Europeans' sexual licentiousness as emblematic of the degenerate and backward character of life in the West Indies and as proof of the evil nature of slavery.[63] Slavery became, within this discourse, the embodiment of the sin that evangelicals wished to purge from the world and slaveholders the living example of it. In their attempts to arouse public outrage against slavery, abolitionists emphasized, in narratives expressly intended to shock English middle-class audiences, the sexual aggression of powerful, degenerate, violent white men—the latter day descendants of Thistlewood—against virtuous, victimized black women. That these narratives valorized a particular type of gender relations in especially voyeuristic and problematic ways did not reduce their effectiveness in the abolitionist crusade against slavery.[64] Thistlewood did not face much criticism in his lifetime for his sexual behavior, but the sexual opportunism that he practised was to become, for a later generation, a perceived flaw in the character of white men in the Caribbean, undermining their fervent defense of the slave system that sustained their fortunes and their pleasures.

NOTES

1. The Thistlewood diary is in thirty seven volumes in Monson MSS, Lincoln County Record Office, England (Monson 31/1–37). Each volume covers a single year. I cite the diary simply by the date of the entry. I wish to thank Lord Monson for giving permission to quote from the diary. A useful introduction to the diary is Douglas Hall, *In Miserable Slavery: Thomas Thistlewood in Jamaica, 1750–86* (London: Macmillan, 1989).

2. For incisive analyses of the significance of interracial sexuality in colonial settings see, in particular, the ongoing work of Ann Laura Stoler: "Rethinking Colonial Categories," *Comparative Studies in Society and History* 31 (January

1989): 134–61; "Sexual Affronts and Racial Frontiers: European Identities and the Cultural Politics of Exclusion in Colonial Southeast Asia," *Comparative Studies in Society and History* 34 (July 1992): 514–51; and *Race and the Education of Desire: Foucault's History of Sexuality and the Colonial Order of Things* (Durham, N.C., and London: Duke University Press, 1995).

3. Trevor Burnard, "Inheritance and Independence: Women's Status in Early Colonial Jamaica," *William and Mary Quarterly* 3d ser., 48.1 (1991): 111–12; "Family Continuity and Female Independence in Jamaica, 1665–1734," *Continuity and Change* 7.2 (1992): 194.

4. Edward Long, *The History of Jamaica* . . . , 3 vols. (London, 1774; rpt. London: Frank Cass, 1970), 2.328.

5. These themes will be developed at length in a future monograph on the society and demography of free people in seventeenth- and eighteenth-century Jamaica. For an initial exploration of some of these themes, see Trevor Burnard, "A Failed Settler Society: Marriage and Demographic Failure in Early Jamaica," *Journal of Social History* 28.1 (1994): 63–82.

6. Hilary McD. Beckles, "White Women and Slavery in the Caribbean," *History Workshop* 36 (Autumn 1993): 69.

7. Barbara Bush, "White 'Ladies,' Coloured 'Favourites' and Black 'Wenches': Some Considerations on Sex, Race and Class Factors in Social Relations in White Creole Society in the British Caribbean," *Slavery and Abolition* 2 (December 1981): 249.

8. These debates, of course, have a long history. The initial positions were laid down by sociologist Melville J. Herskovits and anthropologist E. Franklin Frazier. Frazier, *The Negro Family in the United States*, rev. ed.(Chicago: University of Chicago Press, 1948), 1–69; Herskovits, *The Myth of the Negro Past* (Boston: Beacon Press, [1941] 1958). In regard to Jamaica, Orlando Patterson is the chief exponent of Frazier's position. Patterson argued that the totality of masters' control over slaves, combined with the horrors of the Middle Passage, caused a complete breakdown of all major institutions that could have maintained African-based society or culture. *The Sociology of Slavery: An Analysis of the Origins, Development and Structure of Negro Slave Society in Jamaica* (London: Macgibbon & Kee, 1967). Edward Brathwaite's *The Development of Creole Society in Jamaica, 1770–1820* (Oxford: Oxford University Press, 1971) is an influential application of Herskovits's theories to Jamaica. Brathwaite stresses how persistent African influences were in the creation of a creole culture. A useful synthesis of the two positions that tends toward the Herskovits position is Sidney W. Mintz and Richard Price, *An Anthropological Approach to the Afro-American Past: A Caribbean Perspective* (Boston: Beacon Press, 1992). Richard S. Dunn, in his continuing work on the slaves of Mesopotamia estate, emphasizes that Caribbean slavery was one of the most brutally dehumanizing systems ever devised. "Sugar

Production and Slave Women in Jamaica," in Ira Berlin and Philip D. Morgan, eds., *Cultivation and Culture: Labor and the Shaping of Slave Life in the Americas* (Charlottesville: University of Virginia Press, 1993), 49–72.

9. Philip D. Morgan, "Three Planters and Their Slaves: Perspectives on Slavery in Virginia, South Carolina, and Jamaica, 1750–1790," in Winthrop D. Jordan and Sheila L. Skemp, eds., *Race and Family in the Colonial South* (Jackson, Miss., and London: University Press of Mississippi, 1987), 73–74.

10. For a highly suggestive ethnography of terror as a strategy for cowing slaves in colonial North America, see Rhys Isaac, "On Explanation, Text, and Terrifying Power in Ethnographic History," *Yale Journal of Criticism* 6 (Spring 1993): 217–36. For examples of Jamaican slaves' violent resistance to white power, see Michael Craton, *Testing the Chains: Resistance to Slavery in the British West Indies* (Ithaca, N.Y.: Cornell University Press, 1982), 61–98, 125–39, 172–79, 211–23, 291–322.

11. 28 January, 26 May 1756.

12. For an initial exploration of the significance of violence within the Jamaican slave system, see Trevor Burnard, "'They Do Not Like Their Will to Be Thwarted': The Household and Household Violence in Thomas Thistlewood's Jamaica," in Christine Daniels, ed., *Over the Threshold: Intimate Violence in Early America, 1640–1865* (London: Routledge, forthcoming).

13. It is interesting to compare Thistlewood's inattention to moral self-improvement with William Byrd's obsessive quest for self-mastery. Kenneth Lockridge, *The Diary, and Life, of William Byrd II of Virginia, 1674–1744* (Chapel Hill: University of North Carolina Press, 1987).

14. Lawrence Stone has commented on how infrequently diarists detail their sexual activity. *The Family, Sex, and Marriage in England, 1500–1800* (New York: Harper & Row, 1977), 546–47. For insightful analyses of the sexual lives of other eighteenth-century colonial Americans living in plantation societies, see Kenneth Lockridge, *On the Sources of Patriarchal Rage: The Commonplace Books of William Byrd and Thomas Jefferson and the Gendering of Power in the Eighteenth Century* (New York: New York University Press, 1992); and Kathleen Brown, *Good Wives, Nasty Wenches, and Anxious Patriarchs: Gender, Race, and Power in Colonial Virginia* (Chapel Hill: University of North Carolina Press, 1996), 328–34.

15. 10 November 1759.

16. 17 July 1757.

17. John Thistlewood's diary can be found in Monson 31/38. (See note 1 above.)

18. Thistlewood's sexual history helped determine his sudden decision to leave Lincolnshire in order to travel first to East India and then to Jamaica. On 19 December 1745, Thistlewood was served a warrant charging him with fathering a bastard child. The child was stillborn. Thistlewood left Lincolnshire soon after.

His move to Jamaica seems to have been precipitated by the rejection of his marriage proposal to Bett Mitchell by Bett's parents.

19. On arriving in Antigua en route to Jamaica, Thistlewood noted that "Some black girls laid hold of us and would gladly have had us gone in with them" (13 April 1750). Four days after his arrival, Thistlewood met one of the oldest residents in Jamaica, William Cornish, aged eighty-one, and noted that Cornish "keeps a genteel mulatto girl" (27 April 1750). That this did not affect Cornish's social standing must have been readily apparent even to a newcomer.

20. Wills 52/77 (1786), Island Record Office, Spanishtown, Jamaica.

21. Roger Thompson, *Sex in Middlesex: Popular Mores in a Massachusetts County, 1649–1699* (Amherst: University of Massachusetts Press, 1986), 195–200. For a useful compendium of current knowledge on British North American sexual practices, see David Hackett Fischer, *Albion's Seed: Four British Folkways in America* (New York: Oxford University Press, 1989), 87–93, 298–306, 498–502, 680–83.

22. Stone, *Family, Sex, and Marriage,* 339: Robert Darnton, "Sex for Thought," *New York Review of Books,* 22 December 1994, 65–74.

23. Roy Porter, "Mixed Feelings: the Enlightenment and Sexuality in Eighteenth-Century Britain," in Paul-Gabriel Boucé, ed., *Sexuality in Eighteenth-Century Britain* (Manchester: Manchester University Press, 1992), 9. The similarities between London's sexual culture and Jamaica's are not surprising. Perhaps 60 percent of migrants to Jamaica came from London or the Home Counties. The demography of both places was also remarkably similar. The major difference, of course, was Jamaica's racial makeup. A second difference was the greater variety of sexual possibilities in London. This is discussed further in Burnard, "Inheritance and Independence," 93–114. For sexual subcultures in London, see Randolph Trumbach, "Sex, Gender, and Sexual Identity in Modern Culture: Male Sodomy and Female Prostitution in Enlightenment London," *Journal of the History of Sexuality* 2 (October 1991): 186–203.

24. Long, *History of Jamaica* . . . , 2:328; Philip Wright, ed., *Lady Nugent's Journal of Her Residence in Jamaica from 1801 to 1805* (Kingston: Institute of Jamaica, 1966), 29, 87.

25. For free coloreds and blacks in Jamaica, see Brathwaite, *Development of Creole Society,* 167–75. B. W. Higman estimates that 10 percent of the slave population was colored in 1832. *Slave Population and Economy in Jamaica, 1807–1834* (Cambridge: Cambridge University Press, 1976), 142.

26. Long, *History of Jamaica,* 2:267, 3:542–43; [William Pittis], *The Jamaican Lady; or The Life of Bavia* . . . (London, 1720), 35; John Taylor, "Multum in Parvo or Taylors Historie of his Life and Travells in America and othere parts," MS 105, Institute of Jamaica, Kingston, 1:503; Richard Price and Sally Price, eds., *Stedman's Surinam: Life in an Eighteenth-Century Slave Society* (Baltimore and London: Johns Hopkins University Press, 1988), 242.

27. William Smith, *A New Voyage to Guinea* . . . (London, 1744), 146; J. B. Moreton, *West India Customs and Manners* . . . (London, 1793), 78; Long, *History of Jamaica* . . . , 2:328, 331; [Rev. Isaac Teale], "The Sable Venus—An Ode" (Jamaica, 1765), in Bryan Edwards, *The History, Civil and Commercial, of the British Colonies in the West Indies* 5 vols. (London, 1801), 2:28.

28. 17 July 1750.

29. 26 February, 10 May 1751.

30. 25 and 29 July 1753.

31. Williams entertained Thistlewood with a story about how, after a female domestic had cleaned his hall unnecessarily, "he shit in it and told her there was something for her to clean" (17 July, 1751). His coarseness could slip into brutality: he "killed a Negro girl of his own that had got looseness, stopping her A— with a cornstick" (19 March 1752).

32. 10 July 1753.

33. One exception to this admiring tone is his attitude toward John Cope's indiscretions, but that can be explained by his closeness to Cope's wife, Molly.

34. 11 June 1758.

35. Patterson, *Sociology of Slavery*, 160.

36. Orlando Patterson notes: "I know of no slaveholding society in which a master, when so inclined, could not exact sexual services from his female slaves." Also: "What masters and slaves do is struggle: sometimes noisily, more often quietly; sometimes violently, more often surreptitiously; infrequently with arms, always with the weapons of the mind and soul." *Slavery and Social Death: A Comparative Study* (Cambridge: Harvard University Press, 1982), 173, 207.

37. See Ann duCille, "'Othered' Matters: Reconceptualizing Dominance and Difference in the History of Sexuality in America," *Journal of the History of Sexuality* 1 (July 1990): 116–21, for a trenchant assertion that all interracial relations within slavery "invariably occurred in a climate of sexual domination and despotic rule" (120).

38. 8 January 1751.

39. 1 February 1753.

40. 16 September 1753.

41. 12 March 1755.

42. 20 February 1753.

43. 2–5 May 1756.

44. 5 May 1756.

45. For the idea that public and private transcripts governed discourses within slavery, see James C. Scott, *Domination and the Arts of Resistance: Hidden Transcripts* (New Haven: Yale University Press, 1990).

46. Long, *History of Jamaica* . . . , 2:327.

47. 15 May, 5 June 1754.

48. 13 February, 26 February, 15 October 1755; 24 February, 26 February 1756.

49. 15 March, 25 September 1756.

50. 17 April 1756.

51. Scott, *Domination and the Arts of Resistance*, 13–14.

52. Bush, *Slave Women in Caribbean Society*, 33–45.

53. Inventories, 71/206 (1787), Jamaica Archives, Spanishtown, Jamaica. For examples of Thistlewood borrowing money from Phibbah, see 5 September 1755; 29 February and 3 September 1756.

54. For an amplification of such remarks, see Burnard, "'They Do Not Like Their Will to Be Thwarted.'" An important work on the psychological damage exacted by living under slavery, especially for male slaves, is Bertram Wyatt-Brown, "The Mask of Obedience: Male Slave Psychology in the Old South," *American Historical Review* 93 (December 1988): 1228–52.

55. Madeleine Manoukian, *Akan and Ga-Adangme Peoples* (London, 1950), 26–31; M. D. McLeod, *The Asante* (London, 1981), 30–31.

56. 16 March 1752; 2 April 1757.

57. Michael Mullin, *Africa in America: Slave Acculturation and Resistance in the American South and the British Caribbean, 1736–1831* (Urbana: University of Illinois Press, 1992), 171.

58. Patterson, *Sociology of Slavery*, 178–81.

59. 16 March 1752; 30 June 1755; 2 April 1757.

60. 4–6 February 1765.

61. Thomas Atwood, *The History of Domenica* (London, 1791), 209–10; Long, *History of Jamaica . . .*, 2:327.

62. G. J. Barker-Benfield, *The Culture of Sensibility: Sex and Society in Eighteenth-Century Britain* (Chicago: University of Chicago Press, 1992); K. Sanchez-Eppler, "Bodily Bonds: The Intersecting Rhetorics of Feminism and Abolition," in Shirley Samuels, ed., *The Culture of Sentiment: Race, Gender, and Sentimentality in Nineteenth-Century America* (New York: Oxford University Press, 1992), 92–114.

63. Thomas Coke, *History of the West Indies . . .*, 3 vols. (Liverpool, 1808; London, 1810, 1811), 3:126.

64. For an account of how humanitarianism and the culture of sensibility made the viewing of pain voyeuristic and pornographic, see Karen Halttunen, "Humanitarianism and the Pornography of Pain in Anglo-American Culture," *American Historical Review* 100 (April 1995): 303–34. See also Diana Paton, "Decency, Dependence and the Lash: Gender and the British Debate over Slave Emancipation, 1830–34," *Slavery and Abolition* 17 (December 1996): 163–84.

Chapter 8

Sex, Sexuality, and Social Control in the Eighteenth-Century Leeward Islands

Natalie A. Zacek

A quarter of a century ago, Richard S. Dunn, in what remains the benchmark study of the early development of Britain's West Indian sugar colonies, wrote:

> had the English pioneers been trying to escape from their acquisitive European culture, had they been craving for peace, simplicity, ease, and innocence, they might indeed have found paradise in the Indies. But the English were looking for El Dorado, not Eden. They had geared themselves for wealth, excitement, and violent combat, so they fought and played feverishly in the enervating heat . . . [and] produced a hectic mode of life that had no counterpart at home or elsewhere in the English experience.[1]

Other scholars are far more critical than Dunn in their assessment of the moral character of English West Indian planters and of the societies which they created. Carl and Roberta Bridenbaugh assert that "in the Caribbean men's passions were seldom far from the surface," that "rogues and whores and similar people were the kind generally sent to the Caribbees," and that "good manners and sound morals simply did not exist for the generality of the colonists."[2] A number of more recent monographs have placed a similar emphasis on the seemingly lawless and decadent nature of society in Britain's West Indian possessions, an approach encapsulated by Trevor Burnard's titular description of seventeenth-century Jamaica as "a failed settler society."[3]

The overriding conclusion of these and a host of other scholars is that during the seventeenth and eighteenth centuries the English West Indian colonies were sites of societal failure, especially with respect to the development of behavioral and sexual norms comparable to those which obtained in the metropole. The islanders' unwillingness and/or inability to develop fully those institutions—the Church of England, the courts, the schools—which worked together to regulate social and sexual behavior at home, both caused and was derived from the planters' morally suspect way of life, according to these commentators, and as such is emblematic of the acquisitive and boisterous "Wild West" ethos of these largely male settlements, populated by the dregs of European society.[4] Intent upon making a quick profit and largely unconcerned with replicating European standards of social order, the islanders quickly cast off the restrictions of their home countries and, it seems, devoted themselves to the unrestricted pursuit of drunkenness, gambling, brawling, and, most of all, sex. This idea is exemplified by the lingering legend of Port Royal, Jamaica, a town whose reputation for vice was so great that, when it was completely destroyed by an earthquake in 1692, many observers believed that its ruin was nothing less than the judgment of an angry God on a modern Sodom or Gomorrah.[5]

The idea that early modern English society was sexually restrained and that of the West Indian colonies promiscuous and unfettered is a false dichotomy that has been continuously reified by scholars. This apparently sharp contrast is overdrawn. As Michel Foucault asserts in the first volume of his investigations of the history of sexuality, sexuality is an "especially dense transfer point for relations of power," and as such is never monolithic, even within a particular society.[6] This idea, combined with his conviction that power comes not only from above but also from below, and is constantly diffused through various societal levels and institutions, led Foucault to conclude that there is always and inevitably a significant disjunction between the prescribed sociosexual order and the actual behavior of individuals. Application of this idea within the context of the English Caribbean suggests the possibility that the sexual license of the colonies was not necessarily much greater, and may even in some cases have been less, than that of the metropole.

Early modern Englishmen attempted to frame their society in terms of extreme hierarchy and patriarchy. In their view, society's overriding purpose was to preserve the sacrosanct "Great Chain of Being" and to augment the still limited efficacy of state institutions by encouraging communities to carefully observe and regulate the behavior of their members, particularly in reference to such concerns as bastardy and vagrancy.[7] Ideally, the male head of a household controlled the behavior, particularly the sexual conduct, of everyone resident beneath his roof, including both family members and servants.[8] However, there is considerable evidence that many of these social dictates were observed more in theory than in practice in Britain, particularly in the case of premarital sexual intercourse.[9] On the other hand, sexual practices and taboos were in some respects more repressive in the West Indies than they were in the mother country. One can see such developments at work in the tiny Leeward Island settlements of Antigua, Montserrat, St. Kitts, and Nevis, which never developed as regimented a social or institutional structure as did the larger islands of Barbados and Jamaica, and with which the remainder of this essay is concerned.[10]

It is of course quite apparent that certain expressions of sexual license were far more freely accepted in the islands than they would have been in Britain; this is particularly true in the case of sexual relations between black women and white men. The black woman, whether free or enslaved, was seen almost universally by contemporary white male commentators as predestined by her race and her gender to be of use to white men, so a white man's relations with a black woman required no greater community surveillance or legal regulation than would the man's management of his livestock or other chattels.[11] It was in no way forbidden for a white man to engage in sexual relations with, or even father children by, a black woman; such actions were often deplored by newcomers to the islands, but were accepted as a matter of course by most of the older hands. Even those white men who forswore sexual relations with black women participated in a culture of voyeurism in which the black female body was constructed as a locus of spectatorial pleasure. It was considered perfectly acceptable for white men to savor the spectacle, as they did in the 1750s, of the free black "Bum-boat women"—the double entendre is probably intentional—of English Harbour, Antigua, as they stripped on the docks and swam naked to the Royal Navy warships anchored in the bay, in order to sell their fruits and vegetables to the English sailors. The behavior of these vendors was not a subject of public scandal or censure but was pointed out to male visitors as a picturesque local novelty.[12] Apparently, white male attitudes toward black women's bodies had changed little in the century and a half since Richard Ligon had visited Barbados in the 1640s and found himself utterly enthralled by the sight of the "very large breasts" of young female slaves, "which stand strutting out so hard and firm."[13] Even as thoughtful and open-minded a visitor to the islands as the Scots gentlewoman Janet Schaw believed that black "wenches" were inherently "licentious," based upon her observation that they went about in "little or no clothing" and could "hardly [be] prevailed upon to wear a petticoat."[14]

White women were also commodified as objects of visual pleasure in Leeward society, but in a more subtle manner. Mr. W.S.A.B., a white visitor who attended a Governor's Ball at St. Johns, Antigua, the Leeward seat of government, was sufficiently inspired by the sight of "the sparkling charms of th'Antigonian fair" to compose a lengthy ode in their honor, but his depictions of the women's physical attributes emphasize the modest and innocent appeal of their maidenly beauty, rather than any kind of sexual incitement he might have felt at the sight of it.[15] The charms of these "Beauties" are epitomized in verse by Delia, who "smil'd so innocently gay"; Sacharissa, an "enchanting maid" of "blooming charms"; and Florimel, whose "unaffected innocence . . . unlook'd-for conquest gains."[16] The author's few concrete references to a woman's actual physical appearance emphasize her youth, freshness, and innocence; his mentions of Sacharissa's "soft breast of undissolving snow," Phillida's "soft frame," and "the sweet inclosure" of Amoretta's "ivory teeth," and the substitution of pseudoclassical cognomens for the Antiguan ladies' given names, reveal the idealized nature of his description of the young women and their removal from the arena of casual sexual conquest.

In reality, as W.S.A.B. was quite likely well aware, the Governor's Ball was a well-known entrepôt for the public display of young women of marriageable age, and therefore an important site of the "traffic in women" among the island's elite.[17] Social occasions such as balls were, in fact, highly voyeuristic experiences, but social convention barred male observers from describing female attendees in terms similar to those used to depict the Bum-boat women or slave women at an auction.[18] Such obfuscation, though, does not efface the fact that balls and other elite social occasions were sites of competition based on female sexual attractiveness and male desire. W.S.A.B. may have framed his description of the "Antigonian Beauties" as a paean to their virginal innocence and an announcement of his commitment to maintaining and protecting the chastity of the "innocently gay" against "unlook'd-for conquest," but then, as a mere short-term visitor to Antigua, he was not a participant in this sexual competition, as he was probably not seeking a wife in the islands. Men of the Antiguan elite, though, were most likely assessing the "Beauties" as potential spouses, and therefore as future sexual partners. White women's sexuality was not a contradiction in terms within this society; it was as marked as that of black women, but framed by male observers within the terms of matrimony rather than those of casual conquest.

Sexual values and conduct in the Leeward Islands, then, were structured around a bifurcation in the valuation and treatment accorded to white and black women. As long as these norms were observed, a certain amount of sexual license was allowed, at least to free white men. Difficulties arose, however, when people behaved in a manner which ignored the carefully delineated disjunction between the white virgin or wife and the black Jezebel, particularly when sexual misconduct occurred between white men and white women. The elites of the tiny and inherently unstable white societies of the Leeward Island colonies felt that their dominance was too fragile to withstand the pressures generated by sexually transgressive acts; therefore, sexual behavior among white residents required careful regulation and public enforcement of local laws and mores.[19]

Before we move on to examine cases of sexual transgression among white residents of the Leeward Islands, it is important to stress the always precarious nature of the social order in these islands. Despite their small size, both in land mass and population, the Leeward colonies numbered among Britain's most valued overseas possessions, because of their strategic importance as bulwarks against French, Spanish, and Dutch incursions into the West Indies and the considerable profits which the sugar they produced brought to the mother country. Yet it was these same attributes which made the Leewards tempting prizes and encouraged rival European powers to attack them on numerous occasions, most notably in 1666, when the settlements on Antigua and Montserrat were nearly destroyed by French and Dutch raids. The small size of the white population also encouraged the islanders to constantly fear uprisings of slaves or even of white indentured servants. These fears were in many cases perfectly justified; during the 1666–67 Anglo-Dutch War, Leeward indentured servants, many of whom were Irish by birth and professed Roman Catholics, in several instances turned against their masters and aided the French and Dutch in their raids, while slaves, individually or in groups, frequently rebelled, murdering a particularly brutal master or overseer, destroying property, or, in at least one case, constructing an elaborate plan by which "all the White Inhabitants [of Antigua] . . . were to be murdered, and they [the slaves] intirely to possess the Island."[20] Furthermore, the very geography of settlement in the Leewards created its own particular security problems. Settlers in the mainland colonies of North America knew that they at least possessed the option of flight to the interior if faced with internecine or external attack, but the white inhabitants of the Leewards felt that they had nowhere to which they could run on their tiny islands; even the small interior regions of the several islands promised no refuge, due to their mountainous topography and the presence of hostile encampments of runaway slaves, or maroons.[21]

In addition to these various disadvantages, the Leewards were also weakened by conflicts based on ethnicity and religion, particularly in the cases of St. Kitts and Montserrat. Both of these islands contained significant populations of Irish Catholic servants and ex-servants, who were barred by their religion from owning land and voting for or holding public office. Despised and feared by their fellow islanders, and lacking a material or a political stake in the maintenance of the system, these Irish men and women were seen by wealthier English Protestant planters, often with some justification, as a constant source of discord and rebellion. Moreover, the tremendous upsurge in the profitability of sugar planting which began in the 1660s caused the islands to become increasingly stratified socially and economically, as planters with sufficient capital to invest in the land, slaves, and machinery needed to grow and process the cane slowly forced less prosperous planters off the islands, or at the very least out of the most desirable cane lands.[22]

These various demographic and political constraints, combined with the attitudes about sexuality which the Leeward colonists imported with them from Britain, encouraged colonists to see maintenance of the public order, particularly in the area of sexual behavior, as a priority. Small, isolated, and riven by tensions of religion, ethnicity, race, and rank, the Leeward Islands could not allow sexual transgressions among its white residents to pass unnoticed or unpunished. If community surveillance flourished in a locale such as New England, how much more necessary might it be in the Leewards, colonies "beyond the line" of European statecraft and far more distant both geographically and experientially from the metropole than either the village-based, more demographically balanced settlements of the North or the stable, gentry-dominated plantation societies of the South?[23] New England Puritans might have believed that Satan lurked in the wilderness, but English West Indians feared their own devil of moral and physical corruption, perceived as battening on the hot and humid island climate and the presence of large numbers of blacks.[24] The cost of wealth and imperial dominion in these islands was, it seemed, eternal vigilance, not least against sexual misconduct and the threat which it posed to the already delicate social order.

The forms of sexual misconduct which most troubled the Leeward colonists were: bastardy, incest, adultery, and indecent exposure.[25] Interestingly, prostitution was not a subject of particular public concern, if we may judge from the fact that neither prostitutes nor their clients were fined, imprisoned, or otherwise prosecuted. Prostitution was not considered to be a blameless occupation; at least one Nevis justice of the peace had harsh words for a "common whore," whom he believed was slandering "persons of good Characters," while another Nevisian, one Bartholomew Driscoll, was fined for keeping a "disorderly house," which most likely was some sort of a brothel.[26] On the whole, however, prostitution was not considered to be a truly pressing social problem. Throughout the seventeenth century and into the eighteenth, men tremendously outnumbered women among the white population of the Leewards, so the number of prostitutes at any given time and place was likely to be minimal, and prostitution may have been viewed as a necessary evil to keep unmarried men pacified.[27] Moreover, and perhaps more importantly, these prostitutes were either single women or, in a few cases, widows or women who had been abandoned by their husbands. As such, their availability to a wide variety of men as sexual partners did not impinge as pressingly upon the patriarchal norms of white Leeward society as it might had they not been alone.

In their attempts to maintain social order to the greatest possible degree, island authorities felt it imperative to regulate, and in some cases punish severely, those offenses which they believed directly undermined patriarchal dominance within the family and society. Nonetheless, they were obligated by force of circumstance to allow certain transgressions to pass without censure. These small, fragile societies were in some instances able, if not especially pleased, to accommodate a range of sexual behaviors, particularly miscegenation between white men and black women, which would have been found far less acceptable in England. Nevertheless, the islanders deemed it necessary to resist those expressions of sexual desire which explicitly threatened the ideals of household government and civil society upon which the Anglo-American colonial enterprise was based. In order that some semblance of order might persist in a difficult and frequently threatening physical and cultural environment, the basic rules of social and sexual behavior had to remain fluid, yet at least in some sense meaningful.

The case of Daniel Parke provides a useful illustration of what Leeward society considered the limits of tolerable sexual conduct. Parke, a Virginian by birth, was appointed governor and captain-general of the Leewards in 1705, arrived in the islands the following year, and had served a scant four years of his term when he was murdered by an angry mob of Antiguan residents on December 7, 1710. The assassination of a Crown official by his subjects was a shocking event, and many observers in the mother country saw it as proof positive that the West Indian colonies were degraded and chaotic places, in which the rules of English life and law had fallen into complete disarray.[28]

Parke was in many respects an unsatisfactory head of government for the Leeward colonies. Having hoped to return as governor to his native Virginia, he was extremely dismayed to be posted instead to what he saw as a barbaric and undesirable place of exile.[29] From the moment of his arrival he began to alienate his new subjects, first by antagonizing the powerful and respected Codrington family of Antigua, then by raiding the islands' treasury to build an opulent and much resented Government House in St. Johns. He cemented his ill repute by attempting to establish complete control over appointments to public office in the islands.[30] But however much these actions might have angered Leeward residents, it seems unlikely that in and of themselves they would have led to his murder. After all, an early governor of Montserrat, Roger Osborne, had allegedly murdered Samuel Waad, who was both his brother-in-law and a wealthy island merchant, yet Osborne succeeded in keeping not only his life but even his office. A host of other governors had also been accused of various abuses of power.[31] The aggravating factors in Parke's case, however, related to his sexual behavior in the islands.

As his recent biographer, Helen Hill Miller, has observed, Daniel Parke "had all the vices of a Restoration rake," qualities apparent long before his appointment as Leeward governor.[32] Having spent some years in London in the 1680s and 1690s, he returned to Virginia with an English mistress, by whom he had a son. Returning to England in 1697, Parke abandoned his wife and their legitimate children and brought this consort, whom he attempted to pass off as his widowed "Cousin Brown," with him to London.[33] His relationship with Brown did not escape comment in England and Virginia, but paled in comparison with his behavior in the islands. There Parke, having abandoned Brown, quickly became involved in a large number of liaisons with married women, most notably with Catharine, the wife of Edward Chester, a member of the Assembly of Antigua and the Leeward factor of the Royal African Company.[34]

Parke's affair with Catharine Chester was almost guaranteed to provoke tremendous anger and controversy among members of white Leeward society. Public sympathy took the side of an outraged Edward Chester when he caught Parke in flagrante delicto, "skulking behind the Door of a Room adjoining to Mrs. Chester's bed-chamber." Chester attempted to throw both his erring spouse and her lover out of the house, but when Parke threatened the unarmed man with a sword, the aggrieved Chester was forced to "take in his Wife again, whom he had turned out of doors upon this Occasion."[35] Parke's actions in this altercation showed an utter lack of respect for Chester; they made it clear not only that Parke was carrying on a sexual relationship with Chester's wife, but that Parke was not even sufficiently interested in Catharine to try to bring her into his own bachelor household. By cuckolding Chester to his face and then obliging him through force of arms to continue to live with and financially support an unfaithful wife, Parke displayed complete contempt for Chester as a man and as a husband.

Chester gained still greater reason to detest Parke when, in January of 1710, Parke made a new will, in which he bequeathed "all my estate in these islands, both land and houses, negroes, debts, and so forth . . . for the use of Mistress Lucy Chester, being the daughter of Mistress Katharine Chester."[36] The child in question was clearly a newborn, as "she is not yet christened," yet Parke had already gone to some lengths to make it clear both to Edward Chester and to the community, including the several locally prominent men who served as witnesses to the document, that he, not Catharine's husband, was the infant's father, a claim emphasized by Parke's desire that the child be named Lucy, the name both of Parke's mother and of one of his legitimate daughters in Virginia.[37] As heiress to Parke's substantial fortune and as the namesake of his mother and daughter, the child was brought to public attention as the effigy of Parke's adulterous affair with Catharine Chester, a constant reminder to Edward Chester, and to his community, of Catharine's infidelity.[38]

As no documents remain which might illuminate the affective quality of the relationship between Parke and Mrs. Chester, it is possible to conclude, if impossible to prove, that Parke embarked upon his affair with Catharine at least in part as an attack upon her husband. As the Royal

African Company's representative in the Leewards, Chester controlled the price and availability of slaves to the islands' planters. His position brought him both influence and wealth; he was said to have taunted Parke by informing him that his own annual salary was twice that of the governor, and his power, combined with a talent for clandestine operations, allowed Chester to reap still greater profits as a smuggler.[39] Such a man was an obvious threat to Parke's authority, so what better way was there to symbolically unman and publicly demean him than by cuckolding him and impregnating his wife?[40] The Chester imbroglio, after all, would not have been the first instance in which Parke had chosen to strike at a rival through his wife. In Virginia, having quarreled bitterly with the Reverend James Blair, Parke chose to attack him by seizing the cleric's wife and dragging her from her pew in Williamsburg's Bruton Parish Church in the middle of her husband's Sunday sermon.[41] Although nothing in the historical record implies that Parke was in any way sexually involved with Mrs. Blair, his public manhandling of another man's wife was a sexualized form of assault, even a symbolic rape, and as such brought shame upon the husband who failed to prevent it.

A man could choose to ignore lesser insults, but an undisguised and deliberate assault upon his wife, particularly one of a sexual nature, could not pass unchallenged, especially in a small and competitive society such as that of Antigua. A man's sexual relationship with the lawful wife of another called into question not only the woman's virtue but also her husband's mastery over her, epitomized by his complete control over and unique access to her sexuality and the paternity of her offspring. It is hardly surprising that Governor Parke's adulterous behavior, combined with the host of lesser grievances against him, would inflame "People of such turbulent Spirits and Loose Principles" as those of Antigua to rebellion against and even murder of a royal official.[42] Edward Chester had been overheard to have sworn that he "would gladly lie seven years in Hell to be avenged" against Parke. Such a desire for personal vengeance, when combined with white islanders' various other grudges against Parke, encouraged Antiguans to turn to violence to enforce local norms of sexual behavior against one who blatantly disregarded them.

The married Antiguan women who had consorted with Daniel Parke were judged nearly as harshly by local society for their sexual misconduct as Parke had been. Lucia French, the wife of Parke's close friend and pamphleteering apologist George French, was publicly whipped for her "lewd" and "infamous" behavior, a traditional public punishment for unfaithful wives but one rarely applied to women of the elite.[43] Despite the fact that her husband continued to maintain both her innocence and Parke's probity, the anger and discomfort Parke's behavior had generated within the community required that she be punished for her part in the imbroglio. Elinor Martin escaped physical punishment but was shunned completely by Antiguan society for "having been a known assistant to [Parke] in his lewdness," and was damned further by being accused of having debauched her own daughter.[44] What is significant in these cases is that the accused women were wives; as such, their conduct brought disgrace not only upon themselves but, and perhaps more importantly, upon their husbands, and by extension upon white society itself. Such women did not need to fear for their physical security or freedom but instead suffered a kind of social death when they were excluded from participation at the highest level of their society.

Extramarital sexual behavior was not in itself always an object of censure. The Anglo-Irish adventuress Laetitia Pilkington's memoirs include an anecdote about an aristocratic but impoverished Frenchwoman who served as a lady-in-waiting to the wife of the governor of St. Kitts and who, upon her mistress's death, replaced her both as the governor's hostess and as his lover. Although the man died before his intended marriage to his paramour, the woman in question received no public opprobrium for the liaison; she inherited her lover's entire estate and gained proposals of marriage from a number of eligible islanders.[45] The Frenchwoman's behavior may have been unorthodox, but as an unmarried woman without family in the islands, her conduct did not reflect negatively on a husband, father, or brother and therefore did not merit the sort of punishment meted out to Daniel Parke's married lovers. A woman's extramarital sexual activity was believed, as the case of Daniel Parke has shown, to bring disgrace not merely on her but also, and far more damningly, upon her husband, whose mastery over her, and therefore over all other elements of his existence, would immediately become suspect.[46] The sexual transgressions of an unmarried woman could sometimes be overlooked; those of a wife, never.

The case of Rachel Faucette Levine Hamilton presents an interesting contrast to that of Daniel Parke and his various mistresses. Rachel, the mother of the American statesman Alexander Hamilton, was the daughter of a French Huguenot family of St. Kitts; her father's skills as a physician and his naturalization as an English subject lent the family considerable social standing, despite the financial reverses they suffered shortly after Rachel's birth.[47] In 1745, Rachel, who was then about sixteen, paid a visit to her married sister Ann Lytton in the Danish West Indian colony of St. Croix, where she met the merchant John Michael Levine.[48] Convinced by Levine's "peacock wardrobe" that he was a man of wealth, Mary Faucette, Rachel's mother, urged her daughter to marry the man, despite his being far older than she.[49]

The Levines' marriage quickly devolved into disaster. One of Alexander Hamilton's biographers claims that the problem was simply that "Levine was sedate and elderly; Rachel . . . hot-blooded and young," while another asserts that "Rachel's stubborn nature ran against Levine's desire to dominate and utterly control his wife."[50] Whatever the sources of discord may have been, they were sufficiently powerful that Levine, angered by his belief that Rachel had engaged in extramarital affairs, swore out a formal complaint that she had "twice been guilty of adultery," a claim which resulted in her being confined briefly in the jail of St. Croix's Christiansted Fort.[51] Levine may have meant merely to intimidate Rachel into giving up what he saw as "her ungodly mode of life" and to bend her to his will, but his stratagem backfired. As soon as her husband allowed her to be released from prison, Rachel abandoned him and their young son and, after a short sojourn among friends in Barbados, returned to her mother's home on Nevis.[52]

Shortly after her arrival at Nevis, Rachel met and became romantically involved with her neighbor James Hamilton, a local merchant and a younger son of the Scottish Laird Hamilton of Cambuskeith.[53] Marriage, though, was not an option for the pair; Rachel was still married to Levine, and divorce could only be granted by an act of Parliament.[54] Trying to obtain such a divorce would require far more money and metropolitan influence than either Rachel or Hamilton possessed.[55] Recognizing their predicament, Rachel and Hamilton chose to live together as common-law husband and wife and eventually had two sons.

The couple's relationship was accepted by most of their fellow islanders, and Rachel and Hamilton were treated as man and wife de facto, if not de jure. They appear in the records of the neighboring island of St. Eustatius as "James Hamilton and Rachel Hamilton his wife," having stood as godparents to the son of their friends Alexander and Elizabeth Fraser.[56] The only sign of friction came when their son Alexander became of age to attend the local school; the circumstances of his birth marked him as a bastard and proscribed him from enrolling at a school supervised by the Church of England.

How did Rachel, legally a married woman, manage to avoid the censure of her neighbors for living openly with and bearing children by a man who was not her husband? The answers are several. First of all, Rachel's husband, Levine, was not a resident of the islands; he had been born in Europe and had spent only a few months in the Leewards before returning to the Danish colony of St. Croix, where he had met and married Rachel. Had Levine been in any way a member of their community, the Nevisians might have reacted quite differently to his wife's behavior; the presence on the scene of an angry, cuckolded husband might have brought forth the same kind of public reaction Parke encountered in his entanglement with Edward and Catharine Chester. However, Levine was out of sight and therefore, it seems, out of mind. Furthermore, he was a foreigner, English neither by parentage nor by naturalization, and believed by many to be Jewish.[57] The few Nevis residents who knew Rachel's husband apparently found him to be "a coarse man of repulsive personality," which mitigated any sympathy they may have felt for a dishonored husband.[58] Indeed, it seems that Rachel's most fervent champions were not the Nevisian women, who might have identified with her struggle to escape an unhappy and unwanted marriage and to find a more satisfactory partner of her own choice, but rather the island's men, who chose to see themselves as the protectors of a young, attractive, and, in their opinion, mistreated woman, instead of identifying with a betrayed and abandoned husband.[59] The "patriarchal rage" which might have encouraged Nevis's white male elite to scorn or punish such a publicly unfaithful wife was transmuted into sympathy for Rachel. Admiration of her beauty and intelligence may have played a part in this or indignation at what she had suffered in an unhappy and unwanted marriage, or perhaps a combination of the two.[60]

Secondly, Rachel and Hamilton led a quiet and rather impoverished life, largely outside of the round of social activities. They were not seen by their neighbors as flaunting their unconventional lifestyle, nor did they try to use their connections with well-respected local and European families to demand acceptance into or precedence within the highest echelons of white society. It may be that Rachel's apparent personal unwillingness and/or financial inability to compete for a preeminent position within local society mitigated against her becoming an object of dislike to Nevis's white women. Instead, her readiness to move out of the elite and down the social ladder made it clear to her neighbors that her unorthodox personal life did not threaten the local social order. Finally, it is at least possible that Rachel's unorthodox behavior was excused because she was of French rather than English parentage; if her conduct could be attributed to the influence of her alien blood, it was less threatening to an English settler society.[61] In his analysis of Jean Rhys's island-set novel *Wide Sargasso Sea*, Peter Hulme suggests that English Creole society saw itself as vastly dissimilar from that of white French islanders, whom the former believed to be inherently frivolous, decadent, and amoral.[62]

Rachel Faucette Levine Hamilton escaped the full weight of public censure of her extramarital sexual behavior because her husband, unknown to or disliked by most members of her community, failed to mobilize public opinion against her, and because her transgressions could be viewed as stemming either from her spouse's alleged mistreatment of her or from her non-English background. Rachel's actions may have provoked considerable gossip and at least some disapproval, but they were not perceived as a serious threat to local society and the social order.[63]

The island of Montserrat was the site of another interesting case, one which gave meaning to the old English dictum that "a man's honesty and credit doth depend and lie in his wife's tail."[64] In this case, the issue was not a wife's actual chastity but the fact that a man other than her husband drew attention to her nature as a sexual being by exposing himself to her in front of her husband, thus implying that her spouse did not possess complete control over her sexuality. This volatile situation arose in 1750, when one William Dyett approached George Frye, president of the Council of Montserrat, "under pretense of asking leave to fish in his private pond." Dyett apparently "came up to him [Frye] stark naked when he [Frye] was riding with his wife." Later the same day Dyett, by now presumably clothed, appeared at Frye's house and told him that "the pond in which he had asked leave to fish was not his [Frye's] own but a publick pond, and that he [Dyett] would fish in it in spite of him."[65] At this point, the furious councillor ordered his overseer to whip Dyett, who suffered a few strokes and then ran off.[66] One might assume that the incident would have ended there, but instead its repercussions were felt over the course of the next several years. As late as 1753, petitions and depositions were flying back and forth between Montserrat and London regarding this seemingly trivial event.

The rhetoric in these various communications was in some instances quite heated. Frye asserted that Dyett had appeared before his wife "naked, and with his obscene parts uncovered," while Dyett charged that Frye had ordered his overseer not merely to whip him but to "Kick him in the Ass" and to set dogs upon him. To add to the indignity, as Dyett complained to Mr. Molineux, speaker of the Montserrat Assembly, Frye had ordered that Dyett be whipped not only by the white overseer but also by several of Frye's slaves, an appalling degradation in a slave society, in which whites were empowered to strike blacks but never vice versa.[67] Feeling that he had received a grievous sexual insult, Frye had responded with what he hoped was an equal humiliation: he made Dyett the recipient of a shocking racial insult. Simultaneously, Frye asserted his position at the summit of a hierarchy of white employees, black slaves, and animals by using these various dependents and chattels literally as weapons against someone who dared to challenge his authority.[68]

What becomes apparent from an examination of the documents relating to the case of Frye and Dyett is that their confrontation was not the cause but rather the result of a climate of hostility in Montserrat, in which President Frye was at odds with many of the people he helped to govern. William Dyett was not the only local resident with whom he quarreled; he apparently had also publicly insulted another councillor, Michael White, and had come into conflict with members of such locally prominent families as the Skerretts and the Trants.[69] It seems quite possible that Dyett, whether of his own volition or prompted by other complainants, chose to confront the widely disliked Frye, and to do so in the most insulting manner possible, by exposing his "obscene parts" to Mrs. Frye in the presence of her husband.

Such an act was a tremendous affront to Frye's dignity; it called his manhood and his status as a husband into question, since in theory the only adult male who possessed the right to appear unclothed before a white woman was her spouse. Such an offense was not strictly illegal, as no such eventuality was mentioned in Montserrat's legal codes, but the action served to question Frye's right to hold public office: if the man could not shield his wife from symbolic assault, how could he be trusted to maintain the island's security and prosperity? The fact that Dyett, a small farmer, was of a socioeconomic status inferior to that of the Fryes compounded the insult. Interpreted in such a light, Dyett's action seems as deliberately provocative as Daniel Parke's open cuckolding of his opponent Edward Chester. Like Parke, Dyett entered into a figurative male-to-male conversation which putatively focused on the other man's wife but which in reality struck at his enemy's prestige and symbolically unmanned him. Even the language Dyett used to describe his interest in access to Frye's pond carries a sexual charge. His original taunt can be interpreted as expressing a desire to enter not Frye's pond but his wife, and his subsequent claim that the pond was not really Frye's property but "publick" implies that Frye held no dominion over his wife and that therefore she was open to use by the public, symbolized by Dyett. Given the gravity and depth of such a challenge, it is not surprising that Frye reacted so violently to this symbolic attack, though far less violently than Chester and his comrades chose to avenge themselves against Parke's amours with their wives. Frye's many time-consuming efforts to obtain a judgment against Dyett show how deeply his sense of honor had been damaged by what he clearly saw as a shocking breach of community norms of social deference and respect for the rights of husbands over their wives.

Also from the annals of Montserrat comes our final case of sexually transgressive behavior and the reaction to it by Leeward society, one that took place a few years prior to the outbreak of the conflict between William Dyett and George Frye. In this instance, "about the year 1743 . . . one James Farell, and his sister, children of a Roman Catholick family in the island, were detected in the commission of the horrid crime of incest."[70] Not surprisingly, the siblings' parents were utterly horrified by their discovery of the nature of their son and daughter's relationship; they intended to deal with the situation by placing the girl in a European convent and sending the boy into military service in a European army.

One might assume that the Farrells' fellow Montserratians would be pleased to see such troublesome youngsters depart the island. Incest, after all, made a travesty of the ideal of the orderly patriarchal household; the children were not only engaging in sexual behavior without their parents' knowledge or approval but ignoring the laws of consanguinity, or closeness of blood relationship. The consanguinity issue was sufficiently disturbing to constitute one of the very few grounds in English law for the divorce decree of *a vinculo matrimonii* (from the bonds of marriage), the only legal proceeding which allowed previously wed individuals to marry again in the eyes of the Church of England.[71] One would also think that the inhabitants of such a small white settler society as that of Montserrat, where spousal choice was severely limited, would not mourn the loss of two who were known publicly to have violated the societal taboos against incest.

The events which followed the discovery of James Farrell's affair with his sister and their parents' decision to send both children off of the island, though, were quite different from what one might have expected.

As a contemporary observer wrote, "several of the Protestant families [of Montserrat], and even a majority of the council, hearing of the affair, prevailed on the son and daughter to turn Protestants, under a notion that as such the son might lawfully dispossess his own father of his inheritance."[72] The island establishment, far from scorning the young pair, championed them against their parents, despite the fact that the elder Farrells were behaving in a manner which upheld both the legal and the religious ideals upon which colonial society rested. Supporters of James and his sister "not only maintained the son and daughter, and encouraged and received them into their houses," but even succeeded in convincing Sir William Mathew, the current governor and captain-general of the Leewards, to grant James command of the island's militia, a signal honor for which residents competed jealously.[73] Equally surprising is the fact that "when the chief justice of the island granted a warrant for the apprehension of the daughter (a girl under age) in order to deliver her up to her parents . . . the marshal . . . refused to execute it; threats were publickly given out, that any attempt to put it in execution should be opposed by force; and the chief justice himself, for granting it, was personally threatened and insulted in the streets, and forced to fly to his own house for shelter."[74] Although the law and its servants attempted to uphold the seemingly sacrosanct principle of parental authority over children, most members of local white society claimed that the elder Farrells' inability to prevent their son and daughter from developing an incestuous sexual relationship should cause them to forfeit the privileges of parenthood, which would now devolve onto the champions of these young people.

Why would the residents of Montserrat, including a majority of the members of the island's legislature, overlook the unlawful and, in the eyes of most European observers, immoral behavior of the Farrell siblings to such an extent that they not only financially supported the youngsters but openly flouted all attempts to bring them under the control of the law and of their parents? The Farrell affair, it appears, was an instance in which the entrenched ideals of proper sexual conduct came into direct conflict with political realities, and the latter won out. As has been mentioned briefly elsewhere in this essay, significant tensions existed between English Protestant and Irish Catholic residents of the Leewards. The former generally considered the latter to be "a riotous and unruly lot," particularly in Montserrat, in which the white population throughout the seventeenth and eighteenth centuries was overwhelmingly Hibernian.[75] An opportunity such as that presented by the Farrell case was too good for the

authority and control

English Montserratians to ignore: if they should succeed in persuading James Farrell to join the Anglican Church, he could, by virtue of island law, dispossess the Catholic father he now hated of his property. Such an action would be a classic quid pro quo; James would be able to assert his emotional and financial independence from his father, and the English camp would have the satisfaction of seeing the estate of one of the island's few affluent Irish Catholic families fall into Protestant hands.

Toleration of the crime of incest might be a steep price to pay for such an achievement, but the English of Montserrat were apparently willing to pay it. Accustomed as they were to a steady diet of lurid invective against the allegedly immoral and shameless "Papists," the English interest may have felt that this tolerance set no dangerous precedent regarding violations of the incest taboo. If Rachel Levine's willingness to enter into an extramarital relationship could be attributed to her French background, how much easier might it not be to assert that incestuous behavior was yet another example of the abhorrent practices of Irish Catholics? Patriarchal authority and its control over dependents' sexuality might be a touchstone of colonial society, but that society found it far easier to ignore the furious protests of those individuals it despised—the Catholic Farrell parents; the disliked, possibly Jewish foreigner John Michael Levine—than the rancor of such a prominent member of local society as a George Frye or an Edward Chester.

Previous scholars have made much of the fact that the English colonies in the West Indies lay "beyond the line" of European treaty obligations, and some have proceeded to draw a parallel conclusion regarding an alleged lack of sexual morality in these islands.[76] A careful examination of various cases of unorthodox sexual conduct, though, emphasizes instead that sexual behavior in these settlements, as exemplified by the Leeward colonies, did not lie completely "beyond a line" of European ideals of civilized behavior. The pressing need to adapt to difficult local circumstances meant that certain behaviors had to be tolerated, particularly in relation to miscegenation, but it does not then follow that the sexual behavior of white settlers was anarchic. White society in the Leewards proved itself willing, if not always pleased, to accommodate certain forms of sexual license, but it fervently resisted those which it saw as directly assaulting or mocking the patriarchal ideals upon which colonial British American society was based. Leeward society clearly possessed the ability and the willingness to discriminate in the tenor of its public responses between the varied forms of sexual transgression with which it was obligated to deal.

Had it lacked such capability, it is unlikely that these small and fragile set-tler societies would have succeeded in reconciling their many internal contradictions for as long as they managed to do so.

N O T E S

Versions of this essay have been presented to the Women's Studies Graduate Workshop, Johns Hopkins University, November 1996, and the Mid-Atlantic Conference on British Studies, New York, April 1997. I would like to thank Nuran Cinlar, Toby Ditz, Robert Glen, Alfredo Goyburu, Madhavi Kale, and William MacLehose for their careful readings and comments on several drafts of this essay.

1. Richard S. Dunn, *Sugar and Slaves: The Rise of the Planter Class in the English West Indies, 1624–1713* (Chapel Hill: University of North Carolina Press, 1972), 45.

2. Carl and Roberta Bridenbaugh, *No Peace beyond the Line: The English in the Caribbean, 1624–1690* (New York: Oxford University Press, 1972), 140–41, 394.

3. Trevor Burnard, "A Failed Settler Society: Marriage and Demographic Failure in Early Jamaica," *Journal of Social History* 28 (Fall 1994): 63–82.

4. Orlando Patterson, *The Sociology of Slavery* (London: MacGibbon and Kee, 1967), passim; Richard S. Dunn, "The English Sugar Islands and the Founding of South Carolina," in *Shaping Southern Society: The Colonial Experience*, ed. T. H. Breen (New York: Oxford University Press, 1976), 57–58; Franklin W. Knight, *The Caribbean: The Genesis of a Fragmented Nationalism* (New York: Oxford University Press, 1978), 111.

5. Edward Ward referred to Jamaica as "the Dunghill of the Universe," while a later commentator, George Wilson Bridges, asserted that the earthquake and resulting fire and flood "resembled those visitations of an offended Deity on some cities in the Old World, where an iniquitous race was overwhelmed in sudden and unexpected ruin." See Ward, *A Trip to Jamaica* (London, 1700), 13, and Bridges, *The Annals of Jamaica* (1828; repr. London: Frank Cass, 1968), 1:309.

6. Michel Foucault, *The History of Sexuality*, vol. 1 (New York: Pantheon Books, 1978), 103.

7. On the Great Chain of Being, see E.M.W. Tillyard, *The Elizabethan World Picture* (New York: Macmillan Company, 1944), passim.

8. Susan Dwyer Amussen, *An Ordered Society: Gender and Class in Early Modern England* (Oxford: Basil Blackwell, 1988), 37–38; Mary Abbott, *Family Ties: English Families 1545–1920* (London: Routledge, 1993), 1–2.

9. Peter Laslett, *The World We Have Lost: England before the Industrial Age*, 2d ed. (New York: Charles Scribner's Sons, 1973), ch. 6, esp. 140–41; Keith

Wrightson, *English Society 1580–1680* (New Brunswick, N.J.: Rutgers University Press, 1982), 85.

10. The island of St. Kitts was also known as St. Christopher and St. Christopher's.

11. Deborah Gray White, *Ar'n't I a Woman? Female Slaves in the Plantation South* (New York: W. W. Norton and Company, 1985), ch. 1, esp. 38–39.

12. Anonymous, "Nelson's Dockyard," *Life in Antigua and Barbuda* (St. Johns, Antigua: West Indies Publishing, 1996), 22.

13. Richard Ligon, *A True and Exact History of the Island of Barbadoes* (1657; repr. London: Frank Cass, 1976), 51. White men's fascination with the naked black female body is not surprising when one considers that European women of this era wore many layers of clothing and were rarely, if ever, seen naked, even by their husbands. Despite the sweltering tropical climate of the Leewards, white women, and men as well, generally retained European styles of dress (Dunn, *Sugar*, 281–86).

14. Janet Schaw, *Journal of a Lady of Quality*, ed. Evangeline Walker Andrews and Charles Andrews (New Haven: Yale University Press, 1921), 87, 112.

15. W.S.A.B., *The Antigonian and Bostonian Beauties: A Poem* (Boston: D. Fowle, 1790), 2; emphasis in original. Robert Glen has suggested that W.S.A.B. can be identified as the Antiguan clergyman William Shervington; if this is correct, the Governor's Ball of the poem most likely took place during the 1740s, when Shervington resided in St. Johns (Robert Glen, personal communication, 20 June 1997).

16. *Beauties*, 2–4.

17. For the importance of balls and dances as occasions for sexual competition, see the *Spectator*, 1 June 1711, in which the young West Indian ladies Phillis and Brunetta, "two Rivals for the Reputation of Beauty," compete viciously against one another to obtain the most extravagant ball dresses. See also Rhys Isaac, *The Transformation of Virginia 1740–1790* (Chapel Hill: University of North Carolina Press, 1982), 86; and Cynthia A. Kierner, "Hospitality, Sociability, and Gender in the Southern Colonies," *Journal of Southern History* 62 (August 1996): 468, 471. On the traffic in women, see Gayle Rubin, "The Traffic in Women: Notes on the Political Economy of Sex," in *Toward an Anthropology of Women*, ed. Rayna Reiter (New York: Monthly Review Press, 1975).

18. It comes as little surprise to find that one of the greatest anxieties white settlers felt vis-à-vis the threat of slave rebellion was that male slaves would sexually assault white women—or, worse still, that white women would voluntarily engage in sexual relations with black men. See Hilary McD. Beckles, "White Women and Slavery in the Caribbean," *History Workshop Journal* 36 (1993): 78–79.

19. The tenuous nature of social stability in the Leewards is apparent from such statements as Governor Daniel Parke's observation that "there are so few

People [in the Leewards] that We are Exposed to the Insults of the French from Martinico when ever they please" (28 August 1706; C[olonial]. O[ffice]. 239/1, Public Record Office of Great Britain, unpaginated) and the Nevis Council's apprehension that "the Number of the p[re]sent Inhabitants are so few that in Case of a Warr and Invasion of this Island tis next to an Impossibility we should be able to Defend it" (21 June 1735, C.O. 186/2/36).

20. Dunn, *Sugar*, 124. Dunn also cites an earlier example of Leeward servant revolt; in 1629, servants in the newly established English settlement on Nevis, faced with a Spanish invasion, threw down their arms, crying "Liberty, joyful liberty!" and swam out to the Spaniards' ships to inform the conquerors where their masters had hidden their valuables (Dunn, *Sugar*, 120). For an excellent account of the Antiguan slave conspiracy of 1736, see David Barry Gaspar, *Bondmen and Rebels: A Study of Master-Slave Relations in Antigua* (Baltimore: Johns Hopkins University Press, 1985). The quotation is from the General Report of the Antiguan judges on the aborted conspiracy, cited in Gaspar, *Bondmen*, 3.

21. The Reverend William Smith was warned of the dangers of maroon settlements when he proposed to visit the hills above Basseterre, St. Kitts; see his *Natural History of Nevis, and the Rest of the English Leeward Charibbee Islands* (Cambridge: J. Bentham, 1745), 36. The Shekerley Hills in southwestern Antigua were the site of several small maroon communities; see Gaspar, *Bondmen*, 175–77, and Gaspar, "Runaways in Seventeenth-Century Antigua, West Indies," *Boletin de Estudios Latinamericanos y del Caribe* (June 1979): 3–13. Due to its extremely small size (thirty-nine square miles), Montserrat apparently had no significant maroon settlements; see Howard A. Fergus, *Montserrat: History of a Caribbean Colony* (London: Macmillan Press, 1994), 258.

22. Hilary McD. Beckles, "A 'riotous and unruly lot': Irish Indentured Servants and Freemen in the English West Indies," *William and Mary Quarterly*, 3d. ser., 47 (October 1990): 511, 517–20; Riva Berleant-Schiller, "Free Labor and the Economy in Seventeenth-Century Montserrat," *William and Mary Quarterly*, 3d ser., 46 (July 1989): 546, 562–63.

23. On community surveillance in New England, see Laurel Thatcher Ulrich, *Good Wives: Image and Reality in the Lives of Women in Northern New England, 1650–1750* (New York: Alfred A. Knopf, 1980), 55–57, 96, 102; for gentry dominance in the southern mainland colonies, see Isaac, *Transformation*, 34–42. It is important to keep in mind, however, that community surveillance, though a powerful factor in local societies, was quite capable of overlooking or ignoring certain transgressive behaviors.

24. For discussion of beliefs about the effects of climate on white settlers, see Gary Puckrein, "Climate, Health, and Black Labor in the English Americas," *Journal of American Studies* 13.2 (1979): 179–94; and Karen Ordahl Kupperman, "Fear of Hot Climates in the Anglo-American Colonial Experience," *William and Mary Quarterly*, 3d ser., 41 (April 1984): 213–14. For opinions

about the fear of contagion in black-majority settlements, see Winthrop D. Jordan, *White over Black: American Attitudes toward the Negro, 1550–1812* (Chapel Hill: University of North Carolina Press, 1968), 270–71, 518–21.

25. Although the fear that black men would rape white women was always present in the minds of white islanders, the sole mention of the possibility that a white woman would be raped by a white man is found in the "Martiall Law" articles published in Antigua in 1700, of which Article 32 states that "Whoever shall Force a woman to abuse her, whither she belong to the enemy or not, and the Fact be Sufficiently proved Shall Suffer Death for it." In this instance, a white man's sexual violation of a white woman is framed as a crime which occurs only during wartime. See House of Assembly Minutes, box 316, Archives of Antigua, St. Johns, Antigua.

26. C.O. 241/1, unpaginated. The prostitute is mentioned in a document of 16 April 1726, and Driscoll in one of 20 November 1727.

27. Berleant-Schiller, "Free Labor and the Economy," 557–58. A census of the Leeward colonies taken in 1678 by their governor, Sir William Stapleton, shows the number of white males in the islands as 4613, as compared with a mere 2502 white women. This census is C.O. 1/42/193–243 and has been published in its entirety by Vere Langford Oliver in his *History of Antigua* (London: Mitchell and Hughes, 1894), 1:lviii–lxi, and his *Caribbeana: Being Miscellaneous Papers Relating to the History, Genealogy, Topography, and Antiquities of the British West Indies* (London: Mitchell, Hughes and Clarke, 1910), 2:68–77, 347, and 3:27–35, 70–81.

28. Dunn, *Sugar*, 46.

29. Helen Hill Miller, *Colonel Parke of Virginia: "The Greatest Hector in the Town"* (Chapel Hill: Algonquin Books, 1989), xvii.

30. Miller, *Colonel Parke*, 185–88, 193; F. G. Spurdle, *Early West Indian Government* (Christchurch, New Zealand: Whitcombe and Tombs, n.d.), 39, 187.

31. Spurdle, *Early West Indian Government*, 11; Henry Waad et al., *A Brief and True Remonstrance of the Illegal Proceedings of Roger Osburn* (London, 1654), 1.

32. Miller, *Colonel Parke*, xviii.

33. Ibid., xvi, 70.

34. Algernon E. Aspinall, "The Fate of Governor Parke," in Aspinall, *West Indian Tales of Old* (New York: Negro Universities Press, 1969), 30.

35. Anonymous, *Some Instances of the Oppression and Male Administration of Col. Parke* (London, 1713), 10. It is possible that the term "Male Administration" is a double entendre which refers to Parke's sexual exploits in the islands.

36. Aspinall, "The Fate of Governor Parke," 247. Lucy Chester was to inherit only Parke's Leeward property, as his legitimate children inherited his holdings in Virginia.

37. Miller, *Colonel Parke*, 198. For the social significance of naming a child for its forebears, see Darrett B. Rutman and Anita H. Rutman, *A Place in Time: Middlesex County, Virginia, 1650–1750* (New York: W. W. Norton and Company, 1984), 70, 119.

38. On the concept of the effigy, see Joseph Roach, *Cities of the Dead: Circum-Atlantic Performance* (New York: Columbia University Press, 1996), ch. 2, esp. 36.

39. Miller, *Colonel Parke*, 192, 196.

40. Lawrence Stone, *The Family, Sex and Marriage in England, 1500–1800*, abridged ed. (New York: Harper and Row, 1979), 316–17.

41. Miller, *Colonel Parke*, xvi. As a clergyman, Blair, a commissary of the bishop of London, was immune from challenges to duel, a common method by which man-to-man conflicts were settled.

42. George French, *The History of Colonel Parke's Administration* (London, 1717), 1.

43. Miller, *Colonel Parke*, 203; Stone, *The Family, Sex, and Marriage*, 317; Peter Stallybrass and Allon White, *The Politics and Poetics of Transgression* (Ithaca, N.Y.: Cornell University Press, 1986), 24; George French, *The History of Colonel Parke's Administration* (London, 1717), 1.

44. Miller, *Colonel Parke*, 203.

45. *Memoirs of Mrs. Letitia Pilkington, 1712–1750, Written by Herself* (London: George Routledge and Sons, 1928), 354–55.

46. Describing early modern England, Lawrence Stone asserts that "the honour of a married man was severely damaged if he got the reputation of being a cuckold, since this was a slur on both his virility and his capacity to rule his own household. He became the joke of the village, or at a higher level of his associates, and was defamed and thought unfit for public office." Stone, *Family, Sex, and Marriage*, 316–17.

47. Gertrude Atherton, *The Conqueror* (New York: Macmillan Company, 1902), 3, 5.

48. Jacob Ernest Cooke, *Alexander Hamilton* (New York: Charles Scribner's Sons, 1982), 1.

49. Forrest McDonald, *Alexander Hamilton: A Biography* (New York: W. W. Norton and Company, 1979), 6; Noemie Emery, *Alexander Hamilton: An Intimate Portrait* (New York: G. P. Putnam's Sons, 1982), 15.

50. Nathan Schachner, *Alexander Hamilton* (New York: D. Appleton-Century Company, 1946), 6; Emery, *Alexander Hamilton*, 15.

51. Cooke, *Alexander Hamilton*, 1; Broadus Mitchell, *Alexander Hamilton: Youth to Maturity, 1755–1788* (New York: Macmillan Company, 1957), 7.

52. McDonald, *Alexander Hamilton*, 7.

53. John Chester Miller, *Alexander Hamilton and the Growth of the New Nation* (New York: Harper and Row, 1964), 3.

54. Allan McLane Hamilton, *The Intimate Life of Alexander Hamilton* (New York: Charles Scribner's Sons, 1911), 10.

55. Schachner, *Alexander Hamilton*, 8.

56. Mitchell, *Alexander Hamilton*, 11.

57. Although it is certain that Levine was not an Englishman, scholars have not reached a consensus about his background. Schachner, Hamilton, and Robert Warshow assert that he was a Danish Jew (Schachner, *Alexander Hamilton,* 5; Hamilton, *The Intimate Life,* 8; Warshow, *Alexander Hamilton: First American Business Man* [Garden City, N.Y.: Garden City Publishing Company, 1931], 4), J. C. Miller that he was German (*Alexander Hamilton,* 3), Emery that he was a Dane (*Alexander Hamilton,* 15), and Mitchell that he was a German Jew (*Alexander Hamilton,* 6). Even his surname is a matter of argument; it is given variously as Levine, Lavine, Lavien, Levein, Lawein, and Lavion.

58. Schachner, *Alexander Hamilton*, 11.

59. Mitchell, *Alexander Hamilton*, 6–7.

60. For a discussion of misogyny and gynophobia among colonial British American men, see Kenneth A. Lockridge, *On the Sources of Patriarchal Rage: The Commonplace Books of William Byrd and Thomas Jefferson and the Gendering of Power in the Eighteenth Century* (New York: New York University Press, 1992).

61. The historical evidence points to Rachel's parents being the French Huguenot Faucettes. However, others have asserted that she was either of Jewish descent(Sidney Mintz, personal conversation, 17 October 1996) or African (Mitchell, *Alexander Hamilton*, 11).

62. In his analysis of Jean Rhys's island-set novel *Wide Sargasso Sea*, Peter Hulme suggests that English Creole society saw itself as vastly dissimilar from that of white French islanders, whom the former believed to be inherently frivolous, decadent, and amoral. See Hulme, "The Locked Heart: The Creole Family Romance of *Wide Sargasso Sea*," in *Colonial Discourse/Postcolonial Theory*, ed. Peter Hulme, Francis Barker, and Margaret Iversen (Manchester: Manchester University Press, 1994), 80; and Jean Rhys, *Wide Sargasso Sea* (W. W. Norton and Company, 1982), 17, 80, 134.

63. Many years later, when Alexander Hamilton had grown to adulthood and was involved at the highest level of American politics, his opponents insulted him for what they saw as the immoral characters of his parents and the unorthodox circumstances of his birth and upbringing. John Adams referred to Hamilton as "the bastard brat of a Scotch pedlar," and a widely-circulated pamphlet described him as "the son of a camp-girl." Even Thomas Jefferson, usually relatively tolerant of unconventional modes of life, attacked Hamilton by declaiming that it was "monstruous" that a "foreign bastard" should rise to a position of preeminence in the new nation. These barbs, though, were aimed at an ambitious and feared political rival; no such opprobrium was directed at Rachel Levine and James

Hamilton by those who knew them. See Claude G. Bowers, "Hamilton: A Portrait," in *Alexander Hamilton: A Profile*, ed. Jacob Ernest Cooke (New York: Hill and Wang, 1967), 2; Warshow, *Alexander Hamilton*, 3.

64. Thomas Wythorne, quoted in Stone, *Family, Sex, and Marriage*, 317.

65. Anonymous, *The Case of Captain George Frye, President of the Council of the Island of Montserrat* (London, 1754), 12–13.

66. Ibid., 12–13.

67. C.O. 152/28, 21, 26, 29.

68. In a famous journal entry of 1726, the Virginia planter William Byrd II evoked such a hierarchy, consisting, like that of George Frye, of "my Flocks and my Herds, my Bond-men and Bond-women, and . . . Servants." Quoted in Isaac, *Transformation of Virginia*, 39.

69. C.O. 152/28, 28–29.

70. *Case of Frye*, 9; emphasis in original.

71. Stone, *Family, Sex, and Marriage*, 309; Hamilton, *The Intimate Life*, 10.

72. *Case of Frye*, 9.

73. Ibid., 9–10. For the aristocratic and competitive character of leadership in the Leeward militias, see Richard Pares, *War and Trade in the West Indies, 1739–1763* (London: Frank Cass and Company, 1963), 234.

74. *Case of Frye*, 11.

75. Beckles, "Unruly Lot," 503.

76. Dunn, *Sugar*, 11–12; Bridenbaugh and Bridenbaugh, *No Peace beyond the Line*, passim.

Part IV

Images of Masculinity, Femininity, and Sexuality in the Eighteenth Century

How men and women should behave in the new republic was a topic of much discussion in both public and private discourse. Wayne Bodle focuses on the life and experiences of Erkuries Beatty, paymaster of the First American Regiment, to examine gender roles in post-Revolutionary Pennsylvania. For Beatty and other soldiers, the war exposed them to the larger world but disrupted, or changed permanently, the expectations and plans they had made for their lives. Beatty's correspondence with friends and family reveals the tensions and transformations affecting American society at this time. Through Beatty's often perplexed impressions, readers get a glimpse of the complexities involved in the interactions between men and women.

In her examination of cross-dressing in Charles Brocken Brown's *Ormond*, Heather Smyth also studies tensions in late eighteenth-century American society. For example, Brown expressed interest in advancing women's education, and he suggested that women had capabilities far beyond their usual roles as wives and mothers. Yet he did not really endorse change. Cross dressing permits a blurring between gender and class in the novel, but ultimately, Smyth finds, does not transform gender roles. Martinette de Beauvais may dress as a man, but by doing so, she only reaffirms male and female roles. What Martinette accomplishes when she is dressed as a man, she can do only because others perceive her as a man.

Focusing on seduction tales, Rodney Hessinger further examines post-Revolutionary gender roles and societal anxieties. He finds that as controls over young people were disrupted by the Revolution, a cultural backlash against this youthful freedom occurred. Hessinger argues that seduction literature not only mirrored the fears and tensions existing in society but actually helped to form American culture. In seduction literature, young men were portrayed as immoral seducers. To protect themselves, women, who were pictured as naturally virtuous, had to remain within their "proper" sphere, the home.

As Karen A. Weyler observes, by the late eighteenth century, sexual transgressions were rarely punished by law, as they were in colonial America. However, they did rend the fabric of society by disrupting family life. In seventeenth-century New England, Priscilla Willson and others like her were convicted of fornication in courts of law. Seizing upon the latest medical theories concerning guilt-induced insanity, novelists of the new republic "punished" their female characters who engaged in premarital or extramarital sexual relations by mirroring contemporary attitudes and causing their creations to descend into madness.

Chapter 9

Soldiers in Love
Patrolling the Gendered Frontiers of the Early Republic

Wayne Bodle

In October of 1786 Lieutenant Erkuries Beatty, the paymaster of the First American Regiment, traveled from the Ohio Valley to New York on army business with his old friend Major William North. At a fork in the rugged highway in western Pennsylvania their official assignments took them temporarily down different paths. Beatty keenly lamented the loss of North's company, "as he and I had traveled . . . a great ways together, and I never in my life experienced a more agreeable traveling companion." He was soon overtaken by "a young country fellow but meanly dressed [and] accompanied by a very handsome young girl dressed very genteel." Beatty expressed amazement to see "so well dressed a girl in this country among the mountains, riding a good horse, [with a] saddle . . . and gallanted by such a dirty looking fellow," but the strangers willingly "unveiled" the mystery. The man lived in a roadside cabin that Beatty had just passed, and the woman was a sister, visiting "from the upper parts of [the] Conogocheague" settlement, where she lived with her uncle. Finding Beatty more than willing to escort his sister home, the woodsman left her "entirely in my charge."[1]

Beatty and the woman sparred cautiously. She politely declined to join him for breakfast, but then "very sociabl[y]" told him her name—Bella Barclay—and a little bit about her life as an Irish immigrant who had come to America only two years before. Emboldened, Beatty "endeavored . . . to sport with her good nature and ignorance [but] soon found that she did not deserve the character I had formed of her." Barclay had "a tolerable education" and wits equal at every turn to his own. "Foiled in every attack upon her," and admitting that "in either religion, Philosophy, or History—she got the better of me," he tried an old strategem of both the camp and campus. Pronouncing himself "fatigued," he invited her to stop at a tavern for refreshment. There he "endeavoured to treat her very genteel with plenty of good Toddy and Grog—but her prudence would not suffer her to drink more than was of service to her, and not any to me." He was left lamely to admit that his old friend North "would have enjoyed her company with tenfold the satisfaction that I could."[2]

The pair rode a few miles farther, parting where the road to her uncle's place left the main highway. Beatty's final stab of regret was not one of thwarted seduction or even of wounded intellectual pride; rather, his words spoke ironically to questions of post-Revolutionary gender roles and expectations. Barclay seemed to "regret the loss of my company as well as I did of hers," he recalled, but she had displayed entirely too little respectful curiosity about himself. Although he had "ask[ed] her a great many impertinent questions . . . which she answered with very good nature and freedom," he complained, "never once did she seem any way concerned who I was [or] where I was going."[3]

The encounter did not bring any dramatic changes to Beatty's life. He never mentioned it again and spent six more years of mostly unrewarding military service before carving out a belated and precarious place in the civilian sphere of the new republic. He never became one of the "great white men" once relied on by historians but now suspected as informants about their age, but he did achieve some prominence and a modest stake in his society. The record of his life dwells more than incidentally on his experiences with women, his seemingly endless search for a mate, and his efforts to comprehend the social changes he witnessed.[4]

Career soldiers like Beatty sought order and security in structured, hierarchical institutional environments. Indeed, for some youths caught up unexpectedly by war in 1775, the army, even more than their families, served as a primary socializing agent and a source of personal identity or gender consciousness. But if military culture selected and reinforced "traditional" personality types or values in a society that we now believe was experiencing rapid social change, the relentless geographical mobility of army life could have quite opposite consequences.[5] The Revolution churned through towns and rural areas between 1775 and 1783, disrupting communal patterns and changing relationships between leaders and citizens, masters and servants, and parents and children. Americans who moved west after the war were just as much a self-selected social group as were the soldiers who both policed and protected them. Some may have suffered more disruption and trauma from the war than did their neighbors who remained behind. Others undoubtedly embraced more fully, or more willingly, the myriad new social opportunities offered by the unprecedented rack and ruin of the contest itself. If, as some historians have suggested, the Revolution unleashed a broad range of important, albeit largely unintended, behavioral changes in relations between the sexes during this generation, then the "new west" should provide an ideal place to look for them. And genially uncomprehending military men like Erkuries Beatty may prove to be surprisingly good agents to employ in that search.[6]

The ideological imperatives of the Revolutionary settlement placed these very different groups of Americans into intimate and revealing proximity. Members of the Continental Congress were reluctant even to *have* a postwar army, much less to pay very much for one. They placed the tiny military force that they did authorize at a safe distance, on the Ohio frontier, to serve as a buffer against Indian tribes displaced by and resentful over the war's outcome, to watch over inexperienced settlers, and to guard the national government's own vulnerable property rights in the western lands that were the richest spoil of the Revolution. Evidence of these soldiers' experiences in carrying out those tasks is fragmentary, while reliable accounts of how civilians perceived their encounters with the troops are rarer still. But there is no reason to presume that Beatty's confusion over odd combinations of scruffiness and gentility, or his surprise at meeting women who could discourse and drink with the toughest of his own comrades, were unusual on the frontier. Such cases of cognitive dissonance offer useful barometers of otherwise opaque phenomena. They alert us to disjunctions in social behavior that the broader studies insist *must* have been occurring in these environments, but that we might otherwise miss, because they seemed "normal" to so many of those involved. Conservatives can make ideal, if accidental, ethnographers precisely for their open willingness to marvel at their own cultural befuddlements.[7]

No claims are made here that Beatty's experiences or his reactions to them during the late eighteenth century were "typical" or even broadly representative of soldiers at large, much less of his male contemporaries generally. Case studies willingly sacrifice such macrocosmic authority for more revealing particularities, and this account is no exception. Congress's own parsimony, which rendered its soldiers poor, kept their pay-master constantly in transit between Ohio and the East and eroded his ability to maintain even the transiently stable relationships with civilians that his comrades learned to enjoy. That very mobility, however, pecu-liarly exposed Beatty to the variations in social structure and gender be-havior that were an enduring social echo of the preceding military and political revolutions. His post-Revolutionary experiences, refracted through the wartime adventures of his brothers and a small circle of their friends who temporarily soldiered but then returned to civilian life, pro-vide a revealing lens into the social fluidity that at once underlay and un-dermined any "settlement" of those revolutions.

Erkuries Beatty was born in 1759 in Neshaminy, Bucks County, Pennsyl-vania, the youngest son of Charles Clinton Beatty, a Presbyterian minis-ter and a trustee of the College of New Jersey. His mother died in Scot-land in 1768 and his father during a 1772 mission to Barbados. The older sons among the Beatty children had graduated from or were ready to ma-triculate at Princeton by the latter year, while their oldest daughter was already married. Twelve-year-old Erkuries joined his sister's household and was eventually sent to a private academy in New Jersey to prepare for his anticipated enrollment at Princeton a few years later.[8]

The outbreak of the war upended these plans. In 1775 Beatty enlisted as a private in the New Jersey militia and fought at the Battle of Long Is-land. His brothers subsequently secured him, early in 1777, an ensign's commission in the Fourth Pennsylvania Regiment. He was wounded at the Battle of Germantown on October 4 of that year but recovered in time to winter, uneventfully, at Valley Forge. In 1779 he went on General James Sullivan's punitive expedition into the heart of the Iroquois coun-try in western New York State. In 1781 he marched to Virginia for the Yorktown campaign, then spent the anticlimactic last years of the war back in the north, doing mundane garrison duty and attending to various administrative details.[9]

By 1783 Beatty had come of age in the army and had become virtually a creature of its culture and organizational routines. His facility in ad-justing arcane payroll accounts made him one of the last Continental of-ficers to be discharged late that year, and one of the first applicants when Congress reluctantly decided to raise the successor "First American Reg-iment" in mid–1784. With no bureaucratic civilian sector to absorb their executive talents, soldiers of his background had few incentives to try their luck in the distended postwar economy, and many considered themselves fortunate to remain in military life. Some officers in the peacetime army were able to support families on small salaries, or at least to sustain domestic relationships through the flux of constant mobility and intermittent danger. Others, including Beatty, were figuratively "married" to the service.[10]

What did military life teach soldiers like Beatty about the nature of manhood or the possibilities of relations with women? A surprisingly full, if understandably broken, record survives to illuminate this question. The Continental officers in Beatty's circle were keenly aware that the untimely eruption and uncertain progress of the Revolution affected their ability to accomplish critical tasks of early adulthood. There is no doubt that their hormonal systems were vigorously engaged in the business at hand, and they showed a charming willingness to believe, or even to revel, in the "romantic" dimensions of the project. But beneath their boast and banter lay the sober realization that in an agricultural and artisanal economy, family formation was a pressing necessity, any neglect of which could have lastingly harmful consequences for them. The exigencies of the war might provoke aberrant or impulsive marital decisions that would prove dysfunctional in peacetime, but they could also impose de facto moratoria on serious courtships and thus afford unprecedented opportunities for low-risk sexual experimentation. Serving in different Pennsylvania units, crisscrossing the mobile theaters of war, these youths closely scrutinized each other's activities. They challenged suspicious epistolary silences that might signify ill-advised dalliances, as when John Beatty querulously asked his brother Reading whether an acquaintance was "dead or married." They encouraged, cajoled, counseled, mocked, disclosed, exchanged, explained, and subverted their own and each other's intimate lives in complex patterns of communication that later generations would dismissively categorize as "girl talk."[11]

The spread of the war into the south after 1780 presented the intriguing possibility of liaisons across racial boundaries. Robert Wharry, a surgeon in the Third Pennsylvania Regiment, wrote from Virginia to his fellow doctor, Reading Beatty, in 1781, to announce that he had "a mind to pay my addresses to eight hundred acres of good Land and twenty or thirty *black* Negro's—what would you think of that?" Such fanciful courtships were difficult, however, because of the peripatetic nature of army life. Wharry soon found himself more than seventy miles from camp, where there were "plenty of Ladies, both fair, black and brown;

(but, by the bye) few fair *ones*." But when the army moved into South Carolina, his immobility and isolation only worsened. Some of the "Lads" had "extensive acquaintances," he noted, but his own horseless condition forced him to remain in camp "and not have [it] in my power to pay my devoirs to the nice widows or their bands of Ethiopians."[12]

Reading Beatty's reaction to Wharry's designs or his plight is unrecorded, but his own letters from interior Pennsylvania evoked for his family the potentially uncomfortable specter of interethnic relationships. His brother John questioned Reading's stated intention of making a "spirited attack" on either a "Dutch Girl" or on the "Conostoga Waggon" that symbolized for both the property she might bring to their marital alliance, and wondered how he could separate those two objects of interest. Reading parried John's well-intentioned advice "respecting marrying a Dutch Girl, with a good Plantation and a Conostoga Waggon." But if he "could get the two latter, without the Incumbrance of the former," he acknowledged, "I should hardly pass them by."[13]

Garrison life offered romantic possibilities across the lines of class and culture as well as those of race or ethnicity. Erkuries Beatty told Reading that he might one day find himself in Carlisle, Pennsylvania, and he offered to "introduce" him to "those agreeable fair sex" of that town. He then provided a "character" of *sixteen* Carlisle belles, going up and down the street like a census taker and stopping only because he hesitated to "enumerate" girls between fifteen and eighteen years of age! Betsy Miller was "pretty much inclining to an old maid, not handsome, but very sensible, a great reader," while Sally Posth was "a pretty young lady, possessed of a great deal of sympathy, friendship, and good nature." Hetty Montgomery was "midling handsome, rather given to too much pride, and backbiting, but her favourites will find her very agreeable," but Molly Sergeant was "handsomer and more sociable and genteel," with a "good education." Jenny Blair was "a wild rattling harum-scarum young girl yet possessed of natural wit enough, but very passionate and middling handsome." Sally Sample was a "genteel person, very lively, witty, sociable and kind, possessed of a great deal of love and friendship, she is about 18 years old and not possessed of a very good fortune, tho' Dresses very genteel."[14]

This report, predictably, became the talk of the Beatty clique, and it led to rumors that Erkuries might "Wed a Carlisle Girl." He replied with wonder that his brothers could have taken his "late stile of writing" to suggest that he was "bereft of my Senses, or run stark staring mad," and he denied that he had "the least Idea of marriage in my head, to any Girl in Carlisle."[15] Nevertheless, his friends began to keep a closer watch over him. When Erkuries left Lancaster for "Mount Rock" (possibly Carlisle) in 1783, they guessed that he "has some serious designs on Sally." He had "lately commenc'd Gallant, nothing more common than to catch him in a Tete-a-tete, of an Evening in a Porch with some of our Belles here." But Lancaster's women had recently compiled their own ranked "arrangement of pretty fellows" in the town, a contest in which poor "Ak" Beatty had only finished "No. 3."[16]

This list suggests that Revolutionary soldiers campaigning far from home encountered not only social categories of women who were alien to them but also patterns of female behavior that they had difficulty assimilating with their gendered expectations. The "arrangement" was perhaps the least exotic of such phenomena. In Amelia County, Virginia, the "*Patriotic Fair*" made "*Resolves* . . . in favour of those who have step'd forth in *the service* of their Country" not to "receive the Addresses of any but those." "Could You believe me?" Captain Isaac Van Horne asked Reading. "An Elderly Lady of a very respectable Family (When in Company with a number of our Gentn and a number of Young Ladies of the first Rank), observed was *She* young and to be Maried She would have none but of those who had persevered to the *end of the War*." Lieutenant Samuel Story reported that most women in Savannah, Georgia, were "profess'd Whigs," and asked Reading to imagine "how agreable [is] the situation of a few . . . in such a circle, no request our *delicacy* can permit has been hitherto denied."[17]

We know of other cases of the politicization of the bestowal and denial of sexual access or attention during the Revolution. But the Beattys and their friends were also witnessing much more direct and active political behaviors among these civilian women. In 1782 Major William Van Lear traveled from Carlisle into the Conococheague community. Dismissing Reading's advice to promote his own "acquaintance" with Sally (a "Worthy Girl," whom he would not marry because of her "affluence" and his own "indigence"), he offered the only piece of "domestic" news that was stirring. "Miss Samples" and "Miss Jane Montgomery" had "tak[en] a tour through Conacocheague making interest for her Father against the ensuing Election, as he's a Candidate for the post of Sheriff."[18]

These experiences broadened the cultural frames of reference within which young officers contemplated the work of seeking life partners beyond those they might have employed on Pennsylvania's farms or its blacksmith hamlets had war not arrived just as they began making the transition from late adolescence into manhood. But the evidence suggests that for most of the Beatty circle, military life offered venues for sexual experimentation more than it did avenues toward radically reconfigured social identities. By 1782 Reading Beatty—who had established a reputation for "gallantry" comparable to his brother Ark's—was courting the woman whom he would marry, nineteen-year-old Christina Wynkoop, the daughter of a Bucks County judge from neighboring Newtown. This was a conventional enough match, albeit one with sufficient upward mobility to impress Reading's friends with his good social and economic judgment as well as his personal taste in women. His mates dutifully encouraged Reading's pursuit, but they were not above indulging in mischievous sabotage, or even trying to provoke their friend's helpless jealousy from afar. Isaac Van Horne visited the Wynkoops while on leave in Bucks County, and he advised Reading that "Chrissy, the incomparable . . . look'd charmingly" as she sat at tea, "rather in her disabille." He even admitted that "I sometimes stole a look, not often."[19]

The rest of the group openly envied the sexual success of a comrade whose intended marriage promised both to establish his postwar medical practice and to stabilize his personal life. They continued their frenzied indulgence in "frolics," "kick-ups," "dusts," and other forms of competitive sociability but practiced various kinds of sentimental prophylaxis that reduced their likelihood of making inappropriate matches for themselves. Van Horne actually touted Reading's virtues to one of the Wynkoop girls, admitting that "I can Court much better for my Friend than for myself"—a vestigial rationalization that Erkuries may have been reflexively invoking when he longed for Major North in 1786. Van Horne also insisted that while he was indeed "in love," it was "with all of" the women he met rather than any single one. Their friend James McMichael elevated this point into a maxim. "I Love the whole Sex," he crowed, "and have Long been of Opinion that the Man who had not such a General Philanthropy was incapable of Ever Loving a Single one as he ought." Such easy bromides protected against both indifferent success in the chase and the dangers of accidentally overtaking the wrong quarry.[20]

As the war ground to a halt in 1783, however, most members of the Beatty circle hastened to leave the service and come home, where they adopted lifestyles more in keeping with the realities of a preindustrial economy. They were all civilians by year's end; and in early 1784, when the previously teasing Van Horne was spurned by "Indianna" (who "says she will always esteem me as a friend, but will not suffer me to hope for any thing further"), he could admit that "Tis the D——L to be an old Batchelor."[21]

By now only Erkuries Beatty remained in uniform. The war's end left him in Philadelphia, virtually penniless and struggling to settle the pay accounts of the Pennsylvania troops. The evening of St. Patrick's Day in 1783, he spent in dismal revelry at a Water Street tavern with "a few reduced Continental Officers, Captains of Ships, Irish Volunteers, Hatters prentices . . . Doctor's mates [and] Damn'd droll sinners," feeling fortunate not to have his head broken.[22]

By early 1784 Beatty had been discharged and was living at a Mrs. Stamper's boardinghouse, where his immediate "family" was "a pretty Jolly set of old Continental Officers." The whole capital accumulation of his wartime service consisted of his "depreciation" certificate, a promissory note from the bankrupt Pennsylvania government that was convertible into a land grant in western Pennsylvania after Continental authorities evicted Indian tribes from that area. On April 14, 1784, even this "deprivation note" went up in smoke. When Mrs. Stamper shouted that "a pretty Girl" was passing in the street below, Erkuries raced downstairs and laid the note on top of a hot wood stove. He turned from the window seconds later but saw only a glowing pile of ashes where his fortune had been![23]

Small wonder, then, that Erkuries schemed to get himself appointed as the civilian agent to settle Pennsylvania's army accounts or that he sought a commission in the postwar army. By late May of 1784 he faced eviction from his new household. Mrs. Stamper had "got a Courtier," a disreputable ex-soldier named Captain Wallace. Erkuries returned to the house to find it in an "uproar," with seamstresses making wedding clothes and the motley tenants frantically scrambling to arrange other lodgings. His landlady called him to her room for "a very long *confab*," in which she disclosed "the very great esteem she held me in, rather considered me as a Brother than anything else and wished me to give her serious and Candid advice" on Wallace's proposal. Beatty realized that her mind was made up, however, and thus he refrained form expressing his strong personal distaste for Wallace.[24]

Erkuries and a fellow officer found a house in Spruce Street and hatched a scheme to enter "deeply into speculation in these [land] Certificates."[25] In midsummer, however, he received his commission as paymaster to the First American Regiment, and by that autumn he was in the

Ohio Valley. His main duty there was to shuttle back and forth between the frontier garrisons and the government in the east, begging politicians for the money needed to pay the soldiers. The institutional mendacity and even the occasional outright fraud involved in that process, together with the disruption of his own familial and social relationships at home, kept Beatty in an intermittent state of what now sounds almost like a mild case of clinical depression. He "never was in a worse humour... in all my life," he confessed to his brother on the eve of one sudden departure for the west. "My head is as empty as a calabash. . . . head—head—head—I say this head of mine is not worth a pinch of snuff to night."[26]

In a postwar world, Beatty's profession seemed ill suited to a man who had learned to equate "gentility" with female worth. He valiantly tried to keep up the traditions of the "frolic," but seldom with satisfaction. During his first fall in the West he attended a dance in Pittsburgh, where "the general part of the Ladies in town collected which was about 20." "I conceived 'em to be no great things, chief of them neither dressed, danced nor behaved to admiration," he sniffed, "but as much so as I expected from the disadvantages they labored under." Pittsburgh was emerging as the hub of the trans-Appalachian region, however, and its scrambling gentry elites hardly thought of their impoverished defenders as suitable company for their own daughters either.[27]

After a few months in the West, Beatty developed a serious drinking problem. He and some friends spent St. Patrick's Day of 1785 carousing "till reason had forsaken a number of us." Frontier life fostered a contrapuntal round of male camaraderie and bravado in the garrison, interspersed with polite, but usually abortive, attempts to "pay respects to the Ladies" of the town. In "drinking and shooting contests" at camp, ostentatious forms of deference prevailed, as when the regiment's commander, Colonel Josiah Harmar, outshot all of his subordinates, although Beatty insisted that Harmar had "never shot a rifle before yesterday." In the spring the garrison played "several matches of ball," in which "some officers got hurt," while trips to Pittsburgh brought more "scenes of debauchery" that left Beatty "truly ashamed."[28]

When Erkuries met the Barclays, then, his professed incomprehension at the juxtaposition of frontier leather with Irish lace seems belied by the very telling degree to which it mirrored the western pole of his own nomadic trans-Appalachian life in the 1780's. He struggled almost desperately at times to maintain his ties to the "genteel" world he presumed to remember back in the east. He was both enraged and depressed when sudden orders "to the Westard" forced him to miss the February 1786 wedding of his brother Reading and the universally adored Chrissy Wynkoop. In Philadelphia that December he "sincerely curse[d] the day that ever induced me again to enter in such a rascally service" and sorrowfully confessed to Reading that he "could be happy with the pattern of your good Lady in a place no larger than a Racoon Box living on the toil of my own hands, so that she was happy."[29]

On September 28, 1787, a year after his unfateful encounter with Bella Barclay, Beatty finally met the woman whom he would marry—twelve years later—at a dinner party in Philadelphia. He supped with "Mr. Patterson" and "saw a Miss Ewing there . . . a very sprightly, interesting, and attractive young lady, with Beautiful black eyes [who] sings a good song." He was instantly enraptured but learned that she was "particularly interested in the welfare of "a certain gentleman of my acquaintance," his own brother officer William Ferguson, a captain in the First Regiment. Indeed, she "drank a full bumper of port to [Ferguson's] health, which gave an extraordinary blush to her cheeks and added much to her native beauty," while doing nothing to cool his own ardor.[30]

Beatty's final years of military service and the important circumstances of his belated transition, in early middle age, back into civilian society, are regrettably obscure. He kept no diaries between late 1787 and 1797; and, as his brothers and friends shouldered their own familial responsibilities, their letters begin to disappear as supplementary sources of evidence. Family traditions place Beatty as the commander of the American garrison at Vincennes, Indiana, for two years (1788–90), but available sources do not uphold these claims. He did, however, travel west on the Ohio River from army headquarters, near Marietta, more frequently than east.[31]

Beatty clearly spent some time at Vincennes, and we can only regret the lack of substantive accounts of his experience there. That outpost anchored the American military establishment to the Illinois Country and to the Mississippi Valley, both nominally parts of the nation's Revolutionary inheritance from Britain, but still in culture more like provinces of Spain and France, particularly the latter. At Vincennes, Beatty encountered yet another series of cultural seams between divergent social, linguistic, economic, religious, and political regimes. These were unquestionably as dramatic as any that he had experienced in Virginia (where he saw racial practices different from those he might have beheld in southeastern Pennsylvania) or in Carlisle and Pittsburgh (where he explored the German and Scots-Irish backcountry and saw postwar efforts to Anglicize parts of it), or at various treaty sites in the upper Ohio Valley (where he could observe Native Americans bravely resisting the American onslaught into their homelands).[32] Historians of *le pays des Illinois* have, in particular, remarked on the "enhanced status of women" in the French colony. So did many contemporary visitors to Vincennes, including some American conservatives who hoped to rebuild in the Ohio Valley a replica of the hierarchical and patriarchal society that they believed they remembered from late colonial Anglo-America. John Cleves Symmes, an aggressive land speculator from New Jersey who lived near Cincinnati, saw the Ohio Country as a social sinkhole and Vincennes as its exotic and threatening foreign appendage. The women of that community, he noted in 1790, "are tollerably inviting, they are of good persons and have a most noble gait, far better than is generally met with in New York—their dress is clean and sometimes rich." But "most of the men" struck Symmes as being "wretched in dress and Manners . . . highly imitating the Indians with whom they have since the foundation of their town been largely conversant." This observation, as crabbed and culturally myopic as it undoubtedly was, suggests a communal version of the social pattern that Erkuries Beatty discerned in microcosm on the highway in central Pennsylvania four years earlier.[33]

It was more than dress and demeanor, however, that caused Symmes to characterize relations between the sexes at Vincennes as something suspiciously new on the American landscape:

> The men here are barely one removed from the Indians, and yet they are the greatest slaves to their wives in the world. they milk the cows—cook for the family—fetch and carry and in a word do every thing that is done in doors and out, washing their linnen excepted, while the women spend their time walking about, sitting at their doors, or nursing their children from morning to night, and if one might judge from the contrast I am led to suppose that through the night the men are obliged to observe an humble distance.[34]

Judge Symmes was merely passing through Vincennes while riding circuit across the Northwest Territory. We do not know whether Beatty stayed there long enough to penetrate these ethnocultural mysteries any more deeply or sensitively than Symmes had done. On October 19–22, 1790 under Colonel Harmar and November 4, 1791 under major general and territorial governor Arthur St. Clair, the western troops suffered crushing defeats at the hands of the Ohio Indians near the modern boundary between Ohio and Indiana. Beatty was with the regiment just prior to the latter engagement, but he was sent on a detached mission before the disaster began and thus escaped probable death. Six hundred men and officers, including his friendly rival William Ferguson were killed.[35]

These shocking military disasters forced Congress to fundamentally reconstruct the American frontier defense system, by authorizing the creation of the nation's first real post-Revolutionary army, consisting of more than five thousand men under Major General Anthony Wayne. In 1794, at Fallen Timbers, Ohio, that army avenged the defeats of its predecessor, destroying Native American power in the region. That victory cleared the way for tens of thousands of white settlers to migrate into the Northwest Territory and laid the foundation for the eventual creation of five American states there between 1803 and 1848.[36]

Beatty took no part in either of these military engagements or in the social and political developments associated with them on the frontier. On January 11, 1793, he resigned his commission in the regiment. But he found it no easier to claim a place in civilian life in the 1790s than he might have after the Revolution the decade before. In July of 1792, perhaps while informally negotiating the details of his resignation, Beatty was back at "home" in Carlisle, still "gallanting the Ladies, as I find them very agreeable." His brother John, who left the army in 1780 to begin a medical career and then served in the Congress, helped him to find a farm near Princeton in 1794. But the land was worn out, its "improvements" were in ruins, and husbandry was no fit work for an amateur, much less for a self-characterized "old Stag of a Bachelor."[37] The land's seller, and Beatty's long-time mortgage holder, Reverend John Witherspoon, was a firm believer in the "absolute necessity of marriage" as virtually a requirement of citizenship. Erkuries was by now apparently courting in earnest, but he could barely even *describe* the business, except obliquely, in awkward military terms—"rais[ing] the seige," "retrograde manoeuvers," "out work," "expedit[ing] a surrender," "a state of Blockade," or even "sapping and mining"—much less carry it out successfully. No wonder one object of his "sallies" had "almost knocked [him] up" by observing that "when talking on *Love*. . . . I had got too old to feel in any great degree that powerfull passion or create it in the breast of a *young Lady*," although "she did not doubt but I was worth of a great deal of *es-*

teem and a Lady suitable to my *years* might possibly be persuaded to think so likewise."[38]

Beatty "thought there was too much truth" in this "wicked and malicious Story," and he took the rebuff as "a loud call . . . to be up and doing" on the many fronts of his gentility campaign. He hired several agricultural laborers, both to compensate for his own lack of specialized farming knowledge and to permit him to assume numerous civic and social obligations in the region. In 1798 he even rented the farm for a year to his own cottager. He used that interval to renew his acquaintance with the widow Ferguson, the pretty black-eyed songstress he had met in 1787, who was now the single mother of an eight-year-old daughter. In marked contrast to earlier days, there was little bluster or histrionic strategy in his pursuit of an old, unrequited flame. Beatty simply slipped off to Philadelphia for a week in mid-February of 1799, where their wedding was held, and then he returned to Princeton to prepare his domicile for family life. In late April he brought his bride of two months—already pregnant with his first child—and his stepdaughter home.[39]

They lived in middling happiness ever after. Their home, although a site of hard work and quiet pride, never became much more than a shabby experimental farm before being sold in 1816. Erkuries accumulated dozens of civil, civic, and ecclesiastical offices, as if to make up in functional density for two decades of voluntary exile from the republican life of the new nation. He became, true to his 1784 resolve, "deeply" but not profitably involved in western land speculation, a business that often put him back on the wretched roads over the Pennsylvania mountains that he had traveled in the 1780s. In 1816 he finally made it to Princeton. He sold his farm and moved into town to oversee his son's progress through the college that Beatty himself had never been able to attend. He lost large sums of money on that deal, however; and, although his wife took in boarders to supplement the household income, they never emerged from debt during Erkuries's life. Defying a postwar trend toward abolition, he bought, sold, and occasionally manumitted, African-American slaves throughout his years as a patriarch and gentleman freeholder. Beatty died in 1823, and, as the first mayor of the newly incorporated town of Princeton, he was buried in the town cemetery. His son, Charles Clinton Beatty, was a Presbyterian minister at Steubenville, in the decidedly postfrontier state of Ohio. Susannah Ewing Beatty moved there in 1825 to be with her son, and she lived out her days in a "genteel" household of the sort that her own husband might well have been excluded from only a generation before.[40]

The many contrary women whom Erkuries Beatty and his cohorts met between Philadelphia and Vincennes during the 1780s and 1790s—scouring votes from backwoods valleys, rank-ordering beaus on county seat porches, sustaining tribal resistance to American territorial demands, or just soberly holding down their share of the hard work of the "alcoholic republic"—offer more support to historians who emphasize the tiny behavioral cracks that the Revolution made in the patriarchal template of Anglo-America than to scholars who stress the legal, ideological, or constitutional continuities joining the gendered edifices of the old colonies and the new nation. The threadbare army of that republic, like its paymaster, moved back and forth along this axis doing the business of nationhood, and we can follow its travels, and travails, as with a cursor. Wherever we find puzzled soldiers such as Beatty exclaiming of female conduct that "I did not at all understand this phenomena," or civilian agents of the republic, like John Cleves Symmes, describing odd gender customs "which I never met with before—nor did I think such a one obtained in any part of the World," historians who care about the outcome of this important ongoing debate would do well to set up camp and reconnoiter the area.[41]

Even scholars who pronounce the old glass to have been half-cracked rather than still largely intact would acknowledge that the lack of systematic ideological foundations for redesigning the social roles of men and women prevented post-Revolutionary changes in gender expectations, however many, or varied, or warmly embraced, from becoming substantially cumulative, while rendering them highly vulnerable to predictable reactions and counterattacks. Here, too, the perspectives of soldiers might be enlightening. Beatty and his bluecoated peers witnessed some elements of those backlashes in inland places like Pittsburgh or Marietta, Ohio. Their accounts suggest that these were not solely the work of cranky, land-grabbing men like Judge Symmes, who were usually far too busy filing plat maps or foreclosing mortgages to do much more about "transgressing" women than wonder and whine. Instead, the words of soldiers like Beatty reflected more contentious processes of cultural reconstruction.

When the salons and "*Brilliant* Assembl[ies]" of Pittsburgh began to seem less receptive, or even open, to soldiers than the "frolics" and the "kick-ups" of earlier days, or when Marietta's rude but hospitable cabins were succeeded by frame houses with white fences, flower beds, lace curtains, and locked doors, such transformations were as much the work of *family* as of finance.

The self-imagined "Founding Families" of Pittsburgh, and the late-coming Federalist "pioneers" of Marietta and its imitators, were the true agents of these trans-Appalachian gentrifications. Patriarchy was nowhere more resilient in the post-Revolutionary world than when it was reinforced by consenting adult matriarchs. To whatever extent we are still willing, or able, to imagine the new west on such old analytical frames as "separate spheres" or "domesticity," we should also consider poor soldiers, bounty land notes, empty pay chests, "racoon boxes," and territorial balls, and recall that post-Revolutionary American society, from the conjugal pair to the local community to the nation state itself, was the offspring of both gender *and* social class revisions.[42]

But the entire frontier could not be smoothly plastered over with quarter-section grids, pictures, and patterned wallpapers. Bella Barclay vanished from Erkuries Beatty's sight, life, and, for all we know, memory, into the Pennsylvania forest within seconds after taking her leave of him in October of 1786. Unless she was just a colorful literary artifact of his lonely imagination, we may be able to recover a few facts about her prior or subsequent lives in the Upper Conocoheague Valley. Still, for all of her acknowledged ability to keep his pants on in two languages and at least three academic subjects, this would leave her as one of early America's far too many "inarticulate" souls.

If Conococheague was not destined to be another Marietta, it did earn a reputation as a hearth and exporter of strong-willed, stout-hearted women who never stopped talking back to soldiers. In the nineteenth century the valley was the birthplace of the mothers of two presidents as well as James Buchanan's niece, Harriet Lane, who served as his hostess in the White House. Thus, when the federal union split, the high water mark of the Confederate military surge was *not* at Gettysburg in July of 1863 but at Chambersburg—on the east branch of Conococheague Creek—a few weeks before and one year after that battle. The ranks who received these charges were "manned" largely by Yankee women who might have been a Greek chorus of Barclay's own goddaughters. The southern troops who occupied Chambersburg as a staging area for Gettysburg came predisposed to treat that fallen lady "very genteel," and doubtless with "plenty of good Toddy and Grog" too, but the townswomen were drinking none of those ancient elixirs. The rebels never erased memories of scowling, leering, derisive, and, they concluded, *ugly* German and Scotch-Irish women who mocked their "conquest" of the town and scorned their expectation of deferential conduct from socially inferior civilian subjects.[43]

However, the social price of "gallantries" spurned had risen fiercely in the decades since Erkuries Beatty bemusedly and almost self-deprecatingly recorded his awkward travels with Bella Barclay. In 1864 the rebels returned and burned Chambersburg to the ground! This episode reinforces the substructural continuities that many historians have intuitively perceived between the "Second American Revolution" and the nation's "First Civil War." And it suggests that the genuine settlement of both conflicts required —but ultimately failed to produce—the renegotiation of such fundamental categories of human experience as the "social relations of the sexes."

NOTES

Earlier versions of the essay were presented to the Brown Bag seminar of the Philadelphia Center for Early American studies and the 1998 meeting of the American Historical Association in Seattle. I am grateful to Dr. Edward Baptist for the invitation to present the paper, and to Professor Michael Zuckerman of the University of Pennsylvania, Professor Ann Little of the University of Dayton, and Dr. Greg Knouff of the David Library of the American Revolution, for reading and commenting on subsequent drafts.

1. "The Diary of Major Erkuries Beatty, Paymaster to the Western Army, May 15, 1786 to June 5, 1787," *Magazine of American History* 1 (1877): 314 (entry under September 30, 1786, but probably about October 4, 1786); original MS at the New York Historical Society: BV-Beatty. The "Conococheague Settlement" was apparently located in the valley between the eastern and western branches of Conococheague Creek, in Franklin County, Pennsylvania, just west of the county seat at Chambersburg.

2. Ibid., 314–15.

3. Ibid., 315.

4. Harry B. Weiss and Grace M. Zeigler, in *Colonel Erkuries Beatty, 1759–1823: Pennsylvania Revolutionary Soldier; New Jersey Judge, Senator, Farmer, and Prominent Citizen of Princeton,* (Trenton: Past Times Press, 1958), offer a popular biography of Beatty.

5. Charles Royster, *A Revolutionary People at War: The Continental Army and American Character, 1775–1783* (Chapel Hill: University of North Carolina Press, 1979); and Robert K. Wright, Jr., *The Continental Army* (Washington,

D.C.: U.S. Army, Center for Military History, 1983), explore elements of both the army's social structure and its institutional culture during the era of the American Revolution. See also, Charles Patrick Neimeyer, *America Goes to War: A Social History of the Continental Army* (New York: New York University Press, 1996).

6. The literature on the impact of the Revolution and its role on the status of women in American society, and more recently on the roles of or relations between the sexes generally, is voluminous. Many scholars—most prominently including Linda Kerber and Mary Beth Norton—have argued that while the "fathers" of the Revolutionary resistance did not intend changes in the legal or cultural structures that sustained the patriarchal character of early Anglo-American society, the upheavals of this generation allowed, or often even forced, many individuals to *behave* in ways not countenanced by the prevailing systems of gender relations. An important and still open question involves the stability, permanence, and direction of these behavioral changes in post-Revolutionary society. Kerber has identified an ideological constellation that she calls "Republican Motherhood," created by women themselves and retro-fitted onto American society during the generation after 1776, that sought to stabilize or harmonize this disjunction between intention and result. Much discussion of this subject involves attempts to apply or refine this idea. See Linda K. Kerber, *Women of the Republic: Intellect and Ideology in Revolutionary America* (Chapel Hill: University of North Carolina Press, 1980), esp. chaps. 2–4; Mary Beth Norton, *Liberty's Daughters: The Revolutionary Experiences of American Women, 1750–1800* (Boston: Little, Brown, 1980), esp. chaps. 6–7; Norton, "The Evolution of White Women's Experience in Early America," *American Historical Review* 89 (June 1984): 593–619. Other scholars, notably Joan Hoff (Wilson), have emphasized the many ways in which legal, constitutional, and other structural realities of American society did *not* change in favor of women before the midnineteenth century. See Joan Hoff, *Law, Gender, and Injustice: A Legal History of U.S. Women* (New York: New York University Press, 1991), esp. chaps. 2, 3; Joan Hoff Wilson, "The Illusion of Change: Women and the American Revolution," in *The American Revolution: Explorations in the History of American Radicalism*, edited by Alfred F. Young (DeKalb: Northern Illinois University Press, 1976), 385–445; Elaine F. Crane, "Dependence in the Era of Independence: The Role of Women in a Republican Society," in *The American Revolution: Its Character and Limits*, edited by Jack P. Greene (New York: New York University Press, 1987), 253–75.

7. For accounts of the organization and social composition of this regiment, see William B. Skelton, "The Confederation's Regulars: A Social Profile of Enlisted Service in America's First Standing Army," *William and Mary Quarterly*, 3d ser., 46 (October 1989): 770–85; and Skelton, "Social Roots of the American Military Profession: The Officer Corps of America's First Peacetime Army, 1784–1789," *Journal of Military History* 54 (October 1990): 435–52. The place

of armies in pre- and post-Revolutionary ideological debates is discussed in John Todd White, "Standing Armies in Time of War" (Ph.D. diss., George Washington University, 1978); Lawrence Delbert Cress, *Citizens in Arms: The Army and the Militia in American Society to the War of 1812* (Chapel Hill: University of North Carolina Press, 1982); and Richard H. Kohn, *Eagle and the Sword: The Federalists and the Creation of the Military Establishment in America, 1783–1802*, (New York: Free Press, 1975), esp. introduction and part 1.

8. Weiss and Zeigler, *Colonel Erkuries Beatty*, 1–11. The College of New Jersey was established in Newark, New Jersey, in 1746 but moved to Princeton ten years later. It began to be colloquially known by the name of its host community shortly after that time.

9. Ibid., 12–19. Beatty's brothers, John, Charles, and Reading, joined the Pennsylvania line during the same week that he did. The family was reasonably well connected politically to the Middle Atlantic Whig establishment, including ties of blood to Governor George Clinton of New York and of marriage to the surviving children of the late John Reading, a long-time member of the New Jersey Council and occasionally its acting governor. It is not clear, however, what, if any, specific connections the Beatty family had—except through the Presbyterian establishment—with members of the the emergent radical factions who had seized control of Pennsylvania's government during the crisis of 1776.

10. Royster, *Revolutionary People at War*, chap. 8, esp. 343–45. The supposed disablement of Continental officers for peacetime civilian livelihoods had attitudinal as well as specifically occupational bases; but Erkuries, who had little apparent "aristocratic" pretension in his temperament, seems better to illustrate the latter category. Skelton's, "Social Roots of the American Military Profession" does not provide any systematic data on the incidence of marriage among the officers, although this seems like a fundamental element of social identity. See also his *An American Profession of Arms: The Army Officer Corps, 1784–1861* (Lawrence: University Press of Kansas, 1992).

11. His role as the "babe" of his family made Erkuries the recipient of many of his siblings' solicitous letters and the subject of others. He was also an intermittent diarist during his army years, albeit seldom with the self-reflective clarity he showed on the day he met Bella Barclay. His periodic service in "desk" assignments, with its more regular duty hours, better access to paper, and more varied interaction with civilians than combat duty offered, also helped to create and preserve a record of the growth of his gendered personality. See Joseph M. Beatty, Jr., ed., "Letters of the Four Beatty Brothers of the Continental Army, 1774–1794," and "Letters from Continental Officers to Doctor Reading Beatty, 1781–1788," all edited by Joseph M. Beatty, Jr., *Pennsylvania Magazine of History and Biography* 44.3 (1920): 193–263, and 54.1 (1930): 155–74; "Beatty Letters, 1773–1782," edited by Joseph M. Beatty, Jr., *Proceedings of the New Jersey Historical Society* 80 (October 1962): 223–35, and 81 (January 1963): 21–46.

Also see the following published or manuscript diaries quoted below. John Beatty to Reading Beatty, January 24, 1780, in "Letters of the Four Beatty Brothers," 209 ("dead or married"). For a recent survey of Americans' changing perspectives on the intersections between sexual behavior, family formation, and reproduction during this period, see John D'Emelio and Estelle B. Freedman, *Intimate Matters: A History of Sexuality in America* (New York: Harper and Row, 1988), chap. 3.

12. Doctor Robert Wharry to Doctor Reading Beatty, July 27, 1781, February 6, 1782, March 12, 1782, in "Letters from Continental Officers," 161, 163, 165 (emphasis in original). It is unclear from the context whether Wherry saw African slaves as merely a proprietary by-product of his imagined courtships of wealthy white widows or as potential objects of his own romantic or sexual attention, but there seems to have been a transition from the first meaning to the second as his stay in the South lengthened.

13. John Beatty to Reading Beatty, August 16, 1781; [Reading Beatty to John Beatty], n.d., in "Letters of the Four Beatty Brothers," 221–22.

14. Erkuries Beatty to Reading Beatty, August 19, 1781, in "Letters of the Four Beatty Brothers," 223–26 (emphasis added).

15. Captain Isaac Van Horne to Doctor Reading Beatty, May 18, 1782, in "Letters from Continental Officers," 167; Erkuries Beatty to Reading Beatty, September 12, 1782, in "Letters of the Four Beatty Brothers," 230.

16. James McMichael to Doctor Reading Beatty, June 16, 1783, in "Letters from Continental Officers," 171. For evidence of much younger women evaluating and ranking the soldiers whom they met during the war, see Kathryn Zabelle Derounian, ed., *The Journal and Occasional Writings of Sarah Wister* (Rutherfurd, N.J.: Fairleigh Dickinson University Press, 1987), 46–47.

17. Captain Van Horne to Doctor Reading Beatty, August 13, 1781; Lieutenant Samuel Story to Doctor Reading Beatty, March 6, 1782, in "Letters from Continental Officers," 161, 164 (emphasis in originals).

18. See, for example, Royster, *Revolutionary People at War*, 30. Major William Van Lear to Doctor Reading Beatty, June 9, 1782, in "Letters from Continental Officers," 167–68.

19. Captain Van Horne to Doctor Reading Beatty, October 4, 1782, in "Letters from Continental Officers," 169.

20. Captain Van Horne to Doctor Reading Beatty, May 18, 1782; James McMichael to Doctor Reading Beatty, February 16, 1783; McMichael to Reading Beatty, June 21, 1783, in "Letters from Continental Officers," 167, 170, 172.

21. Captain Van Horne to Doctor Reading Beatty, March 7, 1784, in "Letters from Continental Officers," 173.

22. Erkuries Beatty to Reading Beatty, March 20, 1783; November 19, 1783, in "Letters of the Four Beatty Brothers," 234–35. A letter left for him at a tavern with a *u* inserted into his name, making "Capt *Beautty* of it . . . caused a laugh all thro town," and Erkuries begged his friends to send mail more discreetly.

23. Erkuries Beatty to Reading Beatty, April 14, 1784; May 1, 1784, in "Letters of the Four Beatty Brothers," 242–44.

24. Erkuries Beatty to Reading Beatty, May 1, May 25, 1784, in "Letters of the Four Beatty Brothers," 243, 249–51.

25. Erkuries Beatty to Reading Beatty, May 25, 1784, 250. This proposed enterprise appeared to trouble Beatty profoundly from an ethical standpoint, but he tried to excuse it on the ground that "the rest of the world generally does, to make money by any means."

26. Erkuries Beatty to Reading Beatty, January 24, 1785, and November 29, 1785, in "Letters of the Four Beatty Brothers," 252–56 (quotation on 255–56).

27. Erkuries Beatty Diary, October 1784 to August 1785, BV Beatty, New York Historical Society, entry for November 26, 1784. See Joseph F. Rishel, *Founding Families of Pittsburgh: The Evolution of a Regional Elite* (Pittsburgh, Pa.: University of Pittsburgh Press, 1990), esp. chap. 3.

28. Erkuries Beatty Diary October 1784 to August 1785, passim, esp. entries for November 26–28, 1784; January 27, March 17, 20, 21, 22, 23, 24, 1785.

29. Erkuries Beatty to Reading Beatty, November 29, 1785 and December 12, 1786, in "Letters of the Four Beatty Brothers," 255–56, 258–59.

30. Erkuries Beatty Diary, July 3 to October 25, 1787, entry for September 28, 1787.

31. Charles C. Beatty, *Record of the Family of Charles Beatty* (Steubenville, Ohio: Press of W. R. Allison, 1873), 85; Weiss and Zeigler, *Colonel Erkuries Beatty*, 24, 68–73. As the new federal government's finances stabilized and its problems paying the army eased—and as more garrisons were opened from Cincinnati to the West—the paymaster's duties were increasingly focused on the frontier itself, rather than back in the capital, negotiating helplessly with the nation's civilian political authorities.

32. Judge [John] Law, *The Colonial History of Vincennes, under the French, British, and American Governments* (Vincennes, Ind.: Harvey, Mason, and Company, 1858); Gayle Thornbrough, ed., *Outpost on the Wabash, 1787–1791: Letters of Brigadier General Josiah Harmar and Major John Francis Hamtramck . . . in the William L. Clements Library,* (Indianapolis: Indiana Historical Society, 1957); August Derleth, *Vincennes: Portal to the West,* (Englewood Cliffs, N.J.: Prentice-Hall, 1968).

33. See Susan C. Boyle, "Did She Generally Decide? Women in Ste. Genevieve, 1750–1805," *William and Mary Quarterly,* 3d. ser., 44 (October 1987): 775–89, esp. the sources cited in fn. 1; Winstanley Briggs, "The Enhanced Status of Women in French Colonial Illinois," in *The Quiet Heritage/Le Héritage Tranquil,* edited by Clarence A. Glasrud (Moorehead, Minn.: Concordia College, 1987); John Cleves Symmes to Robert Morris, June 22, 1790, in *The Correspondence of John Cleves Symmes,* edited by Beverly W. Bond (New York: Macmillan Company, 1926), 288–89.

34. John Cleves Symmes to Robert Morris, June 22, 1790, *Correspondence of John Cleves Symmes,* 290.

35. Wiley Sword, *President Washington's Indian War: The Struggle for the Old Northwest, 1790–1795* (Norman: University of Oklahoma Press, 1985), 101–30, 155–92. Ferguson left an infant daughter, Mary, born of his marriage to Susanah Ewing Ferguson two weeks before his death.

36. Ibid., 299–311.

37. *Record of the Family of Charles Beatty,* 86–87; Weiss and Zeigler, *Colonel Erkuries Beatty,* 24–30. Whether Beatty left the army for health reasons (as Wayne's public proclamation implied), in resentment over the promotion of officers by the new regime (as family tradition suggests), or because he felt that he needed to pursue different opportunities in civilian life, is unclear. In a private letter to Secretary of War Henry Knox, Wayne wrote that Beatty had become "totally incapacitated . . . for service by an Avidity to Whiskey." See Richard C. Knopf, *Anthony Wayne: A Name in Arms* (Westport, Conn.: Greenwood Press, 1960), 163. Erkuries Beatty to Reading Beatty, July 22, 1792; Erkuries Beatty to John Beatty, December 29, 1794, in "Letters of the Four Beatty Brothers," 260–61.

38. John Witherspoon, "Reflections on Marriage," *Pennsylvania Magazine,* September 1775, 408, quoted in Jan Lewis, "The Republican Wife: Virtue and Seduction in the Early Republic," *William and Mary Quarterly,* 3d ser., 44 (October 1987): 709; Erkuries Beatty to John Beatty, December 29, 1794, in "Letters of the Four Beatty Brothers," 261 (emphasis in quotation in original).

39. Erkuries Beatty to John Beatty, December 29, 1794, 261; Weiss and Zeigler, *Colonel Erkuries Beatty,* 34–50, 53.

40. This period in Beatty's life is insightfully discussed by Paul G. E. Clemens, in "Rural Culture and the Farm Economy in Late Eighteenth-Century New Jersey," in *Land Use in Early New Jersey,* edited by Peter O. Wacker and Paul G.E. Clemens (Newark: New Jersey Historical Society, 1995), esp. 1–15. See also *Record of the Family of Charles Beatty,* 89–92; Weiss and Zeigler, *Colonel Erkuries Beatty,* 61–67.

41. "Diary of Major Erkuries Beatty," [October 4, 1786], *Magazine of American History* 1 (1877): 314; Symmes to Morris, June 22, 1790, in Bond, *Correspondence of John Cleves Symmes,* 288–89; William J. Rorabaugh, *The Alcoholic Republic, an American Tradition* (New York: Oxford University Press, 1979).

42. Erkuries Beatty to John Beatty, December 22, 1785, in "Letters of the Four Beatty Brothers," 257; Rishel, *Founding Families of Pittsburgh.*

43. George O. Seilhamer, "Old Conococheague Families," *Papers of the Kittochtinny Historical Society* (Chambersburg, Pa.: Public Opinion Print, 1903), 281–303; and George O. Seilhamer, "Early School Girls of the Conococheague," *Papers of the Kittochtinny Historical Society* (Chambersburg, Pa.:

1908), 70–86, esp. 81–83. The women in question were Jane Irwin Harrison, wife of President William Henry Harrison and mother of President Benjamin Harrison; Elizabeth Speer Buchanan, mother of President James Buchanan; and Harriet Lane, Buchanan's niece and the informal "mistress of the White House" during his bachelor presidency. See Everard H. Smith, "Chambersburg: Anatomy of a Confederate Reprisal," *American Historical Review* 96 (April 1991): 432–55.

Chapter 10

"Imperfect Disclosures"

Cross-Dressing and Containment in Charles Brockden Brown's Ormond

Heather Smyth

When Martinette de Beauvais strides onto the stage of Charles Brockden Brown's Gothic novel *Ormond* (1799) in chapter 19, her arrival has been amply foreshadowed by other characters' speculations about her identity. Her revelation that she has dressed like a man to live the life of a revolutionary is also, though less obviously, the culmination of previously foreshadowed themes in the novel. There are, in fact, only two explicit instances of cross-dressing in *Ormond*: the cross-gender dressing of Martinette and the cross-class/cross-racial black chimney-sweep disguise of her brother Ormond. However, the startling effects of these cross-dressing incidents indicate a "category crisis" in the novel, a fundamental conflict that threatens to disrupt social binaries and hierarchies.[1] The destabilization of apparently discrete categories of identity is a larger motif in the novel, and the many instances of disguise in *Ormond*, including the constant replaying of characters' doubling and misrecognition of each other and the novel's emphasis on specularity and the performativity of gender and class, are rehearsals toward these actual examples of transvestiture.[2] Through this unsettling of gender and class hierarchies, Brown's novel offers an important site for the investigation of tensions in early republican discourse.

Set primarily in post-Revolutionary Philadelphia, *Ormond* focuses on the character of Constantia Dudley, an independent, educated, and resourceful young woman who, responsible for her recently blinded and swindled father, struggles with poverty and an outbreak of yellow fever that spreads through the city. During the course of the novel Constantia becomes acquainted with two unconventional figures who are later revealed to be brother and sister: Martinette de Beauvais, a worldly revolutionary who dressed as a man and fought in both the American and French Revolutions; and Ormond, an intelligent, eccentric, and secretive man who is actually a political extremist and a dangerous mercenary. Constantia is also reunited with a long-lost friend, Sophia Westwyn Courtland, who later announces to the reader that she is the narrator of the novel. In the novel's tension-filled final chapters Constantia's father is mysteriously murdered, and Ormond's growing obsession with Constantia leads to his attempted rape of her; but Constantia escapes by killing Ormond in self-defense, and leaves for Europe with Sophia.

Deception is a clear theme in the novel, and the identity of some characters is mobile, often shifting across lines of class and, less frequently, gender.[3] To a certain extent, the cross-dressing in the novel, and the novel's multiple instances of gender blurring or class disorder, suggest that gender and class are constructed, not natural or inherent. Gender and class can be worn like garments and can be confused and mistaken by means of the manipulation of surfaces. This contingency of gender and class undermines the strict hierarchies and divisions that are supported by an understanding of gender and class as inherent features of identity.[4] Brown's text poses this question: if, in *Ormond*, a woman does not have to be conventionally "feminine" (as this category is articulated in republican discourse) and can live like a man merely by dressing as one, and if social class can be mutable rather than fixed and identifiable largely by dress or gesture, what justification is there, especially in the supposedly egalitarian America posited by republican ideology, to maintain strict hierarchies of class and biologically defined roles for men and women?

The questioning of the coherence of identity, particularly as it addresses the lack of transparency of social identity, can be a destabilizing, potentially transformative feature of *Ormond*. Yet cross-dressing and masquerade may only appear to be subversive. Despite the fact that a gap is opened in Brown's text through which the reader may see the contingency of gender and class, Brown's anxiety about disorder and the instability of revolution serves to fix the boundaries of these categories. The text suggests that masks may confuse, but under masks lies "truth" or *real* human nature. Cross-dressing does not finally blur the divisions of gender and class; power and agency remain in the male sphere, and only the privileged have the mobility to move *through* class. The same tropes of disguise, misrecognition, and transformation that can destabilize tax-onomies of gender and class also have the power to reify the systems that underpin these divisions and hierarchies.

At a fundamental level, *Ormond* explores the power of disguise and the susceptibility of perception. It is written in the gothic genre, a form that "question[s] both reason and nature as reliable sources of knowledge" and "prohibits a secure framework for defining the self."[5] Deception, misrecognition, and allusions to the supernatural make reliable knowl-edge impossible in the text. The boundaries between characters blur, and authentic selfhood is questioned. The three female characters, for in-stance, are frequently identified with each other. Constantia and Mar-tinette share a strong resemblance, and Sophia is to Constantia "the image of a being like herself." Once they are reunited, Sophia and Con-stantia are inseparable: Sophia "would not part from her side." Sophia's and Martinette's identities also become confused, for when Constantia is told by her servant that she has a guest, she expects Sophia, but is pre-sented with Martinette.[6] Similarly, Craig, the "confidence man" who swindled Stephen Dudley, claims that he resembles his (fictional) brother, and Constantia recognizes the "points of contact" between herself and Ormond; Ormond asks her, "Is there no part of me in which you discover your own likeness?"[7] And individual characters also have multiple iden-tities that later congeal: Martinette appears as Miss Monrose, then as the purchaser of the lute that Constantia sells for rent money, and finally as Martinette herself; Ormond is Craig's landlord, the chimney-sweep, He-lena Cleves's lover, Martinette's brother, and the youth in the Russian army. By the end of the novel, Ormond's identity has shifted so many times that the reader expects any unnamed, newly introduced character, such as the man who purchases Sophia's picture, to turn out to be Or-mond. The blurring of character boundaries creates confusion in the novel and complication of the plot, and the transgression of borders be-tween characters sometimes also incorporates a transgression of gender and class divisions.

The constant repetition in *Ormond* of disguise, misrecognition of characters and class, and the deceptiveness of surfaces participates in the late eighteenth/early nineteenth-century anxiety about physiognomy. Pro-ponents of the pseudoscience of physiognomy held that the inner charac-ter of a person was visible and interpretable in his or her face and body.[8] Physiognomy also entailed a concern for differences of class and "race" and involved a system of judging moral types by shared physical features.[9] In early industrial America, with its rapid social and technological changes, it became increasingly important to be able to *read* the character of a stranger by appearances. There was a danger, however, that "confidence men" could become adept at mimicking virtuous appearances, "severing the link between surface appearances and inner moral nature."[10] Part of this fear centered on the possibility of people pretending to a higher class or level of respectability, as illustrated in *Ormond* by Craig, whose machinations lead to the Dudleys' poverty. There is a great desire, in *Ormond*, for appearances to be true representations of inherent qualities. Constantia, for instance, prides herself on "interpreting the language of features and looks" and formulating "conclusions as to the coincidence between mental and external qualities."[11] Yet confidence men like Craig and Ormond confound the legibility of appearances and gestures.

Ormond is the figure who most fully embodies the possibilities and threat of unstable identity. He disdains formal recognition of class divisions—"[h]e treated with systematic negligence the etiquette that regulates the intercourse of persons of a certain class"—although he maintains hierarchies by his "condescension."[12] Ormond claims absolute sincerity, but he is actually a master of disguise. His transformations are threatening, for the narrator calls his cross-dressing as a black chimney-sweep a "grotesque metamorphosis." His mutability enables him to "gain access, as if by supernatural means, to the privacy of others"[13]— that is to say, his concealment assists him in uncovering the disguises of others. The frightening thing about Ormond, aside from his uncanny adeptness at masking, is his predilection for using disguise to influence others, usually toward evil ends. Ormond aims to have complete control over the behavior of others, but he chooses to do this by invisible means. When he desires to convert Constantia to his opinions, he veils his ideas from her, revealing them instead in layers: "By piecemeal and imperfect disclosures her curiosity was kept alive." Constantia is caught in the web of this eternal striptease, which is "always new" and "always to be recommenced." He even camouflages himself as "a convert to her doctrines" in order to control her.[14]

In this world of disguise and confidence men, characters know or mistake the identity of other characters by means of appearance. In particular, individuals often explicitly apprehend social class with reference to visual appearance. A neighbor, Sarah Baxter, notes that Constantia is a woman "whom every accent and gesture proved to have once enjoyed affluence and dignity" and despairs that the young woman must perform menial tasks. Similarly, when Constantia meets Mrs. Melbourne, the wife of a wealthy acquaintance, the younger woman's "appearance and conversation" make a deep impression on her hostess: "a consciousness of her own worth, and disdain of the malevolence of fortune, perpetually shone forth in her behavior." Constantia's "person and dress" also attract the notice of the physician attending the sick during the yellow fever outbreak, for her appearance clearly is incongruous with her mean surroundings.[15] Although the emphasis at these moments is on the visual markers of class, such comments would suggest that higher social class, at least, is inherent, and "shines forth" despite reversals of fortune.

Yet class can be mistaken by these same visual signs. Ormond successfully tricks his own household when he "steps from the highest to the lowest rank in society" merely by wearing a chimney-sweep costume and blackening his face.[16] Constantia, too, is frequently thrust into social situations marked by class distinctions. When she ventures outside in her poor neighborhood, she is vulnerable to "the danger of being mistaken by the profligate of either sex for one of their own class."[17] Such a situation occurs at a tavern, where Constantia is mockingly called a "lady" by a servant; when she addresses him as a servant, he is angered at this appellation "coming from a person of her appearance." Her "authoritative tone" does not prevent his "air of familiar ridicule": her poor clothing, for him, is proof of her class. Later, at Ormond's house, another servant treats her with "a politeness to which she knew that the simplicity of her garb gave her no title." Even Constantia, who is "concious . . . of own worth," acknowledges that her clothing entitles her to certain class-specific treatment.[18] That Constantia, previously of a higher social rank, could "become" lower-class merely by a reversal of fortune and could be socially categorized by her dress and appearance suggests that class is not inherent and can be constructed by superficial attributes. She is an unwilling class cross-dresser, and her disguise reveals the mobility of class distinctions.

In his suggestion that social identity could be unstable, Brown draws not only on the gothic tradition but also on a long theatrical history of cross-dressing and gender ambiguity. However, Brown wrote *Ormond* at a particular historical moment in post-Revolutionary America in which the social and political upsets of the Revolution had put into question strict divisions of gender and class. Changing American conceptions of women's roles and class boundaries frame Brown's unconventional treatment of gender and class. In the social chaos of the Revolutionary era, wealthy families could become poor, and newly widowed or deserted women could experience abrupt changes in economic class; the Dudleys' sudden poverty in *Ormond* exemplifies the instability of social class in Revolutionary times. "Revolutionary experience taught that it was useful to be prepared for a wide range of unusual possibilities."[19] Thus, women were sometimes forced to perform "male" tasks. White women crossed the border between the private and public realms when they participated in boycotts, ventured political opinions in print, and successfully managed domestic finance in their husbands' absences.[20] Although they usually performed their political actions under a conventionally "feminine" or domestic guise, their participation in public discourse effected a blurring of the division between male and female roles. Women's public activities during the Revolution may have resulted in "the partial breakdown and reinterpretation of the gender roles that had hitherto remained unexamined. . . . The line between male and female behavior, once apparently so impenetrable, became less well-defined."[21]

It was necessary, in the new republic, to define the qualities of the model citizen, and particularly the model female citizen. The ideal white middle-class republican woman was to be "an independent thinker and patriot, a virtuous wife, competent household manager, and knowledgeable mother."[22] The desire for these qualities in a woman required a reappraisal of white women's education. The character of Constantia, in *Ormond*, represents Brown's exploration of the characteristics of this new woman, including her expanded education. Despite this expansion of the gender roles available to women, however, the post-Revolutionary vision for women coalesced into an image of Republican Motherhood. The Republican Mother was to exercise her patriotism and citizenship through the moral education of her sons. This image of political virtue gave white women a role in the new republic, but it reified their place in the maternal and domestic spheres, ignored the diversities of women's labor, and "at once implicitly granted political effectiveness and explicitly denied it."[23] If the Revolution initiated some blurring of gender roles, it did not prompt a fundamental reexamination of gender hierarchies. A contradiction remained between the individualistic principles of republican ideology and women's continued exclusion from the public sphere as economic and political agents.[24]

Linda Kerber has argued that "[i]t is a measure of the conservatism of the Revolution that women remained on the periphery of the political community."[25] And it is perhaps a measure of Brown's conservatism that his otherwise radical exploration of women's roles in the new republic does not lead to a fundamental rearticulation of gender roles. As Steven Watts notes, "Brown struggled to shape a civic role for women without removing them from their 'natural' domestic setting."[26] In his other writings, Brown often focuses on women's rights and their roles in post-Revolutionary America. In *Alcuin,* for example, Brown stages a dialogue between two characters on the subject of the political and legal rights of women and women's fitness for learning and accomplishment. The dialogue suggests that circumstances and the poverty of women's education, not inherent inferiority, are responsible for women's low status. Despite Brown's treatment of democratic ideas, however, Brown "employed the dialogue form to explore ideas, not to advance or to substantiate them."[27] *Alcuin* represents a "middle way," a "balancing act between responsibility and radicalism."[28] On the issues of gender roles and class hierarchies, Brown similarly maintains a middle ground in *Ormond.*

The issue of women's social roles is a central thematic concern in *Ormond.* The main protagonist, Constantia Dudley, is an independent, intelligent, rational, self-reliant woman. The novel explores her decision not to marry: she fears the loss of personal freedom in becoming "the property of another."[29] Brown illustrates Constantia's intelligence by showing that she is well equipped to engage in spirited debates with men. He demonstrates her independence and self-reliance by highlighting her economic responsibility for herself and her father. Constantia takes a public role when she negotiates with the Dudleys' landlord and when she ventures out into her community to help others during the plague, although her nursing and maternal activities keep her within the bounds for feminine behavior.[30] Martinette de Beauvais and Sophia Westwyn are also strong and rational female characters who participate in the public sphere: Sophia debates political and religious issues, and Martinette fights in both the American and French Revolutions.

Education is the key to the accomplishments of these remarkable women. Stephen Dudley ensures that Constantia has a more rational, worldly instruction than that offered to most women; this "tended to render her superior to the rest of women."[31] Martinette's education is even more unconventional. The two women's learning can be compared to those of other female characters: Helena Cleves, Ormond's former mistress, had academic training that fitted her only "to excite emotions more voluptuous than dignified"; her mind was "uninured to the discussion of logical points and the tracing of remote consequences." Brown notes that her intelligence was comparable to that of "the majority of her sex" but was far inferior to that of "some eminent females" or to that of Ormond himself."[32] The conventional education for women can have even more dire consequences: Sophia blames her mother's passionate, debauched behavior on "early indulgence" and "the embellishments of a fashionable education."[33]

Brown suggests that the three main female characters are capable of exceeding what their society takes to be the limits of gender. When the Dudleys are plunged into poverty, Constantia takes charge, and "the infirmities of sex and age vanished" in the face of the challenges of her new situation."[34] Similarly, when Sophia's mother dies, Sophia successfully handles "obligations and cares little suitable to [her] sex and age."[35] Martinette also moves *beyond* her role as a young woman, for circumstances led her "from the path of ambition and study usually allotted to [her] sex and age." Her circumstances also led Martinette to her involvement in the American Revolution, which the narrator finds unsurprising: it is clear to her that a woman of Martinette's sensibilities would be active in the current revolutionary period, "which called forth talents and courage without distinction of sex, and had been particularly distinguished by female enterprise and heroism." This hinting at gender mobility verges on a suggestion of androgyny when Martinette, speaking of fighting in the American Revolution, claims she felt "as if imbued with a soul that was a stranger to the sexual distinction."[36]

The obvious culmination of this gender crossing is Martinette's crossdressing. She explains, "I delighted to assume the male dress, to acquire skill at the sword, and dexterity in every boisterous exercise. The timidity that commonly attends women, gradually vanished."[37] She joins her husband in the American Revolution[38] and fights alongside hundreds of women in the French Revolution. Male disguise affords Martinette the freedom to act on her political beliefs and her "wild spirit of adventure."[39] In turn, the transvestism offers readers a glimpse of destabilized gender divisions: with only a change of clothes (and a man's education), a woman can do all the things a man can do. Martinette's character is the most radical example in *Ormond* of a new vision for womanhood.

Yet this cross-dressing does not necessarily result in a direct challenge to gender divisions and hierarchies. A gap is opened that allows the reader to see the distance between Martinette's *femaleness* and her transgression of *femininity*, but Brown does not seem prepared to push this to a fundamental questioning of gender roles. In fact, her masquerade becomes incorporated into a more conservative reassertion of gender hierarchies. Literary critics who work on masquerade and transvestiture have noted that cross-dressing can be doublesided. Mikhail Bakhtin, for example, argues that carnival and masquerade are a form of "turnabout," a "temporary suspension, both ideal and real, of hierarchical rank"; carnival is "filled with . . . the sense of the gay relativity of prevailing truths and authorities." Yet carnivals in the early modern era were tolerated, even encouraged, by authority and reinforced rather than overturned social hierarchies,[40] for they provided the masses with an orchestrated outlet for their frustrations that prevented focused critiques of existing power relations. Although role reversal or transvestism offers the illusion of altered social relationships, it leaves in place social hierarchies as well as a given system of representation: "Role-reversal does not deconstruct the dominant ideology; [it leaves] in place the same logic, the logic of sameness."[41] Masquerade may appear an enabling tool for the cross-dresser, but one must inquire into the purpose of a particular act of cross-dressing and the source of its pleasure. When a female transvestite adopts male dress in order to gain freedom of movement or the agency of the gaze, this act, rather than bringing into question her need or desire to cross-dress, may reaffirm the alignment of freedom and agency with male subjectivity in a patriarchal culture. And in Brown's text, only the higher classes cross boundaries: Ormond can *dress down* in terms of race and class without relinquishing his social privileges; and Martinette can not only cross *up* while dressed as a man but also cross *down* by ignoring class distinctions.[42] There is a possibility that, for the privileged, cross-dressing offers the adventurous pleasures of cultural or social border crossing without the responsibility of actual social change.[43] Cross-dressing in *Ormond*, rather than promising a subversion of order, may paradoxically reaffirm existing authority and the foundational terms of representation.

Indeed, despite Constantia's and Martinette's ostensible femaleness, their accomplishments are repeatedly described as masculine; this move reproduces an unbridgeable division between masculinity and femininity and the valorization of the masculine. When Constantia first sees

Martinette (as the purchaser of the lute), she describes her thus: "Hers were the polished cheek and the mutability of muscle which belong to woman, *but* the genius conspicuous in her aspect was heroic and contemplative. The female was *absorbed*, so to speak, in the rational creature."[44] The description asserts binary oppositions between *woman* and *heroic* and between *female* and *rational creature*. Similarly, Ormond praises Constantia for showing "a manlike energy" in reasoning; Constantia claims that Martinette demonstrates "large experience, vigorous faculties, and masculine attainments."[45] Although *masculine* is a valorized term, the narrative often devalues the term *feminine*: Constantia is "not so depraved and effeminate" that she would make an irrational decision.[46] And Ormond, with regard to Helena, states that "to make her wise it would be requisite to change her sex." He claims that, as a woman, Helena's capacity is "limited by nature and . . . the imbecility of her sex." Ormond's opinions are not generally praised in the novel— he is "one of the calumniators of the female sex"[47]—and his position differs from that supported by the rest of the text, which is that women's education and circumstances, not nature, limit their capacity for reason. His remarks, however, appear to be only a more extreme example of those made by other characters.

The litany of comments linking praiseworthy attainments with masculinity makes Martinette's cross-dressing seem less subversive. Her masquerading as a man suggests that she and Constantia, in being rational or adventurous, are acting *more like men*; the foundational terms of gender are not questioned. The frequency with which Constantia's intelligence is called "masculine" leads to a curiosity about whether Martinette is the only character in the text who crosses gender lines. Noah Webster, editor of *American Magazine*, published an unsigned comment in his magazine, which reads as follows: "If we picture to ourselves a woman . . . firm in resolve, unshaken in conduct, unmoved by the delicacies of situation, by the fashions of the times, . . . we immediately change the idea of the sex, and . . . we see *under the form of a woman* the virtues and qualities of a man."[48] The comment sounds suspiciously like a description of a man *dressed* as a woman. In the post-Revolutionary discourse of gender, in which a "firm," "unshaken," and "unmoved" woman is unimaginable, Constantia, in terms of her intellect, appears to be a cross-dressed man. Taking the *American Magazine* contributor's comment to this interesting extreme suggests that Constantia's "cross-dressing" (as a man in female guise), similar to Martinette's cross-dressing, reaffirms the valorized position of masculinity and the policed borders between male and female gender roles.

Martinette seems to be the limit case of an examination of gender roles. She is somehow monstrous, a freak, because she deviates so far from femininity. Her learning and intellect make her a spectacle: "my proficiency, when I allowed it to be seen, attracted great attention." Martinette's comment shows that she recognizes her difference and attempts to hide it from incredulous observers. Her cross-dressing and participation in the American Revolution gain her renown upon her return to Europe: she tells Constantia that the reports of officers "rendered me an object to be gazed at by thousands." She is "exhibited at operas and masquerades, made the theme of inquiry and encomium at every place of resort, and caressed by the most illustrious among the votaries of science and the advocates of the American cause."[49] Although Martinette's cross-dressing may serve as an enabling disguise, bringing her freedom, pleasure, and subjectivity, it also makes her a specular object for upper-class society. She is an object for the viewing (and caressing!) pleasure of others, a display. There is a hint that the experience may be pleasurable for Martinette: although she attempts to hide her difference, she favorably contrasts the luxurious venues of her exhibition with the privations of wartime.[50] However, the disguise does not offer her the liberty or privacy to observe without being in turn observed. In contrast, Ormond can step "from the highest to the lowest rank in society"[51] when he dresses as a black chimney-sweep, yet he still retains the power to control others: he can view them while remaining invisible.

Martinette is also the object of Constantia's gaze and a source of clandestine pleasure for her. Constantia listens "with unspeakable eagerness" to Martinette's tale; she is held back from eager questions by "scruples not easily explained."[52] Martinette excites Constantia's imagination: her stories lead Constantia to "numberless reflections. Her prospect of mankind seemed to be enlarged."[53] Yet when Constantia hears of Martinette's involvement in the French Revolution and learns that she took up arms and was willing to sacrifice her life for her beliefs, she recoils: she "shuddered and drew back, to contemplate more deliberately the features of her guest." She no longer feels a likeness or bond of sympathy with Martinette, yet still "listen[s] greedily, though not with approbation."[54] She conceals her disapproval from Martinette, yet she also seems to be concealing from herself her resemblance to Martinette. Only a few pages later, when Constantia anticipates moving to Europe, the language describing her excitement echoes descriptions of her fascination with Martinette: her mind had gone through "the most signal *revolution*," and the prospect of the move was "ravishing" and "kept her in a state of elevation and awe."[55] On some level Constantia admires and wishes to emulate the life of the revolutionary. Her actions also parallel Martinette's when she kills Ormond at the end of the novel: like Martinette, Constantia is willing to kill in the name of her principles, in this case to protect her honor.

Constantia may also be concealing a desire not just for the adventure of Martinette but for the adventurer herself. Historians suggest that the social practice of "separate spheres" for men and women, particularly in the eighteenth and nineteenth centuries, fostered emotionally intense, often erotic, friendships between women.[56] This explanation, or Brown's own early attraction to men,[57] can partly illuminate the instances of homoeroticism in *Ormond*, but the circumstances of Constantia's fascination with Martinette suggest a more complicated reading. Martinette's cross-dressing disrupts the metonymy of sex-gender-sexuality and can leave not just gender constructions but desire in flux.[58] Before Constantia even meets Martinette, when she only knows her as Ursula Monrose, she speaks of her in romantic terms, imagining that Ursula "would prove worthy of her love." After their friendship begins, Constantia becomes "daily more enamoured" of Martinette. Constantia's passionate friendship with Sophia even more clearly suggests the possibilities opened up by a destabilizing of gender. Sophia demonstrates her commitment to Constantia when she leaves her husband in England the day after her marriage and travels to America to find Constantia. And their reunion is marked by such passionate exclamations as "O precious inebriation of the heart! O pre-eminent love!" and Sophia's firm statement, "Henceforth, the stream of our existence was to mix."[59] Same-sex desire in the novel does not circulate only among the women; it also includes Ormond, who displays homoerotic desire by being most attracted to that part of Constantia that is "masculine."[60]

The homoerotics of the women's relationships in particular highlights the absence of heterosexual romance and marriage in *Ormond*. Constantia's refusal of two male suitors stands in stark contrast to her intense connection with Martinette.[61] Constantia does not marry at the end of the novel but instead leaves for Europe with Sophia; a homoerotic bond thus replaces the usual sentimental ending. On the other hand, if the framing device of the novel, Sophia's letter to I. E. Rosenberg, an acquaintance of

Constantia, is a presentation of the character of Constantia to a potential male suitor (Sophia writes, "I am well acquainted with your motives, and allow that they justify your curiosity"),[62] then the exploration of Constantia as a "new woman" is caught up in the larger project of reinscribing her as a commodity in the marriage market.

Despite Constantia's attraction to Martinette, if her withdrawal of sympathy is the final word on the latter woman's boundary crossings, then Martinette appears abominable, because her "woman's heart" is "inured to the shedding of blood."[63] The extremity of Martinette's unsettling of gender divisions parallels the extremity of her political sensibilities: she goes too far. Although in his youth Brown was an ideological radical, he became a Federalist shortly after writing *Ormond*; in the novel, the French Revolution is the limit case of social upheaval and necessitates a reappraisal of the potential social chaos of post-Revolutionary America. Constantia's rejection of Martinette seems a turning point in the novel. The next scene, in which she finds her father murdered, marks a new role for Constantia. She is transformed and is "recast as a sentimental heroine."[64] She shrieks and swoons too when she sees her father, and swoons upon finding Sophia. Constantia's transformation into a fainting heroine can be seen as a product of Brown's uncertainty about the chaotic possibilities he had unleashed in his novel.[65]

Brown's ambivalence, if that is indeed the cause of this double move of subversion and containment, may be ascribed to his perceived need to clothe (cross-dress?) his unconventional views in a form palatable to his audience. He is undoubtedly writing at an historical moment when a questioning of gender roles is still radical.[66] *Alcuin*, published only a year before *Ormond*, in 1798, was "important in literary history as a 'first', . . . [and] equally important in social history as a 'last.' Brown's initial publishing venture coincided with the end of an era and the climax of discussion on the 'woman question.'"[67] Yet Brown has also shown himself to be, if radical in his views on women's education, conservative in his anxiety about social chaos and revolution. The four novels that he wrote between 1798 and 1799—*Wieland, Ormond, Arthur Mervyn*, and *Edgar Huntly*—progressively document his concerns about the instability of identity and dissolution of social relationships that characterized the tensions between Jeffersonian and Federalist factions in Philadelphia and that marked a transition in his own ideology from republicanism to federalism. After writing these novels, Brown turned to more explicitly sentimental fiction, then renounced fiction altogether and in 1803 became editor of the Christian periodical *Literary Magazine and American Register.* By 1805, Brown had become "a bourgeois moralist in an ascending culture of capitalism."[68] The seeds of this transition are evident in *Ormond*, where the instability of identity that accompanies a questioning of gender and class divisions can be a product of, perhaps also a contributor to, social instability.

Social chaos inverts hierarchies of gender and class, disrupts the chain of acquaintances that permit knowledge of a stranger's character, and confuses the relationship between appearance and identity. Issues of representation and knowability take shape in *Ormond* at the formal level in the treatment of theatricality. The many theatrical references in *Ormond* make explicit the fact that masking is a large concern, even when characters are not actually disguised. Some of these instances are obvious, such as the frequent references to "theater of suffering" and the "actors in the great theater of Europe."[69] Yet theatrical words often appear in ways that suggest that the novel itself is a play: Constantia makes an "entrance" and views a "scene of horrors"; Sophia introduces herself "on the stage" and anticipates meeting Constantia "on that very stage" of London.[70] The main characters are described by their clothes, appearance, or gestures, but rarely by the specificities of their facial features;[71] this has the effect of implying that anonymous actors are inhabiting the characters' roles.

The stagedness of *Ormond* suggests the unreliability of surfaces and appearances. The scene in which Baxter spies on Ursula Monrose/Martinette carrying the dead body of her guardian is a clear example of the theatricality of the text and the undercutting of knowledge gained by visual means. Baxter is (ironically, for this scene) employed as a night watchman. One night, his attention is drawn to the Monrose's house by "the feeble and flitting ray of a distant and moving light." What he sees out his window is a stage: "There was annexed to [Monrose's house] a small garden or yard, bounded by a high wooden fence. Baxter's window overlooked this space." From his seat in what can be called the balcony of this theatre, Baxter sees a figure illuminated by the spotlight: he "caught a glimpse of a human figure passing into the house. . . . This appeared by the light which streamed after him." Significantly, "[t]he person disappeared too quickly to allow him to say whether it was male or female." Baxter grabs a sword and rushes down to the yard and at this point becomes an actor in the scene as well as an observer: he "[raised] his head above the fence," showing his "muscular form and rugged visage," and the narrator notes that "an observer would be apt to admit fearful conjectures." When he finally recognizes that the "spectacle" is Miss Monrose dragging a dead body, he looks at her face and sees "every feature set to the genuine expression of sorrow": "Her senses seemed for a time to have forsaken her. She sat buried in reverie, her eyes scarcely open, and fixed upon the ground."[72]

However, Baxter has misread the scene: he confuses her gender at first, and he also misinterprets the "expression" that is "set" on her face. As Martinette later explains to Constantia, Baxter was a false witness. Martinette "rejoiced" at Roselli's death, because it ended his troubles. She tells Constantia that Baxter's "rueful pictures of my distress and weakness . . . existed only in his own fancy." This revelation leads Constantia to reflections on "the deceitfulness of appearances."[73] In its emphasis on performance and spectacle, the scene suggests that immediate appearances are untrustworthy. The indirect narration of the Baxter scene further highlights the unreliability of its interpretation: the story is passed from Mr. Baxter to Sarah Baxter, to Constantia, to Sophia, and is then redirected from Constantia to Martinette for an alternative interpretation.

The fact that this use of theatricality underlies the novel can be a possible way to keep open the fissures between *natural* and *constructed* gender and class that seem to be foreclosed upon by Brown's ambivalence. Lesley Ferris suggests that "transvestite theater—cross-dressing in performance—is an exemplary source of the writerly text, a work that forces the reader/spectator to see multiple meanings in the very act of reading itself, of listening, watching a performance."[74] Baxter's position as both an observer and player parallels the position of the reader of *Ormond* and necessitates the reader's skeptical interpretation of visible gender and class attributes. The moment at which the artifice of social identity becomes visible is not lost by Brown's reassertion of gender and class hierarchies. Brown is willing to explore, but in the end not endorse, an interpretation of republican discourse that imagines fluid boundaries between sexual roles or divisions of class. However, *Ormond* raises issues of representation and border crossing on multiple levels, so that features such as theatricality or cross-dressing can offer a glimpse of unsettling possibilities and a questioning of conventional terms of representation.

In the end, Brown shows himself to be conducting in *Ormond*, as Davidson notes about *Alcuin*, a "balancing act between responsibility and radicalism."[75] Brown is willing to imagine certain transgressions of gender and class: fuller education for women, more equitable marriages, perhaps greater class mobility. Yet the icons of this transgression—Martinette costumed as a soldier, Ormond as a chimney-sweep—are frightening in their implications of social chaos. *Ormond* is written at the moment of post-Revolutionary America's turning from the egalitarian possibilities of the new republic: "America, during these difficult years, rejected her revolutionary heritage, the alliance with France that was its vestige, and the idealism both bespoke, and turned to a more practical ethic, a politics of survival. *Ormond* allegorizes this tack in the nation's course."[76] Martinette is both the cause and effect of the anxiety produced by social chaos: her characterization reflects a recurring historical pattern in which the unease generated by social change, and particularly the instability of gender and class hierarchies, focuses its energies on the subject of "dress violation," especially women's cross-dressing.[77] Martinette is the realization of the "category crisis" that troubles *Ormond*. She is also the cause of anxiety, for the extremity of her gender transgression necessitates the inscription of her as monstrous. Yet even if the radical possibilities of gender and class mutability are contained by Brown and do not lead to fundamental questions about the distribution of social power, the fissures between inherent and constructed social identities, between the *existential* and the *aesthetic*, have become visible. The emphasis on representation, raised by issues of theatricality, retains these subversive possibilities.

NOTES

I would like to thank Mary Chapman for her detailed comments on drafts of this paper.

1. I borrow the idea of "category crisis" from Marjorie Garber, *Vested Interests: Cross-Dressing and Cultural Anxiety* (New York: Routledge, 1992), 17.

2. While an exploration of racial issues may be a feature of some of Brown's other works, these issues seem to play a smaller role in *Ormond*.

3. Few critics have shifted focus from the theme of deception and disguise to note the category crisis accentuated by cross-dressing in *Ormond*. Many have ignored the instances of cross-dressing and have instead emphasized the disjunction between appearances and "reality," rather than the border crossings that occur during masquerade. Bill Christophersen, for instance, notes that in *Ormond*, disguise and masquerade function as symbols of self-blindness and self-evasion. See

The Apparition in the Glass: Charles Brockden Brown's American Gothic (Athens, Ga. and London: University of Georgia Press, 1993), 168. However, Michael Davitt Bell argues that disguise in the novel represents the "dialectic between innocence and experience[,] between 'sincerity' and 'duplicity,'" or, more generally, "between energy and order." See "'The Double-Tongued Deceiver': Sincerity and Duplicity in the Novels of Charles Brockden Brown," *Early American Literature* 9.2 (1974): 143, 151. Both Alan Axelrod and Michael Davitt Bell suggest that the masquerade symbolizes the mutability of truth that marks creative fiction. See Bell, "'The Double-Tongued Deceiver,'" 159; and Axelrod, *Charles Brockden Brown: An American Tale* (Austin: University of Texas Press, 1983), 126. The critics who do note the border crossings tend not to comment on the radical possibilities opened by cross-dressing and disguise. While *Ormond* may be set in an unstable post-Revolutionary world that threatens "coherent selfhood," Ormond's cross-dressing indicates only his personal forcefulness or eclecticism. This position is articulated by Steven Watts in *The Romance of Real Life: Charles Brockden Brown and the Origins of American Culture* (Baltimore and London: Johns Hopkins University Press, 1994), 95. Although Pattie Cowell offers a useful reading of "[t]he challenging of class and gender hierarchies" in *Ormond*, she does not connect the thematic treatment of this challenge with the structural and symbolic inversion of class and gender hierarchies occasioned by cross-dressing. See "Class, Gender, and Genre: Deconstructing the Social Formulas on the Gothic Frontier," in *Frontier Gothic: Terror and Wonder at the Frontier in American Literature*, edited by David Mogen, Scott P. Sanders, and Joanne B. Karpinski (London: Associated University Presses, 1993), 133.

4. Marjorie Garber usefully notes that "the transvestite is both a signifier and that which signifies the undecidability of signification . . . the figure of the transvestite in fact *opens up the whole question of the relationship of the aesthetic to the existential*" (Garber, *Vested Interests*, 37, 71; emphasis in original).

5. Cowell, "Class, Gender, And Genre," 127–28.

6. Charles Brockden Brown, *Ormond; or the Secret Witness* [1799], edited with an introduction by Ernest Marchand (New York and London: Hafner Publishing Company, 1937), 155, 207, 156. All subsequent references to *Ormond* are from this edition. As this edition is out of print, I encourage readers to consult a new edition of *Ormond* that is forthcoming from Broadview Press. See Charles Brockden Brown, *Ormond*, edited by Mary Chapman (Peterborough: Broadview Press, forthcoming).

7. *Ormond*, 81, 121, 138. The idea that people are equal and therefore similar is an idea central to democratic idealism. I am indebted to Mary Chapman for bringing this point to my attention.

8. Ann Jessie van Sant argues that the "eighteenth-century interest in interior discovery" led to a desire for "transparent bodies," or for a "window" to the heart. She notes the shared belief that "psychological experience was prominently

located in the body." See van Sant, *Eighteenth-Century Sensibility and The Novel: The Senses in Social Context* (Cambridge: Cambridge University Press, 1993), 60–61, 97.

9. Mary Cowling notes that researchers concerned with physiognomy and phrenology undermined "the Lockean-based belief in man's equality." Physiognomy was used to distinguish and justify clear lines of demarcation between social classes. See *The Artist as Anthropologist: The Representation of Type and Character in Victorian Art* (Cambridge: Cambridge University Press, 1989), 121. I put the word "race" in quotation marks to gesture toward the historically specific use of this term as a designation of difference. During the years of the popularity of physiognomy, the Irish, for example, were considered a separate "race" from the English.

10. Karen Halttunen, *Confidence Men and Painted Women: A Study of Middle-Class Culture in America, 1830–1870* (New Haven: Yale University Press, 1982), 42. Van Sant also points out that "one of the principal means of criticizing sensibility lay in revealing the extent to which it could be affected." See van Sant, *Eighteenth-Century Sensibility*, 124.

11. *Ormond*, 62–63.

12. Ibid., 94.

13. Ibid., 110, 96.

14. Ibid., 147–48.

15. Ibid., 49, 90, 42.

16. Ibid., 110.

17. Ibid., 17.

18. Ibid., 77–78, 90.

19. Linda K. Kerber, *Women of the Republic: Intellect and Ideology in Revolutionary America* (Chapel Hill: University of North Carolina Press, 1980), 189.

20. See, for example, Jeanne Boydston, *Home and Work: Housework, Wages, and the Ideology of Labor in the Early Republic* (New York and Oxford: Oxford University Press, 1990), 33. See also Sara M. Evans, *Born for Liberty: a History of Women in America* (New York: Free Press, 1989), 48–53.

21. Mary Beth Norton, *Liberty's Daughters: The Revolutionary Experience of American Women, 1750–1800* (Boston: Little, Brown and Co., 1980), 224–25.

22. Ibid., 256.

23. Evans, *Born for Liberty*, 57; Norton, *Liberty's Daughters*, 298. Boydston also discusses Revolutionary and post-Revolutionary women's labor in *Home and Work*, 43. See also Shirley Samuels, "The Family, the State, and the Novel in the Early Republic," *American Quarterly* 38.3 (1986): 384.

24. Boydston, *Home and Work*, 30, 43–44; Evans, *Born for Liberty*, 55. See also Barbara Bardes and Suzanne Gossett, *Declarations of Independence: Women and Political Power in Nineteenth-Century American Fiction* (New Brunswick, N.J. and London: Rutgers University Press, 1990), 5.

25. Kerber, *Women of the Republic*, 12.

26. Watts, *The Romance of Real Life*, 60.

27. Cathy N. Davidson, "The Matter and Manner of Charles Brockden Brown's *Alcuin*," in *Critical Essays on Charles Brockden Brown*, edited by Bernard Rosenthal (Boston: G. K. Hall and Co., 1981), 82.

28. Ibid., 83.

29. *Ormond*, 69.

30. If, however, the yellow fever is representative of "political upheaval" and revolution, as Bill Christophersen maintains, perhaps Constantia's *fighting* of the plague can be seen as a woman's less conventional actions in time of war, paralleling the involvement of Martinette and other female revolutionaries. This reading would complicate an understanding of Constantia's nursing activities as solely maternal or feminine. On the other hand, although her actions during the plague may appear less conventional (given Christophersen's hypothesis), Constantia's opposition to the revolution throughout the text suggests that her fighting is more conservative. For a discussion of the symbolism of the yellow fever, see Bill Christophersen, *The Apparition in the Glass*.

31. *Ormond*, 28.

32. Ibid., 98–99.

33. Ibid., 187.

34. Ibid., 19.

35. Ibid., 209.

36. Ibid., 166–70.

37. Ibid., 167.

38. There are historical precedents for Martinette's cross-dressing. As Kerber (189), Norton (174, 247) and Evans (52) note, Deborah Sampson Gannett dressed as a man and fought for the rebel army in the American Revolution. See also Julia Ward Stickley, "The Records of Deborah Sampson Gannett, Woman Soldier of the Revolution," *Prologue* 4 (1972): 233–41.

39. *Ormond*, 167.

40. Mikhail Bakhtin, *Rabelais and His World*, translated by Helene Iswolsky (Cambridge: MIT Press, 1968), 10–11, 9.

41. Catherine Craft-Fairchild, *Masquerade and Gender: Disguise and Female Identity in Eighteenth-Century Fictions by Women* (University Park: Pennsylvania State University Press, 1993), 11, 65.

42. It is worth noting that Martinette's expansive personality leads to her transgression of social mores when she visits Constantia. She refuses to wait for the servant to lead her to Constantia, instead entering the room "with careless freedom" (156). Martinette has the upper hand during her visit because she disorients Constantia by ignoring class rituals. Her behavior is reminiscent of Ormond's habitual neglect of etiquette. However, her behavior could also be explained by her "foreignness" as well as her privileged class position.

43. See Gail Ching-Liang Low, "White Skins/Black Masks: The Pleasures and Politics of Imperialism," *New Formations* 9 (Winter 1989): 93.

44. Brown, *Ormond*, 63; emphases mine.

45. Ibid., 131, 157.

46. Ibid., 69.

47. Ibid., 106, 131.

48. *American Magazine* (February 1788), 134. Quoted in Linda Kerber, *Women of the Republic*, 198; emphases mine.

49. Brown, *Ormond*, 166–68. The display and fetishization of Martinette sounds remarkably like that of the "Hottentot Venus." Anne McClintock notes that in 1829 "the 'Hottentot Venus' was the prize attraction at a ball given by the Duchess du Barry in Paris." See *Imperial Leather: Race, Gender and Sexuality in the Colonial Contest* (London: Routledge, 1995), 401, n. 49. McClintock argues that in Victorian Europe, visible stigmata were invented as "a commodity spectacle" that contributed to "the discourse of racial science and the urban surveillance of women and the working class" (41). In 1810, Saartjie Baartman, an African woman also called a "Hottentot," was exhibited in Europe and her genitalia "overexposed and pathologized before the disciplinary gaze of male medical science and a voyeuristic public" (42). The pathologizing of Martinette's crossdressing and "masculine" sensibilities suggests that her exhibition performs the function of disciplining Martinette and other potential gender transgressors, as well as disciplining Constantia as she listens to Martinette's story.

50. Brown, *Ormond*, 168.

51. Ibid., 110.

52. Ibid., 158.

53. Ibid., 170.

54. Ibid., 172.

55. Ibid., 175; emphasis mine.

56. See, for example, Carroll Smith-Rosenberg, *Disorderly Conduct: Visions of Gender in Victorian America* (New York: Alfred A. Knopf, 1985). Smith-Rosenberg argues that "from at least the late eighteenth through the mid-nineteenth century, a female world of varied and yet highly structured relationships appears to have been an essential aspect of American society" (53). Female relationships ranged from sisterly love to "sensual avowals of love by mature women" in a social environment that considered women's intense friendships "both socially acceptable and fully compatible with heterosexual marriage" (53, 59). Smith-Rosenberg suggests that Victorian America was a cultural environment that permitted individuals some movement across a "spectrum of love-object choices" (59). See also Nancy F. Cott, *The Bonds of Womanhood: "Woman's Sphere" in New England, 1780–1835* (New Haven: Yale University Press, 1977).

57. Although I believe that the homoeroticism in *Ormond* supports the disruptions of identity, sexuality, and gender that mark the text, I hesitate to at-

tribute to Brown particular intentions for its inclusion. His interest may have been to titillate his readers. However, Leslie Fiedler argues that *Ormond*'s popular failure was attributable to the inclusion of the homoeroticism between Constantia and Sophia. See *Love and Death in the American Novel* (New York: Dell, 1966), 89. Alternatively, Brown may have explored homoeroticism in his novel for creative, or perhaps personal, reasons. In addition to Brown's early romances with women, Steven Watts notes the writer's intense romantic friendships with two young men, William Woods Wilkins and Joseph Bringhurst Jr. Evidence for romantic attachment includes letters written by the young Brown to these two men, in which he claims to be "absolutely enamoured of [Wilkins]" and asks Bringhurst to "Let me cherish thee, in the same rapture which thou breathest." Brown's sexuality is quoted and the letters quoted in Watts, *The Romance of Real Life*, 33–34.

58. Lisa Moore writes a provocative review of Felicity A. Nussbaum's *The Autobiographical Subject: Gender and Ideology in Eighteenth-Century England* (1989), in which she notes that Nussbaum's tendency, symptomatic of much feminist criticism, to collapse the categories of gender and sexuality leads her to "reinscribe the bipolar heterosexism that insists on the priority of divisions between masculine and feminine, men and women, and assumes that desire is produced in the relations between these two poles and never within them." Nussbaum's reading obscures representations of female homoeroticism in eighteenth-century texts such as the autobiographical *A Narrative of the Life of Mrs. Charlotte Charke* (1759), in which the author's cross-dressing as a man provides evidence, according to Moore, "about the possibility of a female homoerotic sexual identity formed through the unsystematic adoption of various class and gender practices and identities in the service of sexual fantasy and pleasure rather than gender resistance." See "'She Was Too Fond of Her Mistaken Bargain': The Scandalous Relations of Gender and Sexuality in Feminist Theory," *diacritics* 21.2–3 (1991): 93.

59. Brown, *Ormond*, 59, 157, 207–8.

60. I thank Guy Beauregard for this observation.

61. Alan Axelrod has also noted this feature of *Ormond*. See Axelrod, *Charles Brockden Brown*, 120.

62. Brown, *Ormond*, 3.

63. Ibid., 171.

64. G. St. John Stott, "Second Thoughts about Ormond," *Etudes Anglaises* 43.2 (1990): 163. Stott refers to Herbert Ross Brown, who notes that "Only [Constantia's] susceptibility to swoons saved her from becoming 'a new woman.'" In Ross Brown, *The Sentimental Novel* (Durham, N.C., Duke University Press, 1940), 116.

65. Brown, *Ormond*, 177, 184. Her transformation is not complete, however. Although Constantia nearly becomes the feminine victim of Ormond the seducer/rapist, she does, as mentioned above, choose to kill him to save her honor—

a violent action based on principles that resembles Martinette's fighting for liberty.

66. Brown's unease about both the French Revolution and changing gender roles gains texture from Linda Kerber's argument that in the new republic "major changes in women's political life were associated with the radical stages of the French Revolution, and erasure of those changes was associated with the retreat from radicalism." See Kerber, "Separate Spheres, Female Worlds, Woman's Place: The Rhetoric of Women's History," *Journal of American History* 75.1 (1988): 20.

67. Davidson, "Matter and Manner," 72. Paul Lewis similarly argues that, while Brown takes a speculative, rather than clearly radical or conservative, position on gender politics, "the force of his speculation took him into territory rarely explored by his contemporaries, male or female." However, Lewis spends little time exploring the implications of this statement in relation to Brown's work, for his goal in this article is primarily to argue for Brown's inclusion in feminist revisions of the canon of early American writing. See "Charles Brockden Brown and the Gendered Canon of Early American Fiction," *Early American Literature* 31.2 (1996): 183.

68. Watts, *The Romance of Real Life*, 132.

69. Brown, *Ormond*, 49, 154–55.

70. Ibid., 50, 47, 185, 195.

71. Martinette is a notable exception. Constantia's description of Martinette's facial features and complexion (63) highlights the lack of such descriptions of the other characters.

72. Brown, *Ormond*, 54–57.

73. Ibid., 173, 174.

74. Lesley Ferris, "Introduction: Current Crossings," in *Crossing the Stage: Controversies on Cross-Dressing*, edited by Lesley Ferris (London and New York: Routledge, 1993), 8.

75. Davidson, "Matter and Manner," 83.

76. Bill Christophersen, *The Apparition in the Glass*, 80.

77. Jonathan Dollimore discusses this phenomenon in the context of the Renaissance in "Shakespeare Understudies: The Sodomite, The Prostitute, The Transvestite and Their Critics," in *Political Shakespeare: Essays in Cultural Materialism*, edited by Jonathan Dollimore and Alan Sinfield (Manchester: Manchester University Press, 1994), 141.

Chapter 11

"Insidious Murderers of Female Innocence"

Representations of Masculinity in the Seduction Tales of the Late Eighteenth Century

Rodney Hessinger

In January 1801 the *Ladies Magazine and Musical Repository* presented the following song. Entitled "The Men are all Rovers alike," it was sure to strike a familiar chord with its readers:

> To me yet in teens Mamma would oft say,
> That men were deceivers and sure to betray;
> This lesson so strongly she painted to me,
> That lovers I thought all deceivers must be
>   And that men are all rovers alike.
> Young Collin is handsome, good humor'd beside,
> With artless kind offer, would make me his bride;
> Mamma was mistaken I plainly can see,
> And I doubt if all rovers deceivers must be,
>   Or that men are all rovers alike.
> Thus sung the fair damsel, when Collin appear'd
> Her doubts now all vanish'd, no danger she fear'd
> To join in sweet wedlock, the lovers agree,
> Was Miss in the wrong, that hereafter you'll see,
> For the men are all rovers alike[1]

We can not know for sure to what extent, if at all, these lyrics were written tongue in cheek. To the modern reader, at least, there appears to be an almost playful tone in its lines. We can know, however, that the potential humor such a song held would rely on the readers' acquaintance with the themes it touched on.

In the years following the American Revolution, popular novels and periodicals began to define manhood as immoral. The seduction and abandonment of young women by young male predators was a plot line which late eighteenth-century American readers would know quite well. The regularity with which this theme was explored and the seriousness of tone used in such investigations suggest that there was a very real fear underlying these stories. Seduction fiction depicted the difficulties facing young women who had gained a measure of freedom from parents and community but as a result were exposed to greater exploitation at the hands of mobile and unrestrained young men. While seduction fiction may be important as a window into late eighteenth-century American society, northern and older regions in particular, it is of even greater significance because of the formative role it had in shaping American culture. Such fiction not only depicted the seduction and abandonment of young women but attempted to offer solutions to this perceived problem.

This essay shall demonstrate that a variety of cultural strategies were explored in seduction literature to resolve the problem of unaccountable male youth. Some writers held up an ideal of manhood which was steeped in the culture of sensibility. Young men were encouraged to be men of feeling, unashamed to shed a tear or to assist a vulnerable woman. Similarly, writers would ask men to listen to their internal monitors or their consciences, both concepts which were gaining wider cultural currency and marked an ideological shift from former, more coercive patterns of social control. However, writers were not reticent to double their chances by appealing to coercion as well. Visions of otherworldly punishment for male seducers populated seduction tales. Some writers also gave a measure of blame to women and asked them to avoid coquettish behavior which attracted suspect males.

Yet these cultural strategies of control did not prove most popular, in part, at least, because they contradicted the logic of the most popular message to emerge from the seduction tales. Above all else, these tales insisted that young men were immoral, and that as a result, young women needed to seek the protective guidance of parents in seeking prospective partners. It was to young women that these tales were most often addressed, and it was these young women who were increasingly told that women were by nature virtuous and chaste.[2]

While scholars have explored in depth the process whereby woman-hood was redefined as virtuous, the transformation of the definition of manhood has not been given adequate notice. Ruth Bloch has effectively described how in the late eighteenth century the ideological forces of evangelism, moral philosophy, and sentimental literature, when combined with a transmuting philosophy of republicanism, conspired to characterize womanhood as virtuous while removing the concern for virtue from the male-dominated public sphere.[3] Yet some questions remain. As Bloch herself admits, the public sphere did not immediately assume the shape given to it by later writers on domesticity, as an immoral place for worldly men. Most American political theorists believed that the rational pursuit of self-interest would benefit the public at large. Rather than immoral, the public sphere seemed at worst morally neutral. The removal of virtue from the public sphere might have helped men look less moral, but it seems something more was needed to drive home the association of men with immorality. It is the contention of this essay that seduction tales helped forge that association.

As historians have long recognized, the nineteenth century ideology of domesticity relied upon the creation of two opposing poles or spheres, each assigned to a sex.[4] Poststructural theorists have helped emphasize the importance of binary oppositions or dichotomies in the creation of ideologies. One of the central tenets of domesticity was the superior morality of women. As the above discussion has suggested, this notion of female virtue was first clearly articulated at the end of the eighteenth century. The tales of seduction may have been crucial in creating a structuring cultural dichotomy, by providing a pole of male immorality counterposed to female virtue and chastity. These tales were insistent in their notion of female innocence: when women "fell," men were largely to blame. One must consider the costs of this dichotomy.

Nancy Cott has ably argued that by assuming a posture of morality and passionlessness, women were able to advance their position within society and protect themselves from male aggression (even if eventually such a strategy may have backfired).[6] Cott asserts that this strategy represented the best possible option available to women at the time. Where this argument fails is in its assumption that solutions to female vulnerability were only available within characterizations of womanhood. As we step back and look at the negotiation of gender more fully, we will see other options. In seduction fiction we will find possible responses to female vulnerability, such as appeals to male sensibility or conscience or warnings to men about the consequences of their actions. Yet the writers of seduction fiction ultimately eschewed attempts at reforming men and decided to primarily respond to female vulnerability by defining men as evil and urging women to seek protection. In making such decisions, they foreclosed the possibility of building a model of manhood which stressed male accountability and instead fastened men to one pole of an emerging gender dichotomy.

Before directly considering the representation of masculinity in seduction tales, we should consider the social context in which they were written and received. The social history of the late eighteenth century suggests that these novels may have been reflecting recent social developments which marked new problems for young women. One must first consider the changing status of youth within American society. Over the course of the eighteenth century, young adults gained more control over their lives vis-à-vis their parents, especially in the selection of mates.[7] This trend of declining patriarchy was greatly exaggerated by the ideological shifts of the Revolutionary era.[8] The revolution against patriarchal authority represented a newfound freedom for youth, but this freedom was visited with cultural backlash. Seduction fiction expressed grave fears about the newfound freedom of young adults. This ideological "freedom" which the Revolution represented most likely corresponded to economic and geographic changes as well; young men were often relocating in search of occupations in a transitional economy in which inheritance was uncertain and apprenticeship breaking down.[9] Such structural changes of course correlate with the markets where seduction fiction was sold: densely settled northern towns and cities.

In these markets, seduction fiction proved immensely popular. *Charlotte Temple* and *The Coquette*, both seduction novels, captivated American readers when first printed and subsequently through the nineteenth century. While *The Coquette* was a 1797 best-seller and was often reprinted, *Charlotte Temple, the first American best-seller (1794) and reprinted* probably over two hundred times, proved the most popular novel in America until the 1852 printing of *Uncle Tom's Cabin*.[10] If not quite as well documented, the popularity of seduction tales in the periodicals is undoubtable and equally impressive. One close scholar of eighteenth-century periodical fiction noted that the theme of seduction outstripped all other fictional topics in these magazines.[11] Seduction tales also reached many more readers than a consideration of their total sales

popular

and printings would suggest. The number of lending libraries boomed in the final years of the eighteenth century, making fiction available to many nonpurchasers.[12] Also, the colonial tradition of reading literature out loud to assembled groups, such as a number of women at work in the household, persisted into the early national period.[13] While literacy was within the reach of many by the end of the eighteenth century, it was not necessary to have access to the printed word to encounter seduction tales. The seduction plot-line was being presented on the theatrical stage by the first years of the nineteenth century.[14] Advice literature may have also conveyed some of the same messages about seduction. Late eighteenth-century manners books mirrored some of the most important lessons one could find in the fiction of the same period. Specifically, such books often told female readers that they needed to protect themselves against the advances of aggressive males.[15] Overall, seduction tales had the potential for formative influence.

Seduction writers addressed the perceived problem of female vulnerability, but the major cultural strategy they developed to respond to the fear of unrestrained male youth largely failed to address one of its likely determinants, the trend toward a declining influence of the community in courtship.[16] Northern colonial communities had closely watched the courtship process of its youth and provided both formal and informal networks of social control over the pursuits made by men.[17] As the family increasingly privatized, however, such influence would wane, ostensibly leaving young women increasingly exposed to male seducers and less protected by family and community. In fact, from what we know about the changing sexual behavior of single young adults, such changes do seem to have made young women more vulnerable. Premarital pregnancy and bastardy rates reached unprecedented levels in the years during and immediately following the Revolution.[18] While premarital pregnancy might suggest growing sexual freedom for both sexes, or greater vulnerability for women, one suspects that in a society where women in most ways remained dependents and where initiatives for courtship belonged to men, this illicit occurrence was most often a product of the latter.[19] Seduction fiction writers probably did not conceive of their work as a means to curtail the freedom of women through fear; those whom we can identify seemed in their other writings and pursuits to be advocates for the causes of women, particularly female education.[20] Nevertheless, seduction tales depicted young women as vulnerable and most often chose to explain this problem as resulting from exposure to evil men. Thus it appears that seduction tales painted in terms of gendered personal character, problems which may have been essentially structural in form. They resultingly compounded any threats which may have existed to womanhood by making men seem less responsible (because they were naturally immoral).

A warning to women about the predatory nature of men was not the only message which emerged in seduction fiction. A closer look at some of the paths explored, but ultimately not embraced, will demonstrate that alternative options were possible in responding to a perceived female vulnerability. One such path was an appeal to male sensitivity. Seduction fiction was rooted in the culture of sensibility.[21] Initially articulated by moral-sense philosophers, particularly John Locke and David Hume, ideas about sensibility later infused and operated within a broad range of fields, including religion, science, conduct literature, and fiction. All of the varieties of sensibility which emerged shared some basic similarities, most importantly, a belief in and valorization of the ability of human beings to sympathetically feel the pain of others whom they might observe in distress. Particularly in literature, the "man of feeling" emerged as a central figure. Sensibility had the potential to be a gender-neutral model of sensitivity. Tales of seduction did sometimes introduce a theme of male sensibility into their plots. For example, in Susanna Rowson's *Charlotte Temple*, we see Mr. Temple praise the sentimental emotions felt by Captain Eldridge over the loss of his son and wife. Captain Eldridge appears distraught: "But pardon me. The horrors of that night unman me. I cannot proceed. . . . What a mere infant I am! Why, Sir, I never felt thus in the day of battle." To which Temple responds reassuringly, "but the truly brave soul is tremblingly alive to the feelings of humanity." When Eldridge, thus reassured, offers his own justification for a feeling disposition, Temple replies, "This is true philosophy."[22] Sensibility challenged definitions of masculinity based on stoicism. In *The Power of Sympathy*, William Hill Brown employs one of the situations which writers of sensibility repeatedly turned to evoke tears in their characters and audience, a confrontation with slavery. The hero, Harrington, introduces his tale of a meeting with a slave by declaring his sentimental nature: "*I FEEL that I have a soul*—and every man of sensibility feels it within himself. I will relate a circumstance I met with in my late travels through *Southcarolina*— I was always susceptible of *touches of nature*."[23]

Some writers of seduction tales seem to have hoped to reach young male readers in addition to the young women to whom they most obviously directed their stories.[24] By depicting regret and doubt in the characters who committed seduction, authors strived to cultivate sensibility in these potential male readers. Hannah Foster, who has been credited with pushing the seduction story furthest as a vehicle for the cause of women's freedom—a subject to which we shall return—may have actually been more remarkable for her in-depth depiction of a seducer who was also, at times, a feeling man. In Foster's *The Coquette* the seducer Sanford first entertains doubts about his plan of seduction and later experiences extreme regret in seeing its ill effects. In the latter scene he expresses the sentiments usually spoken by the ruined heroines: "Oh, Deighton, I am undone! Misery irremediable is my future lot! She is gone; yes, she is gone for ever! The darling of my soul, the centre of all my wishes and enjoyments is no more!"[25] Susanna Rowson in *Charlotte Temple* also complicates the seducer role by having Montraville express doubts about his seduction schemes and by apportioning some blame to other characters: Belcour (Montraville's evil sidekick) and the unworthy guardian, Mademoiselle La Rue. Before Belcour helps Montraville discard his nagging doubts, Montraville exclaims: "and should I even succeed in seeing and conversing with her, it can be productive of no good: I must of necessity leave England in a few days, and probably may never return; why then should I endeavour to leave her a prey to a thousand inquietudes?"[26]

In their depictions of regret and doubt, these authors often employed the concept of conscience, sometimes referring to it as an "internal monitor." In using such terms, these authors prefigured language which would come to dominate thinking about social control by the middle of the nineteenth century.[27]

In *The Power of Sympathy*, Mr. Harrington (the hero's father), who had been a seducer earlier in life, tries to locate the source of his regret: "From what innate principle does this arise but from the *God within the mind!*" Mr. Harrington goes on to suggest that there comes a time for all individuals when one's actions must be considered within an "hour of reflection" and subsequently judged: "this *internal monitor* sits in judgment upon them and gives her verdict of approbation or dislike."[28] In the words of this same character the ties of the concept of conscience to ideas of sensibility become obvious: "Blessed be that power who has implanted within us that consciousness of reproach, which springs from gentleness and love!—Hail sensibility! Ye eloquent tears of beauty!"[29]

Thus, a few authors at least seem to have applied ideas of sensibility to their male characters, sometimes even to the villain. But only in these few novels is one likely to find such depictions; they appear much less frequently in periodical stories, although it is in periodicals where tales of seduction can be found with great regularity and where they were widely popularized and contributed by a broad range of authors. In the novels discussed above, the authors spent much more time depicting the evils and dangers of men than in upholding a sentimental model for them. Insofar as they addressed male readers, seduction fiction writers were more apt to appeal to potential seducers through fear. To the extent that one finds appeals to conscience in the periodicals, it is more in the form of a threat rather than an extended hand. For example, in one magazine piece, entitled "The Sorrows of Amelia," a direct warning to men is offered: "learn instruction from the fate of Alonzo . . . check the disposition which would prompt you to spread toils for unsuspecting innocence. Guilt will destroy the bliss of the seducer, intrude on his morning pleasure and damp his evening joys."[30] The threat of a guilty conscience could be heightened by depicting its ultimate result as suicide. Thus, in a story in *The Gentleman's and Ladies Town and Country Magazine* which was presented as a letter from the "reformed" rake Edmund to a friend who still practiced the evil arts, the reader learns of the horrible consequences of seduction for the seducer. Edmund relates the story of a young man who felt intense guilt over his seduction of a young woman. This man went to a secluded cabin in the woods, where he worshiped a wax effigy of the woman he had seduced (and who had died) and ultimately commits suicide.[31]

A heavy burden of guilt was not the only potential cost of seduction for men. Authors also used the threat of damnation. In a story in *The Key*, the reader is informed that the libertine will eventually pay for his crime: "But the thunders of heaven will not sleep; injustice will be visited by vengeance."[32] William Hill Brown, in *The Power of Sympathy*, dedicates an extended scene to a dream of Mr. Harrington's in which he visits a Dantesque hell where the worst station is reserved for the seducers:

> In their countenances were depicted more anguish, sorrow, and despair—I turned my head immediately from this dreadful sight. . . . Quivering with horror, I inquired who they were—"These," answered my guide, with a sigh, "are the miserable race of SEDUCERS—Repentance and shame drive them far from the rest of the accursed. Even the damned look on them with horror, and thank fate their crimes are not of so deep a die."[33]

The social fear of seduction is quite palpable in such threats.

While authors appealed to the anxiety of potential male readers more than their sensibility, both strategies must have ultimately seemed futile if men were truly depraved. A story entitled "A Melancholy Tale of Seduction," run in the *Massachusetts Magazine*, displays this tension extremely well. Addressed to a libertine, it starts out by asking him to mend his ways, by appealing to his sensibility: "I hope your mind has not lost all its sensibility, and that there may be a time when this letter shall prove a monitor." It goes on to tell him, in good sentimental fashion, how one of his victims has died of shame. However, any hope of his reform gradually disappears. The author first asks a series of rhetorical questions: "Were there never times when your heart checked you, and obliged you almost to revoke?—Could neither youth; nor beauty, nor innocence, find even a momentary friend in your thoughts? . . . Were your vices only permanent, all your better resolutions transitory?" After posting this final query, the author provides a gloomy response: "They were. To feel for another's wo was a lesson you had never known." At the end of the article the author warns the seducer that eventually he will be racked with guilt: "Pensive moments will come to make you wretched. . . . Be assured, that the burden of misery which awaits yourself, is heavier far than any you have heaped on another."[34] Yet by this point the warning is quite hollow. It seems doubtful whether even the author could believe that this immoral youth, lacking conscience, would ever feel remorse. Since manhood was constructed as immoral, it would seem pointless to ask men to mend their ways. Solutions to female vulnerability would have to be found elsewhere.

While early American writers on seduction sometimes sent messages to potential male readers, it was to young women that they most often addressed their advice. These authors sometimes sought to caution women that the blame for their seduction could be partly laid on their own heads. Warnings against, and depictions of the horrid consequences of, the practice of coquetry were the most frequent forms of such advice. In constructing coquettes, authors rarely portrayed these women as unvirtuous; rather, they practiced flirtatious behavior out of either naivete or a misguided fondness for pleasure. Authors told their intended female readers that simply accepting flattery without a blush could be an invitation to a male predator.[35] In a letter in the *Gentlemen and Ladies Town and Country Magazine* addressed to "the unguarded FAIR of this Metropolis," the author warns that one should show no regard for flatterers: "once you acknowledge the slightest tenderness for him, there is but one step further, from the time of such an acknowledgment, between that and seduction."[36] As this example illustrates, authors portrayed the path to seduction as a slippery one, easily slid down if one false move was made. This seeming slipperiness highlights the lack of reconstructed boundaries and rules of conduct for youth newly freed.

A fondness for luxury and pleasure was often seen as the source of coquetry. It is in these condemnations of young women's appetite for luxury that Jan Lewis's argument for the seduction tales being mostly a dialogue over republicanism seems on surest ground.[37] European aristocratic splendor was weighed against American modesty and virtue in stories condemning coquetry. The choices offered to Eliza Wharton in *The Coquette* are between the modest and respectable minister Boyer and the rakish and aristocratic Sanford. The choice she should have made is abundantly clear. While one can see on American condemnation of European degeneracy in Foster's depiction of Sanford, we might also appreciate the importance of the characteristic which always accompanied seducers such as he: their ability to deceive. Fears of deception were a logical accompaniment to the growing mobility of male youth. Living in a seemingly more anonymous world parents and community had less opportunity to judge the character of male suitors. While Cathy Davidson and Carroll Smith-Rosenberg have both highlighted Eliza's explorations of women's freedom in their discussions of *The Coquette*, it seems doubtful that Hannah Foster or her contemporaries would recognize such a modern reading.[38] Undoubtedly, Eliza was a sympathetic character; her inner goodness was not in doubt. But the choices she made were certainly condemned. Trustworthy friends and family all warned her to leave Sanford and accept the hand of Boyer, and perhaps even more importantly, Eliza herself repeatedly renounces her earlier mistakes through much of the second half of the novel.[39] Hannah Foster was sympathetic to the plight of young women: she wrote her novel, in fact, to warn them of the dangers of men. Coquettes were rarely depicted as immoral; they were mostly naive. They lacked guidance; their parents or guardians were either missing or incompetent.[40] Thus, depictions of coquettes did not often complicate a gender-based polarity of morality, and they also served to emphasize a need for proper parental supervision.

Young women in general seemed to need enhanced supervision because they were facing an untrustworthy sex. Seduction fiction repeatedly constructed the nature of manhood as immoral. Writers did this in conjunction with their insistence on female innocence and virtue. It always required a series of deceptions on the part of the libertine to accomplish his foul end, as the "Story of Philenia" illustrates: "By a long continued series of the most artful insinuations accompanied by the most solemn protestations of eternal love and friendship he triumphed over the innocence and virtue of the once happy, but now abandoned and disconsolate Philenia."[41] In the seduction of the ever innocent Charlotte, it required the machinations of not only Montraville but also Belcour and LaRue to ultimately undo her. The struggle between female innocence and male evil would always end in the loss of the vital possession of chastity; in the words of the title character of "Mathilda", "where is the perfidious man who has robbed my youth of its peace, my mind of its innocence, my once fair frame of its honor. . . . Ah, wretch! he has stolen the deposit, and left the poor cabinet vacant and in ruin!"[42] The most popular metaphor to describe the loss of innocence, as might be expected, was that of deflowering. A *Boston Magazine* story provides a representative example: "her innocence was cropped as the flower of the field, by the early ravages of the mower's hand."[43]

The construction of male immorality was never complete. The tales themselves contain obvious complications: father figures, for example, are often sympathetic characters (and female readers are told to listen to them).[44] Nonetheless, the overall direction the tales were pointing in is clear. One gets a sense of an emerging stereotype by considering the broad range of epithets thrown at the male seducers throughout these tales: "betrayer," "designing villain," "undoer," "monster," "cruel robber," "base dissembler," "wretch," "faithless youth," "betraying enemy," "fiend," "cruel destroyer," "wanton spoiler," or simply "seducer" are just a sample of the epithets employed, not only in these tales, but in poems and didactic essays as well.[45] It also appears that seduction tales were not the only type of fiction to assert men's immorality. Mildred Doyle, in her comprehensive study of early American periodicals, noted that the second most popular theme she found, next to that of seduction, was the abuse of wives by cruel husbands.[46] In this theme, as in seduction, virtuous female characters were constructed in opposition to the male figures. The characterization of male figures in the seduction tales had the potential to spill beyond the tales themselves. Thus, although some authors were careful to draw character distinctions between the male figures in their works, collectively the tales they wrote leave one with an image of male depravity. It is not surprising then, that someone could have penned the lyrics which opened this essay, which declared that "men are all rovers alike."

The slightly more circumspect judgement presented in "Almira and Alonzo" perhaps better represents the collective message of seduction fiction to its female readers: "Your spotless bosoms, the seat of honor, unsuspecting of deceit . . . admit too flattering ideas of men. . . . Few—few indeed, are deserving the confidence they obtain."[47]

Writers of seduction tales did primarily dedicate themselves to warning young women about the nature of men. But in the methods that they chose to pursue this purpose they remained within the tradition of sensibility. Rather than telling tales of seduction because they seemed enticing fare, authors instead hoped to reach young female readers through the principle of sympathy. The tales of seduction which one finds in periodicals of the late eighteenth century and in novels such as *Charlotte Temple*, *The Coquette*, and *The Power of Sympathy* are barely removed from didactic literature. In the periodicals, many stories have only a thin veneer of plot: they are loosely tied to specific names and places, but are primarily lectures, seeking to impart wisdom which might prevent seduction. In fact the line between fact and fiction was often deliberately obfuscated in order to stress the pertinence of the lessons offered. Both periodical articles and novels often claim their tales to be factual "founded upon recent facts," "founded on Fact, veiled only under a fictitious Name" or present the stories as a series of letters between friends.[48] Susanna Rowson frequently intrudes into her story to impart lessons directly to the reader. William Hill Brown and Hannah Foster both have their characters deliver extended lectures to the audience. As implied by the title of William Hill Brown's novel (invoking as it does David Hume's definition of sympathy), these authors felt that the reader could learn lessons from the characters, particularly, the unfortunate seduced, because they had the ability to feel their emotions. Within the body of thought on sensibility, writers such as Hume had developed an elaborate model of sympathy, explaining the ability of human beings to actively feel the emotions of another as if they were their own.[49] The writers of seduction tales sought to use this principle to their advantage, hoping young women would take their lessons more to heart because they could feel the pain produced by seduction. There were competing modes of fiction writing during the eighteenth century. The tales of seduction popular in late eighteenth-century America were clear descendants of the work of Samuel Richardson, not simply because of the shared theme of seduction, but more importantly, because they used fiction to pursue a moral agenda.[50] It is in the context of competing types of fiction that the repeated warnings against novel reading within these novels themselves make sense.[51]

As earlier discussion suggests, American authors did break with the tradition of sensibility in one fundamental way: the hope of male reform was for the most part cast off. Seduction writers challenged the dubious wisdom of Richardson's *Pamela* on the possibility of reforming rakes. Lucy Freeman in *The Coquette* explicitly states what most tales implied in their emphasis on cautioning females rather than reforming males: "'A reformed rake,' you say, 'makes the best husband'" a trite, but a very erroneous maxim, as the fatal experience of thousands of our sex can testify."[52]

The specific responses to the problem of male immorality which seduction fiction writers offered to young women deserve a closer look. Faced with the treacherous villains of their own construction, seduction writers sometimes cried out for the punishment of the seducers. For example, Susanna Rowson wishes for their banishment: "My bosom glows with honest indignation, and I wish for power to extirpate those monsters of seduction from the earth!"[53] The construction of female morality opposed to male immorality has of course at times provoked an attack on male immorality by women reformers. With special regard to the issue of sexual transgression, both Mary Ryan and Carroll Smith-Rosenberg have demonstrated how male brothel visitors could be attacked for their habits by female reformers.[54] Yet the writers of the tales of seduction sought above all else to resolve the dilemma of male immorality through asking young women to seek the guidance of protective parents.[55] In gearing their moral tales toward teaching women to seek parental guidance, seduction authors were abandoning attempts to reform men.

According to these authors, women often suffered the fate of seduction because they lacked parental guidance. Thus Philenia in a *Massachusetts Magazine* story had been left an orphan and was thus exposed to the man who would prove her undoing, Fallacio.[56] Amelia, in a *Baltimore Weekly* story, also lacked parents to guide her: "In her infantine years she was deprived of the tender care of parental affection, and her blossoming beauty was exposed to the all fascinating snares of artful dissimulation."[57] The advice published for the "Unguarded Fair" went so far as to suggest that a young woman in an unprotected state might best be served by not taking the risk of entering the marriage market.[58] For women who were not so unlucky, the lesson was clear. Susanna Rowson repeatedly implores her readers to listen to parental advice in addresses such as this: "Oh my dear girls—for such only am I writing—listen not to the voice of love, unless sanctioned by paternal approbation."[59] In *The Coquette* Eliza finally decides to seek parental guidance and regrets not having done so sooner: "had I done this before, I might have escaped this trouble."[60] Readers of "Almira and Alonzo" are reminded that they can escape Almira's fate of seduction and death by not forsaking parental advice: "remember! had the still small voice of age, the gentle whispers of maternal fondness been heard, the much regretted inhabitant of the silent tomb, might have gladdened a parent's heart."[61]

Writers of seduction literature often emphasized the message of the importance of listening to one's parents by showing the extreme emotional costs of seduction to the parents of a seduced young woman (thus again applying the principle of sympathy). Seduction was always depicted as a crime not only against the seduced but also against her family. William Hill Brown depicts the cycle of pain in poetry: "YOU wound—th'electrick pain extends; To fathers, mothers, sisters, friends."[62] Brown illustrates this pain through the father of the seduced and now deranged Fidelia: "Is not the cause of my woe, a melancholy instance of the baleful art of the SEDUCER?"[63] A *New York Magazine* article goes so far as to depict a parent's death from grief as the result of a daughter's seduction. Expanding the view of parental pain, the reader is told of a dream in which an angel-like creature displays the body of the lost parent, saying, "View the narrow bed, wherein lie mouldering the cold remains of an unhappy parent —the stroke of death was guided by a much-lov'd child!" Upon closer inspection, the corpse possesses a deeply wounded heart: "Here, opening her snowy robe, she displayed a bleeding bosom!"[64] Since one could only evade the evil male seducer through parental guidance, the ultimate mistake a daughter could make was an elopement.[65] Susanna Rowson provides a highly sentimental depiction of the pain of Charlotte's mother on discovering her child's elopement, and the reader is clearly invited to identify with her motherly pain:

> "Oh Charlotte! Charlotte! how ill have you requited our tenderness! But, Father of Mercies," continued she, sinking on her knees and raising her streaming eyes and clasped hands to heaven . . . "of thine infinite mercy, make her not a mother, lest she should one day feel what I now suffer."[66]

Ultimately in the tales of seduction, men could not be reformed. While these tales employed the devices of sensibility, and on occasion portrayed men as possessing sensibility, these works of fiction would help push sensibility into sentimentality by gendering empathy.[67] The gender-neutral model of sensitivity embodied by sensibility would yield to the feminized sensitivity of sentimentalism. Faced with female vulnerability, authors had a range of responses available. By primarily choosing to define men as innately immoral, rather than asking them to assume responsibility for their behavior, they helped construct a lasting gender ideology. Male immorality and female purity mutually reinforced one another as opposites. The type of response engendered by such ideas is well demonstrated by a final example, this time from the real world.

In the year 1800 the Philadelphia Magdalen Society was formed to address the problem of prostitution. The centerpiece of their institution would be an asylum, where, according to their Constitution, they might "aid in restoring to the paths of virtue,—to be instrumental in recovering to honest rank in life those unhappy females, who, in unguarded hour, have been robbed of their innocence."[68] For those who might have questioned the basic innocence of prostitutes, the founders published a defense for them in *Poulson's American Daily Advertiser*: "Is there, I would ask, a village or hamlet in these United States, I might say universe, that has not fostered in its bosom the insidious murderer of female innocence?"[69] The strategy that these founders adopted of protecting and guiding female innocence by building an asylum could be used for all young women. But a preexisting structure, the family home, would increasingly be seen as one as the new century progressed. In a dangerous outside world populated by untrustworthy men, home would become the only safe place for women.

NOTES

I would like to thank William W. Cutler, Margaret Marsh, and Julie Berebitsky for providing early comments which helped focus this essay. P.M.G. Harris, Lisa Wilson, and Dallett Hemphill provided useful criticisms which strengthened my argument. The folks at PCEAS, especially Michael Zuckerman and Sarah Knott, provided helpful leads and comments. Merril Smith and Norah Feeny provided thorough critiques and sound editorial advice.

1. *Ladies Magazine* (New York), January 1801, 40.

2. On the intended audience of seduction fiction see, Cathy N. Davidson, *Revolution and the Word: The Rise of the Novel in America* (New York: Oxford University Press, 1986), 111–25. On the redefinition of womanhood as innately virtuous, see Ruth H. Bloch, "The Gendered Meanings of Virtue in Revolutionary

America," *Signs* 13 (Autumn 1987): 37–58; and Nancy F. Cott, "Passionlessness: An Interpretation of Victorian Sexual Ideology, 1790–1850," *Signs* 4 (Winter 1978): 219–36.

3. Bloch, "The Gendered Meanings of Virtue," 37–58.

4. Barbara Welter, "The Cult of True Womanhood, 1820–1860," *American Quarterly* 18 (Summer 1966): 151–74; Kathryn Kish Sklar, *Catherine Beecher: A Study in American Domesticity* (New Haven: Yale University Press, 1973); and Mary P. Ryan, *Cradle of the Middle Class: The Family in Oneida County, New York, 1790–1865* (New York: Cambridge University Press, 1981).

5. With specific reference to gender ideology, see Joan C. Williams, "Domesticity as the Dangerous Supplement of Liberalism," *Journal of Women's History* 2 (Winter 1991): 69–88.

6. Cott, "Passionlessness," 219–36.

7. Cf. Philip Greven, *Four Generations: Population, Land, and Family in Colonial Andover, Massachusetts* (Ithaca, N.Y.: Cornell University Press, 1970); Daniel Scott Smith, "Parental Power and Marriage Patterns: An Analysis of Historical Trends in Hingham, Massachusetts," *Journal of Marriage and the Family* 35 (August 1973): 419–28.

8. Jay Fliegelman, *Prodigals and Pilgrims: The American Revolution against Patriarchal Authority, 1750–1800* (New York: Cambridge University Press, 1982); C. D. Hemphill, "Age Relations and the Social Order in Early New England: The Evidence from Manners," *Journal of Social History* 28 (Winter 1994): 271–94.

9. Philip Greven's, *Four Generations*, the classic text describing the effects of the declining prospects of land inheritance in one community, has these changes in full swing by the mideighteenth century (175–258). For a more general description of this development, see Kenneth Lockridge, "Land, Population and the Evolution of New England Society, 1630–1790," *Past and Present* 39 (April 1968). On the decline of the apprenticeship system in the early republic, see Sean Wilentz, *Chants Democratic: New York City and the Rise of the American Working Class, 1788–1850* (New York: Oxford University Press, 1984), 23–60; and Gordon Wood, *Radicalism of the American Revolution* (New York: Vintage Books, 1993), 185–86. For a general description of the geographic mobility of youth in the early republic, see Joseph Kett, *Rites of Passage: Adolescence in America, 1790 to the Present* (New York: Basic Books, 1977), 11–110.

10. For a precise explanation of the designation "best-sellers" and a listing of the same, see Frank Luther Mott, *Golden Multitudes: The Story of the Best Sellers in the United States* (New York: Macmillan Company, 1947). On the popularity of *The Coquette*, see Davidson, *Revolution and the Word*, 149–50. The most thorough study of the popularity of Charlotte Temple is R.W.G. Vail, *Susanna Haswell Rowson, the Author of Charlotte Temple: A Bibliographic Study* (Worcester, Mass.: Davis Press, 1933).

278   RODNEY HESSINGER

11. Mildred Doyle, *Sentimentalism in American Periodicals, 1741–1800* (Ph.D. diss., New York University, 1941), 55–61.

Jan Lewis also provides a good sense of the popularity of seduction tales in early national magazines in "The Republican Wife: Virtue and Seduction in the Early Republic," *William and Mary Quarterly* 3.44 (1987): 689–721.

12. Davidson, *Revolution and The Word*, 27–29. Davidson also notes that lending was prevalent among acquaintances.

13. Ibid., 28, 65, 114.

14. Recent work on literacy has suggested that almost all younger New England women were literate by the end of the eighteenth century (thus catching up with men). See Joel Perlmann and Dennis Shirley, "When Did New England Women Acquire Literacy?" *William and Mary Quarterly* 3.48 (1991): 50–67. For a more general consideration of literacy in the late eighteenth century see Davidson, *Revolution and the Word*, 55–79. On adaptations of seduction tales for the stage, see Ann Douglas's introduction to Susanna Rowson, *Charlotte Temple: A Tale of Truth*, ed. Ann Douglas (New York: Penguin Books, 1991; 1st American ed. Philadelphia: M. Carey, 1794). *The Coquette* was transformed into a play as early as 1802; see Nichols J. Horatio, *The New England Coquette: From the history of the celebrated Eliza Wharton: A tragic drama in three acts* (Salem, Mass.: N. Coverly, 1802).

15. Dallett Hemphill, "Women Rising," chapter 6 in "Bowing to Necessities: The History of Manners in America, 1620–1860" (New York: Oxford University Press, forthcoming).

16. A good number of works have tracked the decline of community influence in family affairs in the mid- to late eighteenth century. For a general consideration of this change, see Helena M. Wall, *Fierce Communion: Family and Community in Early America* (Cambridge: Harvard University Press, 1990).

17. Laurel Thatcher Ulrich, *Good Wives: Image and Reality in the Lives of Women in Northern New England* (New York: Knopf, 1980), 94–105, 118–23; Barry Levy, "'Tender Plants': Quaker Farmers and Children in the Delaware Valley, 1681–1735," *Journal of Family History* 3 (1978): 116–35; Lisa Wilson, "'It will not injure you': Men and Courtship in Colonial New England," chapter 2 in *A Useful Member of Society: The Domestic Life of Men in Colonial New England* (prospective title) (New Haven: Yale University Press, forthcoming). Wilson suggests that by the late colonial period a failed courtship could prove quite embarrassing to a young man, because it was largely up to him, rather than his parents, to arrange a marriage. Yet at the same time the oversight of the community and the young woman's family remained; thus a thwarted courtship was visible to the public. This seems to represent an intermediate stage, prior to the one discussed herein, where male youth more easily escaped both parental control and community notice.

18. Daniel Scott Smith and Michael S. Hindus, "Premarital Pregnancy in

America, 1640–1971," *Journal of Interdisciplinary History* 5 (Spring 1975): 537–70; Susan E. Klepp, *Philadelphia in Transition: A Demographic History of the City and Its Occupational Groups, 1720–1830* (New York: Garland Publishing, 1989), 62–137. Smith and Hindus locate the peak of premarital pregnancy rates at the time of the Revolution and suggest that bastardy rates probably followed the same pattern. Susan Klepp, in her thorough demographic study of Philadelphia, locates the peak of illegitimacy in the post-Revolution years, with a subsequent drop in the early nineteenth century.

19. For convincing statements of this position see Cott, "Passionlessness," 228–31; and Christine Stansell, *City of Women: Sex and Class in New York, 1787–1860* (New York: Knopf, 1986), 23–27.

20. On the promotion of female education by novelists, see Davidson, *Revolution and the Word*, 66–74.

21. Discussion of the culture of sensibility, especially in its British manifestation, has boomed in recent years. For two wide-ranging accounts of sensibility, see Markman Ellis, *The Politics of Sensibility: Race, Gender and Commerce in the Sentimental Novel* (Cambridge: Cambridge University Press, 1996); and G. J. Barker-Benfield, *The Culture of Sensibility: Sex and Society in Eighteenth-Century Britain* (Chicago: University of Chicago Press, 1992). For an instructive account of this topic which shows American adoption of this culture, see Karen Halttunen, "Humanitarianism and the Pornography of Pain in Anglo-American Culture," *American Historical Review* 100 (April 1995): 303–34.

22. Rowson, *Charlotte Temple*, 11–12.

23. William Hill Brown, *The Power of Sympathy; or The Triumph of Nature. Founded in Truth*, 2 vols. (Boston: Isaiah Thomas and Company, 1789), 2:29.

24. Cathy Davidson and Jan Lewis both, in fact, suggest that novels and periodical fiction were read by men as well as women. See Davidson, *Revolution and the Word*, 8, 98; and Lewis "The Republican Wife," 692.

25. Hannah W. Foster *The Coquette*, ed. Cathy N. Davidson (Boston: Samuel Etheridge, 1797; reprint, New York: Oxford University Press, 1986), 35, 72, 164.

26. Rowson, *Charlotte Temple*, 4–5.

27. With respect to this change within the family, see Carl Degler, *At Odds: Women and the Family in America from the Revolution to the Present* (New York: Oxford University Press, 1980), 86–110; Rodney Hessinger, "Problems and Promises: Colonial American Child Rearing and Modernization Theory," *Journal of Family History* 21 (April 1996): 125–43.

28. Brown, *The Power of Sympathy*, 2:64–65.

29. Ibid., 59–60.

30. "Sorrows of Amelia," *Baltimore Weekly Magazine*, July 5, 1800, 87.

31. "The Fatal Effects of Seduction," *Gentlemen and Ladies Town and Country Magazine* (Boston), June 1789, 250–51.

32. "Matilda," *The Key* (Fredericktown, Md.), April 14, 1798, 106.

33. Brown, *The Power of Sympathy*, 2:105.

34. "Melancholy Tale of Seduction," *Massachusetts Magazine* (Boston), April 1795, 40–42.

35. For an extended example of this lesson, see Brown, *The Power of Sympathy*, 1:69–80.

36. *Gentlemen and Ladies Magazine*, November 1789, 547.

37. Lewis, "The Republican Wife," 715–21.

38. Davidson, *Revolution and the Word*, 140–50; Carroll Smith-Rosenberg, "Domesticating 'Virtue': Coquettes and Revolutionaries in Young America," in *Literature and the Body*, ed. Elaine Scarry (Baltimore: Johns Hopkins University Press, 1988): 160–84.

39. See especially 26–27, 31, 38, 99, 105, 145.

40. Cf. "Sorrows of Amelia," 86–87; "Sobrina and Flirtirella," *The Key*, April 14, 1798, 108–9; "Gossip LIV," *Boston Weekly Magazine*, February 18, 1804.

41. "Story of Philenia," *Massachusetts Magazine*, December 1791, 729–30.

42. "Matilda," 106.

43. *Boston Magazine*, October 1783, 19.

44. For an excellent exploration of the complications and potential for subversion within one text, see Michael Zuckerman, "Charlotte: A Tale of Sentiment, Seduction, and Subversion" (paper presented at the Philadelphia Center for Early American Studies Seminar, September 11, 1992). The novels do seem to subvert themselves more than the periodical pieces do and to be geared more toward "consumption." Yet while the novels seem to be potentially more enjoyable from the reader standpoint, one is surprised by the degree to which they are steeped in the same stock language one finds in the magazine articles: moral warnings to women about the depraved nature of men were endemic to the form. One might note here also that not all fiction in this period engaged in such moralizing; it was precisely the fictive forms which did not that were condemned by the writers of seduction tales. For a discussion of the discriminatory judgments made by American writers, see Herbert Ross Brown, *The Sentimental Novel in America, 1789–1860* (Durham, N.C., Duke University Press, 1940), 28–29, 75–76; and Doyle, *Sentimentalism in American Periodicals*, 68–74.

45. Cf. "Speech of Miss Polly Baker," *American Museum* (Philadelphia), March 1787, 212–14; "Friendly Hints; or a Letter to a beloved young lady," *Lady's Magazine* (Philadelphia), April 1793, 227–29; "The Dying Prostitute," *Lady and Gentleman's Pocket Magazine* (New York), September 15, 1796, 122–23; "Seduction —An elegy," *American Museum*, August 1787, 205–6; "Treachery and Infidelity Punished," *New York Magazine*, February 1793, 93; "The Seduced Female," *New York Magazine*, January 1796, 13–14; "Story of Amelia," *New York Magazine*, April 1797, 210–15; "Seduction," *Weekly Magazine* (Philadelphia), March 16, 1799, 290.

46. Doyle, *Sentimentalism in American Periodicals*, 50–55.

47. "Almira and Alonzo," *Massachusetts Magazine*, June 1789, 361–64.

48. Cf. "Amelia; or the Faithless Briton," *Columbian Magazine* (Philadelphia), October 1787, 677; "Fatal Effects of Seduction," *New York Magazine* (January 1790), 22; "Story of Amelia," 210. The three major novels considered within this article claimed to be based on fact, and there is ample evidence that this was so. See Brown, *The Sentimental Novel in America*, 9–10, n. 26.

49. Ellis, *The Politics of Sensibility*, 12–14.

50. Ibid., 43–48.

51. William Hill Brown provides a highly illuminating lecture on the various types of novels, deploring some, recommending others. See *The Power of Sympathy*, 1:40–61.

52. Foster, *The Coquette*, 57.

53. Rowson, *Charlotte Temple*, 26.

54. Mary P. Ryan, "The Power of Women's Networks: A Case Study of Female Moral Reform in Antebellum America," *Feminist Studies* 5 (Spring 1979): 66–85; Carroll Smith-Rosenberg, "Beauty, the Beast, and the Militant Woman: A Case Study in Sex Roles and Social Stress in Jacksonian America," in *Disorderly Conduct* (New York: Oxford University Press, 1985), 109–28.

55. If Cornelia Hughes Dayton is correct that one can locate the emergence of a legal "double standard" in mideighteenth-century New England, then the seduction tales helped seal this shift by putting the primary responsibility for preventing seduction on women. See her "Taking the Trade: Abortion and Gender Relations in an Eighteenth-Century New England Village," *William and Mary Quarterly* 3.48 (1991): 19–49. The endorsement of parental involvement in marriage decisions in seduction fiction marked a serious departure from earlier trends in Anglo-American literature; see Fliegelman, *Prodigals and Pilgrims*.

56. "Story of Philenia," 730.

57. "Sorrows of Amelia," 86.

58. *Gentlemen and Ladies Magazine*, November 1789, 547–48.

59. Rowson, *Charlotte Temple*, 26.

60. Foster, *The Coquette*, 94.

61. "Almira and Alonzo," 361–64.

62. Brown, *The Power of Sympathy*, 1:119.

63. Ibid., 136.

64. "Felicia to Her Unfortunate Friend," *New York Magazine*, October 1795, 611–12.

65. Cf. Foster, *The Coquette*, 151; "Amelia; or The Faithless Briton," 677–82, 877–80.

66. Rowson, *Charlotte Temple*, 55.

67. On sentimentalism as feminized, see Ann Douglas, *The Feminization of American Culture* (New York: Knopf, 1977). Sarah Knott explores the transfor-

mation of sensibility at length in "A Culture of Sensibility? Sentiment and Society in Late Eighteenth-Century Philadelphia," Works in Progress Series, Unpublished paper presented to the Philadelphia Center for Early American Studies, October 25, 1996.

68. "Magdalen Society Constitution," Historical Society of Pennsylvania, wj. 37.

69. *Poulson's American Daily Advertiser* (Philadelphia), January 23, 1801.

Chapter 12

"The Fruit of Unlawful Embraces"
Sexual Transgression and Madness in Early American Sentimental Fiction

Karen A. Weyler

Two cultural artifacts, one a painting, the other a medical case history, vividly illustrate the cultural conflation of sexual transgression and madness in the late eighteenth-century transatlantic community and help us understand the repeated appearance of the trope of insanity in early American fiction. The first of these artifacts is Robert Fleury's famous painting *Pinel à la Salpêtriére*, which dramatically illustrates changing medical attitudes toward the insane. This painting depicts Philippe Pinel, a reformer and the leading French psychiatrist of the time, removing the chains from the madwomen at the Salpêtriére, the Paris lunatic asylum. Even as Pinel frees the women, Fleury captures the instability of the moment: passive only momentarily, the women sprawl across his canvas with their clothing in suggestive disarray; drooping stockings display bare legs, and their wild, tangled hair drapes across naked breasts, hinting at untamed, uncontrolled passions.

The second artifact is a brief medical case history drawn from Philadelphia physician Benjamin Rush's 1812 study *Medical Inquiries and Observations Upon the Diseases of the Mind*. In this case history, Rush provides a startling illustration of the cultural conflation of sexual transgression, the conscience, and insanity in the early years of the republic. Discussing the powerful influence of guilt upon the conscience, Rush writes dispassionately about a tragic case of madness: "An instance of insanity occurred in a married woman in this city some years ago, of the most exemplary character, from a belief that she had been unfaithful to

the marriage bed. An accident discovered that the supposed criminal connection was with a man whose very person was unknown to her."[1] The
elusive and ambiguous phrase "whose very person was unknown to her"
invites further question. Does Rush mean that the anonymous man was
literally a person the woman had never met? Or is the remark a (perhaps
unconscious) double entendre, meaning that the woman lacked *carnal*
knowledge of this man, and hence if they were guilty of anything, it was
not of a physical relationship? This second possibility leaves open the option that the anonymous woman might have been guilty of emotional in-
fidelity-that she and the equally anonymous man might have shared some
degree of emotional intimacy, a state of affairs that contemporaneous
American novels portray as dangerous, even illicit.[2] The fate of this
woman remains unexplained, but Rush later makes the provocative claim
that cases of derangement in the United States are *commonly* caused by
"infidelity."[3] This supposedly true episode of guilt-driven insanity is strik-
ingly similar to the pattern of self-punishment for moral transgression
which pervades many early American novels. This self-punishment is
commonly and repeatedly figured as "madness"—a trope that appears to
today's readers as just another tired cliché of early American fiction. Yet
the very repetition of it demands our attention: Why does conscience- or
guilt-induced madness repeatedly appear as a special kind of punishment
for sexual transgression in so many early novels, and what does it tell us
about novelists' engagement with their culture and with other forms of
discourse within it?

As historians of mental illness have demonstrated, madness and insanity are very much culturally constructed states. In *Madness and Civilization*, Michel Foucault describes the complex history of the evolution of
European attitudes toward insanity.[4] To some degree, the American history of insanity parallels that of Europe. Prior to the eighteenth century,
in the British colonies, as in Europe, the insane in many communities
were treated as criminals: incarcerated, beaten, and chained alongside
common malefactors.[5] In other communities, harmless madmen (and
women) were boarded out in the homes of people of the town, while
more violent madmen might be incarcerated in small cottages. The late
eighteenth century, however, was a crucial time in the history of mental
illness, as physicians and reformers such as Rush and Pinel studied insanity, theorized about it, and attempted to decriminalize it. Like Fleury's
painting and Rush's anecdote, early American fiction captures fluctuating
cultural attitudes toward insanity. Cultural associations between madness

and criminality obviously lingered, and contemporary fiction reflects this state of flux, with madness—whether a type of mania, as found in Gothic fiction, or the guilt-driven confessional insanity of the sentimental novel—inevitably associated with transgression.[6] In order to trace evolving American attitudes toward female sexuality, this essay will explore the relationships among sentimental fiction, laws governing sexual behavior, and psychiatric discourse during the years 1790 to 1815, when fictional narratives were assuming an increasingly important and authoritative cultural role.

Much recent scholarship has tended to emphasize the more subversive and feminist aspects of early American sentimental fiction. This trend represents a reaction to the scholarship of earlier decades, which tended to dismiss the sentimental agenda of these novels and criticize them for a lack of "originality."[7] However, the nature of the conservatism of early American fiction has seldom been considered, even though the very "plasticity" of fiction (to borrow Bakhtin's phrase) allowed it to be appropriated and used for a variety of purposes.[8] This essay will examine how several writers with conservative social agendas shrewdly exploit the possibilities inherent in fiction—the multifariousness of the novel and the composition of its audience—demonstrating an astute understanding of their own cultural dynamics and of the readership of fiction. While *The Coquette*, with its multiple voices, allusions to a real-life scandal, and exposé of the economic predicament of women is a complex and fascinating novel, deserving of the attention that it has recently garnered, perhaps more representative of early American sentimental fiction are little-known works such as Samuel Relf's *Infidelity, or The Victims of Sentiment* (1797), the anonymous *Amelia, or The Faithless Briton* (1798), and Sally Wood's *Dorval; or The Speculator* (1801), conservative, even reactionary, texts which treat transgressive sexual behavior in an uncompromisingly harsh manner, killing off entire families in order to portray the devastating effects of women's sexual choices.

Transgressive behaviors such as adultery and fornication impacted both the private and public spheres, for they both disrupted the family unit and broke laws.[9] This intersection between the private and the public, between the family and the community, helps explain the popularity of seduction and sexual infidelity as topics for novelists during the early national period. The parameters of these spheres were far from settled, as Rush's example demonstrates, and novelists, as well as medical writers, mediated between the public and private spheres. As a result of novelists' interest in defining precisely what concerns would be "public," scrutiny of female emotions, conduct, and discipline emerge as primary concerns of sentimental fiction, issues revealing fiction's roots in pedagogical literature. The burgeoning medical discourse of the era also powerfully influenced writers of fiction, as novelists drew upon the authority of this discourse in order to critique fictional models of female sexuality. *Amelia; or The Faithless Briton*, Wood's *Dorval*, and Relf's *Infidelity*, as well as better-known works such as Susanna Rowson's *Charlotte Temple* and *Charlotte's Daughter; or, The Three Orphans: A Sequel to Charlotte Temple* (best known as *Lucy Temple*), all rely upon the theoretical discourse concerning insanity in order to describe and regulate female sexuality. Self-scrutiny, potentially leading to madness as self-punishment for moral transgression, emerges as the ultimate disciplinary tool to regulate female behavior. These novels provide insight into the fluid and dynamic relationship between psychiatric discourse and sentimental fiction. Medical theories about insanity permeate fictional discourse, and it is during the period between 1790 and 1815 that medical and narrative authority increasingly complement and even supplant legal authority governing female sexual behavior.

"Unlawful Embraces": Sexual Transgression and the Ascendancy of Medical and Narrative Discourse

In order to understand the context in which early American fiction was written and read, we must first consider the medical understanding of insanity during the early national period. Through his advocacy of humane treatment and decriminalization of the insane, Benjamin Rush played a crucial role in the reform of medical treatment of the mentally ill during the late eighteenth and early nineteenth centuries. Given his status as a signer of the Declaration of Independence, surgeon general of the Middle Department of the Continental Army, member of the Pennsylvania Convention that adopted the Constitution, and treasurer of the United States Mint, Rush and his work would have been known to most literate people of the early republic. In *Concepts of Insanity*, medical historian Norman Dain dubs Rush a "transitional figure in the history of psychiatry," claiming that his work synthesizes some of the most enduring beliefs of the time about mental illness.[10] While Rush did attempt to systematize established beliefs about mental illness, he also incorporated into his work the new theories about the benefits of "moral treatment," which consisted of meeting the physical and mental needs of patients with sympathy and kindness.[11] There is some debate about the extent to which Rush actually originated new medical ideas, for Rush, Philippe Pinel, and William Tuke (an English Quaker reformer and founder of the York Retreat) were all experimenting with moral treatment at about the same time and each was aware of the others' work.[12] While the degree to which Rush originated new theories of mental illness is thus unclear, he was, without question, at the center of new thought in the United States regarding the function of the brain and mental health and illness. As one of the most prominent physicians of his time, he disseminated his theories and those of his contemporaries through thirty years of teaching at the medical school of the University of Pennsylvania, his private practice, and his scientific writings.[13] Even works on insanity published by other Americans decades before Rush's clearly demonstrate his influence. Edward Cutbush's *Inaugural Dissertation on Insanity* (1794), for example, is little more than a pastiche of Rush's theories with footnotes crediting his lectures, as is Joseph Parrish's *Inaugural Dissertation on the Influence of Passion Upon the Body in the Production and Cure of Diseases* (1805). Moreover, Rush's works were not limited to a professional medical audience; learned individuals of the time such as Thomas Jefferson and John Adams were familiar with Rush's medical theories.

The literate population in general would also have been cognizant of contemporary medical ideas about insanity through works like William Buchan's *Domestic Medicine*, which one medical historian of a later generation claimed was more influential "than any other similar work ever published."[14] Originally published in Britain for a general audience, *Domestic Medicine* was first reprinted in British America in 1772 and in numerous later editions (more than twenty-five prior to 1800) in large cities like Philadelphia and small towns like Halifax, North Carolina. Rush and Buchan use a number of terms to denote the spectrum of mental instability, among them "melancholy" and "mania," but they and others basically agree on general descriptions of these states, as well as the distinctions between hysteria and madness. Rush and Buchan both argue that hysteria is primarily a physical disorder, characterized by convulsions, heart palpitations, and the like.[15] Further, Rush concludes that "hysteria . . . often continues for years, and sometimes during a long life, without inducing madness." Hysteria thus was not part of the spectrum that concluded in madness. Instead, the mildest form of madness was considered to be melancholy, a state characterized by depression and sadness. Madness itself was a further progression on this spectrum. Rush explains that "Madness is to delirium what walking in sleep is to dreaming. It is delirium, heightened and protracted by a more active and permanent stimulus upon the brain."[16] This spectrum of mental illness terminates in mania, a state characterized by violent, often homicidal, tendencies.

Most contemporary medical authorities agreed that great emotion, regardless of cause, was the most dangerous risk factor for inducing madness. Rush provides a fascinating list of the possible causes of mental illness, including intense study and "the frequent and rapid transition of the mind from one subject to another." "But," he explains, "madness is excited in the understanding most frequently by impressions that act primarily upon the heart. . . . They are joy, terror, love, fear, grief, distress, shame from offended delicacy, defamation, [and] calumny."[17] Grief and guilt resulting from infidelity or sexual incontinence were other potential causes of madness. John Haslam, member of the Royal College of Surgeons, apothecary for Bethlehem Hospital, and author of the 1809 *Observations on Madness and Melancholy*, concurs with Rush about these potential risk factors and includes "the long endurance of grief; ardent and ungratified desires; . . . prosperity humbled by misfortunes: in short, the frequent and uncurbed indulgence of any passion or emotion, and any sudden or violent affection of the mind."[18] Further, physicians considered grief to be a particularly dangerous emotion, for although as Buchan explains, it originates as melancholy, unchecked grief "often terminates in absolute madness."[19] Eighteenth-century psychiatry thus tended to reduce certain kinds of mental illness to a direct cause-effect relationship: great emotion stimulates the brain, resulting in corporeal pathologies such as fever or a lesion on the brain, which in turn produce some form of mental disturbance. Thus medical practitioners collapsed and confused the symptoms and possible causes of mental illness.

Central to my argument is the consensus among physicians that the force of the conscience itself could drive people—especially women—to madness. In *Medical Inquiries and Observations Upon the Diseases of the Mind*, Rush explains that "The understanding is sometimes deranged through the medium of the moral faculties. A conscience burdened with guilt, whether real or imaginary, is a frequent cause of madness. The latter [imaginary guilt] produces it much oftener than the former."[20] Rush provides a number of anecdotes about guilt, including the story of a man who killed a friend in a duel, an example of "real" guilt, and the afore-mentioned case of the woman who erroneously believed herself to be involved in an affair, an example of "imaginary" guilt. The end result of unchecked grief and guilt could be particularly dangerous, according to the prevailing medical thought, for grief, often linked with guilt, "sometimes brings on sudden death, without any signs of previous disease, either acute or chronic."[21]

Also commonly accepted by the medical community throughout the late eighteenth and nineteenth centuries was the notion that women, for biological reasons, were more susceptible to mental illness than men. Both British and American physicians promulgated this belief. Rush claims that "Women, in consequence of the greater predisposition imparted to their bodies by menstruation, pregnancy, parturition, and to their minds, by living so much alone in their families, are more predisposed to madness than men"; Haslam concurs.[22] This conflation of medical theory and sociological observation again suggests the permeability of the private and public spheres, as well as the ways in which male medical practitioners established decisive authority over the female body and mind. American authors of sentimental fiction draw upon these medical theories concerning privacy, the conscience, guilt, and madness, as they explore alternatives to the legal system for controlling female bodies and minds.

Rush furthers his sociological view of madness by rejecting the notion that the insane are a public spectacle and emphasizing instead the need for privacy, even secrecy, in the treatment of mental illness.

> Mad people should never be visited, nor even seen by their friends, and much less by strangers, without being accompanied by their physician, or by a person to whom he shall depute his power over them. The dread of being exposed, and gazed at in the cell of a hospital by an unthinking visitor, or an unfeeling mob, is one of the greatest calamities a man can anticipate in his tendency to madness.

Despite his efforts to decriminalize the insane and to treat them humanely, Rush gives in to the impulse to hide mental illness, as if it were still a shameful condition.

> [T]here is another advantage from concealing the persons of mad people from the eye of visitors and the public. . . . Now, by rendering the place in which mad people are confined, private—I had almost said sacred—members of families may be sent there without its being known. Nay, they will

be sent there upon the first appearance of the disease, in order to *prevent* its being known, and the disease thereby be more frequently cured.

Protection from the gaze of others is even more important to the female sex, he hints, because madness has a peculiar effect upon the "moral faculties" of women—yet another link between female sexuality and madness, in this case suggesting that only careful, rational attention and discipline keep women's sexuality contained. Further, Rush argues that if women's madness were hidden, then "The obliquity and convulsions of the moral faculties, which sometimes take place in madness, would in this way never be known, or, if known, would be forgotten, or never divulged." Rush thus argues that for their own benefit, people suffering from any sort of mental illness should not be subjected to public ridicule and humiliation, as they were in British insane asylums such as Bedlam.[23] Nonetheless, mental illness still bore a stigma, for it was something that should be hidden away from the community, in contrast to the common earlier practice of boarding harmless madmen with caretakers in the community. Despite his efforts to counteract the stigma of mental illness, Rush himself reinforces the notion that mental illness is somehow shameful—especially for women, given the immodest actions in which they might engage while mentally troubled—and thus should be concealed from view, if not in a prison, then in an asylum.[24]

Rush, Haslam, and Buchan were remarkably progressive, however, in their view that some kinds of mental illness were curable, even preventable. Haslam, for example, explicitly advocates the role of education and self-control in preventing insanity. He ascribes most causes of insanity to "errors of education, which often plant in the youthful mind those seeds of madness which the slightest circumstances readily awaken into growth." He adds,

> It should be as much the object of the teachers of youth, to subjugate the passions, as to discipline the intellect. The tender mind should be prepared to expect the natural and certain effects of causes: its propensity to indulge an avaricious thirst for that which is unattainable, should be quenched: nor should it be suffered to acquire a fixed and invincible attachment to that which is fleeting and perishable.[25]

That passion could be subject to the will was a commonplace belief of medical practitioners. Joseph Parrish explicitly advocates the importance of the will in the overall health of the body and mind, arguing that cultivated virtue is "the most powerful agent in the prevention of disease."[26]

This is precisely the moral message of many sentimental novels, which show by example the dangers of submitting to passion and desire, of whatever kind.

In order to develop the will and control the passions, much sentimental fiction advocates self-discipline through close examination of the conscience. Epistolary fiction in particular promotes self-discipline as an achievable objective, for the prized qualities of sensibility and virtue (or the absence thereof) can easily be conveyed to readers both inside and outside the text through the process of letter writing. Clearly, through epistolary communication one practices the art of self-scrutiny; over time, self-scrutiny becomes a seemingly natural process, rather than an art or learned skill. Significantly, even those sentimental novels which are not written in epistolary form usually include a number of letters which serve to reveal the transgressions of the writers, because to be most effective, self-examination must be observed by others—it must be publicly validated—a requirement that epistolary fiction readily fulfilled. A more dramatic alternative to epistolary self-scrutiny, however, is the deathbed confession; guilt-driven self-examination and admission of error frequently serve as the focus of deathbed scenes in nonepistolary novels.

This emphasis on self-scrutiny in the early American novel ultimately leads to an overt disciplinary function, particularly affecting female characters, as they examine their conduct and emotional responses in minute detail. Recognition of significant moral failings, such as loss of sexual virtue, necessitates a secularized, but nonetheless ritualistic, process of confession and self-punishment, culminating in "madness" or some other disorder of the sensibilities.[27] Fictional emphasis on the conspicuous, even performative, nature of madness obviously subverts the trend toward privacy in contemporary medical treatments of insanity, particularly given that, despite the moral underpinnings of these episodes, they also serve to enthrall and entertain the reader. This connection between transgressive behavior and madness is not coincidental. Rush's progressive work was indeed crucial in the decriminalization of the insane and in establishing humane treatment for the mentally ill in the United States. Yet even from this intermediary position, Rush views criminal behavior itself as a potential cause for madness, particularly if the person who has broken a law feels intense guilt or remorse.

Rush's conflation of legal and moral transgression is closely related to the broad shift in the sphere of punitive action in America during the late eighteenth century. Prior to 1750, moral sin and crime were virtually synonymous in most of the colonies, for the function of law was to identify sinners. Thus, adultery and fornication were criminalized not just in New England but in virtually all of the English colonies. Dramatic changes occurred in the legal system during the decades immediately before and after the Revolution: although accounts suggest that adultery and fornication increased, criminal punishments for these offenses underwent a sharp decline.[28] One legal historian has concluded that these changing patterns of legal enforcement are not indicative "of significantly more immorality but of a new social and legal attitude toward the immorality that had always existed."[29]

It may indeed be the case that legal attitudes toward immorality were changing, but concomitantly, other evidence indicates that the rates of pre- and extramarital sex were increasing, perhaps reflecting decreased parental authority over children's behavior, ranging from courtship to choice of marriage partner. Ellen Rothman's study of courtship behavior concludes that "Young men and women born in the years after Independence enjoyed a high level of self-determination. This meant not only that they were free to choose their own mates but that they socialized with little parental supervision."[30] Perhaps linked to increased freedom in courtship was freedom in choice of marriage partners. Historian Daniel Scott Smith's study "Parental Power and Marriage Patterns" indicates that there was a decrease in parental authority over children's marriage choices from the late eighteenth century through the nineteenth. For women born to wealthier families between 1781 and 1840, the growing tendencies to delay marriage, to marry out of birth order, and to remain single suggest decreased parental involvement and increased freedom of choice for young women.[31] This changing relationship between parents and children may also have contributed to the striking rise in the incidence of premarital sex during the last decades of the eighteenth century. Daniel Scott Smith and Michael S. Hindus's well-documented study "Premarital Pregnancy in America 1640–1971: An Overview and Interpretation" convincingly demonstrates that there was a dramatic increase at this time in premarital pregnancies (those pregnancies that resulted in a birth before the ninth month of marriage): from 1761 to 1800, 33 percent of all first births to married women occurred before the ninth month of marriage.[32] These factors suggest that young women were indeed exercising increased self-determination and sexual freedom—a situation many writers of sentimental fiction regarded with considerable anxiety.

Understanding contemporary theories of insanity and sociological factors indicating that young women were exercising increased sexual freedom enables us to better interpret the narrative conjunction of sexual transgression and madness in early American fiction. Given these factors, it is significant that the first American-authored sentimental novels appeared at precisely the time that they did, for some of these novels advocate conservative, even reactionary, notions regarding female sexuality, as novelists shrewdly negotiate the complicated politics of fiction in order to reach an audience composed of precisely those young women whose lives they wished to influence. Despite the apparent declension in public morality and legal enforcement regarding the exercise of female sexuality, the American novel during this time assumes a compensatory function by asserting a higher standard of private morality. Paralleling, and at the same time borrowing from, medical theories of insanity, sentimental fiction increasingly employs the trope of madness as a form of narrative punishment for violation of moral codes. This shift in the punitive consequences of sexual transgression is especially striking given the fact that the law is omnipresent in many novels of the period. Even though numerous fictional characters are arrested for forgery, debt, or murder, virtually no one is prosecuted for sexual transgressions, despite the fact that laws governing such behavior remained on the books (and for that matter, still exist today).[33] The increasing irrelevance—if not the removal—of such statutes suggests a broad cultural usurpation of legal authority by a narrative authority, in tandem with medical authority, that locates punitive consequences for sexual and moral transgressions firmly within the private sphere.[34] Many of these novels punish women for both passion and gullibility by death in childbirth, but death in childbirth is an evil that could befall any woman, and within these fictional accounts, plenty of virtuous women die in childbirth as well.[35] Instead, madness acts as a special kind of marker to signal moral failings such as fornication and adultery.

Before I discuss specific novels, there is one last factor connecting insanity and sexual behavior that needs to be considered: syphilis, a disease with complex medical and sociological implications. In its tertiary stage, syphilis may result in meningoencephalitis, commonly called general paralysis or paralytic affection in the medical literature of the time. The timing of this stage varies dramatically; it typically appears from five to twenty or thirty years after the initial infection. Although there was not complete agreement among medical professionals about the exact nature of the relationship between syphilis and madness, a connection between these two conditions was established in the sixteenth century.[36] Numerous physicians reaffirmed this connection in the medical literature of the late eighteenth century. Based upon his experience at Britain's Bethlehem Hospital, Haslam makes the connection between insanity and syphilis explicit in his *Observations on Madness and Melancholy*, claiming: "Paralytic affections are a much more frequent cause of insanity than has been commonly supposed"; he also adds that "a course of debauchery long persisted in, would probably terminate in paralysis."[37] In his chapter on venereal disease, William Buchan, too, makes this connection explicit, matter-of-factly listing "madness" alongside "ulcerous sore throats" and "carious bones" as the result of untreated syphilis. Despite the medical knowledge that syphilis could be contracted in a variety of nonsexual ways, Buchan lists possible means of contracting syphilis only after first explaining that venereal diseases are "generally the fruit of unlawful embraces."[38] In the late eighteenth century, syphilis was, in fact, often transmitted through kissing, shared clothing or utensils, unsterilized medical implements, hereditary infection, and breast feeding.[39] The widespread labeling of syphilis as a "venereal" disease is significant, because this designation carried with it a persistent association with uncontrolled lust and desire.[40] That insanity was a possible consequence of syphilis undoubtedly contributed to the lingering view of the insane as immoral, even criminal, despite the work of physicians such as Rush and Pinel to counteract this view. Statistics are not available to indicate how many people in the late eighteenth century suffered from insanity that had its origins in syphilis. However, numerous studies from the early twentieth century, after reliable tests for syphilis had been developed, but before the discovery of penicillin, indicate that an average of 25 percent of patients in state psychiatric institutions tested positive for syphilis.[41] We can therefore reasonably assume that many cases of insanity in the late eighteenth century were indeed induced by syphilis.

Certainly Americans of this time period had an avid interest in treatments for what the medical literature called the "French disease" (an ironic label, since most studies indicate that a virulent strain of syphilis probably originated in North America and was transmitted to Europe by Spanish and Portuguese sailors). Worldwide, over thirty different works on syphilis were published in English between 1780 and 1820, and many of these works appeared in multiple editions.[42] Numerous works on this topic for both general and scientific audiences were printed in the United

States, including John James Giraud's *Doctor Giraud's Specific and Universal Salt, for the Venereal Disease, and All the Venereal Affections Which are the Result of It* (1797) and William Burrell's *Medical Advice; Chiefly for the Consideration of Seamen: and Adapted for the Use of Travellers, or Domestic Life* (1798).

That no American sentimental novel explicitly details the physical manifestations of syphilis is unsurprising, given that even some doctors avoided the topic. Despite the knowledge that syphilis frequently was contracted nonsexually and even though he intended his *Domestic Medicine* to be a practical handbook to address common ailments, Buchan initially omitted a chapter on venereal disease, owing to the unsavory nature of the topic. In later editions, he included the chapter but felt compelled to justify it: "The unhappy condition of such persons will certainly plead our excuse, if any excuse be necessary, for endeavouring to point out the symptoms and cure of this too common disease."[43] The closest novelists come to mentioning venereal disease is to hint at the debauched state of a character like Madame La Rue of *Charlotte Temple*, whose debilitated condition requires hospitalization, or Edward Somerton, the seducer figure in Caroline Matilda Warren's *The Gamesters*, part of whose narrative retribution is to live out the remainder of his life "prey of the disease" which he caught from the "irregularities of his youth."[44] Indeed, phrases such as "debauched state"—often read by twentieth-century readers as hackneyed clichés—were polite ciphers or codes for eighteenth-century readers, hinting at a whole array of moral transgressions: drunkenness, gambling, and, especially, uncontrolled sexual behavior and consequent disease.[45] Novelists deal with the issue of sexual passion in a similarly coded way, leaving out the lascivious details (in part from fear of giving directions for seduction) and providing readers with just enough information for them to understand the magnitude of the woman's fall from virtue (for example, she becomes pregnant with an illegitimate child). Despite the reticence with which American novelists deal with sexual issues and venereal disease, given the prevalence of this disease and its relatively unsuccessful treatments in the late eighteenth and early nineteenth centuries, which in all likelihood led to a high incidence of syphilitic insanity, we cannot ignore the cultural context in which readers would have perceived any mention of insanity, particularly when explicitly linked to sexual misbehavior.

For readers of the late eighteenth and early nineteenth centuries, then, madness as a literary trope underscored the criminality of the individual character's behavior, for madness both flagged guilty behavior and served as a punishment in and of itself. Sally Wood's *Dorval; or The Speculator* dramatically emphasizes these elements in the novel's treatment of Elizabeth Dunbar. Betrothed to a man chosen by her parents, Elizabeth is only one of the many victims of Dorval, a speculator, bigamist, and murderer. Dorval wears the mask of the sentimental man, and only the truly discerning can see beyond it. Despite the warnings of her dear friend Aurelia against Dorval, Elizabeth elopes with him. Elizabeth is no passive, sexless creature; she readily avows that "from the moment I saw Dorval, my senses were infatuated, my reason obscured by passion."[46] Love and passion properly directed and publicly sanctioned within the context of marriage are not proscribed in this novel. However, Elizabeth's passion is unsanctioned, for as she explains, "The *first* [my emphasis] failing of my erring heart was concealment. Had I made a confidant of my injured mother; had I confided in my friend . . . I had never known the misery into which I have been betrayed by the worst, the vilest of men." In order to further his own financial and sexual ends, Dorval cruelly encourages Elizabeth's passion for him, convincing her to elope with him. Elizabeth again recognizes that it was the secrecy attendant in this relationship that rendered it so dangerous: "I heard his secret vows—fatal beginning! I consented to correspond with him—guilty commerce! I met him in private—incorrigible folly!" Dorval never intended to marry Elizabeth, but in a plot twist borrowed from Samuel Richardson's *Clarissa*, he holds her captive in a house in Philadelphia while he attempts to seduce her. Elizabeth eventually escapes with her physical virtue intact, as she repeatedly asserts to anyone who will listen.

Fatal consequences follow her actions nonetheless. Elizabeth's elopement is a "harbinger" of evils for her family: the deaths of two of her siblings and the loss of her family's fortune.[47] In the midst of her escape from Dorval, Elizabeth learns of these tragedies by overhearing the story of her family's downfall and slanderous rumors about herself. Elizabeth dramatically reenacts this scenario for Aurelia: "I could hear no more. A kind of distraction seized me—I grew raving—a dreadful fever followed—my intellects were unequal to the trial—my reason deserted me." Elizabeth's "broken heart and a guilty conscience" result in her incarceration in a madhouse in Philadelphia, where she slowly regains her rationality.[48] In a seeming testimonial to the efficacy of moral treatment, Mr. Lawson, the superintendent of the asylum, provides her with books, a private room, and rational conversation, thereby aiding in her recovery.

Lawson even reunites her with her friend Aurelia, who finds Elizabeth much changed, her beauty marred by "[h]er trembling limbs, her emaciated form, and her pallid countenance," all of which "declared how much she had suffered." Despite her sympathy, Aurelia finds Elizabeth's situation distasteful: although she expresses her pleasure at seeing her friend, she un-ironically ponders that "surely a mad house was a most undesirable place in which to find her."[49]

Once Elizabeth has learned of the dangers of concealed passions, duly suffered for her transgressions, and confessed them for the benefit of Aurelia's already sterling character, she can be rehabilitated—for she was guilty only of allowing ill-judged passion to induce her to elope with Dorval, not of engaging in actual sexual relations with him. To emphasize this point, Elizabeth repeatedly protests her innocence: "I am wretched, frail, and weak, but not guilty.—The shame of vice has never washed from my cheek the crimson of virtue." Even though Aurelia eventually becomes convinced that Elizabeth is indeed "pure and unspotted," she agrees that marriage is the only means to salvage Elizabeth's reputation and make her acceptable to her parents. Now able to appreciate kindness and virtue, Elizabeth does not return to her erstwhile suitor, Mr. Jones, but instead marries Lawson, the superintendent of the asylum. Fascinated in the asylum by her "melancholy beauty," Lawson falls in love with her, thereby further complicating the novel's erotic equation of sexuality and madness. Is Elizabeth now the only fit mate for Lawson, given his close association with the inhabitants of the asylum? Or, perhaps more likely, is Lawson the only fit mate for Elizabeth? Certainly he is the savior of her reputation, for once they are married, she can escape the asylum, that "scene of shame and sorrow" and return to her parents with her virtue "unspotted." Indeed, her friends urge Elizabeth to marry Lawson, if for no other reason, because "in becoming the wife of so valuable a man, every thing like disgrace would be removed from her character, and all past disagreeable occurrences forgotten."[50] While most early American novelists are concerned with the legal status of the married woman as the feme covert, here Wood is more concerned with how a woman's reputation will be affected by her marriage. In this case, Lawson's moral distinction effectively eclipses the damage to Elizabeth's reputation. But even more important, it seems clear that in Wood's view, Elizabeth's passion can be suitably directed only by a man who has witnessed the results of uncontrolled passions and learned how to tame them.

Uncontained and misdirected passions also cause the tragic madness of a female character in Samuel Relf's novel *Infidelity*. Caroline, the female protagonist, is married to an older "man who never avowed more than a motive of expediency for his addresses, who has ever neglected the offices of a husband, and for whom . . . [she] never felt more than esteem."[51] In modern-day English, the match was arranged, Mr. Franks married Caroline for her money, and neither is particularly happy in this situation. Although Relf coyly avoids describing the exact nature of the husbandly "offices" that Mr. Franks neglects, the narrative hints that, at the minimum, Mr. Franks does not fulfill Caroline's romantic emotional needs; hence he, too, is at fault in this relationship. Caroline remedies her loneliness, amid many a subplot, by falling in love with a young neighbor, named Charles Alfred. The narrative is ambiguous about whether or not Caroline and her neighbor ever consummate their relationship. Obviously, however, Caroline has committed emotional infidelity; she is guilty of permitting another man to become emotionally intimate with her—an intimacy suggested by the secret meetings and clandestine communication between Caroline and Charles.

Upon discovering this relationship, Caroline's husband kills himself. Guilt-stricken, Caroline then begins her descent into madness, which is completed when her brother kills her lover in a duel. After a friend worries that Caroline "will soon fall victim to the ravages of madness," she tells Caroline's brother, "We have sent to town for Dr. R——, that patron of humanity, whose presence imparts health to the patient, and comfort to the distressed." But even the powers of the eminent "Dr. R——"— clearly an allusion to Rush, given that *Infidelity* was published in Philadelphia—cannot save the adulterous, guilt-stricken Caroline. Eventually she, too, dies of grief and guilt, "the fury of madness . . . tearing her soul."[52] Lest the reader misread Caroline's madness as merely an excess of sensibility, Relf carefully ensures that Caroline herself enacts a ritualistic acknowledgment of wrongdoing, as she conveniently drifts into lucidity only long enough to castigate her own behavior and to confess her sin.

Although seemingly a parable about the dangers of arranged marriages, another way to understand this novel is that Caroline's sexuality threatens not only herself but also two families, for the novel ends with the death of Mr. Franks, Caroline, and her lover, Charles Alfred. The exclamation of Caroline's brother makes this interpretation explicit, when he accuses Alfred: "You have murdered the character of my whole family, by insulting the chastity of my sister!"[53] Caroline's father may have abused his authority and exercised poor judgment in arranging her marriage, but according to the narrator, it is Caroline's uncontrolled passion that exacerbates this dangerous situation.

Numerous other early American novels feature similar scenes of deathbed madness and confession—all of which are explicitly linked to sexual transgressions. Charlotte Temple, too, in the novel of that name, rages in a delirious state brought on by grief and shame. After Montraville abandons her, Charlotte writes a poignantly repentant letter to her mother, begging her forgiveness. Made melancholy by her intense solitude and the lack of a female confidant (an absolute necessity, according to the advice literature of the day), Charlotte teeters on the brink of madness. After she gives birth to her daughter in a hovel, guilty visions torment Charlotte; she "rave[s] incessantly" and does not even recognize her own child.[54] In the sequel novel, *Lucy Temple*, it is Charlotte's seducer, Montraville (who has taken Franklin as his surname after marrying Julia Franklin), who succumbs to madness. According to the narrator, his sin is visible on his countenance even to "[a]n indifferent gazer," for he is guilty of "yielding to the impulse of guilty passion." Fittingly, Montraville himself is now haunted by visions of Charlotte, and he "labour[s] under slight fits of insanity." After seeing his illegitimate daughter Lucy, whose true identity is unknown to him, he becomes even more tormented, crying "Take her away, this vision haunts me forever, sleeping or waking, it is still before me."[55]

Once again, sexual transgression is visited upon entire families. Charlotte Temple and Montraville both die after fits of insanity. Montraville's legitimate son, Lt. Franklin, continually tempts death in the pursuit of heroism after learning that his beloved Lucy is his half-sister, and he dies fighting against Napoleon. Lucy, herself guilty of no crime, "did not shrink nor faint, nor fall into convulsions" upon learning that Lt. Franklin was lost to her forever. She merely "[placed] her hand upon her brow, reclined against the mantel piece a moment, and then left the apartment." Although Lucy grieves, she does so rationally: Rowson, like Wood, reserves fits of insanity to identify and punish those guilty of sexual misbehavior. Rowson later has Lucy devote herself to benevolent acts, from which she learns "the great secret of woman's happiness, to enjoy the happiness of others."[56] Despite the narrator's hard sell of this position, readers must understand that, for Rowson, this is the only fate left to the product of a sinful liaison. Lucy's eventual death marks the end of the Temple family, as well.

Even those characters in early American fiction who are victims of trickery or violence are not free of narrative scrutiny, and they too are punished for their gullibility, if for nothing else. The case of Amelia, the female protagonist in a novel entitled *Amelia; or The Faithless Briton*, differs dramatically from that of Elizabeth Dunbar, Caroline Franks, Charlotte Temple, or Montraville. Lillie Deming Loshe was the first of many critics to dismiss this novel, which she calls one of the many "histories of seduction, too common in the fiction of the time."[57] Yet this overtly political and very conservative novel illustrates the engagement of its author with contemporary issues. Amelia is the beloved daughter of the wealthy American merchant, Horatio Blyfield. She, her father, and her brother live on Long Island, where they moved to escape the hostilities of the Revolutionary War. When a battle occurs in their neighborhood, Horatio Blyfield charitably brings home Doliscus, a wounded British soldier. The aristocratic Doliscus, a practiced seducer, repays Blyfield's hospitality by tricking his gullible daughter Amelia into a clandestine mock-marriage ceremony and then abandoning her. When she informs him that she is pregnant, he ripostes: "[Y]ou may be assured, that I still entertain the warmest gratitude for the favours which were there conferred upon me by the virtuous Horatio, and his amiable daughter."[58] His cruel play on the word "favours," hinting at the sexual favors he enjoyed, and the distinction he makes between the "virtuous Horatio" and the merely "amiable" Amelia should signal to Amelia that he does not regard her as his wife, but she vows "publicly to vindicate her honour, and assert her rights." She intrepidly follows Doliscus to England, setting the stage for the final and fatal conflict between her family and Doliscus. After Doliscus rejects her demands for "a public and unequivocal acknowledgment of their marriage," he informs her that their marriage was nothing but "a rural masquerade, at which an honest soldier . . . played the parson, and you the blushing bride—but, pr'ythee, do not talk of husband." This discovery shocks Amelia into a stupor punctuated by "boisterous [laughter]" and "nervous ejaculation[s]."[59] She then gives premature birth to a son, who dies three days later.

The rest of the novel centers around the issue of culpability: to what degree is Amelia responsible for the tragedy that befell her? Amelia continues to assert her righteous innocence; contemplating suicide, she prays,

"Gracious Father! . . . I have been deluded into error; but am free from guilt: I have been solicitous to preserve my innocence and honour. . . . The treachery of him to whom I entrusted my fate, has reduced me to despair." The appearance of her forgiving father prevents her from committing suicide, as he blithely instructs her: "Cheer up, my Amelia! The errors of our conduct may expose us to the scandal of the world, but it is guilt alone which can violate the inward tranquillity of the mind." But guilt *does* "violate the inward tranquillity" of Amelia's mind: Racked by grief, shame, and guilt, she succumbs to a fever, which in turn sends her into a delirious, Ophelia-like state, and she dies amid "peals of loud and vacant laughter" and pathetic fits of singing.[60] In a belated acknowledgment of *his* guilt, Doliscus allows Honorius, Amelia's brother, to kill him in a duel. This act of vengeance precipitates Honorius's own death: to escape the consequences of the duel, Honorius flees to America, where he is immediately killed at the battle of Monmouth.

Responsibility and culpability are central issues in this narrative. Doliscus is obviously at fault for tricking and seducing Amelia, and, readers might tend to exonerate Amelia as the victim of a heartless schemer. The narrative itself discourages this reading: despite Amelia's ostensible innocence, the narrator deliberately dwells upon the "errors" that she committed. First, she erred by allowing passion to obscure her judgment of Doliscus's character. She compounded this error by consenting to marry without her father's permission, in a clandestine ceremony. Aside from the issue of consent, this novel explicitly attacks the belief that romantic love somehow supersedes the bonds that legally and publicly unite individuals and families. Amelia allows herself to be seduced by Doliscus's dangerous rhetoric about the privacy of intimate relationships. He dismisses the need for public rites such as the marriage ceremony and instead asserts the primacy of the private relationship between a passionate couple, arguing, "My Amelia has surely no vanity to gratify with idle pageantry; . . . the privacy of the marriage does not take from its sanctity." Although Amelia recognizes that it is the very public nature of marriage that protects the individual from "the fatal consequences that might arise from the obscurity of the transaction," her passion wins out over her common sense.[61] Doliscus's trickery and Amelia's poor judgment and susceptibility to passion bring about the end of two families. The deaths of Amelia, her baby, Honorius, and Doliscus signal the end of the family line for both the American Blyfields and Doliscus's noble British family.

Readers obviously should learn not one but several moral lessons from
Amelia, for as the narrator explains, the purpose of this narrative is not
merely to entertain but "to improve [its] readers." Once again, madness
appears as a trope to signal the dangers of female choice and unchecked
passion. The narrator also critiques Amelia's political infidelity—her susceptibility to the blandishments of her political enemy—and her belief
that private life can be effectively insulated from public life. Clearly the
fate of the family is linked to the state, as the narrator sets forth in the introduction: "the great events of the late war . . . were chequered with
scenes of private sorrow, and the success of the contending forces was al-
ternately fatal to the peace and order of domestic life."[62] In "Infidelity
and Contagion: The Rhetoric of Revolution," Shirley Samuels argues for
a specific connection between the notion of the family and the nation during the early republican period.

> National concerns were portrayed as domestic dilemmas . . . since to pre-
> serve the nation it was conceived necessary to preserve the family as a care-
> fully constituted supporting unit. Therefore the sexual infidelity that repre-
> sented the greatest threat to the family was presented as a national threat,
> especially after the French Revolution when women were popularly under-
> stood to be the instigators of the dread mob that came to stand for democ-
> ratic rule, and Liberty came to be depicted as a whore.[63]

Although Relf's narrator is much too refined to label Amelia a "whore,"
clearly there is a political element to his critique, for she not only secretly
chooses a husband but chooses a British nobleman, the very antithesis of
her own American merchant family. While contemporary readers might
be tempted to excuse Amelia, given her youth and Doliscus's deliberate
seduction of her, the narrator does not allow such a reading. His emphasis on guilt and culpability shows us that he, at least, finds Amelia partly
responsible for her situation.

Given the manner in which the narrative carefully forecloses sympathetic readings of Amelia's plight, it is simply not possible to read *Amelia*
as protofeminist tract or subversive text, as so many contemporary critics read *The Coquette*, another novel of seduction. In the character of
Eliza Wharton, Hannah Foster complicates matters by showing readers
an aging woman of little means, desperate to marry into a higher social
class, seizing perhaps her last chance at happiness. Amelia, however, is
young, beautiful, rich, and beloved by her father. And, although Amelia,
like Charlotte Temple, is a naive target of deliberate seduction, this cir-

cumstance does not eliminate her responsibility for her actions. To describe them merely as victims of seduction is to deny them agency—something that the narrators and authors of both of these texts are careful not to do. Indeed, these novels betray considerable anxiety about the issue of female agency. While each of these women is in some way victimized by her seducer, each is also partially responsible for her own fate, whether from her fateful passivity (Charlotte Temple), her passion (Amelia Blyfield and Elizabeth Dunbar), or her improperly channeled romantic sensibilities (Caroline Franks). Madness as a repeated trope underscores this reading of the texts and provides a dramatically lurid fate for each transgressive woman.

The delirious state suffered by each of these characters serves a necessary narrative function, for it is the means by which errors are confessed and narrative "truth" revealed. This delirious state—consistent with contemporary medical theory—represents self-annihilation, the utter negation of self, as self-punishment either for misplaced trust, betrayed consent, or transgressive behavior. In each case, madness serves as a means to deliver a narrative verdict on the character, as well as a punishment for his or her errors. Punishment for sexual transgressions via the trope of madness becomes so common, indeed, so *expected* by the reader of early American fiction, that it becomes in a sense almost naturalized. Seduced by these patterns, readers are no longer surprised that the female protagonist's self-censure will drive her into a guilty and ultimately deadly delirium.[64] Thus, this familiarity undermines the strangeness of these texts for modern readers; further, without cultural context, the trope of madness becomes almost indecipherable or untranslatable to modern readers.

The early American novel has long been conspicuous, even notorious, for its reliance on thematic conventions such as conscience- or sensibility-induced madness. Tropical repetition in popular culture serves to reinforce basic cultural norms and values and helps readers "combat ambiguity."[65] In a time of social and political upheaval such as existed in the early republic, thematic repetition thus represents both reliability and the reification of older social codes—shrewdly translated and exported into a new form that would effectively enthrall the exact audience of young women whom writers most wanted to reach. In some cases, fiction itself may have served as a repository for older communal values during the turbulent post-Revolutionary years, thus for a time stabilizing and perhaps enabling a sense of nationally shared cultural values.[66] These early American "tales of truth" reassure readers that those who transgress will be punished in a marked way. Fiction thus acted as a check upon female sexuality, as a cultural force to counter increasingly tolerant legal attitudes toward female sexuality. Further, the lingering cultural associations between madness and criminality render madness a far more powerful and meaning-laden punishment for women than death during childbirth.

During a time in which there was a loosening of legislation concerning private life and sexual mores were becoming private rather than state concerns, fiction assumed an increasingly important role. Fiction became a substitute or surrogate for law, as it helped to provide social continuity during a period of changing attitudes toward arranged marriages and sexual morality.[67] Perhaps we should not be so quick, then, to dismiss the innumerable prefaces which argue for the moral efficacy of American fiction. Many novelists seized upon this issue of sexual transgression precisely because they could advocate a higher standard of sexual morality than that currently enforced by most state legal systems. Novelists provided frightening examples that transgressive behavior such as fornication would not go unpunished, even if that crime were not highlighted by a pregnancy. Civil law might no longer publicly punish those guilty of sexual transgressions, but the novel showed readers the inevitable punishment of those who transgressed against their families and communities. Thus the novel in effect publicized behavior that the legal and medical systems were increasingly relegating to the private realm. Drawing upon the authority of current medical and psychological theories, fiction filled in the gap between the penal code and private morality. By training readers in the art of self-scrutiny, asserting the absolute necessity of confession, and demonstrating the horrific dangers of sexual transgression, novelists finally gave themselves a defensible position from which to assert the virtuous nature of American fiction—a particularly important concern given that fiction was continually under attack by figures of cultural authority, such as Noah Webster and Timothy Dwight.

The fluidity between fiction, "real life," and medical thought during the early national era is indicative of the manner in which early American fiction is deeply embedded within its culture and vice versa. Novelists of the early republic affirmed their engagement with critical and cultural issues of the day by incorporating contemporary scientific beliefs into their work and engaging in critiques of the weakening public control of young women.[68] Sentimental novels such as *Infidelity*, *Charlotte Temple*, *Amelia*, and *Dorval* reflect considerable cultural anxiety about female choice and sexual freedom. Their conservative plots not only reflected but in all likelihood contributed to the growing sexual conservatism of the early nineteenth century. During this time, fiction became an increasingly important link in the nexus of public discourse, able to incorporate the authority of other kinds of discourse and make their power its own. Close study of early fiction reveals the shifting balance and fascinating interplay of forms of cultural authority. These novels delineate the increasing power and ascendancy of medical discourse, while at the same time revealing the extent to which American writers were engaged with their culture as they explored the boundaries of the public and private spheres, and indeed, attempted to make these boundaries permeable.

N O T E S

Research for this essay was supported in part by a 1995–96 Stephen Botein Fellowship from the American Antiquarian Society and by a research fellowship from the Graduate School at the University of North Carolina at Chapel Hill.

1. Benjamin Rush, *Medical Inquiries and Observations Upon the Diseases of the Mind* (1812; reprint, New York: Hafner, 1962), 44. All subsequent references are to this edition. Although not published until 1812, *Medical Inquiries and Observations Upon the Diseases of the Mind* was based upon thirty years of medical experience and clearly reveals its origins in eighteenth-century thought.

2. As social historians have demonstrated, spousal affection was becoming increasingly important in everyday life as well. In "Eighteenth-Century Family and Social Life Revealed in Massachusetts Divorce Records," in *A Heritage of Her Own: Toward a New Social History of American Women*, ed. Nancy F. Cott and Elizabeth H. Pleck (New York: Simon and Schuster, 1976), Cott notes that prior to 1765, divorce petitions did not mention loss of spousal affection; however, after 1765, although by itself not grounds for a divorce, loss of spousal affection became an increasingly important issue in petitions (123). Linda K. Kerber also notes an increase in the mention of spousal affection in post-Revolutionary Connecticut divorce petitions; see *Women of the Republic: Intellect and Ideology in Revolutionary America* (1980; reprint, New York: Norton, 1986), 175. Merril D. Smith also addresses the issue of romantic marital expectations in *Breaking the Bonds: Marital Discord in Pennsylvania, 1730–1830* (New York: New York University Press, 1991), especially 69–75.

3. Rush, *Medical Inquiries*, 65–66.

4. Another useful study is Klaus Doerner's *Madmen and the Bourgeoisie: A Social History of Insanity and Psychiatry* trans. Joachim Neugroschel and Jean Steinberg (1969; reprint, Oxford: Blackwell, 1981). Doerner uses a comparative

approach to describe the origins and evolution of British, French, and German psychiatric treatments for the insane.

5. Albert Deutsch, *The Mentally Ill in America: A History of Their Care and Treatment from Colonial Times* (Garden City and New York: Doubleday, Doran and Company, 1937), 52–53.

6. Generally, madness is constructed differently in more consciously Gothic fiction, such as Charles Brockden Brown's *Wieland* and *Edgar Huntly*. In these novels, madness is not merely a trope; unlike episodes of insanity in sentimental fiction, the violent manias of such characters as Wieland and Clithero provide the action for the plot rather than the moral denouement. In much sentimental fiction, madness is an expedient means of exposing error and disposing of sinful characters. It becomes a convenient and recognizable trope, one that readers could easily decipher, since it operates similarly in numerous novels.

7. Two important early studies are Lillie Deming Loshe, *The Early American Novel* (New York: Columbia University Press, 1907); and Herbert Ross Brown, *The Sentimental Novel in America, 1789–1860* (Durham, N.C.: Duke University Press, 1940). Among recent critics of early American fiction, Cathy N. Davidson has been the strongest proponent of subversive readings of these texts. Drawing upon the work of Mikhail Bakhtin and scholars working in the field of the history of the book, Davidson has persuasively argued that sentimental fiction as a genre was progressive in its advocacy of literacy skills and education for women. See *Revolution and the Word: The Rise of the Novel in America* (New York: Oxford University Press, 1986), 66 and 73; chapter 4, "Literacy, Education, and the Reader," discusses these issues at some length. Despite Davidson's emphasis on the subversive nature of early American fiction, she does point to the disjunctions in a number of sentimental novels between their conservative plots and the sex and situations of their authors. She specifically cites novels by Helena Wells and Sally Wood as fitting this paradigm. Many contemporary figures of cultural authority, as politically diverse as Thomas Jefferson and Timothy Dwight, as well as numerous anonymous writers of newspaper reviews, considered sentimental fiction unambiguously subversive and iniquitous for most readers; they regarded the very nature, subject matter, and status of fiction as topics of grave concern. See Thomas Jefferson, *The Writings of Thomas Jefferson*, ed. Paul Leicester Ford (New York: Putnam's, 1892–99), 10:104; and Timothy Dwight, *Travels in New England and New York* (New Haven: Dwight, 1821), 1:515–18. G. Harrison Orians also attests that fiction was widely criticized for its potentially subversive nature. See Orians, "Censure of Fiction in American Romances and Magazines: 1789–1810," *PMLA* 52 (1937): 195–214.

8. M. M. Bakhtin, *The Dialogic Imagination*, ed. Michael Holquist, trans. Caryl Emerson and Michael Holquist (Austin: University of Texas Press, 1981), 39.

9. By "private" and "public" spheres, I refer to the distinctions that Jürgen

Habermas makes in *The Structural Transformation of the Public Sphere* (1962), trans. Thomas Burger (Cambridge, Mass.: MIT Press, 1989), whereby certain concerns fall under the aegis of the conjugal family within the private realm, while others, such as matters of public opinion, belong to the public area of the private realm. Still other concerns, like laws, fall into the sphere of public authority. As I argue in my essay, the distinctions between the public and private spheres in the early republic were in a state of tremendous flux, particularly with regard to the regulation of female behavior and sexuality.

10. Norman Dain, *Concepts of Insanity in the United States, 1789–1865* (New Brunswick, N.J.: Rutgers University Press, 1964), 15.

11. Dain, *Concepts of Insanity*, 4–5. For more information on the evolution of moral treatment and the rise of institutions in post–1825 America, see Ruth B. Caplan's *Psychiatry and the Community in Nineteenth-Century America: The Recurring Concern with the Environment in the Prevention and Treatment of Mental Illness* (New York: Basic, 1969). Mary Ann Jimenez's *Changing Faces of Madness: Early American Attitudes and the Treatment of the Insane* (Hanover, N.H.: University Press of New England, 1987) discusses the medicalization of insanity as a disease, as well as the rise of moral treatment in America, focusing particularly on Massachusetts.

12. Dain, *Concepts of Insanity*, 12–15; Caplan, *Psychiatry and the Community*, 5. Vincenzo Chiarugi, the Italian contemporary of Rush, Pinel, and Tuke, was also an active advocate during the 1770s and 1780s for humane treatment of the mentally ill, but he was much less influential in America.

13. Dain, *Concepts of Insanity*, 22–24. Citing Nathan G. Goodman and James E. Gibson, Dain estimates that Rush taught three thousand students during his thirty years of teaching and private practice. See Goodman, *Benjamin Rush, Physician and Citizen 1746–1813* (Philadelphia: University of Pennsylvania Press, 1934), 192; and Gibson, "Benjamin Rush's Apprenticed Students," *Transactions and Studies of the College of Physicians of Philadelphia*, 4th ser., 14 (1946): 127–32.

14. Hugh P. Greely, "Early Wisconsin Medical History," *Wisconsin Medical Journal* 20 (1922): 564.

15. William Buchan, *Domestic Medicine; or The Family Physician*, 17th ed.(Halifax, N.C.: Abraham Hodge, 1801), 261. All subsequent references are to this edition.

16. Rush, *Medical Inquiries*, 16, 12.

17. Rush, *Medical Inquiries*, 36–37, 37, 38–39, 44, 66.

18. John Haslam, *Observations on Madness and Melancholy* (1809; reprint, New York: Arno Press, 1976), 210.

19. Buchan, *Domestic Medicine*, 248.

20. Rush, *Medical Inquiries*, 44.

21. Rush, *Medical Inquiries*, 318. Further, several published treatises discuss

the effects of passions such as grief on the body and the mind, including Henry Rose's *An Inaugural Dissertation on the Effects of the Passions Upon the Body* (Philadelphia: Woodward, 1794); and Alexander Anderson's *An Inaugural Dissertation on Chronic Mania* (New York: Swords, 1796).

22. Rush, *Medical Inquiries*, 59; Haslam, *Observations on Madness*, 245–50.

23. Rush, *Medical Inquiries*, 238–39.

24. In *Democracy and Punishment: Disciplinary Origins of the United States* (Madison: University of Wisconsin Press, 1987), Thomas L. Dumm notes that the prison reforms instituted at Philadelphia's Walnut Street Jail in the 1790s closely parallel the reforms taking place in the treatment of mental patients. Penal reforms move from a desire to humiliate prisoners by making them public spectacles to a policy of isolating prisoners in solitary confinement as the first step in the rehabilitation process. Prisoners were removed from the public eye, yet were kept under the constant surveillance and control of prison guards. Such a system was designed to promote order, rationality, and contemplation for the purpose of producing self-regulating republican machines (101–5). Rush's work undoubtedly influenced these penal reforms, as he believed that the same environmental controls would benefit both criminals and the mentally ill, once again demonstrating his and other reformers' continued (albeit unintentional) conflation of these two groups.

25. Haslam, *Observations on Madness*, 237.

26. Joseph Parrish, *An Inaugural Dissertation on the Influence of the Passions Upon the Body in the Production and Cure of Diseases* (Philadelphia: Kimber, Conrad and Co., 1805), 48.

27. In *Worlds of Wonder, Days of Judgment: Popular Religious Belief in Early New England* (New York: Alfred A. Knopf, 1989), David D. Hall discusses the public, ritualistic nature of seventeenth- and eighteenth-century religious and civil confession, which served to relieve sinners of the burden of their transgressions (172–78). The confessional nature of late eighteenth-century sentimental fiction represents the increasing secularization of this behavior.

28. See William E. Nelson, "Emerging Notions of Modern Criminal Law in the Revolutionary Era: An Historical Perspective," *New York University Law Review* 42 (1967): 450–82. The results of his study, which concentrates on Middlesex County, Massachusetts, are startling. Immediately prior to the Revolution, during the period from 1760 to 1774, 210 women were prosecuted for fornication in Middlesex County (452). In 1786, a change in the statutes regarding fornication allowed women guilty of this crime simply to appear before a magistrate and pay their fines without being subject to prosecution. Nelson concludes that even this penalty was no longer enforced after 1791. Further, during the 1790s, women were even able to file paternity suits against the fathers of their illegitimate children without themselves risking punishment. The enforcement of adultery statutes was similarly weakened: even though divorces were

regularly granted after the Revolution for reason of adultery, spouses were seldom criminally punished (455–57). See also Cott, "Eighteenth-Century Family
and Social Life Revealed in Massachusetts Divorce Records," 107–35; and "Divorce and the Changing Status of Women in Eighteenth-Century Massachusetts,"
in *"The American Family in Social-Historical Perspective,* 2d ed., ed. Michael
Gordon (New York: St. Martin's, 1978), 115–39. Cott demonstrates that there
truly was a sexual double standard when it came to marital sexual infidelity. The
differing rates of male and female divorce petitions granted on the basis of adultery suggest that women were judged much more harshly than were men and
that male marital infidelity was more likely to be dismissed. These statistics
begin to change after the Revolution. See "Divorce and the Changing Status of
Women," 122–26. Cornelia Hughes Dayton also notes this sexual double standard in mid-eighteenth-century New England. She suggests that not only were
men no longer being punished for the crime of fornication but that "the sexually irresponsible activities of men in their youth would not be held against them
as they reached for repute and prosperity in their prime." See Dayton, "Taking
the Trade: Abortion and Gender Relations in an Eighteenth-Century New England Village," *William and Mary Quarterly* 48.1 (1991): 22. In *Breaking the
Bonds,* Smith notes that in post-Revolutionary Pennsylvania, women were
"slightly more successful than men in winning divorces on adultery grounds
when they did petition" (85). Nonetheless, Smith also notes the continuance of
a sexual double standard: women were occasionally charged with adultery after
a pregnancy, particularly when local officials became concerned that the child
might be a charge on the community.

29. Nelson, "Emerging Notions," 458.

30. Ellen K. Rothman, "Sex and Self-Control: Middle-Class Courtship in
America, 1770–1870, "in *The American Family in Social-Historical Perspective,*
3d ed., ed. Michael Gordon (New York: St. Martin's, 1983), 394–95. See also
Rothman, *Hands and Hearts: A History of Courtship in America* (New York:
Basic, 1984), especially chapter 1.

31. Daniel Scott Smith, "Parental Power and Marriage Patterns: An Analysis
of Historical Trends in Hingham, Massachusetts, *"Journal of Marriage and the
Family* (August 1973): 419–28. Smith acknowledges that it is difficult to generalize about the rest of the country based upon the study of one town; however, fertility patterns in Hingham are consistent with those at the national level. Jane
Turner Censer's unpublished study of upper-class North Carolina families during
the late eighteenth and early nineteenth centuries supports Smith's conclusions.
Censer, too, notes an increase in the number of women marrying out of birth
order. Censer's work is cited in Carl Degler, *At Odds: Women and the Family in
America from the Revolution to the Present* (New York: Oxford University Press,
1980), 11. Significantly, Smith also argues that illegitimacy rates parallel rates of
premarital sex. While there are currently no statistics available about the rate of

illegitimate births in America during this time, most historians concur with Smith that the number of illegitimate births probably increased as well.

32. Daniel Scott Smith and Michael S. Hindus, "Premarital Pregnancy in America 1640–1971, "*Journal of Interdisciplinary History* 5 (1975): 561. This statistic is particularly dramatic when compared to the years before and after this period. For the period from 1721 to 1760, 22.5 percent of first births to married women occurred before the ninth month of marriage; for the period from 1801 to 1840, 23.7 percent (561). Robert A. Gross notes similar findings in his study of Concord in *The Minutemen and Their World* (New York: Hill, 1976). Gross concludes that 41 percent of all first births between 1760 and 1774 were the result of prenuptial conceptions (217, n. 59). Smith and Hindus hypothesize that this spike is related to "the disintegration of the traditional, well-integrated rural community to the beginnings of economic and social modernization" (559). Religious revivalism of the nineteenth century probably was instrumental in lowering premarital pregnancy rates (551). Further, Smith and Hindus propose that "sexual restraint was compatible with the norms of thrift and abstinence required of the upwardly striving young capitalist. . . . Having internalized the mechanism of delayed gratification in terms of his economic life, the nineteenth-century American male would not risk the consequences of a marriage precipitated by a premarital pregnancy" (552). Smith and Hindus do not, however, consider the powerful influence of fiction in regulating sexual mores and behavior.

33. Although violations of adultery and fornication statutes are seldom prosecuted today, as of 1989, twenty-five states and the District of Columbia still prohibited adultery, while thirteen states and the District of Columbia prohibited fornication, according to Richard Green. See Green, "*Griswold's* Legacy: Fornication and Adultery as Crimes, "*Ohio Northern University Law Review* 16 (1989): 545–49. Many statutes remained on the books in unaltered form for decades, even centuries. For example, until 1973, the statutory punishment for adultery in New Hampshire was whipping and the wearing of the letters "AD" on one's clothing. See "The Scarlet Legislature: For Adulterers Only," *Student Lawyer*, May 1987, 6–7. Needless to say, this punishment had not been enforced for several centuries, but the fact that it remained on the statute books is an indication of how states began deliberately turning a blind eye toward so-called "domestic" crimes during the late eighteenth century.

34. Hayden White suggests that all "narrativity, whether of the fictional or factual sort, presupposes the existence of a legal system against or on behalf of which the typical agents of a narrative account militate. And this raises the suspicion that narrative in general, from the folktale to the novel . . . has to do with the topics of law, legality, legitimacy, or, more generally, authority." See White, "The Value of Narrativity in the Representation of Reality, "in *The Content of the Form* (Baltimore: Johns Hopkins University Press, 1987), 13.

35. Davidson, *Revolution and the Word*, 116. Since, in fiction unmarried

mothers and illegitimate children rarely survive the birth process, seldom is accountability after birth an issue for either mother or father. Mrs. P. D. Manvill's *Lucinda; or The Mountain Mourner* (1807; 2d ed. [with additions], Ballston Spa, 1810) provides a notable exception. After Melvin Brown rapes Lucinda, she bears a daughter. Someone in the town of Greenfield, however, lodges a complaint against her presence; in order to keep her from being committed "to the care of the public, "her parents have to provide bail or demonstrate that moving her would be dangerous to her health (99). Her parents successfully petition to keep her at home until her death. The novel ends once the magistrate confronts Brown, holding him accountable for his actions and forcing him to pay for the care of his child.

36. Claude Quétel, *History of Syphilis* (Baltimore: Johns Hopkins University Press, 1990), 160–62.

37. Haslam, *Observations on Madness*, 259, 208–9.

38. Buchan, *Domestic Medicine*, 303, 285.

39. Buchan, *Domestic Medicine*, 285; and Thomas Parran, *Shadow on the Land: Syphilis* (New York: Reynal, 1937), 75.

40. Quétel, *History of Syphilis*, 71–75.

41. Edward B. Vedder, *Syphilis and Public Health* (Philadelphia: Lea, 1918), 97. Vedder's statistics differ for men and women. He estimates that syphilis was demonstrable among 20–25 percent of white males admitted to insane asylums, but probably present in 25–35 percent of that population. Syphilis was demonstrable in white women in 10–23 percent of the inmate population, but probable in 15–30 percent (97). Parran estimates that by 1937, before the widespread use of penicillin to treat syphilis but after the improvement of alternate treatments for the disease, the number of the syphilitic insane dropped to 10 percent of the total admissions to state psychiatric institutions (301).

42. Philip Ricord's *Illustrations of Syphilitic Disease* (Philadelphia: Hart, 1852) contains a somewhat useful bibliography of works on syphilis, dating from the first appearance of the disease through 1850. This bibliography is more comprehensive for British and European titles than American ones, for it provides only a partial listing of American works and frequently excludes the most important reprints of British works. Some of the more important early works on syphilis published in the United States and intended for a scientific audience include John Hunter's *A Treatise on the Venereal Disease* (1787, 1791); Benjamin Bell's *A Treatise on Gonorrhoea Virulenta and Lues Venerea* (1795); Thomas T. Hewson's *A Complete Treatise on Syphilis* (1815); and Richard Carmichael's *An Essay on the Venereal Diseases Which Have Been Confounded with Syphilis, and the Symptoms Which Exclusively Arise from That Poison* (1817).

43. Buchan, *Domestic Medicine*, 285.

44. Carolina Matilda Warren, *The Gamesters; or Ruins of Innocence* (Boston: Carlisle, for Thomas and Andrews, et al., 1805), 304.

45. Popular in America, William Hogarth's print series *The Rake's Progress*, which depicts the rake's imprisonment and ultimate death in Bedlam, likewise suggests syphilitic insanity resulting from debauched behavior.

46. Sally Wood, *Dorval; or The Speculator* (Portsmouth, N.H., 1801), 213, 214.

47. Wood, *Dorval*, 226, 217.

48. Wood, *Dorval*, 218. By way of contrast, Aurelia, secure in the knowledge of her own virtue, suffers from hysteria when she learns of Elizabeth's elopement. Aurelia "[brooded] over these accumulated evils, till her blood became congealed. It ceased to flow with its usual calmness. Her pulse stopped, and a suffocating sensation, more dreadful than fainting, came over her" (104). This juxtaposition of hysteria with madness emphasizes the physical manifestations of hysteria, while accenting the correlation between transgressive behavior and madness. Hysteria, it seems, is an appropriate state for a virtuous woman.

49. Wood, *Dorval*, 211, 213.

50. Wood, *Dorval*, 213, 223, 212, 224.

51. Samuel Relf, *Infidelity, or The Victims of Sentiment: A Novel, in a Series of Letters* (Philadelphia, 1797), 18.

52. Relf, *Infidelity*, 184, 190.

53. Relf, *Infidelity*, 187.

54. Susanna Rowson, *Charlotte: A Tale of Truth* and *Charlotte's Daughter; or The Three Orphans*, ed. Ann Douglas (1794 and 1828; reprint, New York: Penguin, 1991), 122. All subsequent references to works by Rowson are from this edition.

55. Rowson, *Charlotte*, 230–31, 175, 175.

56. Rowson, *Charlotte*, 238, 238, 260.

57. Loshe, *Early American Novel*, 61.

58. *Amelia; or The Faithless Briton* (Boston, 1798), 14–15.

59. *Amelia*, 16, 19, 20.

60. *Amelia*, 22, 24, 30.

61. *Amelia*, 11–12.

62. *Amelia*, 2, 1.

63. Shirley Samuels, "Infidelity and Contagion: The Rhetoric of Revolution, "*Early American Literature* 22 (1987): 187.

64. Lucy Franklin of *The Vain Cottager; or The History of Lucy Franklin* (New Haven: Increase Cooke and Co., 1807) and Laura of Leonora Sansay's *Laura* (Philadelphia: Bradford and Inskeep, 1809) are among the very few unmarried, sexually active women in early American fiction who do not die. The conclusions of these novels make clear, however, that these women must nonetheless pay a steep price for their transgressions.

65. Jan Radway, *Reading the Romance: Women, Patriarchy, and Popular Literature*, rev. ed. (Chapel Hill: University of North Carolina Press, 1991), 196. See

also Fredric Jameson, "Reification and Utopia in Mass Culture, "*Social Text* 1 (1979): 135–37.

66. In *Imagined Communities: Reflections on the Origin and Spread of Nationalism* (London: Verso, 1983), Benedict Anderson argues that vernacular print culture was essential in establishing "imaginary communities" of widely separated individuals; these "imaginary communities" in turn enabled the rise of modern nationalism. Anderson emphasizes the importance of newspapers as a part of vernacular print culture. Nancy Armstrong and Leonard Tennenhouse extend Anderson's thesis, however, and suggest that fiction was perhaps the more important medium in creating modern communities. See *The Imaginary Puritan: Literature, Intellectual Labor, and the Origins of Personal Life* (Berkeley: University of California Press, 1992), especially 141–48.

67. John Zomchick has argued that "law and narrative both stand as references, guides for adjudicating between personal desires and social demands—the latter understood in the double sense of personal demand for society and social demands upon person." See *Family and the Law in Eighteenth-Century Fiction: The Public Conscience in the Private Sphere* (Cambridge: Cambridge University Press), 4.

68. Medical practitioners were in turn influenced by artistic treatments of insanity. Indeed, Rush's *Medical Inquiries and Observations Upon the Diseases of the Mind* is remarkable today both for the fluidity with which he moves between science and art and for the manner in which he juxtaposes poetry and quotations from Shakespeare's *King Lear* as medical "evidence" alongside his own observations. Similarly, Samuel Coates, a manager of the asylum at the Pennsylvania Hospital from 1785 to 1825, kept a memorandum book in which he noted case histories of patients at the hospital. His narratives are themselves dramatized in a manner reminiscent of contemporary sentimental fiction. See Coates's memorandum book, "Cases of Several Lunatics in the Pennsylvania Hospital" (1785–1825), located in the archives of the Pennsylvania Hospital.

Selected Bibliography

Abel, Elizabeth, ed. *Writing and Sexual Difference*. Chicago: University of Chicago Press, 1982.

Alexander, Flora. "Women as Lovers in Early English Romance." *Women and Literature in Britain, 1150–1500*. Cambridge: Cambridge University Press, 1993.

Amelia; or The Faithless Briton. Boston, 1798.

Amussen, Susan Dwyer. *An Ordered Society: Gender and Class in Early Modern England*. Oxford: Basil Blackwell, 1988.

Anderson, Alexander. *An Inaugural Dissertation on Chronic Mania*. New York: Swords, 1796.

Anderson, Benedict. *Imagined Communities: Reflections on the Origin and Spread of Nationalism*. London: Verso, 1983.

Arens, W. *The Man-Eating Myth: Anthropology and Anthropophagy*. New York: Oxford University Press, 1979.

Armstrong, Nancy, and Leonard Tennenhouse. *The Imaginary Puritan: Literature, Intellectual Labor, and the Origins of Personal Life*. Berkeley: University of California Press, 1992.

Axelrod, Alan. *Charles Brockden Brown: An American Tale*. Austin: University of Texas Press, 1983.

Axtell, James. *Imagining the Other: First Encounters in North America*. Washington, D.C.: American Historical Association, 1991.

Bardes, Barbara, and Suzanne Gossett. *Declarations of Independence: Women and Political Power in Nineteenth-Century American Fiction*. New Brunswick, N.J. and London: Rutgers University Press, 1990.

Barker-Benfield, G. J. *The Culture of Sensibility: Sex and Society in Eighteenth-Century Britain*. Chicago: University of Chicago Press, 1992.

Barnett, Louise K. *The Ignoble Savage: American Literary Racism, 1790–1890*. Westport, Conn.: Greenwood, 1975.

Beckles, Hilary McD. "White Women and Slavery in the Caribbean." *History Workshop* 36 (Fall 1993): 66–81.

Bell, Michael Davitt. "'The Double-Tongued Deceiver': Sincerity and Duplicity in the Novels of Charles Brockden Brown." *Early American Literature* 9.2 (1974): 143–63.

Beverley, Robert. *The History and Present State of Virginia.* Chapel Hill: University of North Carolina Press, 1947.

Bloch, Ruth H. "The Gendered Meanings of Virtue in Revolutionary America." *Signs* 13 (Fall 1987): 37–58.

Boucé, Paul-Gabriel. "Aspects of Sexual Tolerance and Intolerance in Eighteenth-Century England." *British Journal for Eighteenth-Century Studies* 3 (1980): 173–91.

———, ed. *Sexuality in Eighteenth-Century Britain.* Manchester: Manchester University Press, 1982.

Bourne, Russell. *The Red King's Rebellion: Racial Politics in New England, 1675–1678.* New York: Atheneum, 1990.

Bourque, Linda Brookover. *Defining Rape.* Durham, N.C.: Duke University Press, 1989.

Boydston, Jeanne. *Home and Work: Housework, Wages, and the Ideology of Labor in the Early Republic.* New York and Oxford: Oxford University Press, 1990.

Brathwaite, Edward. *The Development of Creole Society in Jamaica, 1770–1820.* Oxford: Oxford University Press, 1971.

Breen, T. H. "An Empire of Goods: The Anglicization of Colonial America, 1690–1776." *Journal of British Studies* 25 (1986): 467–99.

——— *Tobacco Culture: The Mentality of the Great Tidewater Planters on the Eve of the Revolution.* Princeton: Princeton University Press, 1985.

Breitwieser, Mitchell R. *American Puritanism and the Defense of Mourning: Religion, Grief, and Ethnology in Mary White Rowlandson's Captivity Narrative.* Madison: University of Wisconsin Press, 1990.

Bridenbaugh, Carl and Roberta Bridenbaugh. *No Peace beyond the Line: the English in the Caribbean, 1624–1690.* New York: Oxford University Press, 1972.

Brotherston, Gordon. *The Image of the New World: The American Continent Portrayed in Native Texts.* London: Thames and Hudson, 1979.

Brown, Charles Brockden. *Ormond; or the Secret Witness.* 1799. Edited with an introduction by Ernest Marchand. New York and London: Hafner, 1937.

Brown, Herbert Ross. *The Sentimental Novel in America, 1789–1860.* Durham, N.C.: Duke University Press, 1940.

Brown, Kathleen. *Good Wives, Nasty Wenches, and Anxious Patriarchs: Gender, Race, and Power in Colonial Virginia.* Chapel Hill: University of North Carolina Press, 1996.

Brown, Peter. *The Body and Society: Men, Women, and Sexual Renunciation in Early Christianity.* New York: Columbia University Press, 1988.

Brownmiller, Susan. *Against Our Will: Men, Women and Rape.* New York: Bantam, 1975.

Brumm, Ursula. *American Thought and Religious Typology.* New Brunswick, N.J.: Rutgers University Press, 1970.

Buchan, William. *Domestic Medicine; or The Family Physician.* 17th ed. Halifax, N.C.: Abraham Hodge, 1801.

Burke, Charles T. *Puritans at Bay: The War against King Philip and the Squaw Sachems.* New York: Exposition, 1967.

Burkett, Elinor. "Indian Women and White Society: The Case of Sixteenth-Century Peru." In *Latin American Women: Historical Perspectives*, edited by Asunción Lavrin, 101–38. Westport, Conn.: Greenwood, 1978.

Burnard, Trevor. "A Failed Settler Society: Marriage and Demographic Failure in Early Jamaica." *Journal of Social History* 28.1 (1994): 63–82.

———. "Family Continuity and Female Independence in Jamaica, 1665–1734." *Continuity and Change* 7.2 (1992): 181–98.

———. "Inheritance and Independence: Women's Status in Early Colonial Jamaica." *William and Mary Quarterly* 48.1 (1991): 93–114.

———. "'They Do Not Like Their Will to Be Thwarted': The Household and Household Violence in Thomas Thistlewood's Jamaica." In *Over the Threshold: Intimate Violence in Early America, 1640–1865*, edited by Christine Daniels. London: Routledge, forthcoming.

Bush, Barbara. "White 'Ladies,' Coloured 'Favourites' and Black 'Wenches': Some Considerations on Sex, Race and Class Factors in Social Relations in White Creole Society in the British Caribbean." *Slavery and Abolition* 2 (December 1981): 245–62.

Bynum, Caroline Walker. *Holy Feast and Holy Fast: The Religious Significance of Food to Medieval Women.* Berkeley and Los Angeles: University of California Press, 1987.

———. *The Resurrection of the Body in Western Christianity, 200–1336.* New York: Columbia University Press, 1995.

Byrd, William. *Histories of the Dividing Line betwixt Virginia and North Carolina.* New York: Dover, 1967.

Caplan, Ruth B. *Psychiatry and the Community in Nineteenth-Century America: The Recurring Concern with the Environment in the Prevention and Treatment of Mental Illness.* New York: Basic, 1969.

Carson, Cary, Ronald Hoffman, and Peter, J. Albert, eds. *Of Consuming Interests: The Style of Life in the Eighteenth Century.* Charlottesville: University Press of Virginia, 1994.

Christophersen, Bill. *The Apparition in the Glass: Charles Brockden Brown's American Gothic.* Athens, Ga. and London: University of Georgia Press, 1993.

Cohen, J. M. *The Four Voyages of Christopher Columbus: Being His Own Log-*

Book, Letters and Dispatches with Connecting Narrative Drawn from the Life of the Admiral by His Son Hernando Colón and Other Contemporary Historians. Harmondsworth, England: Penguin, 1969.

Cott, Nancy F. *The Bonds of Womanhood:"Woman's Sphere" in New England, 1780–1835.* New Haven: Yale University Press, 1977.

———. "Divorce and the Changing Status of Women in Eighteenth-Century Massachusetts." In *The American Family in Social-Historical Perspective*, 2d. ed, edited by Michael Gordon, 115–39. New York: St. Martin's, 1978.

———. "Eighteenth-Century Family and Social Life Revealed in Massachusetts Divorce Records." In *A Heritage of Her Own: Towards a New Social History of American Women*, edited by Nancy F. Cott, 107–35. New York: Simon and Schuster, 1979.

———. "Passionless: An Interpretation of Victorian Sexual Ideology, 1790–1850." *Signs* 4 (Winter 1978): 219–36.

Cowell, Pattie. "Class, Gender, and Genre: Deconstructing Social Formulas on the Gothic Frontier." In *Frontier Gothic: Terror and Wonder at the Frontier in American Literature*, edited by David Mogen, Scott P. Sanders, and Joanne B. Karpinski, 126–39. London: Associated University Presses, 1993.

Craft-Fairchild, Catherine. *Masquerade and Gender: Disguise and Female Identity in Eighteenth-Century Fictions by Women.* University Park: Pennsylvania State University Press, 1993.

Crane, Elaine F. "Dependence in the Era of Independence: The Role of Women in Republican Society." In *The American Revolution: Its Character and Limits*, edited by Jack P. Greene, 253–75. New York: New York University Press, 1987.

Craton, Michael. *Testing the Chains: Resistance to Slavery in the British West Indies.* Ithaca, N.Y.: Cornell University Press, 1982.

Cutbush, Edward. *An Inaugural Dissertation on Insanity.* Philadelphia: Zachariah Poulson, Jr., 1794.

Dain, Norman. *Concepts of Insanity in the United States, 1789–1865.* New Brunswick, N.J.: Rutgers University Press, 1964.

Davidson, Cathy N. "The Matter and Manner of Charles Brockden Brown's *Alcuin*." In *Critical Essays on Charles Brockden Brown*, edited by Bernard Rosenthal, 71–86. Boston: G. K. Hall, 1981.

———. *Revolution and the Word: The Rise of the Novel in America.* New York: Oxford University Press, 1986.

Davis, Margaret H. "Mary White Rowlandson's Self-Fashioning as Puritan Goodwife." *Early American Literature* 27.1 (1992): 49–60.

Dayton, Cornelia Hughes. "Taking the Trade: Abortion and Gender Relations in an Eighteenth-Century New England Village." *William and Mary Quarterly* 48.1 (1991): 19–49.

Deagan, Kathleen A. "Spanish-Indian Interaction in Sixteenth-Century Florida and Hispaniola." In *Cultures in Contact: The Impact of European Contacts on Native American Cultural Institutions, A. D. 1000–1800,* edited by Willaim W. Fitzhugh, Anthropological Society of Washington Series, 281–318. Washington, D.C.: Smithsonian Institution Press, 1985.

Degler, Carl N. *At Odds: Women and the Family in America from the Revolution to the Present.* New York: Oxford University Press, 1980.

de Léry, Jean. *History of a Voyage to the Land of Brazil.* Translated by Janet Whateley. Berkeley: University of California Press, 1990.

Deliette, Pierre. "Memoir of De Gannes Concerning the Illinois Country." In *The Western Country in the 17th Century,* edited by Milo M. Quaife, 81–171. Chicago: Lakeside, 1947.

Derounian, Kathryn Zabelle. "A Critical Edition of Mrs. Mary Rowlandson's Captivity Narrative." Ph. D. Diss., Yale University, 1972.

———. "The Publication, Promotion, and Distribution of Mary Rowlandson's Indian Captivity Narrative in the Seventeenth-Century." *Early American Literature* 23 (1988): 239–61.

———. "Puritan Orthodoxy and the 'Survivor Syndrome' in Mary Rowlandson's Indian Captivity Narrative." *Early American Literature* 221 (1987): 82–93.

Devereux, George. "Institutional Homosexuality of the Mohave Indians." *Human Biology* 9 (1937): 518, 498–99.

Díaz, Bernal. *The Conquest of New Spain.* Translated by J. M. Cohen. New York: Penguin, 1963.

Dickinson, Olive Patricia. *The Myth of the Savage and the Beginnings of French Colonialism in the Americas.* Edmonton: University of Alberta Press, 1984.

Doerner, Klaus. *Madmen and the Bourgeoisie: A Social History of Insanity and Psychiatry.* 1969. Translated by Joachim Neugroschel and Jean Steinberg. Oxford: Basil Blackwell, 1981.

Dollimore, Jonathan. "Shakespeare Understudies: The Sodomite, the Prostitute, the Transvestite and Their Critics." In *Political Shakespeare: Essays in Cultural Materialism,* edited by Jonathan Dollimore and Alan Sinfield, 129–52. Manchester: Manchester University Press, 1994.

Douglas, Ann. *The Feminization of American Culture.* New York: Knopf, 1977.

Downing, David. "'Streams of Scripture Comfort': Mary Rowlandson's Typological Use of the Bible." *Early American Literature* 15.3 (1981): 252–59.

duCille, Ann. "'Othered' Matters: Reconceptualizing Dominance and Difference in the History of Sexuality in America." *Journal of the History of Sexuality* 1 (July 1990): 102–30.

Dudley, Edward, and Maximilian Novak, eds. *The Wild Man Within: An Image in Western Thought from Renaissance to Romanticism.* Pittsburgh: University of Pittsburgh Press, 1973.

Dumm, Thomas L. *Democracy and Punishment: Disciplinary Origins of the United States.* Madison: University of Wisconsin Press, 1987.

Dunn, Richard S. "The English Sugar Islands and the Founding of South Carolina." In *Shaping Southern Society: The Colonial Experience.* Edited by T. H. Breen. New York: Oxford University Press, 1976.

————. *Sugar and Slaves: The Rise of the Planter Class in the English West Indies, 1624–1713.* Chapel Hill: University of North Carolina Press, 1972.

————. "Sugar Production and Slave Women in Jamaica." In *Cultivation and Culture: Labor and the Shaping of Slave Life in the Americas,* edited by Ira Berlin and Philip D. Morgan, 49–72. Charlottesville: University of Virginia Press, 1993.

Dussel, Enrique. *The Invention of the Americas: Eclipse of"the Other" and the Myth of Modernity.* Translated by Michael D. Barber. New York: Continuum, 1995.

Dwight, Timothy. *Travels in New England and New York.* New Haven: T. Dwight, 1821.

Elliott, Dyan. *Spiritual Marriage: Sexual Abstinence in Medieval Wedlock.* Princeton: Princeton University Press, 1993.

Elliott, Emory. *Power and the Pulpit in Puritan New England.* Princeton: Princeton University Press, 1975.

Ellis, Markman. *The Politics of Sensibility: Race, Gender and Commerce in the Sentimental Novel.* Cambridge: Cambridge University Press, 1996.

Evans, Sara M. *Born for Liberty: a History of Women in America.* New York: Free, 1989.

Fairchild, Hoxie. *The Noble Savage: A Study in Romantic Naturalism.* New York: Russell and Russell, 1961.

Ferguson, Margaret W., Maureen Quilligan, and Nancy J. Vikers, eds. *Rewriting the Renaissance: The Discourses of Sexual Difference in Early Modern Europe.* Chicago: University of Chicago Press, 1980.

Ferris, Lesley. "Current Crossings." Introduction to *Crossing the Stage: Controversies on Cross-Dressing,* edited by Lesley Ferris. London and New York: Routledge, 1993.

Fiedler, Leslie. *Love and Death in the American Novel.* New York: Dell, 1966.

Fischer, David Hackett. *Albion's Seed: Four British Folkways in America.* New York: Oxford University Press, 1989.

Fitzpatrick, Tara. "The Figure of Captivity: The Cultural Work of the Puritan Captivity Narrative." *American Literary History* 3 (1991): 1–26.

Flaherty, David H. "Law and the Enforcement of Morals in Early America." In *Perspectives in American History,* edited by Donald Flemming and Bernard Baylin, Vol. 5, 203–53. Cambridge: Harvard University Press for Charles Warren Center for Studies in American History, 1971.

Fletcher, Anthony. *Gender, Sex and Subordination in England, 1500–1800.* New Haven: Yale University Press, 1995.

Fliegelman, Jay. *Prodigals and Pilgrims: The American Revolution Against Patri-archal Authority, 1750–1800.* New York: Cambridge University Press, 1982.

Foster, Hannah. *The Coquette; or The History of Eliza Wharton.* Edited by Cathy N. Davidson. Boston, 1797. Reprint, New York: Oxford University Press, 1986.

Foucault, Michel. *The History of Sexuality: An Introduction.* Translated by Robert Hurley. New York: Vintage, 1990.

———. *Madness and Civilization: A History of Insanity in the Age of Reason.* 1965. Reprint, New York: Vintage, 1973.

Garber, Marjorie. *Vested Interests: Cross-Dressing and Cultural Anxiety.* New York: Routledge, 1992.

Gerbi, Antonello. *Nature in the New World: From Christopher Columbus to Gonzalo Fernández de Oviedo.* Translated by Jeremy Moyle. Pittsburgh: University of Pittsburgh Press, 1985.

Goldberg, Jonathan. *Sodometries: Renaissance Texts, Modern Sexualities.* Stanford, Calif.: Stanford University Press, 1992.

Godbeer, Richard. "'The Cry of Sodom': Discourse, Intercourse, and Desire in Colonial New England." *William and Mary Quarterly* 52 (April 1995): 259–86.

Gookin, Daniel. *A Narrative of the Troubles with the Indians in New England, From the First Planting thereof to the present Time.* 2 vols. Roxbury, Mass.: S. G. Drake, 1865.

Gowing, Laura. "Gender and the Language of Insult in Early Modern London." *History Workshop Journal* 35 (1993): 1–21.

Green, Richard. "*Griswold's* Legacy: Fornication and Adultery as Crimes." *Ohio Northern University Law Review* 16 (1989): 545–49.

Greene, David L. "New Light on Mary Rowlandson." *Early American Literature* 20 (1985): 24–38.

Greene, Jack P. *The Diary of Colonel Landon Carter of Sabine Hall, 1752–1778.* 2 vols. Charlottesville: University Press of Virginia, 1965.

Greven, Philip. *Four Generations: Population, Land, and Family in Colonial Andover, Massachusetts.* Ithaca, N.Y.: Cornell University Press, 1970.

Gross, Robert A. *The Minutemen and Their World.* New York: Hill and Wang, 1976.

Gutiérrez, Ramón A. *When Jesus Came, the Corn Mothers Went Away: Marriage, Sexuality, and Power in New Mexico, 1500–1846.* Stanford, Calif.: Stanford University Press, 1991.

Hall, David D. *Worlds of Wonder, Days of Judgment: Popular Religious Belief in Early New England.* New York: Knopf, 1989.

Hall, Douglas. *In Miserable Slavery: Thomas Thistlewood in Jamaica, 1750–86.* London: Macmillan, 1989.

Halttunen, Karen. *Confidence Men and Painted Women: A Study of Middle-Class Culture in America, 1830–1870.* New Haven: Yale University Press, 1982.

———. "Humanitarianism and the Pornography of Pain in Anglo-American Culture." *American Historical Review* 100 (April 1995): 303–34.

Hansen, Klaus P. "The Sentimental Novel and Its Feminist Critique." *Early American Literature* 26 (1991): 39–54.

Hartmann, Heidi I., and Ellen Ross. "Comment on 'On Writing the History of Rape.'" *Signs: Journal of Women in Culture and Society* 3.4 (1978): 931–35.

Harvey, A. D. *Sex in Georgian England: Attitudes and Prejudices from the 1720s to the 1820s.* New York: St. Martin's, 1994.

Haskett, Robert. "'Not a Pastor, but a Wolf': Indigenous-Clergy Relations in Early Cuernavaca and Taxco." *The Americas* 50.3 (1994): 293–336.

Haslam, John. *Observations on Madness and Melancholy.* London: J. Callow, 1809. Reprint, New York: Arno Press, 1976.

Hemming, John. *Red Gold: The Conquest of the Brazilian Indians, 1500–1760.* Cambridge: Harvard University Press, 1978.

Hemphill, C. Dallett. "Age Relations and the Social Order in Early New England: The Evidence from Manners." *Journal of Social History* 28 (Winter 1994): 271–94.

Hessinger, Rodney. "Problems and Promises: Colonial American Child Rearing and Modernization Theory." *Journal of Family History* 21 (April 1996): 125–43.

Higman, B. W. *Slave Population and Economy in Jamaica, 1807–1834.* Cambridge: Cambridge University Press, 1976.

Hoff, Joan. Law, *Gender, and Injustice: A Legal History of U. S. Women.* New York: New York University Press, 1991.

Howe, Susan. "The Captivity and Restoration of Mrs. Mary Rowlandson." *Temblor* 2 (1985): 113–21.

Hulme, Peter. "Polytropic Man: Tropes of Sexuality and Mobility in Early Colonial Discourse." In *Europe and Its Others: Proceedings of the Essex Conference on the Sociology of Literature,* vol. 2, 17–31. Colchester, England: Essex University, 1985.

Hurtado, Albert L. *Indian Survival on the California Frontier.* New Haven: Yale University Press, 1988.

Ingram, Nartin. *Church Courts, Sex and Marriage in England, 1570– 1640.* New York: Cambridge University Press, 1987.

Isaac, Rhys. "On Explanation, Text, and Terrifying Power in Ethnographic History." *Yale Journal of Criticism* 6 (Spring 1993): 217–36.

———. *The Transformation of Virgina, 1740–1790.* Chapel Hill: University of North Carolina Press, 1982.

Jefferson, Thomas. *The Writings of Thomas Jefferson.* Edited by Paul Leicester Ford. New York: G. P. Putnam's Sons, 1892–99.

Jennings, Francis. *The Invasion of America: Indians, Colonialism, and the Cant of Conquest.* Chapel Hill: University of North Carolina Press, 1975.

Jimenez, Mary Ann. *Changing Faces of Madness: Early American Attitudes and the Treatment of the Insane.* Hanover, N.H., and London: University Press of New England, 1987.

Karlsen, Carol F. *Devil in the Shape of a Woman.* New York: Norton, 1987.

Karttunen, Frances. *Between Worlds: Interpreters, Guides, and Survivors.* New Brunswick, N.J.: Rutgers University Press, 1994.

Kerber, Linda K. "Separate Spheres, Female Worlds, Woman's Place: The Rhetoric of Women's History." *Journal of American History* 75. 1 (1988): 9–39.

———. *Women of the Republic: Intellect and Ideology in Revolutionary America.* 1980. New York: Norton, 1986.

Kett, Joseph. *Rites of Passage: Adolescence in America, 1790 to the Present.* New York: Basic, 1977.

Kitch, Sally L. *Chaste Liberation: Celibacy and Female Cultural Status.* Urbana: University of Illinois Press, 1989.

Klepp, Susan E. *Philadelphia in Transition: A Demographic History of the City and Its Occupational Groups, 1720–1830.* New York: Garland, 1989.

Knapp, Jeffrey. *An Empire Nowhere: England, America, and Literature from Utopia to The Tempest.* Berkeley: University of California Press, 1992.

Koehler, Lyle. *A Search for Power: The"Weaker Sex" in Seventeenth-Century New England.* Urbana: University of Illinois Press, 1980.

Kolodny, Annette. *The Land before Her: Fantasy and Experience of the American Frontiers 1630–1860.* Chapel Hill: University of North Carolina Press, 1984.

———. *The Lay of the Land: Metaphor as Experience and History in American Life and Letters.* Chapel Hill: University of North Carolina Press, 1975.

Koning, Hans. *Columbus: His Enterprise.* New York: Monthly Review, 1976.

Lahontan, Louis Armand de lom d'Arce. *New Voyages to North America.* London, 1703.

Laquer, Thomas. *Making Sex: Body and Gender from the Greeks to Freud.* Cambridge: Harvard University Press, 1990.

Las Casas, Bartolomé de. *The Devastation of the Indies: A Brief Account.* Translated by Herma Briffault. Introduction by Bill M. Donovan. Baltimore: Johns Hopkins University Press, 1992.

Lawson, John. *A New Voyage to Carolina.* Edited by Hugh Talmadge Lefler. Chapel Hill: University of North Carolina Press, 1967.

Leach, Douglas Edward. *Flintlock and Tomahawk: New England in King Philip's War.* New York: Norton, 1966.

———. "The 'Whens' of Mary Rowlandson's Captivity." *New England Quarterly* 34 (September 1961): 352–63.

LeClercq, Chrestien. *New Relation of Gaspesia with the Customs and Religion of the Gaspesian Indians.* Translated by William F. Ganong. Toronto: Champlain Society, 1910.

Lescarbot, Marc. *The History of New France.* 3 vols. Translated by W. L. Grant. Toronto: Champlain Society, 1907–14. Reprint, Westport, Conn.: Greenwood Press, 1968.

Levy, Barry. "'Tender Plants': Quaker Farmers and Children in the Delaware Valley, 1681–1735." *Journal of Family History* 3(1978): 116–35.

Lewis, Jan. "The Republican Wife: Virtue and Seduction in the Early Republic." *William and Mary Quarterly* 3.44 (1987): 689–721.

Lewis, Paul. "Charles Brockden Brown and the Gendered Canon of Early American Fiction." *Early American Literature* 31. 2 (1996): 167–88.

Lockridge, Kenneth A. *The Diary, and Life of William Byrd II of Virginia, 1674–1744.* Chapel Hill: University of North Carolina Press, 1987.

———. "Land, Population and the Evolution of New England Society, 1630–1790." *Past and Present* 39 (April 1968): 62–80.

———. *On the Sources of Patriarchal Rage: The Commonplace Books of William Byrd and Thomas Jefferson and the Gendering of Power in the Eighteenth Century.* New York: New York University Press, 1992.

Logan, Lisa. "Mary Rowlandson's Captivity and the 'Place' of the Woman Subject." *Early American Literature* 28.3 (1993): 255–77.

Lowance, Mason I., Jr. *The Language of Canaan: Metaphor and Symbol in New England from the Puritans to the Transcendentalists.* Cambridge: Harvard University Press, 1980.

Maccubbin, Robert Purks, ed. *'Tis Nature's Fault: Unauthorized Sexuality during the Enlightenment.* New York: Cambridge University Press, 1987.

Manvill, Mrs. P. D. *Lucinda; or the Mountain Mourner.* Johnstown, N.Y., 1807. 2d ed. (with additions) Ballston Spa, N. Y., 1810.

Martin, Wendy, ed. *Colonial American Travel Narratives.* New York: Penguin, 1994.

McAlister, Lyle N. *Spain and Portugal in the New World, 1492–1700.* Vol. 3 of *Europe and the World in the Age of Expansion.* Minneapolis: University of Minnesota Press, 1984.

McClintock, Anne. *Imperial Leather: Race, Gender and Sexuality in the Colonial Contest.* London: Routledge, 1995.

McLaren, Angus. *Reproductive Rituals: The Perception of Fertility in England from the Sixteenth Century to the Nineteenth Century.* London: Methuen, 1984.

Miller, Perry. *The New England Mind: The Seventeenth Century.* Boston: Beacon, 1954.

Mintz, Sidney W., and Richard Price. *An Anthropological Approach to the Afro-American Past: A Caribbean Perspective.* Boston: Beacon, 1992.

Mirabelli, Philip. "Silence, Wit, and Wisdom in *The Silent Woman.*" *Studies in English Literature 1500–1900* 29.2 (1989): 309–36.

Montrose, Louis. "The Work of Gender in the Discourse of Discovery." In Stephen Greenblatt, ed., *New World Encounters,* 177–217. Berkeley: University of California Press, 1993.

Moore, Lisa. "'She Was Too Fond of Her Mistaken Bargain': The Scandalous Relations of Gender and Sexuality in Feminist Theory." *diacritics* 21.2–3 (1991): 89–101.

Morgan, Edmund S. *The Puritan Family: Religion and Domestic Relations in Seventeenth-Century New England.* New York: Harper and Row, 1966.

———. "The Puritans and Sex." *New England Quarterly,* December 1942, 591–607.

Morgan, Philip D. "Three Planters and Their Slaves: Perspectives on Slavery in Virginia, South Carolina, and Jamaica, 1750–1790." In *Race and Family in the Colonial South,* edited by Winthrop D. Jordan and Sheila L. Skemp, 37–80. Jackson, Miss., and London: University of Mississippi Press, 1987.

Mörner, Magnus. *Race Mixture in the History of Latin America.* Boston: Little, Brown, 1967.

Morton, Thomas. *New English Canaan or New Canaan.* New York: Arno, 1972.

Mullin, Michael. *Africa in America: Slave Acculturation and Resistance in the American South and the British Caribbean, 1736–1831.* Urbana: University of Illinois Press, 1992.

Murray, Judith Sargent. *Story of Margaretta. The Gleaner. A Miscellaneous Production by Constantia.* 3 vols. Boston, 1798.

Namias, June. *White Captives: Gender and Ethnicity on the American Frontier.* Chapel Hill: University of North Carolina Press, 1993.

Nelson, Dana D. Introduction to *Kelroy.* Edited by Dana D. Nelson. 1812. Reprint, New York: Oxford University Press, 1992.

Nelson, William E. "Emerging Notions of Modern Criminal Law in the Revolutionary Era: An Historical Perspective." *New York University Law Review* 42 (May 1967): 450–82.

Norton, Mary Beth. *Founding Mothers and Fathers: Gendered Power and the Forming of American Society.* New York: Knopf, 1996.

———. *Liberty's Daughters: The Revolutionary Experience of American Women, 1750–1800.* Boston: Little, Brown, 1980.

Nourse, Henry. "Mrs. Mary Rowlandson's Removes." *Proceedings of the American Antiquarian Society,* 2d. Ser. 12 (1898): 401–9.

Orians, G. Harrison. "Censure of Fiction in American Romances and Magazines: 1789–1810." *PMLA* 52 (1937): 195–214.

Padden, R. C. *The Hummingbird and the Hawk: Conquest and Sovereignty in the Valley of Mexico, 1503–1541.* Columbus: Ohio State University Press, 1967.

Parran, Thomas, M. D. *Shadow on the Land: Syphilis*. New York: Reynal and Hitchcock, 1937.

Parrish, Joseph. *An Inaugural Dissertation on the Influence of the Passions Upon the Body in the Production and Cure of Diseases*. Philadelphia: Kimber, Conrad, 1805.

Paton, Diana." Decency, Dependence and the Lash: Gender and the British Debate over Slave Emancipation, 1830–34." *Slavery and Abolition* 17 (December 1996): 163–84.

Patterson, Orlando S. *Slavery and Social Death: A Comparative Study*. Cambridge: Harvard University Press, 1982.

Perlmann, Joel, and Dennis Shirley. "When Did New England Women Acquire Literacy?" *William and Mary Quarterly* 3.48 (1991): 50–67.

Pinel, Philippe. *A Treatise on Insanity*. Introduction by Dr. Paul F. Cranefield. Translated by D. D. Davis, M.D. 1806. Reprint, New York: Hafner, 1962.

Porter, Roy. "Mixed Feelings: The Enlightenment and Sexuality in Eighteenth-Century Britain." In *Sexuality in Eighteenth-Century Britain*, edited by Paul-Gabriel Boucé, 1–27. Manchester: Manchester University Press, 1992.

Price, Richard, and Sally Price, eds. *Stedman's Surinam: Life in an Eighteenth-Century Slave Society*. Baltimore and London: Johns Hopkins University Press, 1988.

Quétel, Claude. *History of Syphilis*. Baltimore: Johns Hopkins University Press, 1990.

Quinn, David B., ed. *New American World: A Documentary History of North America to 1612*. 5 vols. New York: Arno and Hector Bye, 1979.

Rabasa, José. *Inventing America: Spanish Historiography and the Formation of Eurocentrism*. Norman: University of Oklahoma Press, 1993.

Radisson, Pierre-Esprit. *Voyages of Peter Esprit Radisson, being an account of his Travels and Experience among the North American Indians from 1652 to 1684*. Edited by Gideon Scull. New York: P. Smith, 1943.

Radway, Janice A. *Reading the Romance: Women, Patriarchy, and Popular Literature*. Rev. ed. Chapel Hill: University of North Carolina Press, 1991.

Ralegh, Walter. *Selected Writings*. Edited by Gerald Hammond. Harmondsworth, England: Penguin, 1986.

Reis, Elizabeth. "The Devil, the Body, and the Feminine Soul in Puritan New England." *Journal of American History* 82.1 (1995): 15–36.

Relf, Samuel. *Infidelity; or The Victims of Sentiment; a Novel, in a Series of Letters*. Philadelphia: W. W. Woodward, 1797.

Rose, Henry. *An Inaugural Dissertation on the Effects of Passion Upon the Body*. Philadelphia: William Woodward, 1794.

Rothman, David. *The Discovery of the Asylum: Social Order and Disorder in the New Republic*. Boston: Little, Brown, 1971.

Rothman, Ellen K. *Hands and Hearts: A History of Courtship in America*. New York: Basic, 1984.

———. "Sex and Self-Control: Middle-Class Courtship in America, 1770–1870." In *The American Family in Social-Historical Perspective*, 3d. ed. Edited by Michael Gordon, 393–410. New York: St. Martin's, 1983.

Rouse, Irving. *The Tainos: Rise and Decline of the People Who Greeted Columbus*. New Haven: Yale University Press, 1992.

Rousseau, G. S. and Roy Porter, eds. *Sexual Underworlds of the Enlightenment*. Manchester: Manchester University Press, 1987.

Rowlandson, Mary. "The Soveraignty and Goodness of God. . . ." In *So Dreadfull a Judgment: Puritan Responses to King Philip's War, 1676–1677*. Edited by Richard Slotkin and James K. Folsom, 301–69. Middletown, Conn.: Wesleyan University Press, 1978.

Rowson, Susanna. *Charlotte: A Tale of Truth* and *Charlotte's Daughter; or, The Three Orphans*. Edited by Ann Douglas. 1794 and 1828. Reprint, New York: Penguin, 1991.

Rush, Benjamin. *Medical Inquiries and Observations Upon the Diseases of the Mind*. 1812. Reprint, New York: Hafner, 1962.

Ryan, Mary P. *Cradle of the Middle Class: The Family in Oneida County, New York, 1790–1865*. New York: Cambridge University Press, 1981.

———. "The Power of Women's Networks: A Case Study of Female Moral Reform in Antebellum America." *Feminist Studies* 5 (Spring 1979): 66–85.

Sagard, Gabriel. *The Long Journey to the Country of the Hurons*. Edited by George M. Wrong. Translated by H. H. Langton. Toronto: Champlain Society, 1939.

Sale, Kirkpatrick. *The Conquest of Paradise: Christopher Columbus and the Columbian Legacy*. New York: Penguin, 1991.

Samuels, Shirley. "The Family, the State, and the Novel in the Early Republic." *American Quarterly* 38.3 (1986): 381–95.

———. "Infidelity and Contagion: The Rhetoric of Revolution." *Early American Literature* 22 (1987): 183–91.

———., ed. *The Culture of Sentiment, Race, Gender, and Sentimentality in Nineteenth-Century America*. New York: Oxford University Press, 1992.

Sanday, Peggy Reeves. "The Socio-Cultural Context of Rape: A Cross-Cultural Study," *Journal of Social Issues* 37.4 (1981): 5–27.

[Sansay, Leonora.] *Laura*. Philadelphia: Bradford and Inskeep, 1809.

"The Scarlet Legislature: For Adulterers Only. "*Student Lawyer*, May 1987, 6–7.

Scott, James C. *Domination and the Arts of Resistance: Hidden Transcripts*. New Haven: Yale University Press, 1990.

Shuffelton, Frank. "In Different Voices: Gender in the American Republic of Letters." *Early American Literature* 25.3 (1990): 289–303.

———. "Mrs. Foster's Coquette and the Decline of the Brotherly Watch." *Studies in Eighteenth-Century Culture* 16 (1986): 211–24.

Sieminski, Greg, Capt. "The Puritan Captivity Narrative and the Politics of the American Revolution." *American Quarterly* 42 (1990): 35–56.

Silverman, Kenneth. *The Life and Times of Cotton Mather.* New York: Harper and Row, 1984.

Simons, Patricia. "Women in Frames: The Gaze, the Eye, the Profile in Renaissance Portraiture." *History Workshop Journal* 25 (1988): 4–30.

Sklar, Kathryn Kish. *Catherine Beecher: A Study in American Domesticity.* New Haven: Yale University Press, 1973.

Slotkin, Richard. *Regeneration through Violence: The Mythology of the American Frontier, 1600–1860.* Middletown, Conn.: Wesleyan University Press, 1973.

Slotkin, Richard, and James K. Folsom. *So Dreadfull a Judgment: Puritan Responses to King Philip's War, 1675–1677.* Middletown, Conn.: Wesleyan University Press, 1978.

Smith, Daniel Blake. *Inside the Great House: Planter Family Life in Eighteenth-Century Chesapeake Society.* Ithaca: Cornell University Press, 1980.

Smith, Daniel Scott. "Parental Power and Marriage Patterns: An Analysis of Historical Trends in Hingham, Massachusetts." *Journal of Marriage and the Family* 35 (August 1973): 419–28.

Smith, Daniel Scott, and Michael S. Hindus. "Premarital Pregnancy in America 1640–1971." *Journal of Interdisciplinary History* 5. 4 (1975): 537–70.

Smith, Merril D. *Breaking the Bonds: Marital Discord in Pennsylvania, 1730–1830.* New York: New York University Press, 1991.

Smith-Rosenberg, Carroll. "Beauty, the Beast, and the Militant Woman: A Case Study in Sex Roles and Social Stress in Jacksonian America." In *Disorderly Conduct*, 109–128. New York: Oxford University Press, 1985.

———. "Domesticating 'Virtue': Coquettes and Revolutionaries in Young America." in *Literature and the Body*, edited by Elaine Scarry, 160–84. Baltimore: Johns Hopkins, 1988.

Somerville, Margaret R., *Sex and Subjection: Attitudes to Women in Early Modern Society.* London: Arnold, 1995.

Stallybrass, Peter. "Patriarchal Territories: The Body Enclosed." In *Rewriting the Renaissance: The Discourses of Sexual Difference in Early Modern Europe*, edited by Margaret W. Ferguson, Maureen Quilligan, and Nancy J. Vickers, 123–42. Chicago: University of Chicago Press, 1986.

Stanford, Ann. "Mary Rowlandson's Journey to Redemption." *Ariel: A Review of International English Literature* 7.3 (1976): 27–37.

Stansell, Christine. *City of Women: Sex and Class in New York, 1787–1860.* New York: Knopf, 1986.

Stern, Steve J. *Peru's Indian Peoples and the Challenge of Spanish Conquest: Huamanga to 1640.* Madison: University of Wisconsin Press, 1982.

Stickley, Julia Ward. "The Records of Deborah Sampson Gannett, Woman Soldier of the Revolution." *Prologue* 4 (1972): 233–41.

Stone, Lawrence. *The Family, Sex, and Marriage in England, 1500–1800.* New York: Harper and Row, 1977.

Taussig, Michael. *Shamanism, Colonialism, and the Wild Man: A Study in Terror and Healing.* Chicago: University of Chicago Press, 1987.

Thickstun, Margaret Olofson. *Fictions of the Feminine: Puritan Doctrine and the Representation of Women.* Ithaca: Cornell University Press, 1988.

Thomas, M. Halsey. *The Diary of Samuel Sewall.* Vol. 2. New York: Farrar, Strauss and Giroux, 1973.

Thompson, Roger. *Sex in Middlesex: Popular Mores in a Massachusetts County, 1649–1699.* Amherst: University of Massachusetts Press, 1986.

Thwaites, Reuben G., ed. *The Jesuit Relations and Allied Documents.* 73 vols. Cleveland: Burrows Bros., 1896–1901.

Tinling, Marion, ed. *The Correspondence of the Three William Byrds of Westover, Virginia, 1684–1776.* Charlottesville: Virginia Historical Society, 1977.

Tobin, Lad. "A Radically Different Voice: Gender and Language in the Trials of Anne Hutchinson." *Early American Literature* 25.3 (1990): 253–70.

Todorov, Tzvetan. *The Conquest of America: The Question of the Other.* Translated by Richard Howard. New York: Harper Torchbooks, 1987.

———. *The Morals of History.* Translated by Alyson Waters. Minneapolis: University of Minnesota Press, 1995.

Toulouse, Teresa A. "'My Own Credit': Strategies of (E)Valuation in Mary Rowlandson's Captivity Narrative." *American Literature* 64.4 (1992): 655–76.

Trumbach, Randolph. "Sex, Gender and Sexual Identity in Modern Culture: Male Sodomy and Female Prostitution in Enlightenment London." *Journal of Interdisciplinary History* 2 (October 1991): 186–203.

Ulrich, Laurel Thatcher. *Good Wives: Image and Reality in the Lives of Women in Northern New England, 1650–1750.* New York: Oxford University Press, 1980.

Vail, R.W.G. *Susanna Haswell Rowson, the Author of Charlotte Temple: A Bibliographic Study.* Worcester, Mass.: Davis, 1933.

The Vain Cottager; or The History of Lucy Franklin. New Haven: Increase Cooke, 1807.

Van Sant, Ann Jessie. *Eighteenth-Century Sensibility and the Novel: The Senses in Social Context.* Cambridge: Cambridge University Press, 1993.

Vaughan, Alden T. *New England Frontier: Puritans and Indians, 1620–1675.* Boston: Little, Brown, 1965.

Vaughan, Alden T., and Edwin W. Clark, eds. *Puritans among the Indians: Ac-*

counts of Captivity and Redemption, 1676–1724. Cambridge: Harvard University Press, 1981.

Vedder, Edward B., A.M., M.D. *Syphilis and Public Health.* Philadelphia and New York: Lea and Febiger, 1918.

Verduin, Kathleen. "'Our Cursed Natures': Sexuality and the Puritan Conscience." *New England Quarterly* 56 (1983): 220–37.

Wagner, Peter. *Eros Revived: Erotica in the Age of Enlightenment.* London: Secker and Warburg, 1988.

Wall, Helena M. *Fierce Communion: Family and Community in Early America.* Cambridge: Harvard University Press, 1990.

Warren, Caroline Matilda. *The Gamesters; or Ruins of Innocence. An Original Novel, Founded in Truth.* Boston: Carlisle, for Thomas and Andrews, et al., 1805.

Watts, Steven. *The Romance of Real Life: Charles Brockden Brown and the Origins of American Culture.* Baltimore and London: Johns Hopkins University Press, 1994.

Welter, Barbara. "The Cult of True Woman, 1820–1860." *American Quarterly* 18 (Summer 1966): 151–74.

We People Here: Nahuatl Accounts of the Conquest of Mexico. Repertorium Columbianum, no. 1. Edited and translated by James Lockhart. Berkeley: University of California Press, 1993.

White, Hayden. "The Value of Narrativity in the Representation of Reality." In *The Content of the Form.*, 1–24. Baltimore: Johns Hopkins University Press, 1987.

Wilentz, Sean. *Chants Democratic: New York City and the Rise of the American Working Class, 1788–1850.* New York: Oxford University Press, 1984.

Williams, Joan C. "Domesticity as the Dangerous Supplement of Liberalism." *Journal of Women's History* 2 (Winter 1991): 69–88.

Williams, Roger. *A Key into the Language of America.* Edited by John J. Teunissen and Evelyn J. Hinz. Detroit: Wayne State University Press, 1973.

Winslow, Ola Elizabeth. *Samuel Sewall of Boston.* Vol. 2. New York: Macmillan, 1964.

Wolfthal, Diane. "'A Hue and a Cry': Medieval Rape Imagery and Its Transformation." *Art Bulletin* 75.1 (1993): 39–64.

Wood, Gordon. *Radicalism of the American Revolution.* New York: Vintage, 1993.

Wood, Sally. *Dorval; or The Speculator.* Portsmouth, N. H., 1801.

Woodfin, Maude H., ed. *Another Secret Diary of William Byrd of Westover, 1739–41: With Letters and Literary Exercises, 1696–1726.* Richmond, Va.: Dietz, 1942.

Wright, Louis B., ed. *The Prose Works of William Byrd of Westover.* Cambridge: Harvard University Press, 1966.

Wright, Louis B., and Marion Tinling, eds. *The Secret Diary of William Byrd of Westover, 1709–12.* Richmond, Va.: Dietz, 1941.

———— *William Byrd of Virginia: The London Diary (1717–1721) and Other Writings.* New York: Oxford University Press, 1958.

Wroth, Lawrence C., ed. *The Voyages of Giovanni da Verrazzano.* New Haven: Yale University Press, 1970

Wyatt-Brown, Bertram. "The Mask of Obedience: Male Slave Psychology in the Old South." *American Historical Review* 93 (December 1988): 1228–52.

Zavala, Iris M. "Representing the Colonial Subject." In *1492–1992: Re/Discovering Colonial Writing,* edited by René Jara and Nicholas Spadaccini. Hispanic Issues, no. 4 Minneapolis: Prisma Institute, 1989. 323–48.

Zomchick, John. *Family and the Law in Eighteenth-Century Fiction: The Public Conscience in the Private Sphere.* Cambridge: Cambridge University Press, 1993.

Contributors

Wayne Bodle is an assistant professor in the Department of History at Indiana University of Pennsylvania. Currently he is NEH/Lloyd Lewis Fellow at the Newberry Library. His book *The Seat of War: Civilians, Soldiers, and Society during the Valley Forge Winter* is forthcoming from New York University Press. He has published articles in the *William and Mary Quarterly* and the *Pennsylvania Magazine of History and Biography* and is currently researching regional development in the Middle Atlantic colonies and states from initial European settlement until 1800.

Trevor Burnard is Senior Lecturer in History at the University of Canterbury, New Zealand. The author of numerous articles on Jamaican and American history, including "Inheritance and Independence: Women's Status in Early Colonial Jamaica," *William and Mary Quarterly* (January 1991), he is currently working on a biography of Thomas Thistlewood and a history of free society in Jamaica before 1780.

Richard Godbeer is an associate professor in the Department of History at the University of California, Riverside. Godbeer's first book, *The Devil's Dominion: Magic and Religion in Early New England* (Cambridge University Press, 1992), won the American Historical Association Pacific Coast Branch Book Award. He is currently working on a second book that will examine attitudes toward sex in early America. He has published exploratory essays on this subject in the *William and Mary Quarterly* (April 1995) and the *New England Quarterly* (September 1995).

Else L.Hambleton is a doctoral candidate in history at the University of Massachusetts. Her dissertation is entitled "'The World Filled with a Generation of Bastards': Unwed Mothers and Pregnant Brides in Seventeenth-Century Massachusetts." She has presented papers at several professional conferences, including *"Massachusetts vs. Appleton and Willson:* An Atypical Fornication Trial," at the Second Carlton Conference on the History of the Family in 1994.

Rodney Hessinger is a doctoral candidate in American history at Temple University. He is completing a dissertation entitled "Seduced, Abandoned, and Reborn: Sexual and Social Stress and the Role of Youth in Defining Bourgeois America, 1780–1850." He is the author of "Problems and Promises: Colonial American Child Rearing and Modernization Theory," *Journal of Family History* 21.2 (1996): 125–43.

Steven Neuwirth is professor of English and coordinator of American Studies at Western Connecticut State University. In 1992–93, he presented Fulbright Lectures in France, Belgium, Sweden, Spain, and Great Britain. He is the author of many articles, including "The Images of Place: Puritans, Indians, and the Religious Significance of the New England Frontier," *American Art Journal* 17 (1986): 42–53.

Gordon Sayre is assistant professor of English at the University of Oregon, where he teaches American Literature, as well as courses on travel and exploration narratives, autobiography, and the Enlightenment. He is the author of *"Les sauvauges américains": Representations of Native Americans in French and English Colonial Literature* (University of North Carolina Press, 1997).

Erik R. Seeman received his Ph.D. from the University of Michigan and is now an assistant professor of history at the State University of New York at Buffalo. He is completing a book, *Laity, Clergy, and the Shaping of Popular Religious Culture in New England, 1700–1775.*

Merril D. Smith, the author of *Breaking the Bonds: Marital Discord in Pennsylvania, 1730–1830* (New York University Press, 1991), teaches history at Widener University. She is currently at work on a study of mothers and daughters in early America and has published some of her findings in an essay, "'Unnatural Mothers': Infanticide, Child Abuse, and Motherhood in the Mid-Atlantic, 1730–1830," in *Over the Threshold: Intimate Violence in Early America,* edited by Christine Daniels (Routledge, forthcoming).

Heather Smyth is a doctoral candidate in English at the University of Alberta. She is completing her dissertation, entitled "Caribbean Women

Writers and the Post-Colonial *Bildungsroman*." She is the author of "Tradition and the Female Talent: A Feminist Response to T. S. Eliot and Harold Bloom," *Queen's Arts and Science Undergraduate Review* 4 (1992): 21–29.

Karen A. Weyler is a visiting assistant professor in the English Department at Wake Forest University. She has published essays in *Early American Literature, Studies in Short Fiction,* and *Southern Quarterly.* She is currently revising a book-length study of the literary culture of the early national era: *Intricate Relations: Regulation of the Self in Early American Fiction.*

Stephanie Wood, coeditor of the forthcoming anthology *Indian Women of Colonial Mexico* (University of Oklahoma Press), teaches courses on Latin American history at the University of Oregon. With the support of the American Council of Learned Societies, she is currently finishing another book about indigenous views of the conquest of Mexico, based on Nahautl-language sources that span the sixteenth through eighteenth centuries.

Natalie A. Zacek is a doctoral candidate in history at Johns Hopkins University. She is completing a dissertation entitled "Dangerous Tenants: Social and Ethnic Conflict in the Leeward Islands, 1670–1763." She has presented several professional papers. Most recently, she presented "Diversity and Unity in the English Leewards: Evidence from a 1678 Census" to the Seminar of the Institute of Commonwealth Studies at the University of London.

Index

Abortion, among Native American women, 42

Adultery, as cause of insanity, 284, 288, 298; changes in laws, 290–91; disruption of family, 285, 298, 299; in early American fiction, 285, 298; in Leeward Islands, 198–203

African and African-American women, advantages to interracial liaisons, 170–71, 178–80, 181; bodies of, 164, 167, 192–92; rapes of, 176–78; seen as sexually insatiable or licentious, 174–75, 193

American Revolution: effect on young men, 218–19, 221, 265; and female behavior, 223; and gender relations on frontier, 219; and romance across racial and ethnic lines, 221–22, 223–24

Appleton, Samuel: background of, 94–95; and honor, 95, 96, 111; life after trial, 109–10; rape of Priscilla Willson, 1, 87; relationship to judges, 95; status as gentleman, 1, 95, 111

Beatty, Erkuries, 3, 215; and Bella Barclay, 217–18; birth and early life, 220; commissioned as paymaster to the First American Regiment, 225; courtship of men in Beatty circle, 224–25; discharged in Philadelphia, 225; farming and courting, 229–30; final years in army, 227, 229; frontier life, 226–27; as lens to observe post-revolutionary gender relations, 218–20, 231; marries, 230; mayor of Princeton, 230; meets future wife, 227; rates women of Carlisle, 222–23; resigns commission, 229

Berdache, 8, 50–51

Byrd, William, 133; attitude toward marriage, 149–52; attitude toward women,

149, 151–53; birth of, 137; fears of sexual inadequacy, 152–53; and female lustfulness, 152–53; flirtations with other women during marriage to Lucy, 141–42; "Inamorato L'Oiseaux," 135; marriage to Lucy Parke, 138, 139–41, 149; marriage to Maria Taylor, 138, 140, 145; older years, 145, 153; preoccupation with control, 147–48, 153; and prostitutes, 142–43; range of sexual experiences, 138; and servants and slaves, 143–45; settings of sexual experiences, 139–40; sexual experiences in London, 142–43; sexual relationship with Lucy, 139–40; sexual relationship in marriage, 150–51; status as gentleman, 1; struggle between spirituality and body, 148; struggles with passion, 133, 147–48; as transatlantic gentleman, 137, 139, 140, 148, 154–55; and venereal disease, 143; writings useful to study sexuality in colonial South, 136–37

Celibacy: and the Bible, 122–23; Christian tradition of, 122, 127, 128; condemnation of, 124, 125; conflicts of laity and priests, 123–24; embraced by Sarah Prentice, 121; and making the body holy, 117, 121, 127; after Reformation, 124; threatens beliefs about women, 126; and women, 117

Children: of black women and white men, 170–71; of Europeans and Native American women, 21, 23; less parental supervision of, 292; provisions made for, 21–22, 27n, 40. See also Gender; Popular fiction

Cortés, Hernando, 17, 18, 20, 21, 25, 73n, 33

Cross dressing, 215, 240, 241, 243, 244, 247–48, 249–50, 251; transvestite theater, 254. See also *Ormond*

de Lahontan, baron (Louis Armand de lom d'Arce): compares and contrasts European and native societies, 48; as cultural and literary innovator in colonial writing, 47; perception of native woman as sexual aggressors, 48–49; and sexual freedom, 49–50
de Léry, Jean, 14; *History of a Voyage to the Land of Brazil*, 46
Diaries, as source of early American sexual attitudes, 136; of William Byrd, 136–37. *See also* Byrd, William; Thistlewood, Thomas
Díaz, Bernal, 16, 17, 19, 20, 21

Explorers' accounts, 35; eyewitnesses differ in accounts, 53. *See also* Native Americans

Fornication: acquittal of Samuel Appleton for, 89; Appleton-Willson trial, 90–92; changes in Puritan laws, 99–100; conviction of Priscilla Willson, 89; loss of honor or status of men, 97, 100; loss of status for women, 98; prosecution in Massachusetts Bay Colony, 89–90; prosecutions in New England, 97–101, 110. *See also* Gender; Popular fiction

Gender: changes in courtship and sexual behavior in late eighteenth century, 266, 278n; construction of, 72–73, 77–78, 81n, 87, 264–65, 272; decline in patriarchy, 265; double standard in laws, 106; expectations in Jamaican slave society, 182; premarital pregnancies, 266, 292; Puritan ideology, 99, 110; relations in post-Revolutionary frontier, 226–28, 231–33; roles in post-Revolutionary period, 215, 231, 234n, 245–52; in seduction tales, 215, 272. *See also* Cross dressing; *Ormond;* Popular fiction
Great Awakening, connection between spirituality and body, 118, 127–28; in Grafton, 118, 119

Homoeroticism, in *Ormond*, 251–52
Homosexuality, and Native Americans, 50–51, 103

Illustrations by Gabriela Quiñones, 13, 18, 19, 22
Immortalists: and the body, 127–28; challenge New England ministerial ideas, 125–26; in southeastern New England, 119–20, 121, 128; and spiritual union, 120. *See also* Celibacy; Prentice, Sarah
Incest, 205–7
Indecent exposure, as insult to husband, 203–5
Insanity: and William Buchan, 287, 288, 290, 294, 295; caused by guilty conscience, 288–89, 296; culturally constructed, 284–85, 286; in early American fiction, 283, 284, 286, 291, 293, 295, 296, 298, 299, 303, 304–5; effect on female sexuality, 290, 297; and John Haslam, 288, 290, 294; induced by emotion, 288; *Medical Inquiries and Observations Upon the Disease of the Mind* (1812), 283–84; moral treatment of, 287; in *Pinel à la Salpêtriére*, 283; and Benjamin Rush, 283–84, 286, 287, 288, 289, 290; women more susceptible to, 289
Ireland, Shadrack: and Immortalists, 120; and Sarah Prentice, 120; death of, 121

Leeward Islands: ethnic and religious conflicts, 195; Rachel Levine Hamilton, 200–203; Daniel Parke and unacceptable sexual conduct, 197–200; precarious nature of social order, 194–95; prostitution, 196; rebellions of slaves and servants frequent, 194–95; regulation of order, 195–96, 207–8; sexual behavior of "outsiders" more tolerated, 207
Lockridge, Kenneth, on William Byrd and early American gender relations, 136–37, 153–54

Masturbation, 103–4, 144, 148
Men: and class, in Puritan fornication trials, 95; and control, 147, 199; cuckolding, 198–99; decline in patriarchy, 265; fear of confidence men, 243; indecent

exposure of, 203–5; opportunities for sexual activities, 133, 194; "patriarchal rage," 153–54, 202; patriarchy of Jamaican planters, 166–67, 172; patriarchy of Spanish and Portuguese, 24; Puritan loss of status, 97; relationships with servants and slaves, 133, 134, 143–45, 163; sexual aggression and, 146–47; sexual exploits denounced in nineteenth century, 183–84. *See also* American Revolution; Byrd, William; Gender; Popular fiction
Midwives, depositions in bastardy cases, 91, 97, 100, 107, 108

Native Americans: and alliances with white traders, 40–41; and William Byrd II, 41, 146–47; chastity of, 39–40; conquest by Europeans, 7; courtship practices, 39; images of, 8, 146; and John Lawson, 40, 41–42; in mid-Atlantic, 36–37; and misunderstandings with Europeans, 36–37; perceived as promiscuous, 41–43, 66; Pueblo Indians, 13, 14; as savages in Mary Rowlandson's narrative, 64, 66, 68, 70, 72, 73–74; sexual freedom of, 49; war in Northwest Territory, 228–29
Native American women: baptism of, 18, 19; in Brazil, 14; as "gifts" to Europeans, 18, 19, 20, 21, 22, 31n, 52–53, 146; La Malinche (doña Marina), 18, 21; perceived lasciviousness of, 12, 14; as prostitutes for traders, 42–43, 46, 47; rape of, 2, 146; as servants and concubines, 17. *See also* Rape
Nudity, of black women, 192–93, 209n, 259n; ethnographic voyeurism, 12; Marc Lescarbot, 44; native women gazing at men, 49; Gabriel Sagard, 45–46; views of Europeans about Native Americans, 44

Ormond: blurring of identities, 241; conservatism of, 252–53; Constantia as republican woman, 245; construction of class and gender in, 241, 244, 247, 249; cross dressing in, 3, 215, 241–42, 244, 248–49, 253–54; disguising characters, 242–43; disrupts social binaries and hierarchies, 240, 251, 255; and education

for women, 246–47, 252; examines tensions in early republic, 240, 244, 246, 254–55; homoeroticism in, 251–52; Martinette as radical example of new woman, 247, 250–51; masculine and feminine divided, 248–50; plot of, 240–41; roles of women, 246–52

Popular fiction: addressed to female readers, 263, 267, 270; appeals to fears of male readers, 269–270, 274; and chastity, 272, 276, 300; and conscience, 291; conservatism of, 285, 293, 304; fears about young people, 265, 266; fears of deception, 271; and formation of late eighteenth-century culture, 263, 265, 266, 276; medical works influence, 286; parental guidance needed, 274–75, 301; politics in, 300, 302; popularity of seduction tales, 265–66, 285; public and private defined, 286, 293, 304–5; punishment of immoral characters, 291, 293, 295–96, 297–302, 303, 304; and sensibility, 263, 266, 268, 273; warnings against coquetry, 270–71; young men as immoral in, 263, 265, 271, 274, 275, 276; young women as virtuous and vulnerable in, 263, 266, 271, 276. *See also* Insanity; *Ormond*
Prentice, Sarah: birth and marriage to Solomon Prentice, 117; celibacy of, 116, 121, 122; challenges gender ideals, 126; conversion experiences, 117, 118; and free love, 119; and Immortalists, 120; rumors about, 116, 119; and Shakers, 121–22, 126
Prentice, Solomon: describes Sarah's reconversion experience, 118; marries Sarah Sartell, 117; seen as too radical by Old Lights, 118
Prostitution: and William Byrd, 142–43; and Native Americans, 42–43, 46, 47; Philadelphia Magdalen Society, 276

Quinnapin, 59, 67, 81n; description of, 68, 69, 70–72, 73; as symbol of all men, 73–75, 77

Rape, 1; accounts of, 11, 12, 36–37, 146–47; in Appleton-Willson trial,

Rape *(continued)*
96–97, 107, 108; in Brazil, 14; in Chile, 15; and conception, 96–97, 110; and conquest, 9, 14, 16, 17, 24, 25; definitions of, 10, 14, 15; in European art, 15–16, 24; *membrus febrilis*, 9, 25; in Mexico, 16, 17, 21; of Pueblo women, 14; protests by clergymen, 15, 16; and racism, 14, 17, 23, 24, 25; Mary Rowlandson and, 64–66, 70–71, 73; silence of European military leaders about, 25; of slaves, 176–78; in Venezuela, 15

Rowlandson, Mary: captivity narrative as commentary on gender, 55; and chastity, 2, 63–65, 69–72, 73, 74; as critic of men, 74–75; as domestic tale, 77–78; feminine voice, 3, 8, 57–58, 67–75; historical Mary Rowlandson, 56, 57; as ideal Puritan woman, 75–78; and Increase Mather, 59–60, 64; masculine voice, 57, 58, 62–63; preface of narrative, 59–60; as "savage," 65, 68, 69; title of captivity narrative, 60–62; and virtue, 70–72

Sex and sexuality: of adolescents, 50; American attitudes towards, 285; and the Bible, 122–23; comparisons of sexual culture in Jamaica, New England, and London, 172–73, 187n, 191–92; confusion about Native American sexuality, 44; defined, 156n; difference between accounts of missionaries, explorers and promoters, 38–39, 43, 46–47; difficulties in evaluating European accounts, 37–38; and early Christians, 123; food and sex, 65–66; and the Great Awakening, 116, 117; images and impressions, 2; interpretation, 4; and marriage, 87, 102, 124–25; in New England, 101–2, 110; premarital sex discouraged, 99; Puritan sexual attitudes, 102–6, 110; "repressive hypothesis," 43, 44, 48; and religion, 116; regulation of, in Leeward Islands, 194; women as sexually dangerous and seductive, 24

Sexual relations between black women and white men, 163–64, 172; accepted in West Indies, 173, 175–76, 192, 194, 196; black women seen as sexually insatiable, 174–75; ruptures in white solidarity, 164–65, 180; unequal power relationship, 176, 177–78

Shakers, and challenges to society, 126–27

Slavery: abolitionists, 183, 184; absence of slave testimony, 167; detrimental effects on slaves, 181–82; in Jamaica, 165–68; molestation of women, 167, 177–78; punishment of male slaves, 166–67; sexual tensions within slave community, 182; violence as part of, 167, 182. *See also* Leeward Islands; Native American women; Sexual relations between black women and white men

Thistlewood, Thomas, 3, 133; beliefs about black women, 175; diary of, 163–64, 167–68, 171; diary of John Thistlewood, 170–71; feelings about white women, 175; interference in sexual lives of slaves, 183; introspection lacking, 167–68, 169–70; Phibbah, 170, 172, 181; as rapist, 176; sexual encounters described, 169; sexual experiences in England, 171; sexual experiences on Egypt estate, 171; sexual practices accepted by planters, 183; as sexual predator, 172, 182

Venereal disease: and William Byrd, 143, 293–95; as God's punishment for sexual freedom, 46; in Jamaica, 179

Virginity: and early Christians, 123; as ideal for New England women and men, 98, 104; illustration, 18; of Native American women, 17–18; in popular fiction, 272; and rape, 97. *See also* Celibacy; Native Americans; Rowlandson, Mary

West Indies: criticized as lawless, 190–91; and regulation of morality, 133–34. *See also* Leeward Islands; Thistlewood, Thomas

Willson, Priscilla, 1, 92–93; as ideal woman, 103, 108; life after trial, 109

Women: bodies of, 64–67, 72–73, 193–94, 289; ideals, 87, 98, 99, 103; challenges to gender ideals, 126; perception as sexual temptresses, 67, 104, 106, 152–53, 174; and planter society, 164–65, 174; and political behavior, 223; role in marriage, 87; role of women's community in New England, 106–7; sexual activity of, 292, 293; subordinate status in New England, 59, 62–63, 103. *See also* African American women; Gender; Native American women; *Ormond*; Popular fiction; *and names of individual women*